Effective Software
Project Management

Effective Software Project Management

Robert K. Wysocki

WILEY

Wiley Publishing, Inc.

Effective Software Project Management

Published by
Wiley Publishing, Inc.
10475 Crosspoint Boulevard
Indianapolis, IN 46256
www.wiley.com

Published by Wiley Publishing, Inc., Indianapolis, Indiana

Published simultaneously in Canada

ISBN-13: 978-0-7645-9636-0
ISBN-10: 0-7645-9636-5

Manufactured in the United States of America

10 9 8 7 6 5 4 3 2 1

1B/QX/QT/QW/IN

For general information on our other products and services or to obtain technical support, please contact our Customer Care Department within the U.S. at (800) 762-2974, outside the U.S. at (317) 572-3993 or fax (317) 572-4002.

Library of Congress Cataloging-in-Publication Data

Wysocki, Robert K.

  Effective software project management / Robert K. Wysocki.

      p. cm.

  Includes index.

  ISBN-13: 978-0-7645-9636-0 (paper/website)

  ISBN-10: 0-7645-9636-5 (paper/website)

  1. Computer software—Development—Management. I. Title.

  QA76.76.D47W97 2006

  005.3'068—dc22

                          2005034341

Robert K. Wysocki, Ph.D., has over 40 years experience as a project management consultant and trainer, information systems manager, systems and management consultant, author, training developer, and provider. He has written 14 books on project management and information systems management. One of his books, *Effective Project Management: Traditional, Adaptive, Extreme, Third Edition* (Wiley, 2003), has been a best-seller and is recommended by the Project Management Institute for the library of every project manager. He has over 30 publications in professional and trade journals and has made more than 100 presentations at professional and trade conferences and meetings. He has developed more than 20 project management courses and trained over 10,000 project managers.

From 1963 to 1970 he was a systems consultant for one of the world's largest electronics components manufacturers. In that capacity he designed and implemented several computer-based manufacturing and quality control systems. From 1970 to 1990 he held a number of positions in both state supported and private institutions in higher education as MBA Director, Associate Dean of Business, Dean of Computers and Information Systems, Director of Academic Computing, CIO, and Senior Planner.

In 1990, he founded Enterprise Information Insights, Inc. (EII), a project management consulting and training practice specializing in agile project management methodology design and integration, project support office establishment, the development of training curriculum, and the development of a portfolio of assessment tools focused on organizations, project teams, and individuals. His client list includes AT&T, Aetna, Babbage Simmel, BMW, British Computer Society, Boston University Corporate Education Center, Computerworld, Converse Shoes, the Czechoslovakian Government, Data General, Digital, Eli Lilly, Harvard Community Health Plan, IBM, J. Walter Thompson, Ohio State University, Peoples Bank, Sapient Corporation, The Limited, The State of Ohio, Travelers Insurance, TVA, the U.S. Coast Guard Academy, Wal-Mart, and several others.

He is a Senior Consultant at the Cutter Consortium where he is an active member of the Agile Project Management Practice. He has consulted widely in agile project management with such companies as Sapient, Wells Fargo, Wal-Mart, Blue Cross Blue Shield of Massachusetts, the TVA, and others. He is vice-president and president elect of APLN, a member of ASAPM and the Agile Alliance. He also serves as advisor to Project Summit and Business Analyst World. He is a member of the Project Management Institute, the American Society of Training & Development, and the Society of Human Resource Management. He is past association vice president of AITP (formerly DPMA). He earned a B.A. in Mathematics from the University of Dallas, and an M.S. and Ph.D. in Mathematical Statistics from Southern Methodist University.

Executive Editor
Bob Elliott

Senior Development Editor
Kevin Kent

Production Editor
Pamela Hanley

Copy Editor
Nancy Rapoport

Editorial Manager
Mary Beth Wakefield

Production Manager
Tim Tate

**Vice President and Executive
   Group Publisher**
Richard Swadley

**Vice President and Executive
   Publisher**
Joseph B. Wikert

Project Coordinator
Ryan Steffen

Graphics and Production Specialists
Denny Hager
Jennifer Heleine
Stephanie D. Jumper
Alicia B. South

Quality Control Technician
Joe Niesen

Media Development Coordinator
Laura Atkinson

Proofreading and Indexing
TECHBOOKS Production Services

CONTENTS

The Declaration of Interdependence (that Bob Wysocki, I, and others co-authored) documents the fundamental principles that underlie an agile-adaptive approach to project management. (See www.apln.org for the complete Declaration.) Two of these principles, are particularly relevant to this book:

- We **improve effectiveness and reliability** through situationally specific strategies, processes, and practices.
- We **expect uncertainty** and manage for it through iterations, anticipation, and adaptation.

No two people are alike. No two teams are alike. No two projects are alike. Yet many organizations and project managers attempt to "standardize" projects, essentially trying again and again and again to pound square pegs into round holes. I've watched team after team attack high-risk, high-uncertainty projects with meticulously laid out plans that were complete and utter fantasy. Furthermore, most team members knew that the plan was fantasy, but if you have only square pegs, you use square pegs.

Bob introduces us to square, round, triangular, and polygonal pegs—just the right one for specific situations. But even better, he helps us figure what kinds of holes we have. It's one thing to have a principle that says "situationally specific," but what are the situations? How many do we have? What are the key characteristics that define a "situation" for a project manager? Bob introduces us to a simple but powerful concept to guide practitioners in defining holes (the situation) and then presents us with a suite of pegs (solutions) that fit each type of hole.

Bob defines project situations using a four-quadrant analysis of the certainty, or uncertainty, of both ends and means. With some projects the ends, the business objectives and specific software requirements that enable us to meet the objectives, are fairly well known. On others, they are ill defined in the beginning and have to evolve over the life of the project as more is learned. Some projects may utilize a well-understood and proven technology, while others employ bleeding edge, state-of-the-art technology. When square peg project managers meet uncertainty, they try to pound out that uncertainty with a detail plan—but in reality that meticulous plan is nothing more than a superstition about the future.

However, when the objectives, requirements, and technology are well known, we should be able to plan the project with some assurances that we can meet the plans for scope, schedule, and cost.

To differentiate projects using a slightly different analogy, when both ends and means are well known, we can utilize a traditional Plan-Do strategy in which we lay out the plan and then execute the steps. When both ends and means are not well known, the strategy could better be described as Envision-Explore. We lay out a rough plan, but we assume that significant changes will occur as we learn more during the project. The problem that many square-peg project managers fail to grasp is that many, if not most, high-risk and high-uncertainty issues cannot be "planned" away—they can only be "executed" away. You have to experiment with different options in order to attack uncertainty.

So the certainty-uncertainty of both ends and means provides us with a framework for identifying holes—specific situations. Bob next turns to the pegs—strategies that fit certain problems—strategy options that are absolutely critical in managing the variety of projects that organizations undertake today.

It is important to recognize that strategies and practices are separate things. Some people incorrectly think a particular practice is "agile," while another is "traditional." However, good practices can be used in either a traditional or an agile project (daily team meetings, for example). The critical factor in project management is strategy—the specific model of delivery one chooses to utilize.

Here again Bob elevates us from the simplistic—traditional or agile solutions—to a wider, richer strategy selection. He identifies four uniquely different strategies—Linear & Incremental, Iterative, Adaptive, and Extreme—and then provides us with the characteristics, advantages, and weaknesses of each.

In particular, Bob spends the bulk of the book delving into the latter three strategies—Iterative, Adaptive, and Extreme—because as the Declaration of Interdependence principle states, "We expect uncertainty and manage for it through iterations, anticipation, and adaptation." Today, when more and more projects occupy the uncertainty of ends and means category (and the highest valued ones also), newer Adaptive and Extreme strategies are needed. Bob not only identifies these strategies, but defines them in enough detail that practitioners can effectively utilize them.

If you are tired of trying to stuff square pegs in round holes, if you are having trouble with projects where uncertainty and high risk create floundering projects, then this is the book you need to read.

Jim Highsmith
Flagstaff, Arizona
November 2005

. . . Global 2000 companies will merge their SDLC (systems development life cycle) and PM (project management) strategies to develop domain specific "ILDEs" (integrated lifecycle and development environments) . . . how dysfunctional large companies are if they run Project Management Institute (PMI) guidance in their Project Management Office (PMO) whilst running Rational Unified Process (RUP) as their SDLC in the IT organization. . . . The most competitive companies will be the ones who merge the two schools of thought to deliver optimal value and efficiency by eliminating dysfunctional competitiveness between the project management process and the software lifecycle process.

Adapted from Melinda-Carol Ballou "Coordinating Project and Software Life-cycle Processes," META Group, November 2003, by David J. Anderson in a private communication

We are experiencing the convergence of two disciplines that will result in the creation of yet another discipline. The two disciplines are software development and project management. It is a convergence that is being formed out of necessity. We call this new discipline *effective software project management* (ESPM). It is the topic of this book.

Why Another Book on Software Project Management?

Modern project management is about 50 years old. It grew out of the engineering discipline as a management approach for construction projects. Concurrent with this development, the computer emerged as a primitive tool for businesses. The concurrent growth of project management, the computer as a commercial tool, and software development brought the need for all three to be merged into a discipline to support the enterprise. Today, that need is even more visible for several reasons:

- The discipline of project management is faced with major challenges especially in its ability to support advances in the software development arena

- There is a need to bring together a unified body of knowledge on project management for the software developer

- The practices of project management and software development need to mature into a strategic partnership to lead the formation of processes for the contemporary enterprise

- There is a need for a practical "how to" book that combines in a balanced framework the best practices from systems development life cycles (SDLC) and project management life cycles (PMLC)

These are the driving forces that led me to write this book. There is no book in the market that treats both of these topics in the integrated fashion and to the balanced depth as does this book.

What Is This Book About?

The literature abounds with books on information technology project management but they give passing treatment to how project management processes are applied to specific systems development methodologies. Similarly, there are a variety of books on specific systems development methodologies that do not provide in-depth treatment of project management as it relates to the systems development methodology. The missing piece is a book that gives equal treatment to project management as applied to specific systems development methodologies. Filling that gap is what this book is all about.

What Is the Purpose of This Book?

There are three purposes for this book:

- **To be a professional reference for software professionals**—The major software development models are discussed in this book along with the specific application of project management best practices to the management of those projects. In one place, software professionals can find everything they need to successfully manage their software development projects. In other words, this book is one-stop-shopping for the software development project manager.

- **To give project management consultants a single source for software development project management principles and practices**—For project management consultants whose clients are in the information technology business this book should be a constant companion. This book is a single source of in-depth application of project management best practices to the various needs of the information technology client.

- **To be a textbook for students of computer information systems and project management**—The companion book is *Effective Project Management: Traditional, Adaptive, Extreme, Third Edition* (Wiley, 2003). It was an experiment to write a book for both the professional reference market and the academic market. That experiment was a success as sales to the professional market continue to be healthy, and our new readers in the academic world adopt the book for their credit and non-credit courses at the undergraduate and graduate level. The book has been adopted in over 50 colleges and universities at the undergraduate, graduate, and continuing education markets. A number of training providers are also using the book as a supplement to their course materials. Our expectation is that this book will enjoy similar success in the academic market.

Who Should Read This Book?

The book is written both as a comprehensive reference for professional software development project managers and aspiring software development project managers and as a textbook for undergraduate and graduate students of computers and information systems and project management. It is my hope that this book will become a *de facto* source for all your software development project manager tool, template, and process needs. Anyone who aspires to successfully manage software development projects or successfully manage those who manage software development projects is a targeted reader. Specifically, the target markets are listed in the following sections, and how this book serves the needs of those markets is briefly discussed.

Seasoned Project Managers

You might have a varied and successful career as a project manager, perhaps serving the needs of the software developer. In this book I bring together in one reference a number of best practices in software development project management. If you are a project manager who is looking for an introduction to the management of software development projects, this book will serve that purpose. It is both introductory and advanced and will have a long and useful lifetime for you.

Frustrated Project Managers

Perhaps you have a history of less than stellar performance in the management of software development projects. In many cases you have tried unsuccessfully to adapt your current toolbox of management practices with limited success. You are no doubt looking for more, and this book is just the place. In this book, a number of best project management practices are adapted to the specific management requirements of various types of software development projects.

"Wanna Be" Project Managers

If you are new to software development project management, this book provides a solid foundation as well as the more advanced topics for the special management needs of more complex software development projects. This book is a fast-track introduction and an in-depth treatment of all you need to launch and grow a successful career as a software development project manager.

Occasional Project Managers

This book is a ready reference for those you project managers who haven't mastered the more complex types of software development project management situations and need a reference that is "recipe oriented." Your need is for guidance from day one to day last in software development projects. This book is an excellent fit for you.

Project Management Consultants and Software Development Consultants

As a consultant, you don't often have the luxury of searching for that seldom needed solution. For you, this book is the reference for every viable integration of software development and project management. This is your "one-stop shopping" source.

Software Developers

Many software developers have depended on the systems development life cycle as a substitute for many parts of the project management life cycle. In many cases, the results have been less than expected. In this book, you will find a practical solution to the integration of software development and project management best practices. The result is to gain the skills and competencies to work smarter, not harder.

Software Development Managers

If you are a software development manager, by integrating project management best practices into the software development life cycle you will have a repeatable framework within which to better manage you business unit. This book contains a number of such management aids to meet your specific needs.

Project Management Instructors and Trainers and Software Development Instructors and Trainers

Because this book is applications-oriented, it can serve as a complete reference and support text for your project management and software development classes and training sessions. Each chapter contains a number of thought provoking discussion questions. Answers to the discussion questions can be found by contacting the author at rkw@eiicorp.com. See the companion Web site for this book at www.wiley.com/go/espm for more support materials as well.

Computer Information Systems Students

The integration of software development and project management is inevitable, and this book aims to be the *de facto* book on the topic. If you are a serious student of ESPM, you will want this book in your library.

Students

Whether you are an independent learner or are taking credit or non-credit course work in software development and project management, this book has something for you and may prove indispensable. It can serve as the primary text or as a supplemental reference text in courses in software development or software project management.

How Will You Benefit from Reading This Book?

In one place, the software developer can learn how project management best practices can support the effective completion of their project.

In one place, the project manager can see the connections between their discipline and effective software development.

In total, the software developer as project manager can reliably and repeatedly deliver software development projects.

How Is This Book Organized?

The book is organized into seven parts. Parts II through VI are structured to be as parallel as possible to facilitate finding, interpreting, and comparing information on different types of software development projects and their project management infrastructures.

NOTE
As you read through the following introduction to how the book is organized, don't be put off if you don't recognize all the terms or concepts mentioned. All these ideas, processes, and models are explained thoroughly as you progress through the book.

Part I: The Evolving State of ESPM

This introductory part provides a survey of both the project management landscape and the software development landscape. Both have been evolving independently of one another. The project management landscape is dotted with approaches that have not met the expectations of customers and clients. The failure rates of projects are beyond reasonable expectations, but little seems to have been done to reduce the unacceptably high failure rates. At the same time the software development landscape is dotted with a myriad of approaches for every conceivable type of software development situation. Some succeed while others fail. There seems to be a gap between the two situations. That gap is the lack of an integrated approach to software development project management.

The literature is filled with books that have a strong focus on software development with only brief treatment of project management. This book fills that gap. It gives equitable treatment to both topics and integrates them at a depth and breadth previously not available in the literature.

The underlying structure of this book is based on the certainty to uncertainty continuum, which is unique to this book. All software development models can be arrayed on this continuum. The linear models of Part II lie at the certainty end of this continuum. Parts III through VI discuss models that fall along this continuum from the certainty end to the uncertainty end.

Part I consists of two chapters.

Chapter 1: The Changing Landscape of Software Development

This chapter provides the conceptual foundation for the entire software development project management (SDPM) discipline. It categorizes projects based on the extent of goal clarity and solution clarity. It defines a four quadrant model as the basis of a discussion of risk, team cohesion, communications, customer involvement, change, specification, and business value.

Chapter 2: SDPM Roadmap

This chapter presents a high-level overview of the five SDPM strategies and the specific models that can be found in each strategy. For each strategy, I discuss the characteristics, strengths, and weaknesses.

Part II: Linear ESPM

Linear approaches to software development started with the definition of the Waterfall model. While the Waterfall model was designed to move sequentially from idea through deployment it was an approach that afforded no looking back. Once a phase was completed and approved, it was not visited again. That works as long as requirements are clearly and completely documented and there are no change requests from the client.

Part II has seven chapters.

Chapter 3: Linear SDPM Strategy

The introductory chapter in each of Parts II through VI defines the software project management life cycle of the project types covered in that part. There will be some variation to the Scope, Plan, Launch, Monitor/Control, and Close Phases because of the nature of the software development process being managed. The Linear SDPM type projects consist of the Standard Waterfall and Rapid Development Waterfall models.

Chapter 4: The Linear SDPM Scoping Phase

Because of the nature of Linear software development projects, requirements are completely and clearly identified and documented. A brief document called the Project Overview Statement is prepared and signed off by client and project manager.

Chapter 5: The Linear SDPM Planning Phase

Across all software development project types, the Planning Phase can run from very formal to very informal. Despite that, all of the tools, templates, and processes will be evident in some part of the Planning Phase. The focus here will be on the WBS, scheduling, and resource requirements.

Chapter 6: The Linear SDPM Launching Phase

Regardless of the software development approach being taken, the team needs to figure out how they are going to work together and establish the rules that will govern the engagement. The unique aspect of the Rapid Development Waterfall model is the use of concurrent development paths. These are called "swim lanes" and are a central focus in this chapter.

Chapter 7: The Linear SDPM Monitoring and Controlling Phase

The project work is underway. The focus in this chapter is on measuring project progress and performance. Part of that includes project review sessions and scope change management.

Chapter 8: The Linear SDPM Closing Phase

Through the acceptance procedures, the client will validate that requirements have been met, and it is time to deploy the software to the users. Lessons learned will be a big part of the closing activities, as will the celebration of success by the team.

Chapter 9: The Linear SDPM Strategy Summary

Each part ends with a chapter that compares and contrasts the models presented. In this chapter I discuss risk, change tolerance of the models, and team structures.

Part III: Incremental ESPM

The next set of variations that I cover involves Incremental models. Here, the full functionality is introduced in chunks. Deliverables are put into production status in sequence—each chunk adding more functionality than the last so that the system grows. In addition to getting business value earlier, the client may discover improvements that can be incorporated into later chunks. Whereas the Linear models are change intolerant, the Incremental models at least allow for some change.

Part III has seven chapters.

Chapter 10: Incremental SDPM Strategy

The Incremental SDPM is nothing more than a string of Linear SDPMs. Each Linear chunk adds another piece to the solution until eventually the complete solution emerges. Other than that, the only other difference is that partial solutions are put into production earlier and business value accrues. The Linear SDPM strategy deploys all functionality at the end of the project. Another way of looking at the difference is that the Linear model is the Incremental model with only one increment. The Staged Delivery Waterfall and the Feature-Driven Development model are the two variations discussed in Part III.

Chapter 11: The Incremental SDPM Scoping Phase

The Scoping Phase of the Incremental model and the Linear model are the same. Requirements are gathered and documented the same way. That means that the choice of Linear or Incremental can be postponed until requirements are gathered. Any concern that requirements may not be complete and clear may lead you to decide on using the Incremental model rather than the Linear model.

Chapter 12: The Incremental SDPM Planning Phase

Planning for the Incremental model requires a strategy for chunking the functionality into separate and dependent chunks. Each chunk should have enough functionality content to make it a useful partial solution that can be put into production status while waiting for the addition of the next chunk. The Function/Feature Breakdown Structure is introduced as an aid to chunking.

Chapter 13: The Incremental SDPM Launching Phase

The project team may change at each increment, which is not the case with the Linear model. That places some additional burdens on each team. They will have to ensure a clean hand-off from team to team as the project moves from increment to increment.

Chapter 14: The Incremental SDPM Monitoring and Controlling Phase

Within each increment, the monitoring and controlling activities are the same as with the Linear model. The major area of concern is scope change management. Scope changes approved in one increment may affect later increments, and that needs to be accounted for in the scope change management process.

Chapter 15: The Incremental SDPM Closing Phase

The Closing Phase within each increment is the handoff activity from one team to another. That handoff will require some documentation different than if it were a Linear model.

Chapter 16: The Incremental SDPM Strategy Summary

There are only three points of comparison and contrast here. The first deals with introducing interim releases at each increment as compared to one for the Linear model, the second with the scope change management process, and the third with the handoff between increments.

Part IV: Iterative ESPM

The differences between the Incremental model and the Iterative model are vast. The Iterative model is used when functionality, requirements, and features are only partially known at the outset, and it is up to the model chosen to clarify that information. In Iterative ESPM the solution as it is known at each iteration is built and deployed. It is used and then modified in the next iteration. This process continues until the required solution is built.

Part IV has seven chapters.

Chapter 17: Iterative SDPM Strategy

An *iteration* is defined here as a development cycle that adds more functionality and/or features to an incomplete solution in order to have it converge on a complete solution. While iteration is easy to define, it has a number of variations that you will have to take into account. For example, you can iterate on any of the following requirements: design, functionality, features, usability, or code. There are four models that fit into the Iterative SDPM strategy group: Dynamic Systems Development Method (DSDM), Evolutionary Systems Development, Rational Unified Process (RUP), and SCRUM (not an acronym but a term used in rugby).

Chapter 18: The Iterative SDPM Scoping Phase

The major departure here from the previous two types of software development projects is the absence of a complete specification of requirements. The remaining three types of software development projects all have this in common but at different levels of incompleteness. These three types are collectively called "agile software development" and they are managed using "agile project management" approaches. The Iterative SDPM strategy is the first of the three I will discuss. Requirements gathering is by definition not something that can be completely done at the outset in an Iterative SDPM strategy. You can complete only part of it and will have to depend on the software development approach you take and the project management infrastructure to identify the remaining requirements. In other words, this and the next two SDPM strategies are characterized by processes of learning and discovery.

Chapter 19: The Iterative SDPM Planning Phase

All of the Iterative software development approaches depend on "just-in-time planning." Only the next iteration will be planned, and it will be planned at the completion of the immediately preceding iteration.

Chapter 20: The Iterative SDPM Launching Phase

The team leadership models and team operating rules are very different for Iterative SDPM projects as compared to those you have studied so far. Even within the group of Iterative SDPM models, the leadership and team operating rules differ widely.

Chapter 21: The Iterative SDPM Monitoring and Controlling Phase

The further out you go in terms of uncertainty in the project the less formal you are in terms of project status reporting. Written reports become quite rare in the uncertain project environment. In these types of projects you are primarily looking for signs that the project is converging to an acceptable solution.

Chapter 22: The Iterative SDPM Closing Phase

Each iteration will have its own Closing Phase. It includes activities with the client to decide how to go forward (or even if to go forward) to the next iteration and what the next iteration will contain.

Chapter 23:The Iterative SDPM Strategy Summary

There are considerable differences between the four models that fall in the Iterative SDPM category. In this chapter, I present those differences and discuss selection strategies.

Part V: Adaptive ESPM

In this part I present two software development project management approaches to those projects whose goal is clear but whose solution is not. In informal surveys the vast majority of respondents confirm that adaptive approaches should be used in more than 75 percent of the software development projects. Unfortunately, many software developers try to adapt linear approaches when they clearly are a bad fit. The result is the high failure rate that accompanies such projects. The most notable difference between Iterative and Adaptive approaches is meaningful customer involvement. While a certain level of involvement is needed for Iterative approaches, that involvement increases dramatically as you transition to Adaptive ESPM.

Part V has seven chapters.

Chapter 24: The Adaptive SDPM Strategy

The Adaptive SDPM strategy is conceptually very different than the Iterative SDPM strategy. First there is the recognition that the solution is only partially known and must be discovered and integrated as the project work commences. Users of The Iterative SDPM strategy may not have to deal with that situation. While both life cycles are iterative, the role of the customer in the latter is direction setting where it is not in the Iterative ESPM life cycle. There are two models that follow the Adaptive SDPM strategy: Adaptive Project Framework (APF) and Adaptive Software Development (ASD). APF is a robust model in that it isn't limited to software development, as is ASD. This chapter also discusses two variations to APF—business case justification and prototyping—and how APF can be embedded in other SDPM models.

Chapter 25: The Adaptive SDPM Scoping Phase

Scoping an Adaptive SDPM project is often a high-level activity. Because the solution is not known or at best partially known, scoping at a detailed level is something that happens over the cycles of the project. That means that requirements gathering and planning are also just-in-time activities.

Chapter 26: The Adaptive SDPM Planning Phase

As you move further into the uncertainty domain, Adaptive processes become lighter. By that I mean less documentation and formality are part of the project management approach. The transition is away from non–value-added work to value-added work. The Adaptive project is on an aggressive timeframe with frequent changes. Daily face-to-face team meetings take the place of internal status reports. Much more of a team aura pervades the project. The WBS becomes a just-in-time activity; dependency diagrams and formal project schedules give way to small team scheduling at the whiteboard. The critical path is meaningless in Adaptive project management.

Chapter 27: The Adaptive SDPM Launching Phase

In Adaptive SDPM, it is important that the team be solid and effective. Roles and responsibilities must be clearly understood. Team leadership becomes more of a coordinating activity because there will be any number of subteams working on some small aspect of the software system. Team leadership may change as the project transitions from phase to phase.

Chapter 28: The Adaptive SDPM Monitoring and Controlling Phase

The major difference here compared to the previous life cycles is that change is an integral part of the life cycle. It is not an add-on. It is a necessity. The solution will not be discovered unless change is driving the process.

Chapter 29: The Adaptive SDPM Closing Phase

At the completion of each iteration of an Adaptive SDPM project there is a checkpoint with the customer. This is a go/no go stage-gate for the project. There is a quality check on what has been done so far and a planning activity as newly discovered requirements, functionality, and features are integrated into the prioritization scheme and plans for the next iteration are formulated.

Chapter 30: The Adaptive SDPM Strategy Summary

The two models discussed in this part are compared and contrasted, and I discuss when to use them and when not to use them.

Part VI: Extreme ESPM

In Part VI, you have reached the models that deal with situations in which very little is known about the goal and perhaps nothing about the solution. Several ideas may be floating around as to what might generate a solution, but you may have little evidence to support those contentions. Think of it as a pure R&D situation, and you won't be far off the mark.

Part VI has seven chapters.

Chapter 31: Extreme SDPM Strategy

The life cycle looks much like the Adaptive SDPM life cycle. The difference comes as you look inside each of the phases. Part VI covers several extreme-type models including INSPIRE and extreme programming.

Chapter 32: The Extreme SDPM Scoping Phase

In most cases scoping involves setting the boundaries of the project in terms of time and cost, cycle length, and other general parameters.

Chapter 33: The Extreme SDPM Planning Phase

Planning is just-in-time and not very detailed. The team and its subteams are left to direct their part of the project as they see fit. There are few standards because these would tend to stifle creativity.

Chapter 34: The Extreme SDPM Launching Phase

These are the activities that get the team started on the next iteration. There may be hand offs as new teams come into the picture to replace the previous cycle's team.

Chapter 35: The Extreme SDPM Monitoring and Controlling Phase

Just as in the Adaptive SDPM, this is an informal process that is carried out among the team in its daily meetings. Customer involvement is very high and so little can be done that will stray from the project directives. Constant redirection and replanning is evident, even within an iteration.

Chapter 36: The Extreme SDPM Closing Phase

There are two Closing stages here. One is the Closing activities that pertain to the just completed iteration. The other is the Closing Phase that pertains to the project itself. The iteration closing activities consist of a review of what has been completed, an evaluation of whether or not the deliverables are converging on a solution, and a consideration of what should be done in the next iteration (assuming there is a next iteration). The project closing activities include the standard tasks: business value verification, post-implementation audit, and lessons learned.

Chapter 37: The Extreme SDPM Strategy Summary

The two models discussed in this part are compared and contrasted, and I discuss when to use them and when not to use them.

Part VII: In Summary

This is a comprehensive look back at the models in each of the SDPM strategies. I include an overall comparison, discuss the challenges yet to be faced, and offer suggestions of how you might approach each of the models.

Part VII has two chapters.

Chapter 38: Where Are You?

This is a closer look at the status of software development project management, its strengths and weaknesses, and the challenges yet to be faced.

Chapter 39: Where Do You Want to Go and How Can You Get There?

This is an attempt to envision an end state for software development project management and a plan to get there.

Appendixes

In addition to the chapters, you have two appendixes that can help direct you to further information and resources. Appendix A, "What's on the Web Site," explains what you will find if you surf to the Web site that's associated with this book at www.wiley.com/go/espm. Then, in Appendix B, "Bibliography," you will find a list of related materials for further reading.

Following these two appendixes are a number of appendixes that contain introductory materials for those who want to refresh their knowledge of the basics of project management. These appendixes include "The Project Overview Statement," "Requirements Gathering," "Work Breakdown Structure," "Estimation," "The Project Network Diagram," "The Resource Schedule," "Organizing the Project Team," "Project Performance Reporting," and "Business Process Flow Diagramming."

What Are the Features of the Book?

This book is written in the same style and standards as my previous best-selling book: *Effective Project Management: Traditional. Adaptive. Extreme. Third Edition* (Wiley, 2003). This means the book has the following features:

- It is practice- and applications-oriented.
- It is readable.
- It provides intriguing and useful discussion questions.
- It makes figures and tables available for teacher/instructor use.

Practice- and Applications-Oriented

While all of my previous books have been grounded in concepts and principles, they all are practice- and applications-oriented. I've tried to maintain the research tradition in all that I write and at the same time spare you the task of translating theory to practice. At the same time I try to provide comparisons of different approaches to a problem so that you always know which approach to take and why. I will warn you of the traps. My vision is that you will have my books opened to the pages that discuss the "how to" aspects of a tool, template, or process as you are trying to implement them in your project.

Readable

In keeping with the practice and applications orientation, my writing style is conversational. I want you to feel like we are sitting across from one another having a conversation about some issue or topic. What I try to avoid is giving you a tome to read just to get a few nuggets of information. I am not verbose. I don't have the time to write all those words, and you don't have (or want) to spend the time to read them.

Discussion Questions for Instructors

The third edition of *Effective Project Management: Traditional, Adaptive, Extreme* departed somewhat from the second edition in that I tried to make that edition more appealing to the academic market while not sacrificing the professional market that had already been established with the second edition. By all measures that approach was successful, and the same style will be used here.

Each chapter ends with a few discussion questions that might be used by instructors to create some dialog with the class or might be used for written assignments. These are not your favorite "list the ten causes of the Civil War" type questions, but rather they are questions that I hope will be thought provoking. There are no right answers, although there are plenty of wrong answers. An answer file has been created for instructors. Just e-mail me at `rkw@eiicorp` `.com`, identify yourself as a legitimate instructor or faculty member, and I'll send you the answer file. I'd love to hear from you and hear how you are using the book and its materials.

Files of Figures and Tables

For the benefit of instructors and others who might want to use the figures and tables from the text, I have prepared files containing all of that information. All I ask is that you give the proper attributions for the source of your materials.

What's on the Web Site?

A registered Web site has been built for readers of this book. There you will find the files of figures and tables previously mentioned. This Web site may be accessed at www.wiley.com/go/espm.

How Should You Read This Book?

Front to back would be a straightforward approach to reading this book and would support the needs of the academic market. The typical credit course might cover the book from Chapter 1 through Chapter 39. However, if you or your students need some background in project management, the appendixes can be quickly reviewed.

However, if you have more specific needs, each part can be read and referenced independently of any other part. Each part is targeted to a specific model type to accommodate the reference and application needs of the professional market. Each part is self-contained so that the practicing professional need refer only to the part appropriate to their project application. There is no need to read the entire book if your need is for a specific strategy.

Summary

My intent with this book is to bring together a breadth and depth of materials on software development life cycles and the project management tools, templates, and processes to support them. I have integrated the two disciplines. As far as I know this is the first book that can make that claim. I'll let you be the judge as to whether or not I have met that objective and provided you with a unique reference book on the new and emerging discipline of software development project management. Good luck and may all your software development projects be effective and successful!

The Evolving State of ESPM

No one would argue that software development has undergone a major change in the past decade. On what seems to be a continuous basis you are bombarded with the latest and greatest models, tools, templates, and processes. You may be confused and wonder which of these, if any, make any sense. Should you use this one or that one or maybe the same one for all software development projects?

In this part I will lay the groundwork for what proposes to be the introduction of a new discipline—one that fully integrates software development life cycles and project management life cycles. This is the first attempt at defining such a discipline. Much remains to be done. But at least I can lay claim to trying to bring some order out of the seeming chaos faced by software developers and their project management partners.

CHAPTER 1

The Changing Landscape of Software Development

We're trying to change the habits of an awful lot of people. That won't happen overnight but it will bloody well happen.

John Akers, CEO
IBM

Chapter Learning Objectives

After reading this chapter, you will be able to:

- ◆ Explain the software development landscape
- ◆ Know the definition of software development project management strategy
- ◆ Understand the four quadrants of the software development landscape
- ◆ Know what project management approach is compatible with each quadrant
- ◆ Explain the relationship of complexity and uncertainty and the software development project management landscape
- ◆ Know how risk, team cohesion, communications, customer involvement, change, specification, and business value are affected by the complexity/uncertainty domain
- ◆ Explain the importance of balancing people, process, and technology in the organization
- ◆ Explain staff-driven, process-driven, and technology-driven environments

The software project management landscape is ever-changing. It is defined by no less than five interdependent variables: the characteristics of the software project itself, the software development life cycle, the project management life cycle, the profile of the project team, and the technology that supports the whole. While this may seem overwhelming, it isn't. I'll explore the complexities of this multidimensional landscape with you and show you how to obtain and sustain an effective presence in this changing landscape.

Software development processes and modern project management processes are both about 50 years old. Both are adolescents. Both are trying to earn a seat at the corporate strategy table. Both are sure that they can contribute to the success of their enterprise. Unfortunately, both have a reputation for failing to live up to expectations. Both are struggling, and both face tremendous odds against making any positive impressions.

The equation that says you must strike a balance between people, process, and technology holds the clue as to where you should look. People are smart. Of that there is no doubt. How many times have you heard an executive say, "Just put five of our smart people together in a room, and they will solve any problem you can give them." That may be true, but I don't think anyone would bet the future of their enterprise on the continuing heroic efforts of the anointed few. Technology is racing ahead faster than any organization can absorb, so that can't be the problem. Process is the only thing left, and it is to process that you turn in this book. But it isn't just your normal everyday processes that have your attention. It is the integration of software development processes and project management processes that will demand your attention throughout this book. The result of that integration will be a type of discipline—effective software project management (ESPM). This book is about the concepts and principles of ESPM and its application to real software development problems.

Despite their brief history, software development and project management practitioner groups have never taken the pains to seriously integrate what they have learned with one another. Software developers use their systems development life cycle as a surrogate for project management. Traditional project managers are locked into the construction and engineering mindset that initially defined and continues to define the project management discipline. The impact of the construction and engineering practices on project management continues to be a roadblock to the further development of project management in the software development discipline. As a result, most software developers dismiss most project managers as incapable and irrelevant to meeting their needs. What is needed is to have traditional project managers think openly and creatively about how to effectively serve their customers and deliver business value as their prime directive.

That suggests a fresh approach to managing software development projects. I hope to do that in pages that follow. But right now that that doesn't mean creating new tools, templates, or processes. What we have now is sufficient. What we do not have is the awareness, skills, and creativity to integrate project management life cycles (PMLC) and software development life cycles (SDLC), and the courage to stay the course in implementation of the resulting integrations.

In this book, I take the position that the characteristics of the software development project drive your choice as to the project management tools, templates, and processes that should be used. This is not a recipe book to be blindly followed. Rather, it is a book that teaches you how to create a recipe. In other words, one of my objectives is to help you think like a great project manager.

What Is a Software Development Project?

Several types of software development projects are within the scope of this book. They range from repeatable projects that have been done many times before to projects that are cutting edge problem solving projects. Each presents its own special challenge to the developer. The example given below will be the staging area for exploring effective approaches to software development project management (SDPM).

DEFINITION: SOFTWARE DEVELOPMENT PROJECT

A software development project is a complex undertaking by two or more persons within the boundaries of time, budget, and staff resources that produces new or enhanced computer code that adds significant business value to a new or existing business process.

Although this is a restrictive definition, it does define the types of software development projects that are addressed in this book. The criteria for these projects are that they have the potential of adding significant business value and are not trivial undertakings. These development projects will have significant business value, be highly visible, be of moderate to high complexity, and were needed yesterday.

Examples of Two Software Development Projects

I've crafted a hypothetical case study that will be a referent as I apply the SDPM strategies presented in this book. I hope that this will help you further align yourself with using the models and approaches that this book addresses. I'll incorporate more details to the case study as needed. Any resemblance to past or present companies is strictly coincidental. The case study is purely hypothetical and written to illustrate the use of the concepts and principles in this book.

Introducing the Case Study

Pizza Delivered Quickly (PDQ) is a 40-store local chain of eat-in and home delivery pizza stores. Recently PDQ has lost 30 percent of sales revenue due mostly to a drop in their home delivery business. They attribute this solely to their major competitor who recently promoted a program that guarantees 30-minute delivery service from order entry to home delivery. PDQ advertises one-hour delivery. PDQ currently uses computers for in-store operations and the usual business functions but otherwise is not heavily dependent upon software systems to help them receive, process, and deliver their customers' orders. Pepe Ronee, their Manager of Information Systems, has been charged with developing a software application to identify "pizza factory" locations and create the software system needed to operate them. In commissioning this project, Dee Livery, their president, said to pull out all the stops. She further stated that the future of PDQ depends on this project. She wants the team to investigate an option to deliver the pizza unbaked and "ready for the oven" in 30 minutes or less or deliver it pre-baked in 45 minutes or less.

These pizza factories would not have any retail space. Their only function would be to receive orders, and prepare and deliver the pizzas. The factory location nearest the customer's location will receive the order from a central ordering facility, and process and deliver the order within 30 or 45 minutes of order entry, depending on whether the customer orders their pizza ready for the oven or already baked.

There are two software development projects identified here:

- The first is a software system to find pizza factory locations.
- The second is a software system to support factory operations.

Clearly the first is a very complex application. It will require heavy involvement by a number of PDQ managers. The goal can be clearly defined but even at that the solution will not be at all obvious. The second focuses on routine business functions and should be easily defined. Off-the-shelf commercial software may be a big part of the final solution to support factory operations.

These are obviously very different software development projects requiring very different approaches. The pizza factory location system will be a very sophisticated modeling tool. The requirements, functionality, and features are not at all obvious. Some of the solution can probably be envisioned, but clearly the whole solution is elusive at this early stage. Exactly how it will do modeling is not known at the outset. It will have to be discovered as the development project is underway. The operations system can utilize commercial off the shelf (COTS) order entry software, which will have to be enhanced at the front end to direct the order to the closest factory and provide driving directions for delivery and other fulfillment tasks on the back end. The requirements, functionality, and features of this system may be problematic.

As the case study unfolds in later chapters, you will see that this simple yet realistic case study is rich with learning opportunities. I expect to draw heavily on it for practical illustrations of the concepts and principles presented here.

What Is Software Development Project Management?

Now that you have a clear idea of what a software development project is, it's important to clearly define what software development project management is.

DEFINITION: SDPM

Software development project management is the discipline of assessing the characteristics of the software to be developed, choosing the best fit software development life cycle, and then choosing the appropriate project management approach to ensure meeting the customer needs for delivering business value as effectively and efficiently as possible.

At the risk of cluttering up your vocabulary, I have coined a phrase that reflects the thinking process that I follow to craft a management approach to software development. The definition that follows is unique to this book but important to add to your vocabulary. From now on, any use of the term *SDPM strategy* refers to the definition given here.

DEFINITION: SDPM STRATEGY

A SDPM strategy is an integration of a software development life cycle and a project management life cycle into a customer-facing approach that will produce maximum business value regardless of the obstacles that may arise.

I want you to think of SDPM as an emerging discipline. It is new, although the two components that define it are not new. What is new is the integration of those components to produce an effective SDPM environment. The SDPM strategy for making this happen will be developed in this book.

The title of this section poses a question that is not trivial and certainly not a rhetorical question. I know several project managers that would like to have a working definition of exactly what constitutes software development project management. And further to the point, they would like to know how to do it. This book is a first attempt, but certainly not the last, to answer both questions. My expectations for the effective management of software development projects lie not only in the answer to these questions but also in the answer to three questions that are more operationally focused:

- What are the characteristics of the software to be developed?
- What software development approach is appropriate for building the software?
- What project management approach is appropriate for managing the chosen software development process?

The questions are meant to be answered in the order listed. Each one is dependent on the answers to the previous questions. Furthermore, in execution all three are dependent upon one another. Compare this to the situation where both the software development approach and the project management approach are fixed. Given those two constraints, what do you want us to develop? Do you operate like a solution out looking for a problem? Wouldn't you rather let the characteristics of the problem drive your choices for solution approach? I would hope so. That is the focus of this book.

What Are the Characteristics of the Software to Be Developed?

When I think of the software development landscape, I think of it in very simple terms. I see it as a two-dimensional grid like the one shown in Figure 1-1.

The first dimension relates to the goal of the software development project. The goal is either clearly specified (therefore known) or it is not clearly specified (therefore not known). It's an all or nothing situation. The boundary between clear and not clear is more conceptual that actual. The same is true of the second dimension, which relates to the solution or how you expect to reach the goal. That also has two categories. The solution is either clearly specified (and therefore known) or it is not clearly specified (and therefore not known). If you intersect these two dimensions as shown in the figure, then you have defined a four-category classification of software development projects. This classification is simple but inclusive of every software development project. That is, every software development project that ever has been or ever will be must fall into one and only one of these four categories.

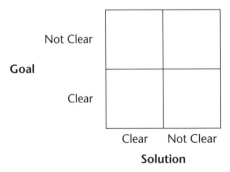

Figure 1-1: The software development landscape

Why is this important? First and foremost, the characteristics of the software to be developed will play an important role in determining the model that will be used. Each of these quadrants presents the development team with a number of decisions regarding how to go forward. The next sections briefly examine each quadrant and the salient aspects of clarity or lack thereof with respect to goal and solution.

Quadrant 1: Goal and Solution Are Clearly Specified

How could it be any better than to clearly know the goal and the solution? This is the best of all possible worlds, but it is also the least likely to occur in today's fast-paced, continuously changing business world. Software development projects that fall into this quadrant are familiar to the organization. Perhaps similar projects have been done several times before. There are no surprises. The client has clearly specified the goal and how to reach that goal. Little change is expected. A variety of approaches is in use for such software development projects. They are all of the design-build-test-implement variety or some variation of the linear concept implied by these approaches. Such projects also put the team on familiar technology grounds. The hardware, software, and telecommunications environments are familiar to the team. They have used them repeatedly and have developed a skilled and competent developer bench to handle such projects.

The limiting factors in these plan-driven approaches are that they are change-intolerant, are focused on delivering according to time and budget constraints, and rely more on compliance to plan than on delivering business value. The plan is sacred, and conformance to it is the hallmark of a successful project team.

Because of the times we live in, these approaches are rapidly becoming dinosaurs. At least the frequency of their application is diminishing rapidly. They are giving way to a whole new collection of approaches that are more customer-focused and deliver business value rather than adhere to a schedule and budget plan.

In addition to a clearly defined goal and solution, software development projects that correctly fall into this quadrant have several identifying characteristics as briefly identified here.

Low Complexity

Other than the fact that the project really is simple, this will often be attributable to the fact that the software development project rings of familiarity. It might be a straightforward application of established business rules and therefore take advantage of existing designs and coding. To the developer it might look like a cut-and-paste exercise. In such cases integration and testing will be the most challenging phases of the development project.

You can still find situations where the project is complex but still well-defined. However, these are rare.

Well-Understood Technology Infrastructure

A well-understood technology infrastructure is one that is stable and has been the foundation for many software development projects in the past. That means that the accompanying skills and competencies to work with the technology infrastructure are well-grounded in the development teams.

Low Risk

The total environment for development projects in this quadrant is that it is known. All that could happen to put the project at risk has occurred in the past, and you have well-tested and well-used mitigation strategies in place. Experience has rooted out all of the mistakes that could be made. The customer is confident that it has done a great job identifying requirements, functions, and features, and they are not likely to change. Except for acts of nature and other unavoidable events, the project is protected from avoidable events. You find few unanticipated risks in software development projects in this quadrant.

Experienced and Skilled Developer Teams

Past projects have been good training grounds for the teams. They have had opportunities to learn or to enhance their skills and competencies.

NOTE I'll have much more to say about teams in the chapters that discuss the Launch Phase of each SDPM strategy. They are a critical success factor in all software development projects. As the characteristics of the software to be developed changes, so also does the profile of the team that can be most effective in developing that software.

Quadrant 2: Goal Is Clearly Specified but Solution Is Not

You have a host of incremental, iterative, and adaptive approaches to SDPM that can be used when the goal is clearly defined, but how to reach the goal—the solution—is not. As you give some thought to where your projects would fall in this landscape, consider the possibility that many if not most of them are really these types of projects. If that is the case, shouldn't you also be considering using an approach to managing these projects that accommodates the goal and solution characteristics of the project rather than trying to force fit some other approach that was designed for projects with much different characteristics?

I contend that the adaptive and iterative class of projects is continuously grow-ing. I make it a practice at all "rubber chicken" dinner presentations to ask about the frequency with which the attendees encounter Quadrant 2 projects. With very small variance they say that at least 75 percent of all their projects are Quadrant 2 projects. Many of them try to adapt Quadrant 1 solutions to Quadrant 2 projects and meet with very little success. The results have ranged from mediocre success to outright failure. Quadrant 2 projects present a differ-ent challenge and need a different approach. For years I have advocated that the approach to the project must be driven by the characteristics of the project. To reverse the order is to court disaster. With the addition of the Quadrant 2 approaches discussed in Parts IV, V, and VI of this book, I cover the project landscape with a full complement of approaches for every conceivable type of project.

Quadrant 3: Goal and Solution Are Not Clearly Specified

Quadrant 3 extends to the remotest boundaries of project types. Quadrant 3 projects are those projects whose goal and solution cannot be clearly defined. What little planning is done just in time, and the project proceeds through sev-eral iterations until it converges on an acceptable goal and solution. If instead there isn't any prospect of convergence, the customer might pull the plug and cancel the project at any time and look for alternative approaches.

Quadrant 4: Goal Is Not Clearly Specified but the Solution Is

The fourth category represents projects whose goals are not known but whose solutions are. This is an impossible situation. It would be equivalent to solutions out looking for problems. Nevertheless, we all have had experiences working with professional services organizations that practice such approaches. They advocate a one-size-fits-all approach, which has never shown to be very successful. I have always discouraged a one-size-fits-all approach with my clients. Most see the wisdom in adopting this position.

What Software Development Approach Is Appropriate for Building the Software?

The characteristics of the software development project will play an important role in determining the software development model to be used. Here I give a generic description of the model characteristics. In Chapter 2 I peel back the onion to the next level of detail and present the five classes of software devel-opment approaches. That sets the stage for a detailed discussion of the soft-ware development approaches in each of the five classes, which is the topic of Part II through Part VI of the book.

Quadrant 1: Goal and Solution Are Clearly Specified

Because all of the information that could be known about this development project is known and is considered stable, the appropriate development model is the one that gets to the end as quickly as possible. Based on the requirements, desired functionality, and specific features, a complete project plan can be developed. It specifies all of the work needed to meet the requirements, the schedule of that work, and the staff resources needed to deliver to the planned work. Quadrant 1 projects are clearly plan-driven projects. Their success is measured by compliance and delivery to that plan.

Quadrant 2: Goal Is Clearly Specified but Solution Is Not

As the solution moves from one that is clearly specified toward one that is not clearly specified, you move through a number of situations that require different handling. For example, suppose only some minor aspects of the solution are not known—features, perhaps; how would you proceed? An approach that includes as much of the solution as is known at the time should work quite well. That approach would allow the customer to examine, in the sense of a production prototype, what is in the solution in an attempt to discover what is not in the solution but should be. At the extreme, when very little is known about the solution, development projects are higher risk than those where a larger part of the solution is known. A solution is needed, and it is important that a solution be found. How would you proceed? What is needed is an approach that is designed to learn and discover the solution. Somehow that approach must start with what is known and reach out to what is not known. The anchor to this approach is that the goal is clearly specified.

Quadrant 3: Goal and Solution Are Not Clearly Specified

If goal clarity is not possible at the beginning of the project, the situation is much like a pure research and development project. Now how would you proceed? In this case you use an approach that clarifies the goal and contributes to the solution at the same time. The approach must embrace a number of concurrent probes that accomplish both. The concurrent probes might be the most likely ones that can accomplish goal clarification and the solution set at the same time. Depending on time, budget, and staff resources, these probes might be pursued sequentially or concurrently. Alternatively, the probes might eliminate and narrow the domain of feasible goal/solution pairs. Clearly Quadrant 3 projects are an entirely different class of projects and require a different approach to be successful.

Quadrant 4: Goal Is Not Clearly Specified but the Solution Is

Here is that nonsense quadrant again. You have the solution; now all you need is to find the problem. This is the stuff that academic articles are often made of. Post your solution and hope somebody responds with a problem that fits it. It has happened. Take the 3M Post-it Note saga, for example. The product sat on the shelf for several years before someone stumbled onto an application. The rest is history.

In summary, you have to answer the first of the three questions posed earlier: "What are the characteristics of the software to be developed?" Because the landscape has been defined in terms of four categories, it should be easy to identify the quadrant that the development project belongs to. If there is any doubt about the quadrant, err on the side of choosing a higher numbered quadrant. I'll have more to say on that strategy throughout the book.

What Project Management Approach Is Appropriate for Managing the Software Development Process?

Now that the first question has been answered and you know what quadrant the project lies in, you can answer the second question, "What project management approach is appropriate for managing software development projects in this quadrant?" As you move through the quadrants from clarity to lack of clarity, the project management processes you use must track with the needs of the project. As a general word of advice as you move through the quadrants, remember that "Lots is bad, less is better, and least is best." In other words, don't burden the project manager and team with needless planning and documentation that will just hinder their efforts. As my colleague Jim Highsmith has said to me conversationally: "The idea of enough structure, but not too much, drives agile managers to continually ask the question, 'How little structure can I get away with?' Too much structure stifles creativity. Too little structure breeds inefficiency." Quadrant 1 projects are plan-driven, process-heavy, and documentation-heavy. As you move to Quadrants 2 and 3 projects, heaviness gives way to lightness. Plan-driven gives way to value-driven, rigid process gives way to adaptive process, and documentation is largely replaced by tacit knowledge that is shared among the team members. These are some of the characteristics of the many approaches that fall in the *agile project management* taxonomy. Several approaches fall under the umbrella of agile. Each is discussed in detail in Part II through Part VI.

I've always felt that the project manager must see value in a project management process before she is willing to use it. Burdening the project manager with what they perceive as a lot of non-value-added work is counterproductive and to be avoided. This becomes more significant as you move from Quadrant 1 to 2 to 3. Furthermore, project managers will resist, and you will get a token effort at compliance. My overall philosophy is that the less non-value-added time and work that you encumber your project managers with the better off you will be. Replacing non-value-added work with value-added work increases the likelihood of project success. Time is a precious (and scarce) resource for every software development project. You need to resist the temptation to add work that doesn't directly contribute to the final deliverables. Up to a point the project manager should determine what is a value add to their project processes and documentation. Make it their responsibility to decide what to use and when to use it. This is the mark of a successful manager of project managers—that they make it possible for the project manager to be successful and then stay out of their way.

Project management methodologies include a number of tools, templates, and processes and the rules for their use. The process of integrating those tools, templates, and processes into software development processes is actually quite straightforward to define. It isn't quite that simple as far as implementation is concerned and that is what motivated me to write this book. In this book, you will learn how to do that integration effectively and how to deal with the various demons that raise their heads during that implementation.

The Complexity/Uncertainty Domain of SDPM

Each quadrant of the software development project landscape has different profiles when it comes to risk, team, communications, customer involvement, specification, change, business value, and documentation. In this section, you examine the changing profile of each domain as you move from quadrant to quadrant.

Complexity and uncertainty are positively correlated with one another. As software development projects become more complex, they become more uncertain. That follows from at least four other relationships, as commented on in the next four sections.

In the Quadrant 1 models you know where you are going, and you know precisely how you are going to get there. It's all in the requirements, functionality, and features. Your plan reflects all of the work, the schedule, and the resources that will get you there. No complexity here. As soon as you move away from a clearly specified solution and are in Quadrant 2, the world is no longer as kind to you as it was while you were in Quadrant 1. The minute you have uncertainty anywhere in the project complexity goes up. You have to devise a plan to fill in the missing pieces. There will be some added risk—you might not find the missing piece, or when you do, you find that it doesn't fit in with what you already have built—go back two steps, undo some previous work, and do the required rework. The plan changes. The schedule changes. A lot of the effort spent earlier on developing a detailed plan has gone to waste. By circumstance it has become non-value-added work. If you had only known.

As less and less of the solution is known, the realities of non-value-added work become more and more a factor. Time has been wasted. Quadrant 2 models are better equipped to handle this uncertainty and the complexity that results from it. The models are built on the assumption that the solution has to be discovered. Planning becomes less of a one-time task done at the outset to a just-in-time task done as late as possible. You have less and less reliance on a plan and more reliance on the tacit knowledge of the team. That doesn't reduce the complexity, but it does accommodate it. So even though complexity increases as you move from Quadrant 1 to 2 to 3, you have a way to deal with it for the betterment of your customer and your sanity as a project manager.

Requirements

As project complexity increases, the likelihood of nailing requirements decreases. This follows logically from the fact that the human brain can retain in memory only about seven pieces of information. The dimensions of complexity are likely to far exceed that constraint. In a complex software product the extent of the number of requirements, functionality, and features can be staggering. Some will conflict with each other. Some will be redundant. Some will be missing. Many of these might not become obvious until well into the design, development, and even integration-testing tasks.

Flexibility

As project complexity increases, so does the need for process flexibility. Increased complexity brings with it the need to be creative and adaptive. Neither is comfortable in the company of rigid processes. Quadrant 2 projects are easily compromised by being deluged with process, procedure, documentation, and meetings. Many of these are unrelated to a results-driven approach. They are the relics of plan-driven approaches. Along with the need for increased flexibility in Quadrant 2 and 3 projects is the need for increased adaptability. Companies that are undergoing a change of approach that recognizes the need to support not just Quadrant 1 projects but also Quadrant 2 projects are faced with a significant and different cultural and business change. For one, the business rules and rules of the project engagement will radically change. Expect resistance.

Flexibility here refers to the project management process. If you are using a one-size-fits-all approach, you have no flexibility. The process is the process is the process. Not a very comforting situation if the process gets in the way of commonsense behaviors and compromises your ability to deliver value to your customer. Wouldn't you rather be following a strategy that allows you to adapt to the changing situations?

Quadrant 1 development projects generally follow a traditional project management methodology. The plan is developed along with a schedule of deliverables and other milestone events. A formal change management process is part of the game plan. Progress against the planned schedule is tracked, and corrective actions are put in place to restore control over schedule and budget. A nice neat package isn't it? All is well until the process gets in the way of product development. For example, if the business situation and priorities change and result in a flurry of scope change requests to accommodate the new business climate, an inordinate amount of time is then be spent processing change requests at the expense of value-added work. The schedule slips beyond the point of recovery. The project plan, having changed several times, becomes a contrived mess. Whatever integrity there was in the initial plan and schedule is now lost among the changes.

Quadrant 2 is altogether different. Project management is really nothing more than organized commonsense. So when the process you are using gets in the way, you adapt. The process is changed to maintain focus on doing what makes sense to protect the creation of business value. Unlike Quadrant 1 processes, Quadrant 2 processes expect and embrace change as a way to a better solution and as a way to maximize business value within time and budget constraints. That means choosing and continually changing the SDPM strategy to increase the business value that will result from the project. Realize that to some extent scope is a variable in these types of SDPM strategies.

Quadrant 3 projects are even more dependent upon flexible approaches. Learning and discovery takes place throughout the project, and the team and customer must adjust how they are approaching the project on a moment's notice.

Adaptability

The less certain you are of project requirements, functionality, and features, the more need you will have to be adaptable with respect to process and procedure. Adaptability is directly related to the extent to which the team members are empowered to act. The ability of the team to adapt increases as empowerment becomes more pervasive. Remember to make it possible for the team members to be productive and stay out of their way. Don't encumber the team members with the need to get sign-offs that have nothing to do with delivering business value. Pick them carefully and trust them to act in the best interest if the customer.

Change

As complexity increases so does the frequency and need to receive and process change requests. A plan-driven software development project is not designed to effectively respond to change. Change upsets the order of things as some or all of the project plan is affected. Resource schedules are compromised. The more that change has to be dealt with, the more time is spent processing and evaluating the changes. That time is lost to the project. It should have been spent on value-added work. Instead it was spent processing change requests.

You spend so much time developing your project plan for your Quadrant 1 project that the last thing you want is to have to change it. But that is the reality in Quadrant 1 projects. Scope change always seems to add more work. Did you ever receive a scope change request from your customer that asked you to take something out? Not too likely. The reality is that the customer discovers something else they should have asked for in the solution. They didn't realize that or know that at the time. That leads to more work, not less. The call to action is clear—choose Quadrant 1 models when specifications are as stable as can be. The architects of the Quadrant 2 and 3 models knew this and so designed approaches that expected change and were ready to accommodate it. You'll see that in more detail in Parts 2 through 6 of the book.

Risk Versus the Complexity/Uncertainty Domain

Risk increases as you move from Quadrant 1 to 2 to 3. In Quadrant 1 you clearly know the goal and the solution and can build a definitive plan for getting there. The exposure to risks associated with product failure is low. The focus can then shift to process failure. A list of candidate risk drivers would have been compiled over past similar projects. Their likelihood, impact, and the appropriate mitigations is known and documented. Like a good athlete, you have anticipated what might happen and know how to act if it does.

As the software development project takes on the characteristics of Quadrant 2, two forces come into play. First, the SDPM strategy becomes more flexible and lighter. The process burden lessens as more attention is placed on delivering business value than on conformance to a plan. At the same time, the product risk increases, as illustrated in Figure 1-2. Risk increases in relation to the extent to which the solution is not known. On balance that means more effort should be placed on risk management as the software development project moves through Quadrant 2 and looks more like a Quadrant 3 project. You will have less experience with these risks because they are specific to the product being developed. In Quadrant 3, risk is the highest because you are in a research and development environment. Process risk is almost nonexistent because the ultimate in flexibility has been reached in this quadrant, but product risk is extremely high. You will have numerous product failures because of the highly speculative nature of Quadrant 3 projects, but that is okay. Those failures are expected to occur. Each product failure gets you that much closer to a functional solution, if such solution can be found within the operative time and budget constraints. At worst those failures eliminate one or more paths of investigation and so narrow the range of possible solutions.

Team Cohesiveness Versus the Complexity/ Uncertainty Domain

In Quadrant 1 the successful team doesn't really have to be a team at all. You assemble a group of specialists and assign each to their respective tasks at the appropriate times. Period. The plan is sacred, and the plan guides them through their task. It tells them what they need to do, when they need to do it, and how they know they have finished their task. They are a group of specialists. They each know their discipline and are brought to the team to apply their discipline to a set of specific tasks. When they have met their obligation, they often leave the team to return later if needed. Period.

The situation quickly changes as the project is a Quadrant 2 or 3 project. First of all, you have a gradual shift of the team makeup from a team of specialists to a team of generalists. The team takes on more of the characteristics of a self-directed team. They become self-sufficient and self-directing as the project moves from a Quadrant 2 to a Quadrant 3 project. Quadrant 1 teams are not co-located. They don't have to be. Quadrant 2 and 3 teams are co-located. Research has shown that co-location adds significantly to the successful completion of the project. Figure 1-3 reflects this shift from a loosely formed team to one that is tightly coupled.

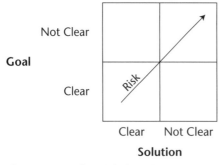

Figure 1-2: The Risk domain

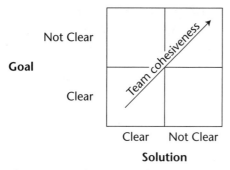

Figure 1-3: The Team Cohesiveness domain

Communications Versus the Complexity/Uncertainty Domain

Lack of timely and clear people-to-people communications has been shown to be the single most frequent reason for project failure. I include both written and verbal communications media in making that statement. Figure 1-4 reflects my thinking.

As you move in the direction of increased complexity and heightened uncertainty, communication requirements increase and change. When complexity and uncertainty are low, the predominant form of communications is written. Status reports, change requests, meeting minutes, issues reporting, problem resolution, project plan updates, and other written reports are commonplace. As uncertainty and complexity increase, written communications give way to verbal communication. The burden of plan-driven approaches is lightened, and the communications requirements of value-driven approaches take over.

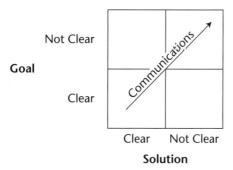

Figure 1-4: The Communications domain

Value-driven communications approaches are the derivatives of meaningful customer involvement where discussions generate status updates and plans going forward. Because projects that are high in complexity and uncertainty depend on frequent change, they have a low tolerance of written communications. In these project situations, the preparation, distribution, reading, and responding to written communications is viewed as non-value-added work. It is to be avoided and the energy spent on value-added work.

Customer Involvement Versus the Complexity/ Uncertainty Domain

Consider for a moment a project from your experience where you were most certain of the goal and the solution. You would be willing to bet your first-born that you had nailed requirements and that they would not change. Yes, that type of project might just be a pipe dream, but give me the benefit of the doubt. For such a project you might ask: Why do I need to have my customer involved except for the ceremonial sign-offs at milestone events? A fair question and ideally you wouldn't need their involvement. How about a project at the other extreme where the goal is very illusive and no solution would seem to be in sight? In such cases the complete involvement of the customer, as a team member perhaps, would be indispensable. What I have painted here are the extreme cases in Quadrant 1 and Quadrant 3.

Quadrant 1 projects are team-driven projects. Customer involvement is usually limited to answering clarification questions as they arise and giving sign-offs and approvals at the appropriate stages of the project life cycle. It would be accurate to say that customer involvement in Quadrant 1 projects is reactive and passive. But all that changes as you move into Quadrant 2 projects. The customer must now take a more active role in Quadrant 2 projects than was their role in Quadrant 1 projects. For Quadrant 3 projects, meaningful customer involvement is essential. In fact, the customer should take on a proactive role. The project goes nowhere without that level of commitment from the customer. Figure 1-5 reflects the gradual shift from passive to very active across the project domain.

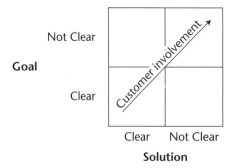

Figure 1-5: The Customer Involvement domain

Finding the solution to a software development project is not an individual effort. In Quadrant 1, the project team under the leadership of the project manager is charged with finding the missing parts of the solution. In some cases the customer is passively involved, but for the most part the team solves the problem. The willingness of the customer to even get passively involved depends on how you have dealt with them so far in the project. If you bothered to include them in the planning of the project, they might have some sympathy and help you out. But don't count on it. Beginning with Quadrant 2 and extending through Quadrant 3, you find more and more reliance on meaningful customer involvement. In your effort to maintain a customer-focus and deliver business value, you are dealing with a business problem not a technology problem. You have to find a business solution. Who is better equipped to help than the customer? After all, you are dealing with their part of the business. Shouldn't they be the best source of help and partnership in finding the solution? This involvement is so critical that without it you have no chance of being successful with Quadrant 3 projects.

Meaningful customer involvement can be a daunting task for at least the three reasons cited in the subsections that follow.

The Customer's Comfort Zone

The customer has been trained ever since the 1950s to take up a passive role. That training went well, and now you have to retrain them. In many instances their role was more ceremonial than formal. They didn't understand what they were approving but had no recourse but to sign. The sign-off at milestone events was often a formality because the customer didn't understand the techie-talk, was afraid not to sign off because of the threat of further delays, and didn't know enough about development to know when to ask questions and when to push back. Now you are asking them to step into a new role and become meaningfully engaged in the software development life cycle. Many are not poised to take up that responsibility. That responsibility is ratcheted up a notch as the project moves further into Quadrant 2 toward Quadrant 3, with less and less known about the solution. The project team is faced with a critical success factor of gaining meaningful customer involvement throughout the SDLC and PMLC. In Quadrant 3 their involvement is even more proactive and engaging. Quadrant 3 projects require that the customer take a co-leadership role with the project manager to keep the project moving forward and adjusted in the direction of increasing business value.

At the same time, the customer's comfort zone is growing. He or she has become smarter. It is not unusual to find a customer who was once more technically involved. They go to conferences where presentations often include technical aspects. They know how to push back. They know what it takes to build software solutions. They've built some themselves using spreadsheet packages and other applications tools. That has two sides. They can be supportive, or they can be obstacles to progress.

Ownership by the Customer

Establishing ownership by the customer of the project product and process is critical. I often ensure that there is that ownership by organizing the project team around co-managers—one from the provider side and one from the customer side. These two individuals are equally responsible for the success of the project. That places a vested interest squarely on the shoulders of the customer manager. This sounds really good, but it is not easily done. I can hear my customers saying, "This is a technology project, and I don't know anything about technology. How can I act in a managerial capacity?" The answer is simple, and it goes something like this: "True, you don't have a grasp of the technology involved, but that is a minor point. Your real value to this endeavor is to keep the business focus constantly in front of the team. You can bring that dimension to the team far better than any one of the technical people on the team. You will be an indispensable partner in every decision situation faced in this project." This ownership is so important that I have postponed starting customer engagements because the customer can't send a spokesperson to the planning meeting. When they do, you have to be careful that they don't send you a weak representative who wasn't busy at the time or who doesn't really understand the business context of the project. Maybe there's a reason that person wasn't busy.

Customer Sign-Off

This is often the most anxiety-filled task that you ever ask of your customer. Some customers think that they are signing their lives away when they approve a document or a deliverable. You are going to have to dispel that perception. This world is one of constant change, high-speed, and high risk. Given that, how could anyone reasonably expect that what works today will work tomorrow? Today's needs might not even come up on the radar screen next week. No matter how certain you are that you have nailed the requirements, you wouldn't expect them to remain static for the length of the project. It simply won't happen. That means that you had better anticipate change as a way of life in SDPM.

Specification Versus the Complexity/Uncertainty Domain

What does this mean? Simply put, it advises you that the choice of SDPM strategy should be based on an understanding of the confidence you have that the specifications have been completely and clearly defined and documented and that scope change requests will not arise from any shortcomings in the specifications documents. As that specification certainty diminishes, your best choices lie in the iterative strategies that populate Quadrant 2—those that allow the solution to become more specific and complete as the project commences or that allow you to discover the solution as the project commences. Finally, if you have very little confidence that you have clearly and completely documented the specifications, then your SDPM strategy takes on the flavor of the research and development strategies that populate Quadrant 3. Figure 1-6 reflects this shift in understanding about specification clarity and completeness.

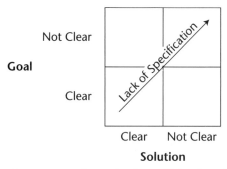

Figure 1-6: The Lack of Specificity domain

The SDPM strategies that require a high level of specification certainty tend to be change intolerant. Consider the situation where a significant change request comes early in the project life cycle. That could render much of the planning work obsolete. A large part of it will have to be done over. That contributes to the non-value-added work time of the SDPM strategy you have chosen. If changes like that are to be expected, an SDPM strategy that is more tolerant and supportive of change should be chosen. The non-value-added work could have been greatly diminished or removed altogether.

If you look inside the specifications document, you can find more detailed information that might help you decide on the best software development model. Specifications are composed of requirements, functions, and features. These array themselves in a hierarchical structure much like that shown in Figure 1-7.

Uncertainty at the requirements level has more impact on choice of software development approach than does uncertainty at the functionality level, which has more impact than that at the features level. Despite all of these efforts, you still have changes on any of those fronts that could have significant impact on our best efforts. That's life.

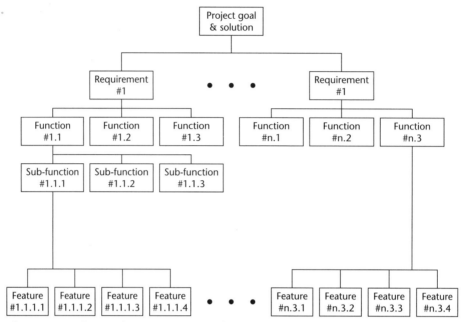

Figure 1-7: The requirements, functionality, and features breakdown structure

Change Versus the Complexity/Uncertainty Domain

The less you know about requirements, functionality, and features, the more you have to expect change. In Quadrant 1 you know everything there is to know about requirements, functionality, and features for this development project. The assumption, then, is that there will be little or no internal forces for change during the development project. Externally, however, that is not the case. Actions of competitors, market forces, and technological advances can cause change, but that is present in every project and can only be expected. The best the enterprise can do is maintain a position of flexibility in the face of such unpredictable but certain events. Figure 1-8 reflects the frequency of change as projects move across the landscape.

Quadrant 2 is a different story altogether. Any change in this quadrant comes about through the normal learning process that takes place in any software development project. When the customer has the opportunity to examine and experiment with a partial solution, he or she will invariably come back to the developers with suggestions for other requirements, functionality, and features that should be part of the solution. These suggestions can be put into one of two categories: either they are "wants" or they are "needs."

"Wants" might be little more than the result of a steak appetite on a baloney budget. It is up to the project manager to help the customer defend their want as a true need and hence get it integrated into the then solution. If they fail to do that, their suggestion should be relegated to a wish list. Wish lists are seldom revisited. If, on the other hand, they demonstrate its value and hence transfer it to a true need, it is up to the project manager to accommodate that new requirement, functionality, or feature into the solution set. It might have to be prioritized in the list of all needs.

In Quadrant 3 you have a further reliance on change to affect a good business-valued product. In fact, Quadrant 3 projects require change in order to have any chance at finding a successful solution. Change is the only vehicle that will lead to a solution.

Business Value Versus the Complexity/Uncertainty Domain

This domain would seem to be trivial. After all, aren't all projects designed to deliver business value. These projects were commissioned based on the business value they would return to the enterprise. This is all true. However, traditional project approaches focus on meeting the plan-driven parameters: time, cost, scope. When originally proposed the business climate was such that the proposed solution was the best that could be had. In a static world that condition would hold. Unfortunately, the business world is not static, and the needs of the customer aren't either. Bottom line, what will deliver business value is a moving target. Quadrant 1 development projects aren't equipped with the right stuff to deliver business value.

It follows then that Quadrant 1 projects deliver the least business value and that business value increases as you move from Quadrant 1 to Quadrant 2 to Quadrant 3. Figure 1-9 illustrates that point quite clearly. At the same time, however, as you move from quadrant to quadrant, risk increases and that means that higher-valued projects need to be commissioned as you move across the quadrants. Remember that the expected business value of a project is the product of (1-risk) and value. Risk here is expressed as the probability of failure and the probability of success is therefore (1-risk).

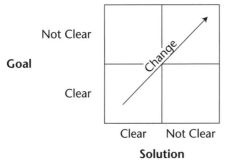

Figure 1-8: The Change domain

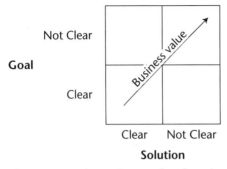

Figure 1-9: The Business Value domain

What does this mean? Simple—whatever SDPM strategy you adopt for the project, it must be one that allows redirection as business conditions change. The more uncertainty present in the development project, the more you need to be able to redirect to take advantage of changing conditions and opportunities.

As projects move through Quadrants 1 to 2 to 3, they become more customer-facing. The focus changes from conformance to plan to delivery of business value. The Quadrant 1 models focus on conformance to plan. If they also happen to deliver maximum business value it would be more the result of an accident than the result of a clairvoyant project plan. The focus on delivery of business value is apparent in all of the Quadrant 2 and 3 models. It is designed into the models.

Balancing Staff, Process, Technology

In this book, I adopt the model shown in Figure 1-10. Staff, or rather the skill and competency profile of the project team, drives the choice software development process and project management process to be employed, and together staff and process drive the choice of technology infrastructure to be employed. This is critical to forming the environment in which the project work will be undertaken. These three factors together form the SDPM strategy.

Figure 1-10: Achieving balance in the SDPM environment

This balance is achieved by first assessing the available staff resources as compared to the skill and competencies needed for the project. The chosen project team then determines the SDPM strategy that best meets the needs of the project and aligns with the team's capacity to deliver. Knowing that, the team can now select the technology infrastructure that best supports the team's capacity to deliver using the chosen SDPM strategy. That technology infrastructure includes software choices (programming languages and other support software, hardware, data communications hardware, and so on).

The balance achieved by these choices is represented by the triangle shown in Figure 1-11. It shows the three coordinates (staff, process, and technology). Those coordinates are constrained to the inside of the triangle because there is a linear constraint on the metric that measures each coordinate. In this example the sum total of the assessed values of each coordinate is 200.

The notation requires some explanation. The three letters (S, P, and T) denote the following: S is for staff, P denotes SDPM strategy, and T denotes technology. The ordering of the three letters is meaningful. The proximity of each vertex to the data point determines the ordering. For example, in Figure 1-11 the current state is closest to the Process vertex, next closest to the Technology vertex, and furthest from the Staff vertex. That results in the labeling PTS. All of the data points that have that property fall in the zone labeled PTS.

By the time this book is published, a beta version of the assessment tool will be available. The assessment tool consists of twenty questions, each with three possible answers. A question is answered by distributing ten points across the three possible responses with the highest point value given to the response that most represents the situation being assessed. The questions are asked twice—once for describing the current state of the environment and once for describing the ideal state of the environment. Figure 1-11 displays a possible result.

Knowing the current state and the ideal, or desired, end state, you can develop a plan that will migrate the organization to its desired end state. Figure 1-12 summarizes what some of those migration strategies might look like

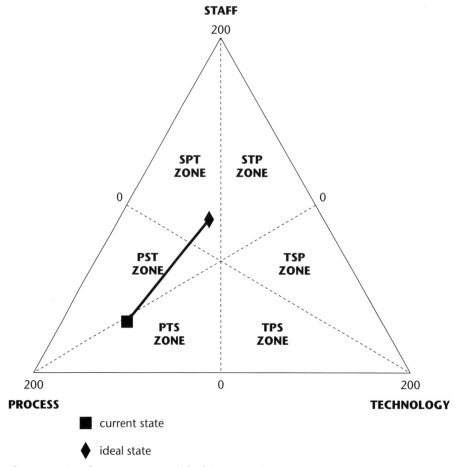

Figure 1-11: The current versus ideal SDPM environment

Note that the migrations are between neighboring zones only. For example, if the current state is zone TPS and the desired zone is SPT, then the migrations would be from zone TPS to TSP to STP to SPT.

Please contact me for further information on how you can learn more about the beta version. My e-mail address is rkw@eiicorp.com.

Now you'll take a look at the various driver sequences and what happens when this balance is compromised.

From Zone	To Zone	Comments on the Transition
TPS	TSP	In this situation technology may have constrained the formation of project management processes because there was little or no input from staff. To correct this situation staff could be empowered to improve project management processes. This may result in some reversals or prior technology decisions.
TSP	STP	Even though technology might be a constraint, staff has had an opportunity to define project management processes. Staff needs to be empowered to make decisions regarding the appropriate technology as it relates to project management processes.
STP	SPT	In this situation the staff are in a enviable position. The remaining task is to create a more balanced relationship between process and technology. That will require slow changes so that the technology environment is adjusted to provide better support for project management processes.
PTS	PST	There may be good coherence between project management processes and the technology to support it but it would have happened without much priority given to the role of staff. That situation can begin to change by commissioning the staff to work on technology improvement initiatives. This may result in reversing prior decisions.
PST	SPT	This is a strong starting position. Project management processes are a high priority for the organization. Technology has been implemented to support both process and staff. The remaining step is to move staff into a higher priority position for further enhancement of the project management environment and the technical support of it.

Figure 1-12: Migration strategies

Staff-Driven Environments

Figure 1-13 illustrates the two people-driven environments that might be encountered.

In the first case (denoted by the star) staff drives SDPM strategy, and together staff and SDPM strategy drive technology. This should be the ideal state for all organizations. It is clear that by using this model you are leveraging the skill and competency capacity of your team and the characteristics of the project to decide how to approach the project from an SDPM perspective. The team should make that decision. The technology platform that they choose to use will take advantage of and build on the earlier decisions on SDPM strategy.

In the second case (denoted by the circle) staff drives technology, and together staff and technology drive process. The only problem with this model is that the choice of SDPM strategy will be constrained by the earlier decision on technology infrastructure. If the earlier decision on technology infrastructure is reversible, then the second case really morphs into the first case.

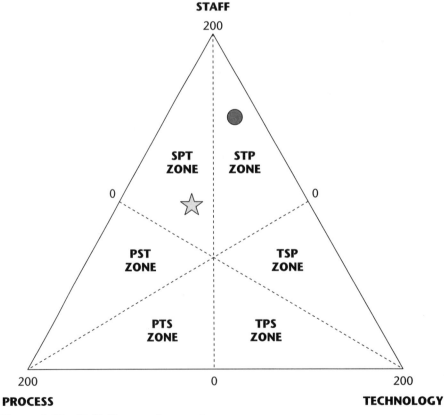

Figure 1-13: Staff-driven environments

Process-Driven Environments

Figure 1-14 illustrates the two process-driven environments that might be encountered.

In the first case (denoted by the star) choice of SDPM strategy drives staff, and together staff and SDPM strategy drive the choice of technology infrastructure. This case reminds me of organizations that might have only one SDPM strategy—a one-size-fits-all approach. In an iterative, adaptive, or extreme world, that can spell disaster. I have long advocated a project classification rule that puts the decision on SDPM strategy in the hands of the project team where it should be. To reverse the order is to put the organization in Quadrant 4—a solution out looking for a problem.

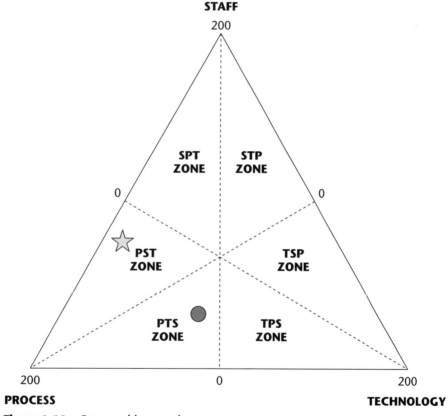

Figure 1-14: Process-driven environments

In the second case (denoted by the circle) SDPM strategy drives the choice of technology infrastructure, and together SDPM strategy and technology infrastructure drive the choice of staff. The die is cast early in the process and now the organization must have an effective and timely recruiting, hiring, and professional development plan in place to assure that project teams are staffed with capable members. This might not be a problem, but if it is, it is a problem that could have been avoided altogether. Why create your own problems when there are enough of them going around?

Technology-Driven Environments

Figure 1-15 illustrates the two technology-driven environments that might be encountered.

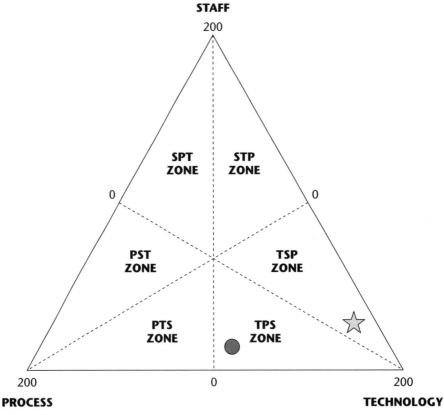

Figure 1-15: Technology-driven environments

In the first case (denoted by the star) the technology infrastructure drives the choice of staff, and together staff and technology infrastructure drive the choices for SDPM strategy. As long as the technology infrastructure doesn't prove to be a binding constraint on good project performance, the situation is workable. Most organizations find themselves in this or closely related situations. Earlier technology infrastructure decisions define the world of the software developer and to some extent the world of the project manager. In the short-term that constraint is fixed. The staff will have been chosen to be compatible with that infrastructure, and that is as it should be. The last variable, the SDPM strategy, is thus constrained to that environment. That might be no issue at all or it might be a serious constraint.

In the second case (denoted by the circle) technology infrastructure drives the choice of SDPM strategy, and together the technology infrastructure and SDPM strategy drive the process choice of staff. This can be made to work. It all depends on the earlier choices and how ready the staff is to embrace those decisions. If staff is given the authority to adapt the SDPM strategy to the project situation, this will work. If the SDPM strategy has been defined to accommodate further adaptation, the teams will have a better chance of success.

Discussion Questions

1. For years there has been debate over whether the development team should be a team of specialists or a team of generalists. Given what you have learned about the software development landscape, what are your thoughts about specialists versus generalists? Does your opinion change depending on which quadrant the project is in? Why or why not? Be specific.

2. What relationship, if any, exists between risk and business value for projects in Quadrant 1, 2, or 3?

3. Many teams have problems getting and maintaining meaningful customer involvement. What have been your experiences—both good and bad?

4. If the frequency of scope change requests is beyond your expectations and it has seriously compromised the project, would you ever consider changing the approach from a linear/incremental one to an iterative/adaptive one? Why or why not? If not, how would you deal with the problem? Be specific.

5. What type of organization do you work for? Is it staff-driven, process-driven, or technology-driven?

6. What type of organization do you work for? Is it staff-driven, process-driven, or technology-driven? What types of problems have you seen that may be the direct result of the type of organization? How might you go about correcting the problems?

SDPM Roadmap

In differentiation, not in uniformity, lies the path of progress.

Louis Dembitz Brandeis, 1856-1941
U.S. Supreme Court Justice

Chapter Learning Objectives

After reading this chapter, you will be able to:

- ◆ Understand the relationship between Linear, Incremental, Iterative, Adaptive, and Extreme software development project management (SDPM) and the complexity/uncertainty domain

- ◆ Explain the Linear, Incremental, Iterative, Adaptive, and Extreme software development project management strategies

- ◆ Recognize several example models in each of the five strategy categories

- ◆ Be able to discuss the characteristics, strengths, and weaknesses of each of the five strategy categories

---

In the previous chapter, I set the stage from the highest vantage point in the software project landscape. In this chapter, I would like to try to move in closer from that point to the next level of detail. In this chapter, I introduce five generic types of development projects that span this landscape. That sets the stage for a brief look at the models that populate each type. The details of each of those models are covered in Parts II through VI.

At the same time, this chapter serves as a guided tour and preview of the models developed in the remaining parts and chapters of the book.

The Contemporary Software Development Landscape

Software development "ain't what it used to be." The early days when the waterfall model was the only act in town are gone. Structured programming has come and gone. The role of the customer has changed from passive to active to proactive. The processes and tools in use are far more sophisticated. In the place of these practices are a variety of models that arise out of the need to be fast, to be right, and to be ready to change on a moment's notice. That doesn't mean throwing out the old ways to make room for the new. Rather you can integrate the old into the new. Much can be gained from the legacies left by your predecessors.

Additionally, to be useful, the process models must adapt to changing conditions and the project must change on a moment's notice as business conditions change. That's a tall order in the face of the rigidity espoused by the traditional waterfall models you are all familiar with. In the absence of suitable alternatives, developers are constantly trying to adapt the waterfall models to problems whose characteristics simply do not fit the models. The results are far less than satisfactory and end up in outright failures in many cases. If you peel back the onion one layer and take a closer look at the software development landscape as described in the previous chapter, you can see what it is really telling you that you ought to be doing.

Figure 2-1 is the foundation that will direct all of the discussions in this book. It shows on two axes all of the significant relationships between SDPM models (Linear, Incremental, and so on) and project landscape variables (complexity and uncertainty). For example, if project complexity is moderately high and the solution only partially identified, the choice of an adaptive model is advised. To use an incremental model instead would be like putting square pegs in small round holes. They don't fit, and no heroic effort can make them fit. Another example of figure's use would tell you that if the specification certainty is low and you have chosen an incremental approach, you might be in for trouble. Another choice (adaptive) would have been better.

I'm covering the software development landscape with five different SDPM strategies ordered from Linear to Extreme. Within each there are a number of software development life cycle models that are in current vogue. These are the models that will be discussed in detail in Parts II through VI. They are introduced here by name with a brief description to follow.

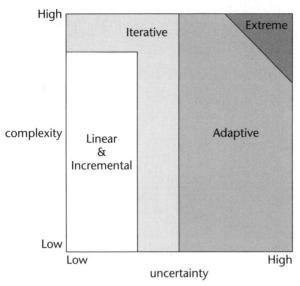

Figure 2-1: The contemporary software development landscape

Linear

The Linear SDPM strategies are found in Quadrant 1.

The Linear SDPM model is the longest lived of all the models you will be considering. Until the early 1990s this was the overwhelming choice of software developers. Developers had few alternatives at that time. Because of its longevity it has become habit with many developers. Even though a number of alternatives exist today, often developers don't consider changing. They would rather force-fit the old when the new would be the better choice. Old habits die hard! That is unfortunate because all of their attempts to modify the linear approach to accommodate software development projects that don't fit the conditions ultimately lead to failure or sadly disappointed customers.

DEFINITION: LINEAR SDPM STRATEGY

A Linear SDPM strategy consists of a number of dependent phases that are executed in a sequential order with no feedback loops. The complete solution is not released until the final phase.

Figure 2-2, the Standard Waterfall model, and Figure 2-3, the Rapid Development Waterfall model, are two examples of linear models.

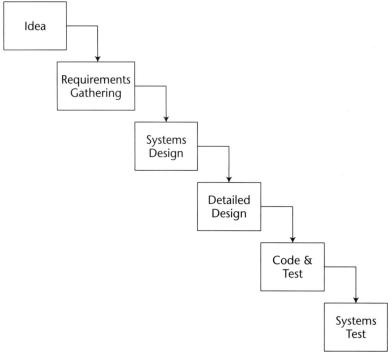

Figure 2-2: Standard Waterfall model

Although the original definition of the Waterfall approach did allow for feedback, the more popular interpretations do not. As the name suggests, water flows only downhill. The Standard Waterfall model shows the sequence of phases that define it. Once a phase is complete, the process moves to the next phase. Phases are not repeated, and no feedback is returned to prior phases. The linearity of this model is clear.

In cases where deadlines are tight or have changed to earlier dates in mid-project, a modification of the Standard Waterfall model is called for. Figure 2-3 depicts the Rapid Development Waterfall model. You face several complications in adopting this alternative. They will be discussed in Part II. For now it is sufficient to know that the development tasks are split into groups of development tasks that can be done in parallel and concurrently. With one exception, that doesn't change the amount of work; it just changes the schedule to complete it sooner than would be the case in the Standard Waterfall model. The last parallel swim lane that is complete determines the completion date of the development project. In keeping with the Standard Waterfall model, work always moves forward, and no feedback is returned. Other than the parallel development effort, the two models differ only in that the Rapid Development Waterfall model has an added task, integration testing. I'll have more to say about that in Part II because it does introduce some complications as well. The linearity of this model is clear.

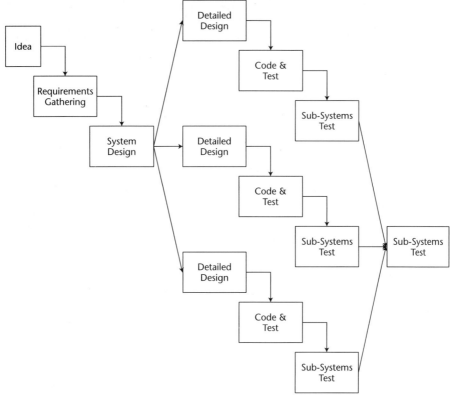

Figure 2-3:   Rapid Development Waterfall model

Characteristics of Linear SDPM Strategy Projects

The characteristics of software development projects that produce a good fit with the linear models are discussed in the following list:

- **Clearly defined goal, solution, and requirements**—Linear models are all based on the assumption that you need to have a clear definition of what the customer needs. That is found in clear and complete documentation of the project goal, the requirements that the solution must meet, specific functionality that underlies those requirements, and the particular and detailed features of each piece of functionality.

  Whether or not this characteristic is present in a project is a subjective call. If the project is cutting-edge and highly leveraged by market conditions, you might expect change even though you feel confident the goal, solution, and requirements have been fully and clearly documented. Such projects might be better served with an approach that can accommodate change. On the other hand, a project that is on familiar ground and isn't leveraged by market conditions might work quite well using one of the linear models. Such projects would have a heavy internal focus. For example, they might be infrastructure projects. Once defined, little change is expected. Your confidence level in each case is quite different, and your decision should be tempered with that information.

- **Few scope change requests**—Given the preceding preconditions the developers do not expect to see many scope change requests. That applies to internal changes. As far as external changes are concerned, that is beyond their control. Those applications that can be impacted by external factors might want to choose a different model.

- **Routine and repetitive projects**—Some development projects will have a lot in common with development projects from the past. These past projects will be of great help. Astute organizations will have anticipated the value of past projects and made provisions for their documentation, archiving, and retrieval.

- **Uses established templates**—Those projects that are routine will have built a risk and issues history with mitigation strategies and a depository of reusable code, use cases, test data, and so on that will greatly simplify the present project. All of these serve as templates for the present project. That helps.

Strengths

Although the proportion of software development projects that fall into the Linear SDPM category is clearly decreasing, Linear SDPM strategies do have a number of strengths that encourage their use as long as the project satisfies the necessary conditions. Some of these choices might be very appropriate given the organization's situation. I count among the strengths the following:

- **The entire project is scheduled**—This is important for those projects that produce deliverables that will be used in other projects as well as those that will share scarce staff resources with other projects that are running concurrently.

- **Resource requirements are known**—Projects that are approved and managed within a portfolio of projects will have to estimate resource requirements for the benefit of other projects in the portfolio. This is mandatory for those portfolios that allocate resources across competing projects in addition to allocating funding across projects.

- **Does not require the most skilled resources**—Development tasks can be partitioned so that lesser skilled staff can work on the simpler tasks. This is a useful option in situations where skilled staff resources are in short supply. Those situations seem to be more frequent as people move from job to job.

- **Team members can be distributed**—Again, work can be partitioned so that individual staff can work on individual tasks wherever they might be physically located and transfer completed work to the appropriate team members. With proper partitioning of the development work, the dependence between tasks can be reduced to the point where real-time interaction between team members can be significantly reduced and even eliminated in selected cases. The likelihood of co-locating your team members might be low and so the Linear SDPM strategy might be the most promising choice even if all the conditions are not met. The trade-offs might be tolerable.

Weaknesses

On the other hand a few weaknesses come with the choice of using a Linear SDPM strategy. The weaknesses I have identified and that are worth mentioning include:

- **Plan and schedule do not accommodate change very well**—The complete plan and schedule provide detailed information about staff allocations and scheduled assignments. Change upsets that order and can require significant revision. That is non-value-added work, and it eats away at the time that can be devoted to value-added work. Plan revisions require a recommitment of staff resources against a revised schedule.

- **Costs too much**—Simply put, all of the money is spent before you have any deliverables against which to measure goal attainment. If the deliverables do not meet requirements, you have no recourse. Money has been spent with nothing acceptable to show for it.

- **Takes too long**—This is the companion to "costs too much." The project has reached the eleventh hour before any deliverables are produced. If any changes had surfaced, it would be difficult to accommodate them inside the time and cost constraints without sacrificing some other requirements or functionality.

- **Requires detailed plans**—Linear plan-driven approaches require heavy documentation. Documentation includes such things as:
  - ◆ All change requests and their resolution
  - ◆ Regular status reports
  - ◆ An issues log and resolution
  - ◆ A risk log and mitigation
  - ◆ Meeting minutes
  - ◆ Planning documents and their updates

  The documentation requirements are demanding and viewed as an onerous task. In practice many teams don't devote the attention required and documentation is done just to satisfy what seems to be a non-value-added burden.

- **Must follow a defined set of processes**—Whether the project management methodology is a one-size-fits-all methodology or offers options depending on project size, complexity, duration, and so forth, it requires compliance by the team. Project performance reports and project reviews are often put in place to ensure that compliance.

- **Is not focused on customer value**—Plan-driven approaches focus on delivering against the plan. That means meeting schedules and budgets. Whenever variances from schedule and budget occur, the process requires that corrective action steps be defined, documented, and monitored.

Incremental

Incremental SDPM strategies are also found in Quadrant 1.

DEFINITION: INCREMENTAL SDPM STRATEGY

An Incremental SDPM strategy consists of a number of dependent phases that are repeated in sequential order with no feedback loops. Each phase releases a partial solution.

Because Incremental SDPM strategies are found in Quadrant 1, their goal and solution must be clearly defined and documented as a condition for using the models described as follows. Figure 2-4, the Staged Delivery Waterfall model, and Figure 2-5, the Feature-Driven Development model, are two examples of incremental approaches. Both models require the complete documentation of requirements, functionality, and features.

The Staged Delivery Waterfall model provides for the early release of chunks of functionality so that the customer can begin to realize business value without having to wait for the single release of the complete solution.

The Feature-Driven Development (FDD) model provides for the early release of chunks of features so that the customer can begin to realize business value without having to wait for the single release of the complete solution. It differs from the Staged Delivery Waterfall model in that the releases consist of groups of features that have a technical relationship to one another. You might have several cycles of development before the customer is satisfied that the cumulative features list has enough business value to be released as in the sense of the Staged Delivery Waterfall model. FDD models might use concurrent swim lanes, sequential phases, or some combination of the two.

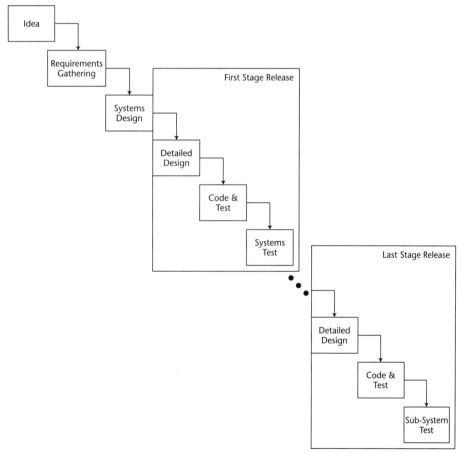

Figure 2-4: Staged Delivery Waterfall model

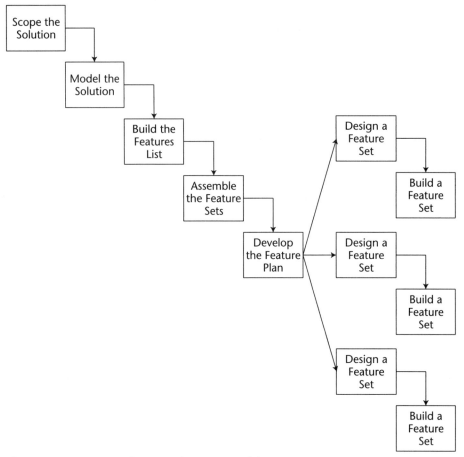

Figure 2-5:   Feature-Driven Development model

Characteristics of Incremental SDPM Strategy Projects

Projects that otherwise would use a linear model but must deliver business value earlier in the development life cycle can modify the model to take advantage of incremental approach. The characteristics of software development projects that produce a good fit with the incremental models are discussed in the following list:

- **Same as Linear SDPM strategy projects**—The same conditions that apply to Linear SDPM strategies apply to Incremental SDPM strategies. Requirements, functions, and features must be clearly defined and a complete plan for their delivery must be put in place. Because the deliverables are deployed in phases, you have some room for accommodating change.

- **The need to release deliverables against a more aggressive schedule**—The primary reason for choosing an incremental over a linear approach is to release business value earlier in the project life cycle. By properly defining what deliverables belong in each phase, you can build a plan to have early releases of deliverables. This allows the business unit to go to the market early and begin generating revenues or other business value.

You might face situations where a Linear SDPM strategy was the approach that launched the project, but at some point in the life of the project it became necessary to accelerate delivery and the strategy was changed to an Incremental SDPM strategy. An at-risk project that has fallen significantly behind schedule might be saved by changing strategies. This will not come without some penalties however. Additional planning to adjust in-process deliverables to fit a phased model will be required.

Strengths

Incremental SDPM strategies are the first that I discuss that are *customer-facing*, that is, they consider what brings value to the customer as the overarching driver for the strategies. I count among the strengths the following:

- **Produces business value early in the development life cycle**—The customer is always anxious to get something out and on the street. The Linear SDPM strategy isn't designed to do that. By moving some of the Return on Investment (ROI) to the front of the development life cycle, business value is assured.

- **Better use of scarce resources through proper increment definition**—A scarce resource can be scheduled to work from increment to increment. That relieves some of the resource contention and scheduling obstacles that the Linear SDPM strategy has to deal with.

- **Can accommodate some change requests between increments**—With the deliverables from an earlier increment deployed and in production status you can get some early feedback on how well the product works and how well it is received by the end users. That feedback can be integrated into the development cycle of a later increment. While that is not the reason why the Incremental SDPM strategy is used, it is a side benefit.

■ **More focused on customer value than the linear approaches**—The early release of partial solutions is more customer-facing than the one-time-only release from the Linear SDPM strategy. The customer feels more a part of what is taking place and has an opportunity to provide some early feedback to the development team. Getting comfortable with a solution one phase at a time removes some of the anxiety around the all at once release of the Linear SDPM strategy.

Weaknesses

On the other hand, a few weaknesses come with the choice of using an Incremental SDPM strategy. The weaknesses I have identified and are worth mentioning include:

■ **Requires heavy documentation**—An Incremental SDPM strategy is more complex than a Linear SDPM strategy because the incremental model development work must be partitioned so that it can be done in phases. With rare exceptions succeeding phases are dependent upon preceding phases. If the original decomposition and allocation of development tasks to the phases is correct, then the approach has a good chance of succeeding. If not, then you face the possibility of re-work and rendering as obsolete previously completed work. Changes have to be accommodated as a result of problems that arise from previously undiscovered function, feature, and code dependencies between increments. That means documentation and more of it than would be normally produced in a Linear SDPM strategy.

■ **Follows a defined set of processes**—To avoid the potential problems identified previously, the team has to follow a rigorous and detailed set of processes. You need a number of checks and balances and rigorous documentation of compliance.

■ **Defines increments based on function and feature dependencies**—This might seem trivial but take a closer look. Despite the team and the customer's due diligence, dependencies will be overlooked. Despite your best efforts you can never be sure you got them all! In complex situations those dependencies are often not even observable. They are discovered in the context of development. The minimum impact is that it simply slows the schedule. Before proceeding, you have to wait for the dependencies to be resolved. That usually means taking a side step to build some functionality not planned for this increment. If you then have a domino effect to other previously undiscovered dependencies . . . well, you get the idea.

- **Requires more customer involvement than the linear approaches**—Part of the decomposition of functions and features to the various increments is the need for those increments to contain sufficient business value to be released to the customer or end user. A good and detailed process flow diagram that shows how all of the functions and features are related from a technical and business perspective is worth its weight in gold. That means more documentation.

- **Partitioning the functions and features might be problematic**—This is the last step in defining the contents of each increment. Each increment must make sense from a technical as well as a business perspective. The two may be at odds with one another. If to that mix you have to consider the capacity of the team to deliver the contents of an increment, the partitioning gets more complex. So you see that pay a price for releasing business value early. The price is in terms of increased risk, more detailed planning, more complete documentation, and more customer involvement. It is a business decision that must be taken seriously.

Iterative

Iterative SDPM strategies are found in Quadrant 1 and 2.

DEFINITION: ITERATIVE SDPM STRATEGY

An Iterative SDPM strategy consists of a number of phases that are repeated in groups with a feedback loop after each group is completed. At the discretion of the customer, the last phase in a group might release a partial solution.

This definition allows for several types of iteration. Iteration can be on requirements, functionality, features, design, development, solutions, and others.

You can see four examples of iterative approaches in Figure 2-6, the Evolutionary Development Waterfall model; Figure 2-7, SCRUM; Figure 2-8, the Rational Unified Process (RUP); and Figure 2-9, the Dynamic Systems Development Method (DSDM).

Iterative SDPM strategies definitely fall in the class of learn and discover. In the Evolutionary Development Waterfall model, the learning and discovering experience is obvious from Figure 2-6. With each iteration more and more of the depth of the solution is revealed. That follows from the customer having an opportunity to play with the "then" solution.

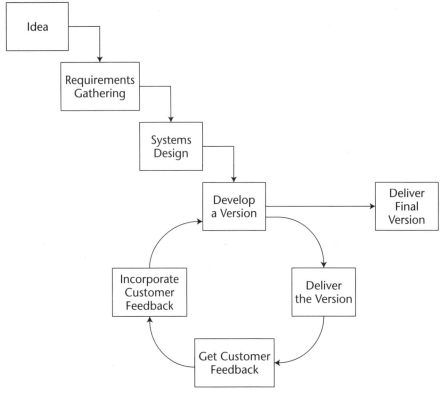

Figure 2-6: Evolutionary Development Waterfall model

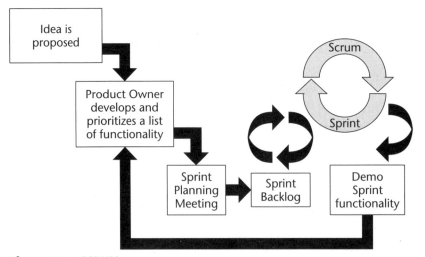

Figure 2-7: SCRUM

SCRUM is a rugby term. It represents what appears to be a chaotic movement of the huddled team toward the goal. Of all the development models discussed in this book, SCRUM is possibly the most customer-driven approach. It is the customer who defines the functions and features that the team prioritizes into phases and builds a phase at a time. The process allows the customer to change functions and features as more of the solution depth is uncovered through the previous iterations.

The Rational Unified Process (RUP) is probably the most well-known of the Iterative software development processes. It adapts quite well to a process approach that is documentation-heavy or to one that is documentation-light. The foundation of RUP lies in the library of reusable code, requirements, designs, and so on. That library will have been built from previous project experiences. That means that RUP can have a long payback period. The library must be sufficiently populated to be useful from an ROI perspective. Four to five completed projects might be enough to begin to see some payback.

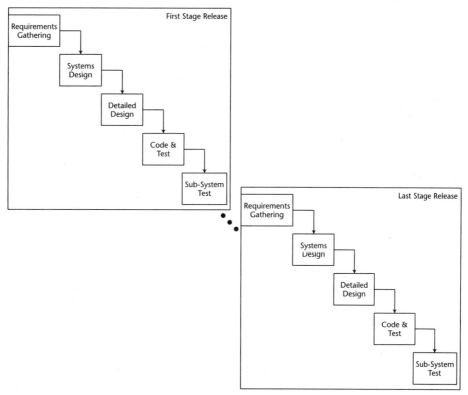

Figure 2-8: Rational Unified Process

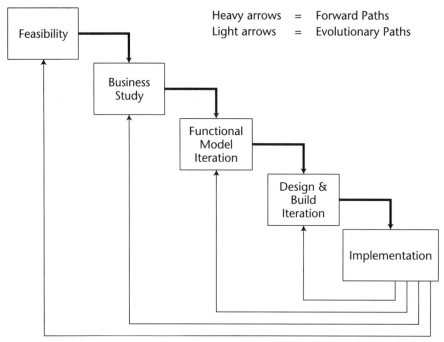

Figure 2-9: Dynamic Systems Development Method

Dynamic Systems Development Method (DSDM) is the Standard Waterfall model in a gravity-free world. Feedback loops are the defining features that separate DSDM from the Standard Waterfall model.

Characteristics of Iterative SDPM Strategy Projects

The Iterative SDPM strategy kicks in when not all of the solution is clearly known. This strategy requires a solution that broadly covers the requirements but might be missing some of the details. In other words, the functions are known and are built into the solution but the details (the features) are not completely known or implemented. The missing or detailed features come to light as the customer works with the most current solution in a prototyping sense. As is true of other Quadrant 2 strategies, the Iterative SDPM strategy is a learn-by-doing strategy. The use of intermediate solutions is the pathway to discovering the details of the complete solution.

Strengths

The Iterative SDPM strategy departs from the Linear and Incremental strategies in that the complete solution is no longer defined. What is defined is a solution whose breadth spans the expected solution but whose depth does not.

This affords some breathing room not provided by linear and incremental strategies. Iterative SDPM strategies do have a number of strengths that encourage their use as long as they satisfy the necessary conditions. I count among the strengths the following:

- **Customer can review current solution for suggested improvements**— Over the years, I have learned that the best way to get the customer thinking about the solution is to show them something concrete. They don't respond to conceptual discussions or to diagrams on paper. They respond to something they can hold in their hands, work with, try out, and get a sense of how it will look and feel on the job. Prototypes were developed for just that reason. The deliverable from an iteration is a prototype, but a very special kind of prototype. It is a working system despite the fact that it is not fully functioned or feature-rich. That will come with later iterations.

- **Accommodates scope changes between iterations**—Let customers try it. If they like it, keep it. If they don't, either fix it or remove it. For customers who are unwilling or unable to clearly define requirements, functions, or features, some flavor of iterative approach is the best way. In the Iterative SDPM strategy you have the requirements and most functions and need only to fill in the gaps to produce a complete solution. The Iterative approach gives the customer a solid foundation on which to learn and discover what is missing. You expect them to change their minds or add functions or features. That is the purpose of this strategy.

- **Adapts to changing business conditions**—What the customer wants in the solution is discovered through the iterations. Because of changing business conditions, what the customer needs in the solution might change. The iterative nature of this strategy provides an opportunity to build those changing needs into the solution at the next or some succeeding iteration.

Weaknesses

On the other hand, you find a few weaknesses that come with the choice of using an Iterative SDPM strategy. The weaknesses I have identified and that are worth mentioning include:

- **Requires a more actively involved customer than Quadrant 1 projects**— As you move to the outreaches of Quadrant 2 and into Quadrant 3, the customer takes on a critical role. Solutions become more evasive in the outreaches of Quadrant 2. To find them you need to bring all of our resources together to focus on finding a solution. That means the customer has to be involved. Involvement is not enough; it must be meaningful involvement. This is probably the hardest thing to have happen. In your brief but turbulent history, the customer has probably never been meaningfully involved. Their involvement was limited to cursory reviews of things they didn't really understand or sign-offs on completed deliverables that they had not had a chance to try in the work place. That is not the involvement I am calling for here. Here the customer must be a principal in the project. They must be a decision maker just as the project manager is a decision maker. The customer brings the business perspective. The project team brings the technical perspective. Both perspectives are integral parts of the solution. Getting and sustaining that involvement is a major challenge that is not to be treated lightly. I have had occasions in my consulting practice where I postponed a client project because they weren't ready to make the needed commitment of time and involvement. Gone are the days when the cop-out was "Oh, that's a technology project and I don't understand technology. Just get it done and I'll look at it then."

- **Final solution cannot be specified at the outset of the project**—Up to a point you know what will be delivered, but you cannot specify the deliverables completely. They are discovered as part of the doing of the project. And so the customer is correct in saying, "You mean I'm going to give you one year and $10 million and you can't tell me what I am going to get?" Up to a point they are correct. The dilemma is that you have to do something. Remember the project is high-visibility and critical to the organization. Under the circumstances and with what you know of the project, the Iterative SDFPM strategy is your best hope of success. Comparing it to the traditional way of thinking about projects is neither fair nor relevant.

Adaptive

The Adaptive SDPM strategies are found in Quadrant 2 and 3.

DEFINITION: ADAPTIVE SDPM STRATEGY

An Adaptive SDPM strategy is one that proceeds from iteration to iteration based on very limited specification of solution. Each iteration learns from the proceeding ones and redirects the next iteration in an attempt to converge on an acceptable solution. At the discretion of the customer an iteration can release a partial solution.

Figure 2-10, the Adaptive Project Framework (APF), and Figure 2-11, Adaptive Software Development (ASD), are two examples of adaptive approaches.

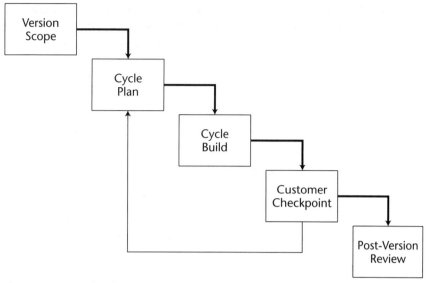

Figure 2-10: Adaptive Project Framework

The Adaptive Project Framework (APF)—as found in *Effective Project Management: Traditional, Adaptive, Extreme, Third Edition,* by Robert K. Wysocki and Rudd McGary (Wiley, 2003) and in Robert K. Wysocki's *Adaptive Project Framework: A Common Sense Approach to Managing Complex Projects* (AMS Press, 2004)—unlike most of the approaches in Quadrant 2 is not limited to software development. Although some of its uses are beyond the scope of this book, APF is equally at home with software development, process improvement, product development, and research and development projects.

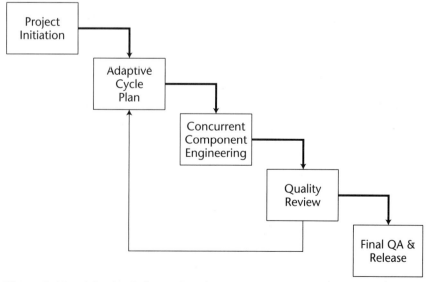

Figure 2-11: Adaptive Software Development

Adaptive Software Development (ASD) was introduced by James Highsmith III in *Adaptive Software Development: A Collaborative Approach to Managing Complex Systems* (Dorset House, 2000). While his focus was on software development, ASD can be extended to product development.

Characteristics of Adaptive SDPM Strategy Projects

The Adaptive SDPM strategy, like other adaptive approaches, is best-suited to projects whose solution is only partially known. The degree to which the solution is known might vary over a wide range from knowing a lot but not all to knowing very little. The less that is known about the solution, the more risk, uncertainty, and complexity are present. To remove the uncertainty associated with these projects, you have to discover the solution. That happens through a continuous change process from iteration to iteration. That change process is supposed to create a convergence on a complete solution. In the absence of that convergence, adaptive projects are frequently cancelled and restarted in some other promising direction.

The success of Adaptive SDPM strategies is leveraged by accommodating frequent change. Change is the result of learning and discovery by the team and most importantly by the customer. Because change will have a dramatic impact on the project, only a minimalist approach to planning is employed. Planning is actually done just in time. There is no wasted effort planning the future. The future is unknown, and any effort at planning that future is viewed as non-value-added work. All Quadrant 2 approaches minimize non-value-added work.

Adaptive SDPM strategies can also be applied to new product development, process improvement, and research and development projects. This is especially true of APF.

Strengths

Adaptive SDPM strategies as defined here are new. They address a class of projects heretofore ignored in most treatises on the subject. Because of this, they bring some unique strengths to the table. I count among the strengths the following:

- **Does not waste time on non-value-added work**—Adaptive SDPM strategies avoid wasting time and effort in every way possible. Planning is done just in time. Because the future is unknown, any time or effort spent on detailed planning of the unknown might be a waste of time, so it is not done. When parts of the future are revealed, the planning associated with that now known future is done.

- **Provides maximum business value within the given time and cost constraints**—The customer is the driver of the Adaptive SDPM strategy. At the completion of every iteration, the customer and the project team review what has been done and what has been learned. That information directs the functions and features to be added in the next iteration. That translates into the deliverables being the best that can be produced given time and cost constraints. The decision on what is best is the customer's to make, and the team merely makes it happen.

Weaknesses

On the other hand, a few weaknesses come with the choice of using an Adaptive SDPM strategy. The weaknesses I have identified and that are worth mentioning include:

- **Must have meaningful customer involvement**—Easy to say but oh-so-difficult to implement. The customer has been trained over the decades to be a passive member of the project. They were given sign-off opportunities at various milestone events. Many of those turned out to be ceremonial at best because the customer didn't really understand the technology parts of the solution and why certain things could or couldn't be done the way they requested. Now you are telling them that the old ways no longer apply and they need to be an integral part of the project team. Most customers would find that they are taken out of their comfort zone and into a world they don't really understand. Their resistance is not unexpected.

- **Cannot identify exactly what will be delivered at the end of the project**—Variable scope flies in the face of everything you have been taught about good project management. Write the specification, estimate time and cost, and deliver what the customer requirements have defined. That is a nice neat package and puts the project team in their comfort zone. But the realities are different as you know. Requirements can't be defined as crisply as they once could. Functions and features aren't fully baked either. The only way out is to assure the customer that as the details become known you will adjust your solution to accommodate those changing situations and produce the best solution you can within the limits that the budgeted time and money will allow. You posit that as long as the customer can define "best value" at each iteration, you will guarantee the best results. That might be a difficult argument and defense to sell, but that is the best that can be done. Remember that this is a critical mission project. It must be successfully completed. You don't know the details but can only work to discover them, so you don't know what the final solution will look like. A certain amount of trust and faith is involved here. If you and the customer can agree to work as a team and to always make the decision that is best for the business, your chances of success improve.

Extreme

The Extreme SDPM strategies are found in Quadrant 3.

DEFINITION: EXTREME SDPM STRATEGY

An Extreme SDPM strategy is one that proceeds from iteration to iteration based on very limited specification of goal and solution. Each iteration learns from the proceeding ones and redirects the next iteration in an attempt to converge on an acceptable goal and solution. At the discretion of the customer an iteration may release a partial solution.

Figure 2-12, INSPIRE, is an example of an extreme approach.

At first glance you might wonder, "What is the difference between an Adaptive SDPM strategy and an Extreme SDPM strategy?" First, and foremost, is goal clarity. Adaptive SDPM strategies require a clearly defined goal while the Extreme SDPM strategies do not. That places Extreme SDPM strategies in a research and development mode. Translated into application I would expect to see a number of parallel investigative swim lanes in the early stages of an Extreme SDPM strategy. The number of those parallel swim lanes decreases as the project moves forward. The reason for the decrease is due to the elimination of several swim lanes as feasible directions for goal and solution discovery. I'll have much more to say on this in Part V.

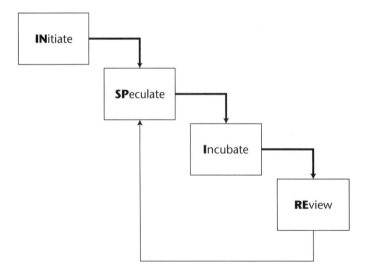

Figure 2-12: INSPIRE

Characteristics of Extreme SDPM Strategy Projects

The Extreme SDPM strategy lies at the outpost of the software development landscape. It serves the needs of those development projects where very little is known about the details of the development effort. Three characteristics characterize these projects:

- **Goal and solution not known**—To be successful these projects must figure out how to emerge from the darkness into the light. "I'll know it when I see it," says it all. Unfortunately, that is not what a development team wants to hear. It doesn't give them any sense of feasible direction. That has to be discovered as part of the work of the project. There are approaches that will provide some direction. These are explored in Part VI.

- **Critical mission projects**—Obviously, the preceding comment on goal and solution makes these projects very high risk. Failure rates will be high. So high in fact that only critical mission projects will choose this approach. If the organization has to find a solution, this is the only alternative.

- **Typical of R&D projects**—Any research and development project will adopt this strategy. Those projects cannot define a solution. They can define a number of possible solutions and depend on iterative investigations to weed out those possible solutions that seem to be dead ends. In doing that, new possible solutions might arise and they, too, will have to be subjected to the same iterative approaches to assess their utility. After some time you will find evidence of some convergence to an acceptable solution. The absence of that will usually lead to abandoning the current approach and looking for an alternative.

Strengths

The Extreme PM strategy might be the last resort. You have reached the point where both goal and solution are not defined enough to use any of the previous strategies. You have nothing left. I count among the strengths the following:

- **Keeps options open as late as possible**—An Extreme SDPM strategy frequently begins with a number of initiatives being pursued in parallel. These are chosen because they represent the most likely directions in which to find a solution. Some will prove fruitful others will not. Those that are fruitful suggest refinements or even other related initiatives to try. An initiative is then open for further investigation until it has been shown to be a dead end.

- **Offers an early look at a number of partial solutions**—The iterations that produce these intermediate results will be short—1 to 4 weeks is typical. The early look gives the customer a way to evaluate the feasibility of the project and the approaches being taken. That opens the way for an early kill decision on the project. Time and money are saved as compared to the linear and incremental strategies.

Weaknesses

On the other hand a few weaknesses come with the choice of using an Extreme SDPM strategy. The weaknesses I have identified and are worth mentioning include:

- **May be looking for solutions in all the wrong places**—So much of the success of the Extreme SDPM strategy depends on having chosen a feasible approach or approaches. In the most complex of cases, that calls for a healthy dose of creativity on the part of the customer and the project team. If they are too far off target, the solution might never be found.

- **No guarantee that any business value will result from the project**— Because of the preceding observations you have no guarantee that a solution or even a partial solution will be found. For critical mission projects this is not a comforting feeling. Let's face it, however; the customer and the team might be trying to solve an unsolvable problem. You'll see that again in the PDQ case study example as you proceed.

A Generic Template for Discussing SDPM Strategies

At the risk of oversimplifying the complexity of software development and the supporting project management processes, I am going to posit a template that will be the basis of my discussion of life cycles in the remainder of this book. I feel that this is necessary to have a basis for contrast and comparison of the models the book covers. This also gives you a foundation for integrating the project management life cycle. The software development life cycles will be imbedded into the project management life cycles to provide our basis for discussing SDPM strategies. Figure 2-13 is that template.

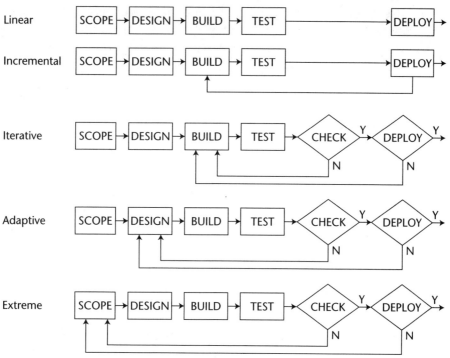

Figure 2-13: A generic software development life cycle

The generic development life cycle is a six-phase life cycle. Each phase takes on a different profile and set of tasks that depend on the particular type of SDPM strategy and model being considered.

Discussion Questions

1. Consider a hypothetical situation in which a project is done following the Waterfall model and is also done independently by another team following the Adaptive Project Framework. Assume both teams are equally skilled. Which approach would you expect to be completed earlier? Why?

2. Assume you work in an organization that is well-steeped in a Linear and Incremental SDPM strategy. What arguments would you put forward to get your organization to adopt an Iterative SDPM strategy? An Adaptive SDPM strategy? Be specific.

3. Assume you work in an organization that is well-steeped in Linear, Incremental, and Iterative SDPM Strategies. What arguments would you put forward to get your organization to adopt an Adaptive or Extreme SDPM strategy? Be specific.

4. Would it be preferable to have teams specialize in one of the five strategies or should each team be specialists in all five? What arguments would you put forth to support each side of the question?

5. Can you envision a project that might use more than one of the strategies? Why or why not? If you answered yes, give an example. Be specific.

PART TWO

Linear ESPM

When software developers first emerged from the primordial swamps and started building software products, they settled on a simple and straightforward model known as the Waterfall model. It is one of several models that I am classifying as Linear—that is, they move through a sequence of steps in a prescribed order with no feedback loops. Once a step is complete the development process moves to the next step. There is no going back for any reason. Some software development projects meet the criteria for using such approaches. This part discusses the generic model as well as several special cases.

CHAPTER 3

Linear SDPM Strategy

A manager . . . sets objectives, . . . organizes, . . .
motivates, . . . communicates, . . . measures, . . . and
develops people. Every manager does these things—
knowingly or not. A manager may do them well or may
do them wretchedly but always does them.

Peter Drucker

Chapter Learning Objectives

After reading this chapter, you will be able to:

- ◆ **Explain the Linear SDPM strategy**
- ◆ **Have a high-level understanding of the Standard Waterfall model and the Rapid Development Waterfall model**

Linear approaches to software development and the project management of such projects have been around the longest of all the models I discuss in this book. These linear approaches date back to the 1950s and 1960s when the traditional Waterfall approach and modern project management had just lit their candles and arose out of the darkness. This chapter serves as an overview of the Linear SDPM strategy and leaves for later chapters in this part the detailed discussion of each phase in the life cycle of a Linear SDPM strategy.

The Linear approach is the longest lived of all the approaches I consider in this book. Until the early 1990s this was the overwhelming choice of software developers. There were few alternatives at that time. Because of the Linear approach's longevity it has become habit with many developers. Even though a number of alternatives exist today, developers don't give second thoughts to changing. They would rather force fit the old when the new would be the better choice.

Old habits die hard. That is unfortunate because all of their attempts to modify the Linear approach to accommodate software development projects that don't fit the conditions ultimately lead to failure or sadly disappointed customers.

The Linear SDPM Strategy

The Linear SDPM strategy is the simplest and most intuitive of the five strategies discussed in this book. It assumes having as nearly perfect information about goal and solution as can reasonably be expected. The strategy is based on that assumption and does not easily accommodate any deviations. The Linear project management life cycle consists of five phases performed in a linear fashion. Figure 3-1 provides an overview of the Linear SDPM strategy. Chapters 4–9 will explore these phases in more detail.

Scope Phase

First, note that the scoping phases for both the linear software development life cycle and the project management life cycle are concurrent. They are also integrated. Depending on the nature and size of the project, the scoping phase can be anything from a few hours across the table by the customer and the project manager to a week-long planned agenda meeting attended by the core project team and several representatives from the customer side. For the simpler case, the Conditions of Satisfaction (see Appendix D) would work quite nicely. For the more demanding case, the week-long planned agenda meeting might cover project scope, business case, requirements gathering, Project Overview Statement (see Appendix C), and a high-level project schedule with perhaps milestones identified.

Plan and Launch Phases

For the simpler case, a half-day planning session with the core team and the customer can produce the Work Breakdown Structure (see Appendix E) and the initial project schedule. The key to the success of this phase is meaningful customer involvement. That idea will be stressed throughout all the models discussed. In fact, it becomes more critical as you move toward models that are more complex and more uncertain. For the more demanding case, the planning session might require as many as 3–5 consecutive days. It involves the same planning team as the simpler case and produces the same deliverables. The Launch Phase involves the entire project team. They establish the team operating rules; make final assignments, roles, and responsibilities using the RASCII Matrix (see Chapter 6); plan the final resource loaded schedule; and write the appropriate work packages. Project work can then begin.

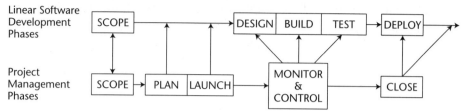

Figure 3-1: The Linear SDPM strategy

Monitor and Control Phases

The design, build, and test phases of the software development life cycle are executed linearly against a project schedule and are monitored and controlled for conformance to that project schedule. Schedule slippages resulting from unforeseen events and scope changes brought on by external factors require the team and the customer to revisit the project schedule and make the necessary adjustments to bring the project back on schedule.

Close Phase

The Close Phase is started when the acceptance test criteria have been demonstrated. The deliverables are put into production status and formal closing activities are done. This includes a post-implementation audit to assess conformance to the plan and achievement of the success criteria. In many cases the success criteria cannot be demonstrated until well after the deployment phase. Lessons learned with respect to the deliverables and the process for creating the deliverables are documented and posted for others to use as appropriate.

Types of Linear SDPM Strategies

Two fundamental models fall into the Linear class, the Standard Waterfall and the Rapid Development Waterfall. Both are introduced here. In addition to the models themselves, I have included a graphic of the Linear SDPM strategy as applied to each. The details of those strategies are discussed in Chapters 4 through 9.

Standard Waterfall Model

Figure 3-2 was displayed in Chapter 2 and is reproduced here for easy reference.

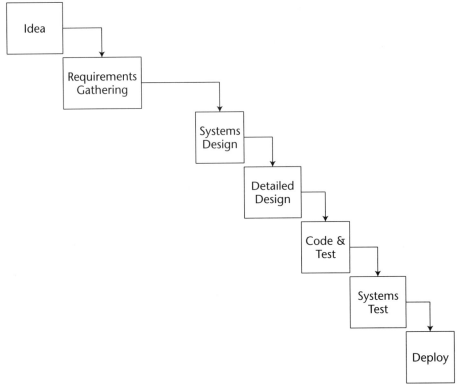

Figure 3-2: The Standard Waterfall model

The first thing to note about this version is that each phase must be complete before the next phase can begin, and that once a phase is complete there is no returning at some later point to revise work completed earlier. That might be acceptable until a change is introduced at which time potential scheduling disaster might result.

Figure 3-3 illustrates the Linear SDPM strategy for the Standard Waterfall model.

Variation to the Standard Waterfall Model

A variation of the Standard Waterfall model somewhat alleviates the non-overlap situation of the Standard Waterfall Model. It is shown in Figure 3-4.

Note the overlap between successive phases. That brief period of time where you have concurrency between successive phases allows, for example, the Build Phase to begin while the Design Phase is still incomplete. That time when you have concurrency is also a time when some feedback can be given, but it is restricted to feedback to the almost completed phase. So if early in the Build Phase the developers come across an alternative design that makes the system more responsive or easy to code, they can inform the design team. There is no guarantee that the design team can implement the changes and still keep to the planned schedule, but at least that possibility exists. All of this assumes that the design team is separate from the build team. If they are in fact the same team, then any advantage that derives from this concurrency is lost. What isn't lost is the improved design that might still be implemented but with some negative impact on the schedule. In situations in which the build team finds a significant improvement from an alternative design, the added design time might be offset with the reduced coding time. In those cases, you find a distinct advantage to the revised Standard Waterfall model. It allows for a sanity check on a phase nearing completion, and it does offer some relief, although limited.

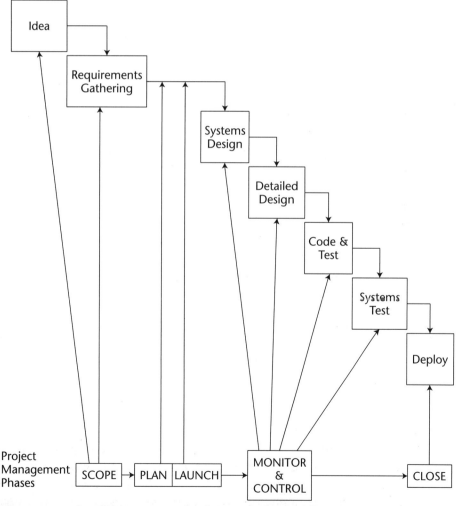

Figure 3-3:   Linear SDPM strategy for the Standard Waterfall model

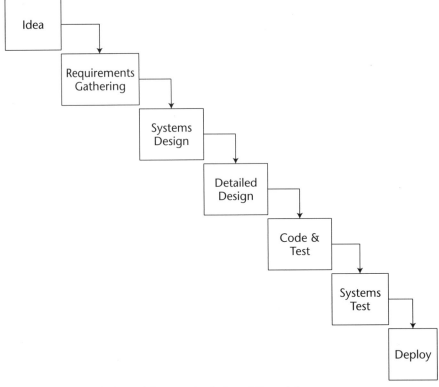

Figure 3-4:   A variation of the Standard Waterfall model

Figure 3-5 illustrates the Linear SDPM strategy for the variation to the Standard Waterfall model.

WARNING

There is good news and bad news associated with the variation. On the good news side are a form of check and balance introduced and some economies of schedule. However, those small gains can easily be overridden by the bad news. Whenever work is compressed into a smaller window of time, several related things begin to happen. First, you face the likelihood of resource contention as one person might be required to work on concurrent tasks from the neighboring phases. That might be trivial or problematic but needs to be considered in any case. Second, risk increases. That happens because you have less time to recover from mistakes made in the more compressed schedule. The degree of overlap is the causal factor. Small overlap will have minimal impact on risk. As the degree of overlap increases so does risk. Take the extreme case where the overlap is such that both design and build occur almost in parallel. While this makes little sense and no one would even contemplate doing it, it does illustrate the indirect correlation between schedule reduction and risk increase. In the hypothetical situation, risk will be at a maximum. The Build

Phase will have very little information from the Design Phase on which to begin coding. That means mistakes will be made and code will have to be redone or even scrapped as the design unfolds. So you do find a distinct trade-off between reduced time and increased risk.

You will see this trade-off in many other models later in the book. Here, in the simplest of situations, it still can be operative.

Rapid Development Waterfall Model

Figure 3-4 (and the ensuing discussion) has a lot in common with the Rapid Development Waterfall model shown in Figure 3-6, which was introduced in Chapter 2 and is reproduced here for ease of reference.

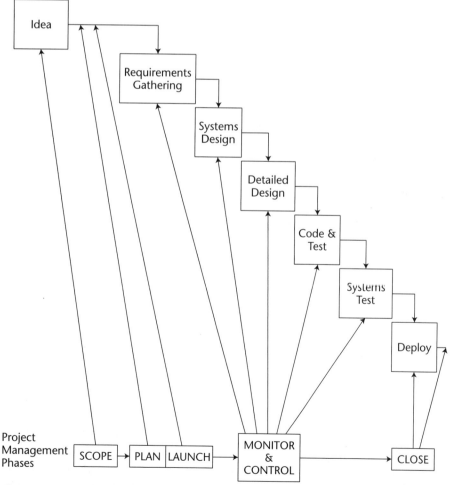

Figure 3-5:   Linear SDPM strategy for the variation to the Standard Waterfall model

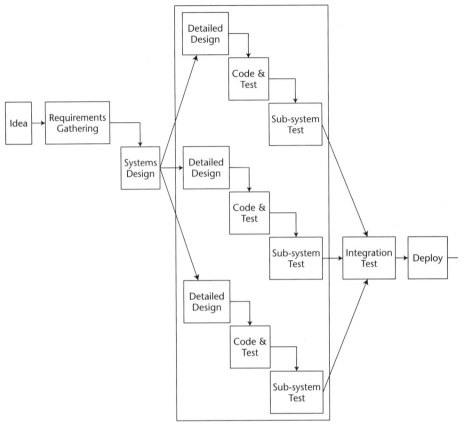

Figure 3-6: Rapid Development Waterfall model

The first variation of the Standard Waterfall model is one in which the project schedule can be compressed. That is done by creating parallel "swim lanes" of development activity. The linearity of the process is still maintained with these parallel swim lanes. Figure 3-6 depicts those parallel swim lanes. You need to consider several things in creating such a development schedule. The first is risk. By squeezing the work into a shorter timeframe the incidence of errors and staff scheduling conflicts increases. The amount of work has not decreased; it just must be completed in a shorter time frame. The last parallel swim lane that is complete determines the completion date of the development project. In keeping with the Standard Waterfall model, work always moves forward, and there is no feedback. Other than the parallel development effort, the two models differ only in that the Rapid Development Waterfall model has an added task, integration testing. I'll have more to say about that in Chapter 7 because it does introduce some complications as well.

Figure 3-7 illustrates the Linear SDPM strategy for the Rapid Development Waterfall model.

It shows the results of integrating the project management life cycle into the Rapid Development Waterfall model. Note that the only difference as compared to the Linear SDPM for the Standard Waterfall model is that the monitoring and control phase now extends to several parallel swim lanes of design, code and test, and sub-system test. The last swim lane that completes determines the start of the integration test phase of the Rapid Development Waterfall model life cycle.

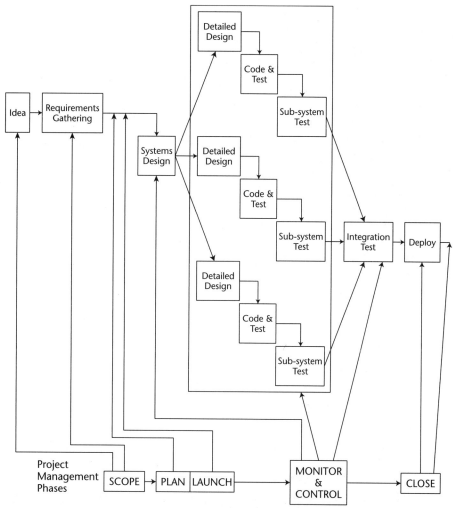

Figure 3-7: Linear SDPM strategy for the Rapid Development Waterfall model

Chapters 4 through 8 discuss the details of each of the five project management phases as they integrate into the Linear software development life cycle. Chapter 9 summarizes the high points of the Linear SDPM strategy.

Case Study

MEMORANDUM

     DATE: **November 9, 2005**

     FROM: **Dee Livery**

     TO: **All PDQ Employees**

     SUBJECT: Status Report

I just wanted to update you on the company-wide business improvement project. As you know, we hired Hype, Hype, and Morehype, a local marketing research and planning company, to ascertain our situation in the marketplace and our business processes. I have seen the draft of their report and wanted you to be aware of certain steps I feel are necessary and must be implemented without further delay.

Their final report will be distributed next week but I wanted you to hear from me before copies of that report begin to circulate. First of all, they have done an admirable job in meeting all of our major issues. They were a good choice. Here are the salient points in their report:

From their interviews, competitor surveys, and analyses they have verified that we do have the best pizza in our market area. We ranked higher than the competition in all categories (taste, variety, appearance, price, and quality of ingredients). The survey also suggested that we add a selection of oven-baked sandwiches to our menus.

From the same market survey, we were second only to our major competitor in our home delivery service. The survey pointed out that our time to deliver and pizza temperature at delivery were the only areas needing improvement.

The market survey also asked about delivery of unbaked pizzas. The results were:

We would definitely use the service	28%
We would probably use the service	31%
Not sure if we would use the service	20%
We would probably not use the service	10%
We definitely would not use the service	11%

The unbaked pizza market is not served by our competitor, and we should move immediately to take advantage of this window of opportunity.

From the analysis of our sales data over the past 30 months, we learned that our home delivery sales began to drop a few months after our competitor moved into the market and has continued to drop at a fairly steady pace. Over the past 18 months we have lost more than 30 percent of our revenues in the home delivery business. That impact has hit all four of our stores about equally. Our eat-in and carry out sales have remained steady over that same period of time.

The summary level data is shown below.

| STORE | 2003 | | 2004 | | 2005 |
	JAN/ JUNE	JULY/ DEC	JAN/ JUNE	JULY/ DEC	JAN/ JUNE
#1 (OPENED IN 1999)					
In	$1.2M	$1.3M	$1.3M	$1.2M	$1.3M
Del	$0.7M	$0.5M	$0.5M	$0.4M	$0.3M
#2 (OPENED IN 1992)					
In	$1.2M	$1.1M	$1.1M	$1.1M	$1.0M
Del	$0.8M	$0.6M	$0.5M	$0.5M	$0.4M
#3 (OPENED IN 1975)					
In	$1.1M	$1.0M	$1.0M	$0.9M	$1.0M
Del	$0.7M	$0.9M	$0.8M	$0.7M	$0.6M
#4 (OPENED IN 1984)					
In	$0.7M	$0.7M	$0.8M	$0.9M	$0.9M
Del	$0.7M	$0.8M	$0.8M	$0.6M	$0.5M
ALL					
In	$4.2M	$4.1M	$4.2M	$4.1M	$4.2M
Del	$2.9M	$2.8M	$2.6M	$2.2M	$1.8M
TOT	$7.1M	$6.9M	$6.8M	$6.3M	$6.0M

Our major competitor began opening stores at the rate of one per month beginning in January 2004. They now have 20 stores. Every PDQ store has lost home delivery sales over that 18 month period and continues to lose sales. In-store sales, which include take-out, have held fairly steady over the past 18 months.

Our marketing consultants have shown how an advertising campaign would boost sales. They also suggest a discount coupon program to introduce our new home delivery services. I like their ideas and recommend we try them out.

(continued)

Case Study *(continued)*

The business process improvement program has identified two problems. First, we need to implement a preparation area where pizza ingredients are sliced, chopped, diced, and otherwise prepared for the production line. As you know, our kitchens are already cramped for space, so I am going to use the four pizza vans to be that staging area. They will service the inventory needs of all four stores from the two pizza factories. The pizza factories will have the main inventory that supplies the pizza vans. The pizza vans will carry inventory destined for the stores and for their own production needs. This is expected to be a continuous service. Second, in order to make room for growth, we need to replace the ovens in all four stores. The new ovens will be rotary ovens that occupy the same footprint as our current ovens but can handle 50 percent more volume. I've had several of our regular customers sample the pizzas baked in these new ovens. As long as we baked the pizzas on pizza stones they didn't notice any differences. Customers who order unbaked pizzas will be given a complimentary pizza stone for their future orders of unbaked pizza. The ovens are on order and will be delivered in one month.

Our major competitor has just introduced 30-minute order entry to order delivery time. We do not have any details on how they expect to meet that goal, but we must counter their program with one of our own.

Based on all of this information and my 30 years of successful experience in this business, I have made an executive decision as to how we are going to proceed. The details will follow but here are the actions we are going to take:

We will open two pizza factories to add capacity to our home delivery line of business. The four existing stores will continue to offer home delivery. Two take-out businesses recently closed and their fully equipped properties were put on the market with 5-year renewable leases with an option to buy at any time. One was the German store Schnitzels-R-Us and the other was the Cambodian store Sprouts-To-Go. Their locations are strategically located in our growing market areas. I have signed a leasing agreement for both of those properties. They are available immediately.

I have been informed by our long-time supplier that they are outfitting trucks to bake pizzas for a small chain on the west coast. I talked with the owner of that chain who said that the early sales figures exceeded their forecasts. I have asked our vendor to customize four of these pizza vans for us. They will be delivered in 6 weeks. Two of them will operate out of our existing four stores and the other two out of our new pizza factories. We'll continue to use the four vans that now service our four stores. At this time they will not be retrofitted to bake pizzas but that option is open to us if it is deemed to be a good business decision. This will be the pilot for further expansion of pizza factories and/or pizza vans.

We have been studying our telephone system. It needs to be replaced with a system that receives all orders from a single number and routes them to the appropriate store, factory, or pizza van for processing.

We need a point of sale (POS) system to handle all data collection (in-store, pick-up, and home delivery) and analyze the collected data to help us make further decisions about pizza factory locations and pizza vans. The network that will service our business going forward must link all information and physical systems into a single system. We haven't used information technology to our advantage in the past, but we must do so in the future if we intend to succeed in this highly competitive business. I need your teams to be limited only by their own creativity.

Since all orders are routed to a store, pizza factory, or pizza van we will need a hardware/software/communications/data system to handle all scheduling and routing in real time.

Inventory replenishment will require an order to be routed from the store to the appropriate pizza van for fulfillment. This order should be initiated by the POS system since it will be constantly monitoring store inventories as a result of orders.

We will also announce a 30-minute order entry to order delivery service as soon as we get our pizza factories and pizza vans in operation. This will be announced through a major advertising blitz in our markets.

I recognize that this action pre-empts the work you are now doing. Please be assured that your work to date with the marketing consultants has been exemplary and solidified my thinking and made these decisions possible. Your work is far from done and we will need to closely monitor our sales and performance to make sure we can reach our goal of recouping and surpassing the lost revenues from the past 18 months.

As always my door is open to all of you, and I welcome your input. We have a significant challenge ahead of us and the business needs all of us pulling together as a team.

Discussion Questions

1. What would you do if the frequency of customer scope change requests were increasing to the point where you felt that the project was now at risk?

2. What might you do to protect the project schedule against too frequent customer scope change requests?

3. Suppose the team uncovered a design change that would significantly increase the business value of the project but would render the project schedule obsolete if introduced. How would you handle this situation?

The Linear SDPM Scoping Phase

Define the problem before you pursue a solution.
John Williams, CEO
Spence Corporation

Chapter Learning Objectives

After reading this chapter, you will be able to:

- ◆ Identify one or more solutions to meeting the project goal
- ◆ Define a functional requirement
- ◆ Define a non-functional requirement
- ◆ Define a global requirement
- ◆ Define a constraint requirement
- ◆ Understand customer sign-off concerns
- ◆ Prepare a Project Overview Statement
- ◆ Ensure that a Linear SDPM strategy is correct

The Linear Scoping Phase is the initiation of the project. It is here that the customer and the project manager come together to define the project at the highest levels. The process of defining encompasses four major tasks:

- Solution definition
- Requirements gathering
- Customer sign-off on requirements
- Writing the Project Overview Statement (POS)

Solution Definition

Defining the solution at the highest level of abstraction is akin to problem solving. I have used parts of the problem-solving model to get this high-level solution definition for years. It works and it is discussed here.

Defining the Problem

Many organizations have a tendency to exclude the computer folks from the early efforts to define the solution. It is certainly true that the problem is first a business problem to be defined and only then is it a technology problem to be solved. However, such an approach overlooks the likelihood that synergy can result from integrating the problem definition from both perspectives simultaneously. A better solution will always follow from the collaborative efforts of the business side and the technology side.

Exactly what is the problem? The more specific we can be in making this definition, the better off we will be in later parts of the project. It is too easy to stray from the problem. Scope creep becomes our worst enemy. A definition that is equivalent to solving world hunger won't work either. That leads to a very long project and opens the possibility of changes in the business climate that lead to scope changes in the project. Perhaps the strategy is to narrow the problem or at least narrow what you are going to do about the problem. It isn't necessary to solve the entire problem in one project. Oftentimes, a sequence of dependent projects works better than one giant project.

For the PDQ case study, the problem statement comes from the narrative background information (which is found in full in Chapter 1). I quote:

> Recently PDQ has lost 30 percent of sales revenue due mostly to a drop in their home delivery business. They attribute this solely to their major competitor who recently promoted a program that guarantees 30-minute delivery service from order entry to home delivery. PDQ advertises one-hour delivery.

For our purposes the problem statement will be:

> PDQ has lost 30 percent of its sales revenue primarily because of a too long elapsed time from order entry to order delivery.

What kind of a problem is this? Is it purely an operational problem and the business side will have to find a way to make pizzas faster? Is it purely a technology problem and the technology side of the house will have to find a way that the computer can provide more efficient processing of the order and its delivery? Or might it just be a business/technology problem? Is there some way to combine the two disciplines to produce yet a third solution? Perhaps we can dig a little deeper into the problem and isolate some possible causes and then begin to formulate a solution or solutions.

Determining Causes

I have been successful using Root Cause Analysis for this step. The major cause is assumed to be the competition and their 45-minute fulfillment time. Root Cause Analysis would have us ask: "Why?" Continue to ask why until it makes no sense to ask it. The results are the root causes. It is those root causes that become the basis for generating solution ideas. For the PDQ case study, a Root Cause Analysis was done with the following results:

- PDQ is too far away from its customers.

- PDQ has not changed its production process since the company was founded.

- PDQ has not been able to leverage technology to improve its market position.

Generating Ideas for Solutions

This is generally a brainstorming session to get all ideas out on the table for ultimate discussion and prioritization. To get credible results the participants must be free to offer any ideas they think might hold promise of solving the problem or at least part of the problem. Here are some of the ideas that came from the brainstorming session for the case study:

- Assemble and bake the pizzas in trucks that continuously move about the city.

- Deliver pizzas ready for the customers to bake in their own oven.

- Add more stores nearer the customers.

- Fully automate all operations wherever possible.

- Obtain a comprehensive computer system to run all operations.

Prioritizing Ideas

In many projects that are focused on solving a problem for the enterprise, it is not necessary to solve the entire problem. Other proposals will address other parts of the problem. It will be senior management's responsibility to pick the mix of proposals that will solve the entire problem, if it is solvable. In the case study, the management team decided to break the project into two projects listed as follows:

Project 1

Fully automate all operations wherever possible.

Obtain a comprehensive computer system to run all operations.

Project 2

Assemble and bake the pizzas in trucks that continuously move about the city.

Deliver pizzas baked or ready for the customer to bake in their own oven.

Decision postponed

Add more stores nearer the customers.

The first two ideas are related and can be acted upon quickly. It looks like a technology problem, and the team will find a technology solution. The two ideas were put into one project and a Linear SDPM strategy was chosen. Project 2 is far more complex. It certainly is a business problem that the project addresses but wait. There is a technology infrastructure that is needed to enable the business solution. The technical requirements will not be easy to define. For those that are identified, a solution is not at all obvious. This project will be launched after Project 1 is complete and will follow an Adaptive SDPM strategy. For the time being, adding more stores wasn't seen as a good business decision. The results of Project 2 might shed more light on that idea.

Requirements Gathering

The structure that I recommend goes something like this:

Problem⇨Goal⇨Solution⇨Requirements⇨Functions⇨Features

If you are reasonably certain that all features have been identified and defined, use a Linear or Incremental SDPM strategy. If you think all functions have been defined and some features have not been defined, use an Iterative SDPM strategy. If some or most parts of the requirements (and hence of the solution) have not been defined, use an Adaptive SDPM strategy. If the goal and solution have not been clearly defined, use an Extreme SDPM strategy. This is the hierarchy followed throughout the book. In this part, I will use the case study to illustrate several concepts. The focus will be on Project 1. Project 2 will be covered in more detail in the chapters on the Adaptive SDPM strategy (Chapters 24-30).

Defining and Managing Customer Requirements

You can go about defining and managing customer requirements in two ways. In simpler situations, you can use Conditions of Satisfaction (COS) described in Appendix D. COS scales up to a certain point where the complexity of the project makes COS a poor choice and something a bit more sophisticated is required. You might prefer to use a more structured approach to gathering customer requirements. That would be the Volere process, which is also defined in Appendix D.

Gathering Customer Requirements

Simply put, project teams that make a concerted effort to manage customer requirements do so because they want to satisfy their customer needs by having their projects succeed. Research studies find that the majority of project failures are related in some way to changing customer requirements.

The section that follows is derived from a modified Volere requirements process and its associated specification template. I have found this to be a best practice. Originally designed for use in systems application development, the process is a generic requirements gathering and specification process whose principles can be applied to small and large projects across varied industries. These processes are discussed in detail in Appendix D. First, we need to put a few definitions in place.

What Are Requirements?

Requirements are the things that you should discover before starting to fully design, build, or execute a project. Discovering the requirements during execution/construction is so inefficient and detrimental that no competent and right-thinking person would do so.

DEFINITION: REQUIREMENT
A requirement is something the product or service should do or produce or a quality that it must have.

A requirement exists either because the type of product demands certain functions or qualities, or the customer wants the requirements to be part of the product/project delivery.

Project requirements start with what the customer really needs and end when those needs are satisfied. In the end-to-end chain of specifications, you face an ongoing danger of misunderstanding and ambiguity. This often leads to nonessential or over-specified requirements. Figure 4-1 illustrates the point I am trying to make.

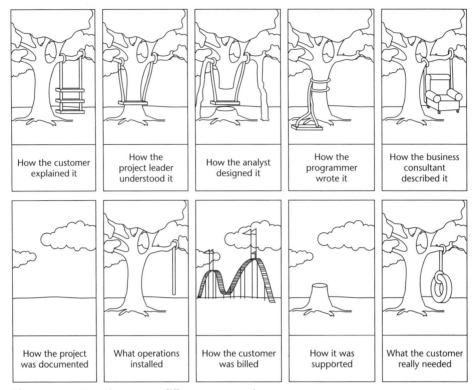

Figure 4-1: Requirements—different perspectives

The point of all of this is—be very careful how you go about defining requirements. As is clear in the figure, not everybody has the same interpretation of
words commonly used. For example, in my technology training classes I used
to ask people to write down their definition of *implementation*. They could
define it in terms of what it included or didn't include. The results were sur-
prising. There were as many definitions of implementation as there were people in the class, and these were people who could hardly utter a sentence
without using the word "implementation." Not even they knew what they
were talking about. Pity the poor customer who has to make sense out of all
this gibberish.

What Kinds of Requirements Are There?

Requirements define the product or service that is the deliverable of the project. These requirements are the basis for changes that a customer is seeking. At
this stage, after stakeholder assessment, the project lead and the project team
are now tasked with going through the steps to establish the requirements
baseline. This process is a systematic step-by-step effort that requires diligence. It will be these requirements that will be used for estimating the cost

and time for the project. Ultimately, these requirements drive acceptance of the product or service by the customer.

There are four types of requirements.

Functional Requirements

Functional requirements specify what the product or service must do. They are actions that the product or service must take, such as check, calculate, record, and retrieve.

DEFINITION: FUNCTIONAL REQUIRMENTS
■■■■ **Functional requirements specify what the product or service must do.**

For the case study, the following is a subset of the functional requirements identified:

- The computer system must report revenues and expenses by line of business.
- The computer system must generate bi-weekly payroll for all employees.
- The computer system must track and reorder inventory automatically.

Non-Functional Requirements

Non-functional requirements demonstrate the properties that the product or service should have to do what it must do. These requirements are the characteristics or qualities that make the product or service attractive, or usable, or fast, or reliable. Most non-functional requirements are associated with performance criteria and are usually those requirements that establish the product or service boundary. Non-functional requirements can sometimes be generated by the refinement of a global requirement. Non-functional requirements are usually associated with performance criteria that set the parameters for how a system is to function.

DEFINITION: NON-FUNCTIONAL REQUIRMENTS
■■■■ **Non-functional requirements demonstrate the properties that the product or service should have in order to do what it must do.**

For the case study, the following is a subset of the non-functional requirements identified:

- The computer system must use PDQ fonts.
- The computer system must use existing PDQ equipment wherever possible.

Global Requirements

Global requirements describe the highest level of requirements within the system or project. Global requirements will describe properties of the system as a whole. During the initial stages of a project, many requirements end up being global requirements. They require the project lead and the team to refine them through the methods of requirement generation. *Global requirements* is a relatively new term. In the past, these have been called general requirements or product constraints or constraining requirements. The caution with global requirements is that in most cases they can be turned into a non-functional requirement simply by asking the questions associated with what, why, or how. In fact, it is wise to move a global requirement to a non-functional requirement to focus in better on what the requirement really is.

DEFINITION: GLOBAL REQUIREMENTS

Global requirements describe the highest level of requirements within the system or project.

For the case study the following is a subset of the global requirements identified:

- The computer system must be intuitive.
- The computer system must not require training by anyone with reason to use it.
- The computer system must be scalable.

Constraints

Constraints are those requirements that, on the surface, resemble design constraints or project constraints. Design constraints are those pre-existing design decisions that mandate how the final product must look or how it must comply technologically. Project constraints cover the areas of budget and schedule along with deadlines and so on. One important note here is that product constraints can be listed as global requirements, but project constraints are *not* because they do not deal with the requirements of the product but rather the process that delivers the product. The two are quite different.

DEFINITION: CONSTRAINTS

Constraints are those requirements that must be met by the entire product or service.

For the case study, the following is a subset of the constraints identified:

- The computer system must not exceed $4 million.
- The computer system must have a response time less than 3 milliseconds.

It is very important to realize that requirements identification and categorization is critical to understanding the direction of the project. It is now that the framework for the project begins to take shape.

Case Study

Based on the memorandum from Dee and further discussions with the customer, the following sub-systems were identified and their requirements identified.

Sub-system #1: Order Entry—The customer enters an order.

1.1 Identify customer

    1.1.1 New or returning

    1.1.2 Customer history

    1.1.3 Name, address, etc.

1.2 Get order

    1.2.1 Products requested

    1.2.2 Quantity and size ordered

    1.2.3 Display options

    1.2.4 Baked or unbaked

1.3 Get delivery instructions

    1.3.1 Delivery location

    1.3.2 Delivery options

    1.3.3 Delivery time requested

1.4 Price order

    1.4.1 Promotions

    1.4.2 Calculate price

    1.4.3 Maintain pricing table

1.5 Confirm order

    1.5.1 Accept, cancel, modify

    1.5.2 Payment type

    1.5.3 Display order

1.6 Submit order

    1.6.1 Submit order

    1.6.2 Confirm order acceptance

(continued)

Case Study *(continued)*

Sub-system #2: Order Fulfillment—Based on current workloads, the system decides where to prepare the order.

2.1 Choose prep location

    2.1.1 Get prep location workload

    2.1.2 Get order data

    2.1.3 Determine location

2.2 Transmit order

    2.2.1 Submit order to prep location

    2.2.2 Confirm location

2.3 Send prep location data

    2.3.1 Update Logistics Management Sub-system

Sub-system #3: Order Routing—Based on current workloads the system decides how to deliver the order.

3.1 Get delivery instructions

    3.1.1 Get delivery location

    3.1.2 Retrieve order detail

3.2 Get workload data.

    3.2.1 Get delivery queue statistics

    3.2.2 Prioritize new order

3.3 Compute real-time route

    3.3.1 Determine route

    3.3.2 Transmit driving directions

    3.3.3 Driver confirmation

3.4 Order status

    3.4.1 Confirm order delivery

    3.4.2 Confirm payment receipt

Sub-system #4: Logistics Management—This sub-system continuously monitors workloads across all preparation locations and all delivery alternatives. It is used by the Order Fulfillment and Order Routing sub-systems.

4.1 Get order entry data

    4.1.1 Retrieve record

    4.1.2 Update record

4.2 Update prep data

    4.2.1 Retrieve record

    4.2.2 Update record

4.3 Update delivery data

    4.3.1 Retrieve record

    4.3.2 Update record

4.4 Update customer information

    4.4.1 Retrieve record

    4.4.2 Update record

Sub-system #5: Inventory Management—This sub-system monitors real-time inventory levels at all locations and automatically issues replenishment orders to the trucks to replenish location inventories and automatically re-orders inventory from the vendor.

5.1 Update on-hand inventory

5.2 Identify reorder needs

    5.2.1 Determine location for inventory reorder needs

5.3 Issue reorder

    5.3.1 Confirm vendor receipt

5.4 Inform location

    5.4.1 Transmit reorder

    5.4.2 Display reorder

    5.4.3 Confirm reorder receipt from location

5.5 Confirm inventory receipt

Customer Sign-Off on Requirements

You will encounter two sign-off situations.

Customer Willingly Signs Off

This is what you hope for, but be careful. The sign-off says that the customer believes that all requirements, functions, and features have been identified and documented. In other words, except for external events over which no one has control, no scope change requests will be made. This is important input to your decision to go forward with a linear strategy. Make sure you are comfortable that the customer really does attest to the fact that all requirements, functions, and feature have been defined and documented.

Customer Unwilling to Sign Off

First of all, the customer equates a sign-off as their approval for what has been documented. Many have the mistaken notion that no changes will be accepted. Obviously that is a myth. The choice of a Linear SDPM strategy assumes there will be no scope changes, and it is designed around that fact. The reality is that no matter how complete the requirements specification, the customer will still make scope change requests. In so doing they need to understand that accommodating the change request will result in scheduling problems. That is the first reason for not signing off. The second reason for not signing off is that they cannot attest to completeness of requirements, functions, and features. That is your signal to find another approach. Either an Iterative or Adaptive SDPM strategy would be preferable.

Case Study

Dee reviewed the requirements with the project team and signed off as follows:

- **Sub-system #1: Order Entry—Dee approved the functions without much discussion. The project team felt that this sub-system was fairly straightforward and felt confident that they could develop the code without incident.**

- **Sub-system #2: Order Fulfillment—Dee was comfortable with all of the requirements except 2.1.3 Determine location. While the rest of the sub-system development could take place as usual, the developers felt that some other approach to coming to closure with the determination of the best location to prepare the order would have to be developed. Just how they were going to approach that requirement would be dealt with at a later time.**

- **Sub-system #3: Order Routing—While both the customer and the developers knew that some type of Global Positioning System (GPS) would be employed, they all knew that the problem was far more complex than the technology they would employ. They could define what the end product would have to do but weren't at all confident that they knew how to attain it. A creative approach would surely be needed.**

- **Sub-system #4: Logistics Management—This sub-system was just a database that housed all the current operational data and would have to be constantly updated. Both parties were comfortable with the requirements and expected development to take place rather routinely. There were no outstanding concerns from either Dee or the developers.**

- **Sub-system #5: Inventory Management—This was the simplest of the five sub-systems. There was even the possibility of acquiring a commercial off-the-shelf solution that could be easily modified.**

Project Overview Statement

One of the deliverables from the solution definition and requirements gathering exercises is the Project Overview Statement (POS). The details of generating this document are given in Appendix C. This document will serve as the baseline for the project as it goes forward to the Planning Phase. Figure 4-2 shows POS for the case study.

PROJECT OVERVIEW STATEMENT	Project Name Operations Rebirth	Project No. 2006-01	Project Lead(s) Pepe Ronee
Problem/Opportunity PDQ has lost 30% of its sales revenue due primarily to a too long elapsed time from order entry to order delivery.			
Goal Implement a comprehensive computer system to automate all operations.			
Objectives 1. Implement a computer system that automates all business operations. 2. Implement a computer system that is intuitive and requires no training by the users. 3. Implement a computer system that is scalable. 4. Implement a computer system that monitors and automatically reorders inventory.			
Success Criteria 1. The rate of operational errors will decrease by at least 8% from current levels no later than 3 months after implementation. 2. The rate of operations execution will decrease by at least 14% from current for all operations no later than 3 months after implementation.			
Assumptions, Risks, Obstacles 1. All current employees will accept the new system. 2. All current employees will evaluate the new system as an improvement in operations over the current one. 3. The total cost of the new system will be lsess than $4M for the first 3 years.			
Prepared By Pepe Ronee	Date 1/12/06	Approved By Dee Livery	Date 1/16/06

Figure 4-2: POS for the PDQ case study

Ensuring That a Linear SDPM Strategy Is Correct

The decision that a Linear SDPM strategy is the correct decision for the project is as much art as it is science. From the science perspective you must have all positive data supporting the decision. The first thing you want to think about is the requirements sign-off. Obviously you must have customer sign-off. Without that it is a done deal, and some other strategy should be chosen. With that sign-off you still might not be clear on the decision to adopt a Linear SDPM strategy. For example, if you got some pretty strong signals that the customer was a bit reluctant to sign off, you need to dig into that and try to find out the reasons. Suppose you do that and are comfortable with what you learned. You are still not ready to make the decision. The next step is to validate that the project will not be affected by any exogenous factors. Projects that involve building software for commercial purposes will be highly affected by changes in the business environment, such as actions by your competitors. For these projects you might want to give some strong consideration to another strategy. The Iterative or Adaptive strategies might be better choices. Erring on the side of adopting a more complex or uncertain strategy is always safe. Erring on the side of adopting a less complex or more certain strategy can have negative results. Projects that have an internal focus only are likely candidates for the Linear SDPM strategy. If you do choose that strategy and it turns out that there are too many scope change requests, you always have the option of switching to a more complex or uncertain strategy. Again the Iterative or Adaptive would be good choices. Both of these strategies have a number of specific models from which to choose.

WARNING

I have encountered organizations, usually large ones, where the business side of the enterprise works on scoping tasks independent of the technical side of the enterprise. True, the early stages of project definition are from the perspective of the business of the enterprise, and technical people are not seen as necessary. But that doesn't last very long. There is no substitute for having the business and technical people collaborate on problem definition and solution. In fact, many of today's systems-related projects are such that the problem definition and the solution come about in parallel. One informs the other. That won't happen without a collaborative effort. If your methodology does not involve both business and technical people together as soon as possible in the project life cycle as possible, you may have a problem.

Discussion Questions

1. The customer was eager to sign off, and you were comfortable that the requirements, functions, and features had been completely defined and clearly documented. But that has changed. The customer is requesting scope changes at an increasing rate, and you do not see any convergence in their actions. You are thinking about changing the strategy to an Iterative SDPM strategy. What considerations would you have to make?

CHAPTER 5

The Linear SDPM Planning Phase

Let all things be done decently and in order.
1 Corinthians 14:40

Chapter Learning Objectives

After reading this chapter, you will be able to:

- ◆ **Understand when to use alternative forms of the work breakdown structure**
- ◆ **Decompose a deliverables-based Work Breakdown Structure (WBS) for the Rapid Development Waterfall model**

The output from the Scoping Phase is a Project Overview Statement (POS) and a clearly defined requirements document. Using these documents as input to the Planning Phase, you develop a plan following accepted principles and practices of Traditional Project Management. With the design, build, and test phases as the highest level of decomposition in the WBS a complete decomposition down to the task level is done. To complete the Planning Phase, estimates of task duration and resource requirements are made, and an initial project schedule is put together.

So, the requirements have been specified and the choice made to follow the Linear SDPM strategy. Now what?

Work Breakdown Structure Template

There are several approaches to building a complete WBS. A popular choice is the deliverables-based approach recommended in the Project Management Institute (PMI) Project Management Body of Knowledge (PMBOK) standards. While you could certainly take that approach in the Linear SDPM strategy, it will almost certainly overcomplicate the project. The approach I am recommending for the Linear SDPM strategy is to have the first-level breakdown be design, build, test, and implement, or some variation of it. The second and following levels of decomposition could then be a deliverables-based approach within each of the major phases of the particular linear model you are using. There is no point in making the WBS structure any more complicated than it needs to be. By following this approach, the opportunity to use templates from past projects increases significantly. Figure 5-1 is an example template for a Waterfall model.

The template can be modified for a specific project. The real value in this approach is that you can leverage all past experiences of projects that used this template. That extends to task duration estimation, dependency diagramming, estimation of resource requirements, and even a complete risk management plan. As another side benefit, you could use the template as a structure for archiving estimated and actual task duration. That becomes a good foundation for future task duration estimating.

Rapid Development Waterfall Model

The template might be useful here, but another approach to building the WBS might even be more useful. Because you know the project work will be divided into concurrent swim lanes with each swim lane working on a different part of the deliverables, doesn't it make sense to build a deliverables-based WBS? Of course it does; that's a no-brainer. So the first-level WBS should be the major deliverables. From there you can follow one of two alternatives. You might further partition the deliverables into subdeliverables and then consider functions and features as the next lower levels of the WBS. Alternatively, you might decompose the major deliverables into functions and features.

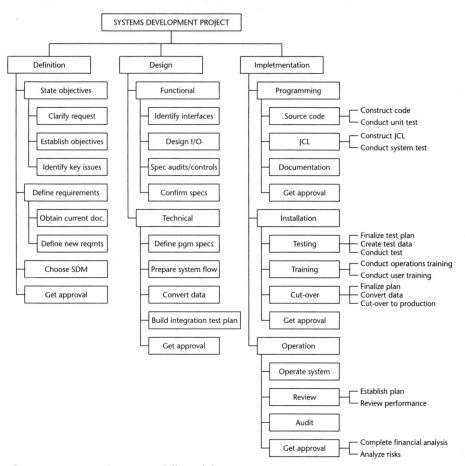

Figure 5-1: WBS for a Waterfall model

The deliverables-based WBS lends itself to the creation of concurrent swim lanes much better than the design-build-test-implement WBS structure. One of the benefits will be in building the dependency diagram, which is the topic of the next section of this chapter.

Here is a hybrid that you might want to consider. I have used this structure many times and have always been satisfied with the results. It gives the project manager an intuitively obvious basis on which to manage the entire project. Figure 5-2 shows the WBS that combines the design-build-test-implement structure with the deliverables-based structure.

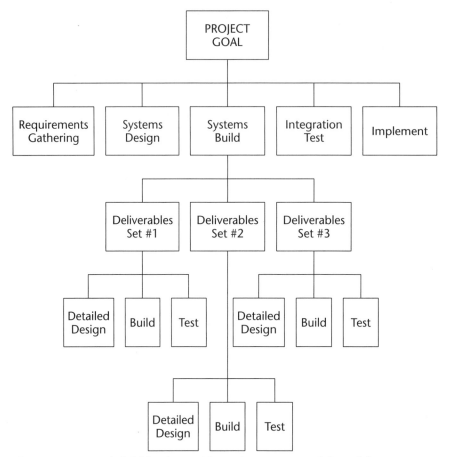

Figure 5-2: WBS hybrid for the Rapid Development Waterfall model

Note that all I have done is embed the deliverables-based WBS in the level one build activity. The hybrid is better aligned with the Linear SDPM strategy for the Rapid Development Waterfall model. The illustration of that was given in Chapter 3 and is repeated here as Figure 5-3 for easier reference.

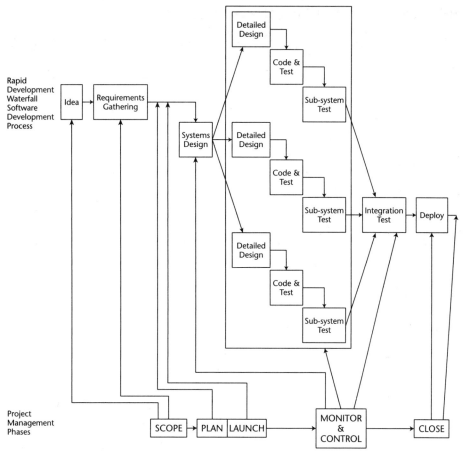

Figure 5-3:   Linear SDPM strategy for the Rapid Development Waterfall model

Dependency Diagramming

The dependency diagram is built using the lowest level of decomposition in the WBS. In this book, tasks define these lowest level decompositions. For the Standard Waterfall model, the straightforward application of dependency diagramming does the job quite nicely. See Appendix G for a quick refresher if you need it. The Rapid Development Waterfall model presents a rather different set of problems, as discussed in the next section.

Rapid Development Waterfall Model

The first thing you have to do is partition the deliverables into sets of deliverables that can be worked on concurrently. Obviously, dependencies between deliverables sets will have to be taken into account to construct these sets of deliverables. You want to avoid as many cross–deliverable set dependencies as possible. Ideally you would want none. A few dependency diagram configurations are worth discussing. Two simple cases are illustrated in Figures 5-4 and 5-5.

Figure 5-4 illustrates a situation where there are design dependencies across two deliverables sets. Detailed Design #2 is dependent upon Detailed Design #1. The net effect of this is to push deliverables set #2 work out to the date when Detailed Design #1 is complete and the Build of Deliverables set #2 out to the date when the Build for Deliverables set #3 is complete. Because final Integration Testing can't start until the last deliverables set is built and tested, you might want to add resources to the swim lane that will complete last in order to protect against a too long delay in Integration Testing.

The structure illustrated in Figure 5-4 should be done repeatedly until the deliverables sets produce a dependency diagram that produces swim lanes that are as independent of one another as possible. The less dependency between deliverables sets, the less risk you have in the Linear SDPM strategy for the Rapid Development Waterfall model than you have in the Linear SDPM strategy for the Standard Waterfall model. Risk containment is important in any project where there are concurrent swim lanes in the plan. The aggressive nature of strategies such as the Rapid Development Waterfall model introduces risk by its very nature.

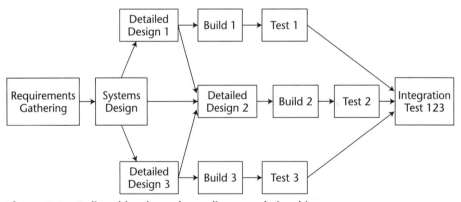

Figure 5-4: Deliverables dependency diagram relationships

Cohesion and Coupling

To minimize the problems associated with cross–deliverable set dependencies you turn to the concept of cohesion and coupling. *Cohesion* is a conceptual measure of the degree to which two or more entities are related to one another. *Coupling* is a conceptual measure of the dependency that exists between two entities. If the entities are deliverables sets, then you have the following as a principle to strive to attain: you should define the deliverables sets so that cohesion is maximized within a set and the coupling is minimized between any pair of sets. Figure 5-5 is an example of this condition. Here each deliverables set can be developed independently of any other (a property of minimal coupling) and the deliverables within a set can be developed together (a property of maximum cohesion). This is the best of all possible worlds in the Linear SDPM strategy for the Rapid Development Waterfall model. Achieving it might not happen very often, but nevertheless you should strive to get as close as possible.

WARNING
Define the deliverables sets so that cohesion is maximized within a set and the coupling is minimized between any pair of sets.

Figure 5-5 depicts a situation where Detailed Design #1 is the predecessor of all other Detailed Design activities. In other words all deliverables are dependent on Detailed Design for Deliverable Set #1. This is a fairly straightforward situation once Detailed Design #1 is completed.

In this example, once the Detailed Design #1 activity is complete, all three swim lanes are free of any cross–deliverable set dependencies. Except for any resource constraints that might affect the scheduling across swim lanes, each swim lane can be scheduled independent of any other swim lane. In deciding how deliverables should be grouped, your first concern will be to minimize cross–deliverable set dependencies. The next section covers this in greater detail.

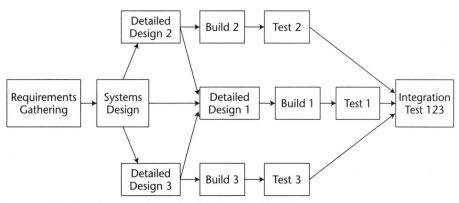

Figure 5-5: Maximum cohesion and minimum coupling

Creating Independent Deliverables Sets

There isn't any algorithm that I know of that will do the job of grouping deliverables into sets that are as independent of one another as possible. I use a trial and error approach that seems to give suitable results. Figure 5-6 provides an example.

Figure 5-6 is the initial schedule for our example project. This would be the network diagram if you were to follow the Standard Waterfall model using a deliverables-based WBS. The final deliverables are the set (A5, B5, . . . G5). A6, D6, and F6 are integration tasks, as is the END task. Most network diagrams, regardless of the WBS from which they were built, will have patterns much like the example. There will be naturally occurring swim lanes based solely on the predecessor/successor relationships that exist among the tasks. If you examine this network diagram, you can group the deliverables into sets that are as independent of one another as possible. Clearly, tasks C1 and D1 are critical to the grouping decisions. If you schedule C1 and D1 early in the project, then you can create two sets of independent deliverables. One set will comprise A, B, and C. The other set will comprise D, E, F, and G. Within each one of those sets you can schedule based only on resource availability. The more resources you have at your disposal, the more independent set of deliverables you can create. The example is simple, yet it will apply in many situations. Try it.

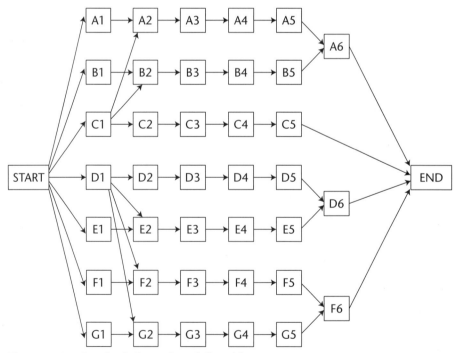

Figure 5-6: Creating independent deliverable sets

Project Scheduling

Scheduling is rather straightforward for both models. However, you do need to consider a few minor differences and points.

Standard Waterfall Model

In the Linear SDPM for the Standard Waterfall model, the skills required in the team change from architects to developers to test technicians as the project moves through its life cycle. Because you have no feedback loops or scope change requests, the architects can move on to other projects once they have finished their work on a project that follows the Linear SDPM model. Their deliverables (design documents) are handed off to the developers.

Rapid Development Waterfall Model

Because of the likelihood that you will have dependencies between deliverables sets, the schedules of each concurrent development swim lane will be related. Resource contention will restrict the flexibility you have in scheduling tasks that require the same skills and competencies.

Resource Requirements

These two models have a number of similarities and a number of differences as well when it comes to resource requirements and scheduling.

The Linear SDPM strategy does not require co-located teams and does not require highly skilled experts. That affords some latitude when assigning and scheduling team members. You find some differences, however, when considering the Linear SDPM for the Standard Waterfall model versus the Linear SDPM for the Rapid Development Waterfall model.

Standard Waterfall Model

The sequential structure of the Standard Waterfall model and the fact that you have no feedback loops means that different skill sets are needed along the project timeline. Once the architects have completed their design work and it has been approved, they can be assigned to other projects. You might encounter resource contention problems only if the architects are assigned to more than one project at a time. Some collaboration and joint scheduling will have to be done between the affected project managers.

Rapid Development Waterfall Model

For the Rapid Development Waterfall model the situation is a bit more complicated. Fortunately you have the advantage of being in control of the cross dependency set schedules. Figure 5-4 illustrates one such situation where cross dependency set scheduling conflicts might arise. Consider the three detailed design activities. If you had but one architect on the project, their time would have to be concurrently spent across three detailed design activities. The scheduling conflict centers on the scheduling of Detailed Design #3 to not conflict with Detailed Design #1 or its successor Detailed Design #2. Because of the architect resource constraint, you might be required to sequence the three detailed design activities in series rather than in parallel. The same situation can occur as you schedule the build and test activities. Will you be limited to one resource for each of these activities and hence be forced to schedule each of them in series rather than in parallel? Furthermore, what happens when schedule slippage occurs in one of the swim lanes? That will further aggravate an already conflict-ridden schedule. The bottom line here is that by choosing to follow a Linear SDPM for the Rapid Development Waterfall model instead of the Standard Waterfall model you affect two things.

- On the positive side you bring product to market sooner and hence return on the business investment.

- On the negative side you increase project risk through the added possibility of resource contention.

One way out is to add resources to the Rapid Development Waterfall model team as compared to the Standard Waterfall model team.

Discussion Questions

1. You are Pepe Ronee, and you have run the Linear SDPM strategy Scoping Phase by the book. But you have this gnawing feeling that what Dee Livery, the client, wants is not what she needs. Within the context of the Linear SDPM strategy what could you do?

CHAPTER 6

The Linear SDPM Launching Phase

When a team outgrows individual performance and
learns team confidence, excellence becomes reality.

Joe Paterno, Football Coach
Penn State University

Chapter Learning Objectives

After reading this chapter, you will be able to:

- ◆ Choose between the Hierarchical and Team Leader models for your Linear SDPM strategy
- ◆ Apply the RASCI Matrix to the Linear SDPM strategy
- ◆ Establish the appropriate team meeting rules
- ◆ Manage concurrent swim lanes

Linear SDPM strategy projects are by-the-book projects. That is, most if not all of the processes and templates will be established and will have been used many times over. These projects have little to offer in the way of surprise, at least until you discover that you really should have chosen another strategy.

The Launching Phase gets the full project team identified. Rules are established for how they will operate. There are two major tasks in this phase.

- The first is to line up the skills and competencies of the team with the specific needs of the project.
- The second is to align the project schedule with the team members' availabilities.

In the Linear and Incremental SDPM strategies, teams might not be co-located, so the scheduling aspect is not all that straightforward. The details for the Linear SDPM strategy will be discussed in this chapter.

Team Leadership Model

In terms of leadership models, the Hierarchical Leadership or Team Leader models are the preferred choice. Small projects that are following the Linear SDPM strategy and have unusually low levels of uncertainty and complexity lend themselves to the Hierarchical Leadership model. Communications between the project manager and individual team members will be very common with little need for cross–team member communications. As complexity and uncertainty increase, the better choice becomes the Team Leader Model. Complexity and uncertainty introduce the need for more decision making and problem solving, which requires interaction among the team members.

The choice as to which leadership model makes the most sense is often a personal one rather than one based on project characteristics.

Hierarchical Leadership Model

While this model might seem somewhat dated and not at all in keeping with worker empowerment and self-determination, it does have an application in the simpler Linear SDPM strategy projects. However, I believe in minimalist overhead, especially when it comes to management. In the simpler cases it tends to be the micromanagement and non-value-added work time that plagues many projects. This happens often as a result of the direct communications between project manager and team member. The team member receives all her assignments directly from the project manager and reports all results back to the project manager. Micromanagement is a temptation that many project managers cannot avoid. Projects all have aggressive delivery dates, and you shouldn't be adding useless baggage in the way of management oversight, meetings, and status reports of all descriptions. So watch out for those pitfalls if you choose this model.

WARNING The Hierarchical Leadership model encourages micromanagement so be careful.

Team Leader Model

As projects take on more complexity and uncertainty, the need for inter-team collusion and collaboration increases. The Hierarchical Leadership model gives way to the Team Leader model. Whereas the Hierarchical Leadership model was obviously hierarchical the Team Leader model is not. Team members are treated more as equals with the team leader making decisions based on each member's input unlike in the Hierarchical Leadership model. This structure is more in keeping with contemporary thought on worker empowerment.

WARNING
When using this model, the project manager has to make sure he or she is in the loop on any exchanges that take place between team members. The last things you want as project manager are surprises. Include in your operating rules some mechanism that assures that you stay in the loop.

Organizing the Linear SDPM Strategy Project Team

Now that you have identified the individuals who will become the project team, it is time to make them function as a team. Remember right now that they are a herd of cats; they are not yet a team. First, I want to share a few words on authority and responsibility; then I will address several procedural matters that the team has to discuss and agree on.

Authority

Authority and responsibility go hand in hand. To have one and not the other makes no sense. How often have you been in situations where you were responsible for making a certain thing happen but had no authority over the resources needed to make it happen or no authority to make and carry out a decision? To be effective, the project manager must have authority over the project. It is his or her job to get the project done on time, within budget, and according to specification. That authority is often delegated, but it is the project manager who is ultimately responsible.

The major difficulty that project managers have is that the project team is not their line responsibility. Team members are assigned based on their expertise but report to other managers. This means that the project manager will have to exercise the best leadership skills and diplomacy to get the job done. The key is in the project planning activities that schedule resources to windows of time. It is here that the resource manager makes the commitment of people resources. Honoring that commitment within the time allotted reduces the incidence of problems. If the project manager remembers to keep the resource managers involved and aware of all project changes, negotiations will proceed better when circumstances warrant.

Standard Waterfall

For the Hierarchical Leadership model or Team Leadership model, all authority rests with the project manager. None is vested in the team members. With that authority goes the accountability for the project deliverables. When using a Linear SDPM strategy, you should prefer one of these leadership models, but do not default to this structure without good reason.

Rapid Development Waterfall

As a minimum, the project manager must vest authority for each swim lane in a team member. Because the team members might not be highly skilled, that choice is an important one. Lacking the appropriately skilled team members, the project manager might want to employ the Hierarchical Leadership model.

Responsibility

There is no question where the responsibility lies. This cannot be delegated. The project manager assigns activity management responsibility to team members. They are then responsible for completing their assigned activity within its scheduled window of time and for producing the activity deliverables on time according to specification. It is the project manager, however, who is ultimately responsible for completing the project as expected. In conveying this sense of responsibility to each team member, the project manager must exercise sound leadership and management skills. He or she will do this by maintaining a consistent level of interest in and communication with each of the activity managers, by involving them and engaging them in planning, change management deliberations, and problem resolution. He or she will keep everybody on the team informed of project status.

The Linear SDPM strategy has an interesting property that is not shared by other strategies. The early analysis and design phases are staffed by the most senior and most experienced members of the IT unit. As you move from analysis and design into development, the developers tend to be less senior and less experienced than those who worked in the analysis and design phases. As you move from programming into testing, you often find the least experienced and least skilled members. And finally the maintenance team members are often the most junior members of the IT unit. New hires are often assigned here as a way to get up to speed with the current applications. Apply this concept as you choose your staff. Know where you should enlist the more senior members and where you have the luxury of stepping down to less experienced team members. This may offer you some negotiating room with the resource managers that are supplying your team members.

RASCI Matrix

Regardless of the SDPM strategy you have chosen, it is necessary that you set up a roles and responsibility matrix. The more disparate the location of the team members, the more important this matrix. Once established, every team member should have one posted at their work station. Figure 6-1 illustrates a simple example.

Note that each deliverable has a team member who is assigned the responsibility of delivering it. Also, each integration has a person responsible for seeing the integration through to completion. Post the RASCI Matrix in a spot that is frequented by the team. Posting it in the team war room would be ideal.

Developing a Team Development Plan

Your team has been assembled, and you have assessed each member on all of the characteristics important to achieving balance, on their skills, and on their competencies. Unfortunately, the picture is not very pretty. In several areas the team is noticeably weak. While your job as project manager is not necessarily to be a career or professional development manager of your team members, you still have to get the project done, and the imbalance on the team is a barrier to your success. Identify the high-risk areas that are not offset by a balanced team that can deal with those types of risks. As part of your risk management plan, put a development plan in place for selected members of the team.

TASK	PEPE	ALAN	BETH	CARL	DEE	EARL	FRAN	GAIL
Project Mgr	R		S		A			
Deliverable A	I	R	I					
Deliverable B	I	C	I	R				
Deliverable C	I	C	I	R				
Deliverable D	I		I			R	C	
Deliverable E	I		I				C	
Deliverable F	I		I				R	
Deliverable G	I		I				C	R
Deliverable A6	I	R			I			
Deliverable D6	I				I	R	C	
Deliverable F6	I				I		R	
Deliverable A7	I	R			I			

R = Responsible   A = Approval   S = Support for the R   C = Coach   I = Informed

Figure 6-1:   Example of a RASCI Matrix

Once you have assessed the strengths and weaknesses of each team member you can assign tasks according to the team profile. For example, suppose you have a team member whose interpersonal skills are marginal and one whose interpersonal skills are excellent. Any negotiations with the customer should be assigned to the person with the excellent interpersonal skills. Suppose another team member does not have good planning skills. You might have them shadow someone on the team who does have good planning skills. By observation they should begin to pick up those skills.

Team Meetings

Team meetings are held for a variety of reasons, including problem definition and resolution, scheduling work, planning, discussing situations that affect team performance, and decision making. The project manager defines team meetings in terms of the following:

- **Frequency**—How often should the team meet? Too frequently and precious work time is lost. Too infrequently, and the window of opportunity for having a meeting to deal with problems that might have arisen will be closed and the project manager risks losing management control over the project. Meeting frequency varies as the length and size of the project varies. There is no formula for frequency. The project manager must simply make a judgment call.

- **Length**

- **Meeting dates**

- **Submission/preparation/distribution of the agenda**—Project teams fortunate enough to have a project administrative assistant can have that person receive agenda items and prepare and distribute the agenda. Otherwise, the assignment should be rotated to each team member. The project manager might want to set up a template agenda so that each team meeting covers essentially the same general topics.

- **Who calls the meeting**—A team member can serve as meeting coordinator. Just as agenda preparation can be circulated around to each team member so can the coordination responsibility. Coordination involves reserving a time, place, and equipment.

- **Who is responsible for recording and distributing the minutes**—As with the previous two duties noted in this list, the project manager should establish a rotation among the team members for recording and distributing the meeting minutes. Make no mistake—meeting minutes are an important part of project documentation. As the evidence of discussions of problem situations and change requests, the actions taken, and the rationale for those actions, when confusion arises in the project and clarifications are needed, the meeting minutes can settle the issue. Recording and distributing the minutes are important responsibilities and should not be treated lightly.

As the preceding list implies, the entire team needs to participate in and understand the rules and structure of the meetings that take place over the life of the project. Different types of team meetings, with perhaps different rules governing their conduct and format, might occur.

As the chosen SDPM strategy moves from Linear through Incremental through Iterative and to Adaptive and Extreme, the frequency of team meetings will increase and the formality of those meetings will decrease. But more on that throughout several later chapters.

Managing Concurrent Swim Lanes

The Linear SDPM strategy for the Standard Waterfall model has but one swim lane, so it doesn't have many of the problems that accompany the Linear SDPM strategy for the Rapid Development Waterfall model. Because the major phases are linear, scheduling problems arise when one phase is delayed for whatever reason. The delay is passed forward to the next phase where there is an expectation that the delay will somehow be nullified. Maybe, but most likely not. More likely, it will be passed forward again until the life cycle has run its course and the project completes late.

If there are any additional scheduling problems with the Linear SDPM strategy, it will be with the Rapid Development Waterfall model. Delays in the Linear SDPM strategy for the Rapid Development Model cause the same scheduling difficulties as delays do in the Linear SDPM strategy for the Standard Waterfall plus a few more. When a delay occurs in one of the swim lanes and that swim lane has downstream tasks that are predecessors to tasks in other swim lanes the scheduling slippage on the home swim lane now spreads to the dependent swim lane(s). The results can be catastrophic. Because various types of skilled resources are working in parallel, their cross–swim lane schedules are highly dependent upon one another. A slippage in just one swim lane can reverberate through the entire project.

Discussion Questions

1. You are Pepe Ronee, and you have just met your full team for the first time. It is not what you expected. There are 15 inexperienced members and only 2 experienced developers. You do not have the option of replacing any of them. Within the context of the Linear SDPM strategy what could you do?

CHAPTER 7

The Linear SDPM Monitoring and Controlling Phase

If two lines on a graph cross, it must be significant.

Ernest F. Cooke
University of Baltimore

Chapter Learning Objectives

After reading this chapter, you will be able to:

◆ Discuss the role of project reviews in the Linear SDPM strategy life cycle

◆ Implement strategies to protect the project form scope change requests

◆ Understand the role of the scope bank and management reserve and when to use them.

◆ Adapt milestone trend charts to the Linear SDPM strategy

Because the Linear SDPM strategy is a plan-driven strategy, conformance to plan is of the utmost importance. That calls for a structured project performance reporting system. Such reporting will mostly be electronic or hardcopy reports distributed on a scheduled basis, in versions for immediate managers, senior managers, customers, and other stakeholders. Reports within the team will usually be electronic. A high-level reporting will take place at milestone events, which typically line up at the completion of each of the design, build, and test phases.

Project Review Sessions

At milestone events, a project review should be held. The purpose of these review sessions is to ascertain the performance of the project against the project plan. A typical review session will be attended by three or more senior project managers who do not have a vested interest in the project being reviewed, by a manager from the Project Management Office (if there is a PMO), the project manager of the project being reviewed, and any other persons who are associated with the project being reviewed and who the project manager feels would have valid input. These are serious sessions. In them the project manager must review the project plan and the status of the plan; if there are problems, there should be a presentation of them, their cause, and the fix that is in place. At the next project review it is expected that the project manager will update the reviewers as to the outcome of the fix. The reviewers have three purposes in mind for these sessions:

■ **Compliance to the established project management processes**—The project manager must show how that has been achieved or establish a rationale for whatever departure from the process was taken and why it was taken.

■ **To review status against plan**—They will be looking for variances that might foreshadow problems or continuing trends that need the attention of the project team.

■ **To offer suggestions and strategies to address any issues raised in the previous two paragraphs**—If such are offered, it will be incumbent on the project manager to either reject them with good reason or adopt them and report the outcome at the next project review.

Both the Standard Waterfall and the Rapid Development Waterfall offer several milestone events at which these sessions can take place.

WARNING
■■■■■■■ Reviews can often present unexpected problems. It is easy to politicize reviews. They provide a forum for others to jockey for positions of power or set the stage for their own self-serving purposes. Reviews can expose hidden problems in the enterprise that others would just as soon keep hidden. Thus, the review becomes a formality without any real reason for being done. In some organizations, reviews are intimidating. The project manager is raked over the coals, many times for problems outside his or her scope of authority and control. Finally, however, a review can present a significant opportunity to share lessons learned. Don't miss the opportunity.

Linear SDPM Strategy for the Standard Waterfall Model

Refer to Figure 7-1; the project reviews should come at the completion of each major phase in the software development process.

That would mean project reviews should come at the milestone events where sign-off has been obtained for Systems Design, Detailed Design, Code and Test, and Systems Test.

Linear SDPM Strategy for the Rapid Development Waterfall

Refer to Figure 7-2; the project reviews should come at the completion of each phase in the software development process.

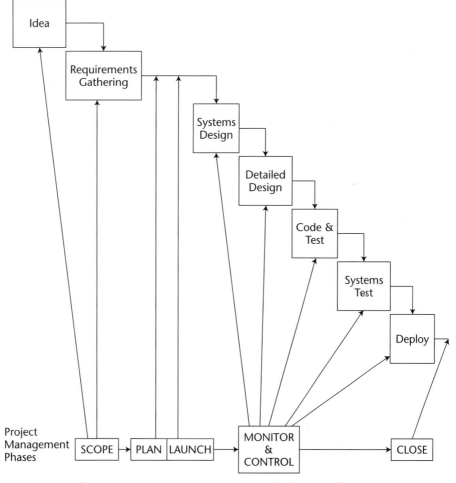

Figure 7-1:   The Linear SDPM strategy for the Standard Waterfall model

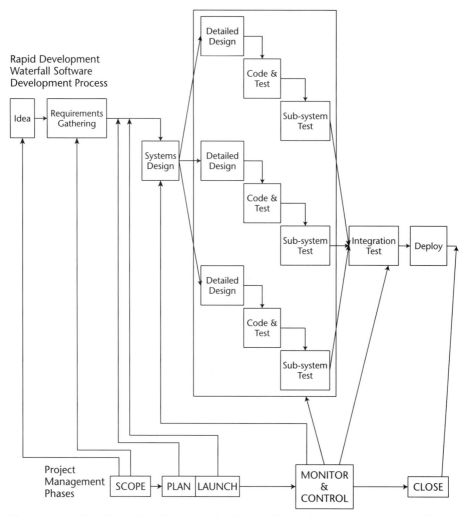

Figure 7-2: The Linear SDPM strategy for the Rapid Development Waterfall model

That would mean project reviews should come at the milestone events where sign-off has been obtained for Systems Design and Integration Test. Other reviews might be scheduled for the concurrent swim lanes to ensure those efforts are moving along according to the plan.

When a project becomes distressed, it is common practice to schedule additional project reviews with the purpose of correcting the problem and restoring the project.

The target is to bring all the swim lanes to completion on schedule so as not to delay the start of integration testing. The latest-to-complete swim lane drives the start of integration testing.

WARNING
Be prepared to move resources from one swim lane to another in order to bring the latest swim lane to completion as early as possible. However, these reassignments are not without their price. Every reassignment adds a bit of transition and ramp up time to the tasks that are inherited by the resource you have moved. The most talented and adaptive of your team members should be the ones you consider for these reassignments.

Scope Change Management

Why have this section in this chapter since you assume requirements, functions, and features are completely and clearly defined and documented? Well, things aren't always what they seem to be. Even though your assumption holds, the world doesn't stand still for you. The business world changes and some of those changes can affect your project. So despite the fact that you weren't expecting any changes, you shouldn't be overly concerned that they will happen. These changes will generally have more of an impact on the Linear SDPM strategy for the Standard Waterfall model than for the Linear SDPM strategy for the Rapid Development Waterfall model. The next sections discuss just why this is so.

WARNING
The customer has a very different view of change than does the developer. Customers tend to view change as simpler than the developer. They don't see the system ramifications for what appears to be a very simple request. Developers, on the other hand, see all sorts of ghosts and goblins in even the simplest of requests. The request can indirectly have an impact on all uses of the variables or parameters that are directly affected. The design is compromised and must be revised. The database design and layout is affected because of longer character strings resulting from the change request, and so on.

Standard Waterfall

A change at any point will have reverberations that will be felt all through to the end of the project life cycle. The later the change appears in the life cycle, the more impact it can have. First of all, consider the trivial case. The change is to some design or development work that has been scheduled but not yet been done. The impact will be to adjust the schedule going forward and perhaps re-align some of the team members to the new work. You have time to adjust the schedule so that the impact on the completion date might be minimal or none at all. The worst case is where the change has an impact on design or development work that has already been done. That means rework as some of the work completed earlier will no longer be viable and has to be replaced.

Rapid Development Waterfall

As mentioned earlier a change at any point can have reverberations through perhaps only one swim lane as long as that swim lane is not a predecessor of any other swim lane. In those cases consider yourself as having dodged a bullet. More likely, however, is the case where the change-impacted swim lane is a predecessor to other swim lanes. You now have a scheduling problem to resolve. It can be particularly complex if the resources are aggressively scheduled across several impacted swim lanes.

Protecting the Linear SDPM Strategy Project Against the Impact of Scope Change

To protect against the impact of scope change I would like to call to your attention to two different strategies. The first is what I call "management reserve." The second strategy is to change to either an Incremental or Iterative SDPM strategy. The next sections take a look at each one.

Management Reserve

Management reserve is not a new idea. It has been around for several decades. You first saw an example of it in your departmental budgets and later in your project budgets. Simply put it means to allocate a small percentage of your total budget to any unforeseen expenses that might arise but that could not be forecasted at planning time. That percentage was generally a figure in the range of 7–12 percent of the total budget that would be added to the budget as a contingency. If it wasn't spent, it was returned to the budgeting authority. The analog for the project schedule is to allocate that same percentage to the schedule. Add up all the labor time estimated for the project and take, say, 10 percent of that figure. Put that in a task at the end of the project. That moves the scheduled completion date out by as many days as are in the management reserve task. The name of that task will be "management reserve." This is to be used for all of those unforeseen schedule slippages or adjustments resulting from scope change requests that are approved. In some enterprises it is also used for the time spent analyzing scope change requests. As project manager, you treat management reserve as a resource available to you in emergency situations—like scope change. Your objective as project manager is not to spend that time, in which case you will bring the project in earlier than estimated. Now isn't that a novel idea?

If you have trouble selling the idea of management reserve to your management, try the Scope Bank approach that follows.

Creating a Scope Bank

On the surface this looks like management reserve in disguise with one significant difference. At project-planning time, establish a bank and deposit some number of hours in that bank. The purpose of the Scope Bank is to have schedule time available for processing scope change requests and absorbing any schedule impacts. The same 10 percent that we used for management reserve can be used for the Scope Bank deposit. The Scope Bank 10 percent has a bit different cast to it than the management reserve 10 percent. The project manager is willing to assume that the 10 percent of time in the Scope Bank can be absorbed into the project schedule without adversely affecting the schedule. In other words, it can be absorbed into the project plan. That is critical to the success of this approach. As scope changes arise, the balance in the Scope Bank Account covers all processing time. Once the balance reaches zero, the customer must make a deposit before they can make a withdrawal. They make a deposit by substituting development time for lesser priority functions or features.

If you have trouble selling the Scope Bank approach, your last protection against scope change will be to change SDPM strategies.

Changing SDPM Strategies

If you had assumed there would be no changes or that, if there were, they would have minimal impact and you didn't fare too well with that assumption, then one last option is to move on to a strategy that is a bit more supportive, a bit more favorable to the actual project. For minor infractions of the "no change" assumption, consider changing the project approach to the Incremental SDPM strategy, and for more serious infractions consider changing the project approach to the Iterative SDPM strategy.

This will not be an easy sell to management, especially if the project has already slipped behind schedule because of too frequent scope change requests. Face it; you chose the wrong strategy at the beginning. Maybe you didn't have the background information you needed and what you did have led you to a decision that seemed correct at the time. The worst thing to do is continue on your present course. Bite the bullet and make your case to the customer and senior management, but do it positively. Show how what has happened is for the greater good of the deliverables but could not have been foreseen at the beginning of the project. Sell the customer and senior management on the long-term benefits of the change.

Incremental SDPM Strategy

Although the Incremental SDPM strategy is a Linear strategy and bound by the same conditions as other Linear strategies, you can bend the rules a bit and accommodate change. Here is how that would be done. First of all, you need to package the deliverables into increments and develop these packages one at a time in some prioritized sequence. You can read about that in Chapters 10–16. Once you have defined the increments, you must gain customer approval for this change of project approach. (That might not be an easy task, by the way.)

Iterative SDPM Strategy

If a change to the Incremental SDPM strategy wasn't radical enough to protect the project from scope change requests, you'll have to take the next step and change to the Iterative SDPM strategy. This change is fairly straightforward. The primary change will be in the accommodation of scope change requests between iterations. That was not part of the Incremental approach. It will obviously affect the completion date of the project, but that is the price you pay for accommodating the discovery of new features for inclusion in the solution. A more detailed discussion of this strategy is the topic of Part IV of this book.

WARNING

The Linear SDPM strategy is a formal strategy. It defines phases that must be done in a prescribed order with no feedback. There are no variations that waver from this linearity requirement. A problem arises then when it is discovered during the course of the project that there is a better way of doing something or there is a piece of functionality that could be done more effectively if adjusted properly. All well and good, but the formality of the Linear process prohibits that from happening. It must be left to the next release of the deliverables and business value is lost or at best postponed to later.

Milestone Trend Charts

Among the several reporting tools you might typically use, I would like to illustrate how the milestone trend chart can be used for the Linear SDPM strategy for the Rapid Development Waterfall model. See Appendix J if you need a refresher on milestone trend charts. Chapter 38 also has some specific applications of milestone trend charts. Figure 7-3 is the preferred way to track progress in a Rapid Development Waterfall project.

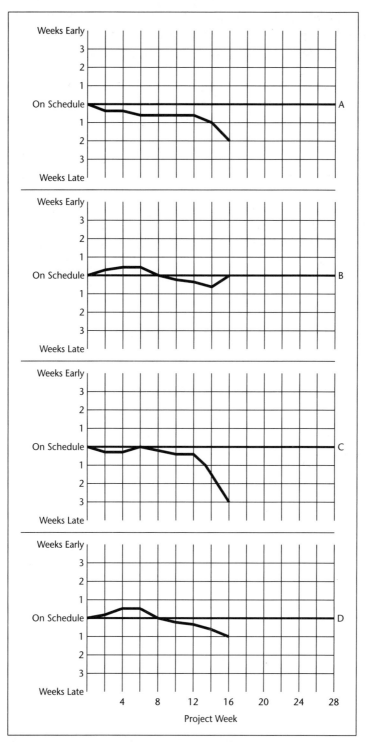

Figure 7-3: Using milestone trend charts in a Rapid Development Waterfall project

This project has three concurrent swim lanes that may have cross–swim lane dependencies. Milestone trend charts do not show any cross–swim lane dependencies, but that does not compromise the usefulness of the charts. In this case, for example, the first three panels show the status of each swim lane with respect to completing on schedule. The fourth panel shows the status of all the swim lanes with respect to being completed on schedule. Looking at Figure 7-3, you can see that Swim Lane A has slowly drifted behind schedule and is now two weeks behind schedule. Because it has two weeks of slack in its schedule, it has exceeded that and placed the project one week late. Swim Lane B, which is on the critical path, has returned to on-schedule status as of the most recent report date. Its completion drives the beginning of the integration test activities. Because it is on schedule, some other swim lane must be the reason for the project schedule slippage. Swim Lane C is another story. It has trended down for four consecutive report periods and that is what would have triggered a closer look at the reason why and what might be done to return the project to an on-schedule status. Also, if you are tracking status using the bottom panel, then the four consecutive reporting periods with a trend in the same direction is your clue that there is a problem and some action will be required. Because the integration test activity will be started one week late, the culprit must be one or more of the swim lanes. It happens that both Swim Lane A and Swim Lane C will be late. Swim Lane A will be two weeks late, but it has only one week of slack. It will push integration testing out one week beyond its scheduled start. Similarly, Swim Lane C will be three weeks late and it has only two weeks of slack. It will also push integration testing out one week beyond its scheduled start. Swim Lane B is on schedule, so it will not likely have any resources that can be reassigned to bring Swim Lanes A and C back on schedule. You have 12 weeks remaining before the integration testing is scheduled to start. A solution will have to be found within that time frame.

Discussion Questions

1. There are too many scope change requests, and they are taking away from project work time to the point where the schedule is now in jeopardy. You did not include management reserve time or a Scope Bank at the beginning of the project. Is it too late to introduce them now? Which one do you think would have a better chance of gaining senior management support and the support of the customer? Do you have another suggestion for protecting the project schedule?

The Linear SDPM Closing Phase

*We cannot afford to forget any experiences, even the
most painful.*

Dag Hammerskjold
Secretary of the United Nations

Chapter Learning Objectives

After reading this chapter, you will be able to:

- ◆ **Explain the significance of the customer sign-off**
- ◆ **Structure the acceptance test procedure for meaningful closure**
- ◆ **Discuss the four deployment strategies**
- ◆ **Understand the dilemma posed by documentation**
- ◆ **Know why lessons learned is so important**

Once the customer has signed off that the requirements have been satisfactorily met, the Closing Phase begins.

Requirements Validation

Requirements validation should be done by comparing the actual features and functions against the planned features and functions. All of this would have been documented in an acceptance test procedure developed and approved by the customer and the project manager during the Planning Phase. As long as that document is kept current, the validation involves nothing more than demonstrating that all items on the acceptance test procedure list have been checked off. If the document has not been kept current, validation becomes a shooting contest, and the customer usually wins. Because the Linear SDPM strategy is based on the assumption of clearly defined and documented requirements, validation should be straightforward. But that doesn't mean it should not be a formal process from initial definition through to final acceptance.

There must be some assurance throughout the project life cycle that the current requirements are in fact what the customer expects. It sounds like it should be simple and straightforward, but that is far from reality. It all depends on what you—the project manager and project team—have done to ensure alignment between what the customer expects and what you are delivering. The first step to this assurance is to have the customer meaningfully involved throughout the project life cycle. That means frequent touch-points with the customer. At those touch-points, both of you should be verifying that the previously agreed requirements are still valid. The customer should sign off as part of project initiation that the requirements list was completely and clearly defined and documented and that it wasn't expected to change. Despite all of the due diligence that might have been done, in 40+ years of practicing project management I have never had a project that didn't have a requirements change somewhere along the project life cycle.

The Conditions of Satisfaction (see Appendix D for a refresher) is the key. You should have used them during project initiation. Now use them again as a routine part of your project reviews. Verify that they are the same or have changed. If they have changed, revise the project plan accordingly.

Acceptance Test Procedures

This should always be a collaborative effort by the project team and the customer. The acceptance test procedure is written collaboratively with the customer and the project team participating. Constructing test data might be an individual or a collaborative effort. The customer will have some testing to do with their end users to ensure that the system is "friendly" and responds as expected. The project team will have some testing to do with the technical team to ensure performance is as expected and that the system is technically sound.

As part of every project review and every change request you must revisit the acceptance test procedures. I recall a situation several years ago that taught me a lesson about change that I have never forgotten. I was the CIO, and the situation involved one of my junior programmers and a customer who was never satisfied. In fact, it was common knowledge that our Information Systems Division wasn't numbered among their friends. A manager from that customer's department ran into a junior programmer in the hallway one day and innocently asked: "John, I forgot to tell you in our requirements gathering session yesterday that we also need to see that sales activity report broken down by product line within sales territory and we need it reported monthly."

Before responding, John thought to himself: This is a great opportunity to win some points with this manager. I'm going to be in here on Saturday doing some clean-up work on the very code that he is talking about. I can take care of his request in a matter of an hour or so. So John responded, "No problem, I'll take care of that in a matter of a few days. Don't worry about forgetting to mention it in the meeting. I'll cover you." The manager nodded and walked off. John felt great. He figured he had scored a lot of points with that manager and would be forever in his good favor. John was so excited about his little victory that he forgot to make any mention of the change in the acceptance test procedure. The testing people never picked up on it either, so it went unnoticed in the requirements documentation until test time. The message here is that every change request must be treated as a major request until proven otherwise. That means it must be processed through a formal change request process and the appropriate decisions and followup actions taken.

Customer Sign-Off

Customer sign-off can be ceremonial or formal, as described in the following sections.

Ceremonial Acceptance

Ceremonial acceptance is an informal acceptance by the customer. It does not have an accompanying sign-off for completion or acceptance. It simply happens. Two situations fall under the heading of ceremonial acceptance.

- In the first situation the customer must accept the project as complete at the deadline date, whether or not the project meets specification. For example, if the project was to plan and conduct a conference, the conference will happen whether or not the project work has been satisfactorily completed. When it comes to software, there is no ceremonial acceptance. The acceptance follows a very formal process. If the deliverable doesn't meet the criteria it is not accepted and returned for further work

- In the second situation a project deliverable requires little or no checking to see if specifications have been met—for example, planning and taking a vacation. Often there will be a brief description of desired features of the vacation, but in the end, whatever is planned is accepted. The acceptance is very informal.

Formal Acceptance

Formal acceptance occurs in those cases involving an acceptance procedure, either written by the customer or in many cases, especially computer applications development projects, written as a joint effort by the customer and appropriate members of the project team. Typically this done very early in the life of the project—during project planning is a good time. This acceptance procedure requires that the project team demonstrate compliance with every feature in the customer's performance specification. A checklist is used and requires a feature-by-feature sign-off based on performance tests. These tests are conducted jointly and administered by the customer and appropriate members of the project team. The checklist is written in such a fashion that compliance is either demonstrated or not demonstrated by the test. It must not be written in such a way that interpretation is needed to determine whether compliance has been demonstrated.

The Closing Phase

Closing a project is often the most overlooked of the phases of the project life cycle. You have another project waiting for you, and you are behind schedule. Your current project is finished, and there is nothing you can do about it any longer. It seems hard to devote any time to a completed project when you have a new one staring you in the face.

Both Linear SDPM strategies have the same closing activities. Once requirements have been validated and the acceptance test procedures met, the project enters the formal part of the Closing Phase. There is the sign-off by the customer that the project can truly enter the closing activities.

Deployment Strategies

The deliverables are deployed into production status. For both the Linear SDPM strategy for the Standard Waterfall model and the Linear SDPM strategy for the Rapid Development Waterfall model there will be only one deployment. All deliverables are put into production status at one time. For cases where you have multiple releases, you can refer to the Iterative, Adaptive, and Extreme SDPM strategies later in the book. Deployment in the Linear SDPM strategy can happen following one of four different strategies.

- **Phased Approach**—The Phased Approach decomposes the deliverable into meaningful chunks and implements the chunks in the appropriate sequence. This approach would be appropriate in cases where resource limitations prevent any other approach from being used.

- **Cut-Over Approach**—The Cut-Over Approach replaces the old deliverable with the new deliverable in one action. To use this approach the testing of the new system must have been successfully completed in a test environment that is exactly the same as the production environment.

- **Parallel Approach**—In cases where the new system might not have been completely tested in an environment exactly like the production environment, this approach will make sense. It allows the new system to be compared with the old system on real live data.

- **By Business Unit Approach**—Like the phased approach, this approach is chosen when resource constraints prohibit a full implementation at one time.

Project File

For the Linear SDPM strategies, the project file will contain all of the information collected during the course of the project. Typical documents found in the project file include meeting minutes, scope change requests and actions, problems and their resolution, risk issues, system documentation, final project report, and lessons learned.

WARNING

Documentation ranks right up there in popularity with root canals. Analysts, architects, developers, and testing folks do not look forward to having to produce documentation. The temptation to do a sloppy job and get it over with is a strong driver for many. Yet the Linear SDPM strategy depends heavily on having clear and complete documentation.

Lessons Learned

Lessons learned are part of the post-implementation audit. I mention it here because there are some issues around the strategy that you chose that you should consider. What did you do to verify that the requirements were clearly defined and completely documented? Was it a process? Were there forms with questions that the customer was required to answer? Was it an open discussion between you and the customer? Did you miss any physical signs that were really a valid signal that things weren't exactly as they were represented? Maybe you made some wrong choices for this project, but if you paid attention, the signs were there and you shouldn't repeat the error the next time.

What you did that ended up being the wrong choice is just as valuable a lesson learned as your having chosen an action that turned out to be right. Given the same situation on another project, would you do the same thing or would you take a lesson from the past and choose some other course of action? Most people will have a hard time documenting an action that didn't work as expected. That's too bad because often that is the most valuable information, especially if you can articulate why the action might not have worked. Why take chances on repeating an action and expecting a different outcome? Someone once said that was the definition of insanity.

Discussion Questions

1. Management will always pressure you to get to the next project before you have closed the books on the current project. How would you sell the practice of lessons learned to senior management?

CHAPTER 9

The Linear SDPM Strategy Summary

Experience is not what happens to you; it is what you do with what happens to you.

Aldous Huxley
English novelist and critic

Chapter Learning Objectives

After reading this chapter, you will be able to:

- ◆ Understand risk and how it affects the Linear SDPM strategies
- ◆ Understand scope change and how it affects the Linear SDPM strategies
- ◆ Understand team structure and how it affects the Linear SDPM strategies
- ◆ Know why there is a communications gap built into the Linear SDPM strategy

You've now spent the last five chapters exploring the Linear SDPM strategy and, in particular, looking at variations for the Standard Waterfall model and the Rapid Development Waterfall model. In this summary chapter I'll discuss a few major points regarding both models and draw some conclusions about their further use and adaptation.

Comparing and Contrasting the SDPM Models

The two models are the same in that both the goal and solution are clearly defined and documented. That is the entry criteria for using these two models. If you know ahead of time that these criteria will be compromised, you have better choices for strategies. Software development projects for the consumer would be examples where change might be inevitable as a result of changing market conditions over which we have no control. Software development projects for internal consumption and where no external factors are operative are good candidates for both models. You might choose one of the two models over the other solely because of deadlines. The more aggressive the deadline, the more likely you would opt for the Linear SDPM strategy for the Rapid Development model. The scarcer the resources, the more likely you would opt for the Linear SDPM strategy for the Standard Waterfall model.

Points to Remember

As I look back at the chapters in this part, I want to emphasize a few key points that you need to consider as you deliberate on the strategy to use in your project.

Risk Situations

Risk in the Linear SDPM strategy is minimal as compared to the other classes of projects I discuss later in the book. For the Linear SDPM strategy for the Standard Waterfall, the only risk specific to the strategy is the risk that you have not completely defined and clearly documented all requirements. I'm excluding exogenous factors because you have no control over them. They are going to happen regardless of the strategy you have adopted. But if you have chosen the wrong strategy and internal factors result in scope change requests, that is a different matter. So what are the consequences of that risk? Three significant ones are worth calling to your attention.

Schedule Slippages

This is probably the least costly of the three. You are going to add more work to accommodate added scope. The thinking project manager will present the customer with two alternatives.

- Keep the same schedule by reprioritizing requirements, removing the lowest priority one, and replacing it with the new scope request.
- Add the new scope request and move the schedule out far enough to accommodate it.

There is a third alternative, but that requires major surgery on the project plan. Briefly put, you change the approach to an Incremental one, release the current functionality for the first increment, add the new scope request, and integrate it into the second increment. All of this assumes that dependencies are behaving and the currently built functionality has business value to the customer. This might have additional risk associated with it that results from the added complexity and the fact that the team is being taken out of its comfort zone.

Rework

Next in terms of impact would be those scope change requests that render previously completed work obsolete or no longer needed. The time invested in the now obsolete work is lost and cannot be recovered. Some additional work needs to be done to back out the now obsolete functionality and replace it with the new. This is obviously more costly than the previous situation. If this added work is significant, you might want to give some thought to changing the approach to the Incremental, as was an option in the preceding situation.

Resource Contention

This problem seems to plague every project except the simplest ones, regardless of how you approach it. For the Linear SDPM strategy for the Standard Waterfall model, the problem occurs in two places:

- **If you need to re-engage the architects to revise the design completed and approved earlier**—Their availability could be problematic.

- **If you need to reassign developers to accommodate the scope change—** This is where the schedule will be affected. Their workload will almost always be increased and result in a schedule extension.

If you are following the Linear SDPM strategy for the Rapid Development model, the two reasons are intensified. The design change can have an impact on all of the swim lanes if it affects any dependency relations across swim lanes. The added developer time will have to fit into an already complex resource schedule.

Change Intolerance

I keep finding reasons to come back to change and its relationship to linear models, but it is the bane of all linear models. I don't need to repeat those arguments, but it is instructive to put that foremost on your mind as you go about deciding what strategy makes sense for your project. If you have any suspicions that change will be a factor in your project, do not use a Linear strategy. Period. If you have any suspicion that the customer has doubts about what has been defined and documented for requirements, do not use a Linear strategy. Period. Other strategies will serve you better and give the project a better chance at succeeding.

In the face of all these signals to choose another strategy, what if you go ahead and still choose a Linear strategy? Maybe you had no choice given your environment and the team that you have been given. In that case, recall that we talked about the Scope Bank and management reserve. Use either or both of them. They might be your saving strategy.

Team Structure

It seems like all I have to summarize with are cautions and warnings about pending disaster. Well I've saved the positive news for last. Linear SDPM strategies are the least demanding on team strength and capacity. As you move into the Incremental and Iterative and beyond strategies, you lose that positive aspect. Team strength, capacity, generalist skills and competencies, and co-location become the requirements for success of the approach. But more on that later. For the Linear SDPM strategy for the Standard Waterfall model, you will have the maximum freedom in team member skills, experiences, and team structure. A few well-chosen senior architects and senior developers might be all that you need to be successful. You will, of course, depend on them to rally the rest of the team. They will be your team leaders in both the design and development phases.

WARNING

Communications among the team members has always been a problem with Linear SDPM strategies. The "throw it over the wall" structure is the culprit. Each phase of the software development life cycle is worked on by team members with different skills. For example, once the business systems analysts finish their work, they document it and "throw it over the wall" to the systems analysts who finish their work, document it, and "throw it over the wall" to the system architects, and so on. Rather than depend on one-on-one communications, these team members rely on the written documentation that they pass forward. There are several opportunities for this type of communications to run into problems without anyone even realizing it.

The Standard Waterfall model variation introduced in Chapter 3 can reduce the problem somewhat. Recall that that figure presented a variation of the Standard Waterfall by having successive phases overlap one another. By having the overlap, you have an opportunity to have one-on-one communications to handle any points of confusion, but that is only if those points of confusion are discovered during the period of overlap.

Knowing the potential problems that can occur is a forewarning that the hand-off between phases might be modified to have some type of review or joint meeting between the affected team members so that the potential problem might be short-circuited.

Discussion Questions

1. Your management isn't too keen on the idea of management reserve or the Scope Bank. It has never been presented as a logical alternative to the scheduling problems that run amok in your organization. Create a logical argument and presentation to convince your management to let you test the idea on a couple of pilot projects. Give some thought to what's in it for them.

PART THREE

Incremental ESPM

The models discussed in this part must meet the same criteria as in the Linear approach. In the Linear approach the software product is deployed at the end of the development life cycle. In the Incremental approach market conditions require early release of product. To accommodate that, the incremental approach decomposes the software product into chunks of code—each one having some business value. These chunks are released as they are built. Finally the end product is fully released at the end of the development cycle, just as would be the case for the Linear approach.

CHAPTER 10

Incremental SDPM Strategy

I find the great thing in this world is, not where we stand, as it is in what direction we are moving.

Oliver Wendell Holmes
American physician and popular writer

Chapter Learning Objectives

After reading this chapter, you will be able to:

- **Explain the Incremental SDPM strategy**
- **Have a high-level understanding of the Staged Delivery Waterfall model and the Feature-Driven Development model**

The first variation from the linear models of Part II is the Incremental model, which is discussed in this part. Incremental models arise out of the customer's need to deliver partial functionality at intermediate points along the software development timeline. For a variety of business reasons, customers cannot wait until the end of the development cycle to get their glimpse of the product and begin to derive business value. Market forces have put them in a position where they need to generate business value early. In many cases it might simply be a positioning strategy. They want to get to the market first and establish an early position for themselves.

The Incremental SDPM strategy is accomplished by "chunking" the functionality and features into meaningful parts so that each part offers marketable business value. Several increments might be defined so that the released product grows in functionality over time.

The Incremental SDPM Strategy

Incremental approaches must meet the same requirements as linear approaches. The goal and the solution must both be clearly defined. An incremental approach is chosen so that results can be delivered in stages over the life of the project. Figure 10-1 illustrates the generic Incremental SDPM strategy. Later in this chapter, I adapt it to the Staged Delivery Waterfall model and the Feature-Driven Development model.

Situations will arise where business value needs to be delivered early and often. In these cases the total solution is decomposed into "chunks" of deliverables. Each chunk provides enough functionality to be of business value in a production sense. These chunks are released sequentially until all functionality has been released to production status. These sequential releases offer opportunities to modify functionality in future increments.

Because Incremental SDPM strategies are found in Quadrant 1, their goal and solution must be clearly defined and documented as a condition for using the models described below. Figure 10-2 (Staged Delivery Waterfall model) and Figure 10-4 (Feature-Driven Development model) are two examples of incremental approaches. Both models require the complete documentation of requirements, functionality, and features.

For projects that otherwise would use a linear model but must deliver business value earlier in the development life cycle, you can modify the model to take advantage of an Incremental approach.

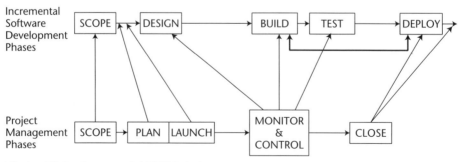

Figure 10-1: Incremental SDPM strategy

Scope Phase

As in the case of the Linear SDPM strategy, this is an integrated activity with the Scope Phase from the software development life cycle and the project management life cycle. You have one added task, however. The decision to deploy the deliverables in increments adds some complexity to the scoping activities. The increments must be defined. That definition has two parts:

- The first is the definition of deliverables sets that have business value.
- The second, which is not independent of the first, is to sequence the deliverables sets so that no technical dependencies are violated.

Plan and Launch Phases

The Plan Phase is more complex for the Incremental SDPM strategy than it is for the Linear SDPM strategy. The difference is due to resource scheduling. In the Linear SDPM strategy, a particular resource (say, the developers) can do their programming work and move on to other projects. In the Incremental SDPM strategy their work is not done contiguously. It comes in chunks. If the schedule for an early increment slips, it affects the resource schedule for all subsequent increments. In most cases the development resources will have already made commitments to other projects and might not have the flexibility required to meet the new schedule demands of the revised project. The complexity now extends to more than one project, as decisions have to be made regarding the relative priorities of the affected projects.

Monitor and Control Phases

The Monitor and Control Phases for the Incremental SDPM strategy are a bit more complex than in the case of the Linear SDPM strategy, for two reasons:

- First is the scheduling and resource management of the increments. The resource schedules have to be considered as fixed and any slippages have to be recovered within the given schedules.
- Second, as the customer uses the deliverables from an increment, they will undoubtedly discover other features they would have liked to include in the original scope but didn't have in mind at the time. Only by using the released deliverables did the customer discover the new features. The assumption that led to choosing this strategy was that such discoveries wouldn't happen. All functions and features were defined up front—or so it was assumed. Nevertheless, this situation will occur and you must deal with it.

You might want to include some portion of the typical close activities as each increment is deployed. That would be done as part of the monitoring and control phase, however. It would involve an acceptance test procedure to cover the deliverables deployed at the end of each increment. That leaves open the possibility that a deliverable set might not meet the acceptance criteria and cause some revisions to be made in subsequent increments. The same risk is present whenever the customer or end user has an opportunity to work with a partial solution and give feedback to the developers. Changes will be suggested if you have given the customer an opportunity to do so. You have been warned, so be ready.

Close Phase

The Close Phase is exactly the same as in the case of the Linear SDPM strategy, in that it involves demonstrating acceptance test criteria, putting deliverables into production status, and performing formal closing activities, including a post-implementation audit to assess conformance to the plan and achievement of the success criteria. This will occur after the last increment has been deployed.

Types of Incremental SDPM Strategies

Incremental SDPM strategies are little more than the variation you would expect when the Linear SDPM strategies are not as responsive to business conditions as the customers would want them. The motivation for adopting an incremental approach is to deliver business value earlier than would be the case with linear approaches. In some cases this early introduction gives the enterprise an opportunity to test market new products and perhaps make modifications in later increments. Two types of strategies deserve mention in this context. They are introduced here at a high level and detailed in the chapters of this part that follow.

Staged Delivery Waterfall Model

The Staged Delivery Waterfall model provides for the early release of chunks of functionality so that the customer can begin to realize business value without having to wait for the single release of the complete solution.

Figure 10-2 is adapted from Steve McConnell's book *Software Project Survival Guide* (Microsoft Press, 1998).

This model works well in those situations where it is to your advantage to deliver business value early. If that is the case, you should prioritize the functionality to phases to deliver maximum business value. The stages could be long or short depending on the needs of the client. The other reason for adopting this model is to give you some breathing room in case the early releases give the client a reason to suggest changes. In other words, you are protecting yourself against requirements not having been completely defined and agreed to.

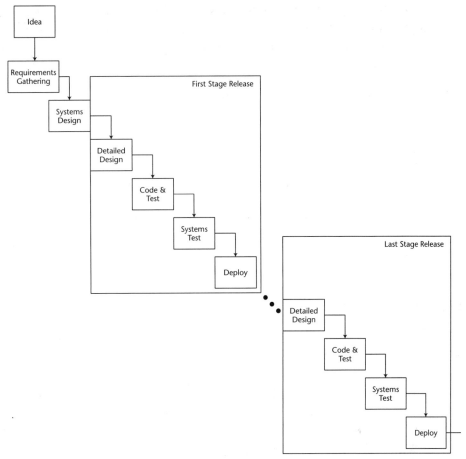

Figure 10-2: Staged Delivery Waterfall model

Figure 10-3 illustrates the Incremental SDPM strategy for the Staged Delivery Waterfall model.

Within each of the stages, the linearity of the Standard Waterfall model is clearly present. This makes the integration rather straightforward. The only difference between the staged model and the standard model is the intermediate release of incomplete but functioning deliverables.

Feature-Driven Development

Feature-Driven Development (FDD) first appeared in *Java Modeling in Color with UML* by Peter Coad, Eric Lefebvre, and Jeff DeLuca (Prentice Hall PTR, 1999). A more comprehensive treatment of FDD can be found in *A Practical Guide to Feature Driven Development* by Stephen R. Palmer and John M. Felsing (Prentice Hall PTR, 2002).

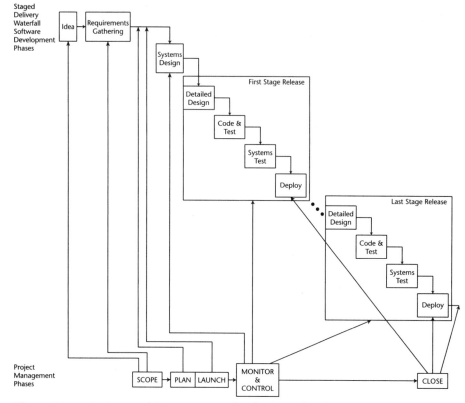

Figure 10-3: Incremental SDPM strategy for the Staged Delivery Waterfall model

The high-level process view of FDD is shown in Figure 10-4. Note that the solution must be known in order to use FDD effectively. A model of the solution is developed and used to create the functional Work Breakdown Structure (WBS). The functional WBS contains a very detailed list of features. The features list is grouped into similar features and prioritized for development. FDD iterates on the design and building of the groups of features.

Much like the Rapid Development model, FDD prioritizes parts of the solution. But this time it is features-driven. With the addition of features code to the solution, the solution grows in terms of business value. Intermediate production solutions can be released as part of this approach. As in the Rapid Development model, you can have multiple design/build swim lanes running concurrently in the Feature-Driven Development model.

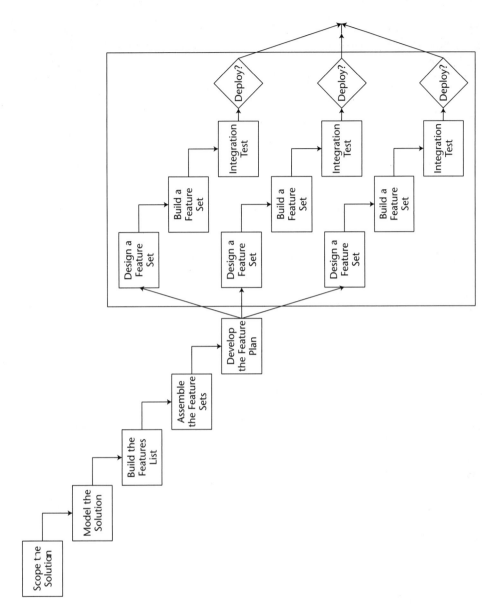

Figure 10-4: Feature-Driven Development model

FDD provides for the early release of chunks of features so that the customer can begin to realize business value without having to wait for the single release of the complete solution. It differs from the Staged Delivery Waterfall model in that the releases consist of groups of features that have a technical relationship to one another. Several cycles of development might occur before the customer is satisfied that the cumulative features list has enough business value to be released as in the sense of the Staged Delivery Waterfall model. FDD models might use concurrent swim lanes, sequential phases, or some combination of the two.

Figure 10-5 illustrates the integration of the project management life cycle into the Feature-Driven Development life cycle.

WARNING
Resist the temptation to use the increments to solve the problem. That is not the purpose. You must have a clearly defined goal as well as a clearly defined solution to use these approaches. If the solution is not clearly defined, iterative and adaptive approaches will serve you better.

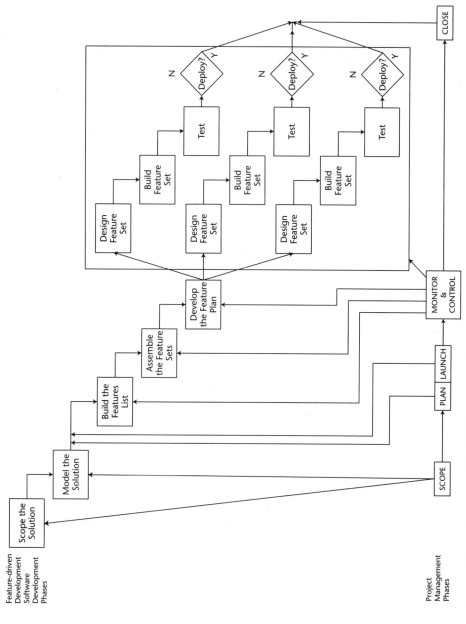

Feature-driven
Development
Software
Development
Phases

Scope the
Solution

Model the
Solution

Build the
Features
List

Assemble
the Feature
Sets

Develop
the Feature
Plan

Design
Feature
Set

Build
Feature
Set

Test

Deploy?

N

Y

Design
Feature
Set

Build
Feature
Set

Test

Deploy?

N

Y

Design
Feature
Set

Build
Feature
Set

Test

Deploy?

N

Y

CLOSE

Project
Management
Phases

SCOPE

PLAN

LAUNCH

MONITOR
&
CONTROL

Figure 10-5: Incremental SDPM strategy for the Feature-Driven Development model

Discussion Questions

1. How would you go about the task of decomposing the project into meaningful business chunks? Speak to the rules you might employ.

2. You have completed the first few increments and released deliverables to the customer. The customer is now coming to you with changes to what has been released. These changes make sense but will cause your project to go off schedule if integrated into the future increments. What would you do?

CHAPTER 11

The Incremental SDPM Scoping Phase

I find the great thing in this world is, not where we stand, as it is in what direction we are moving.

Oliver Wendell Holmes
American physician and writer

Chapter Learning Objectives

After reading this chapter, you will be able to:

- ◆ Explain the Scoping Phase of the Incremental SDPM strategy
- ◆ Conduct the Scoping Phase of the Staged Delivery Waterfall model
- ◆ Conduct the Scoping Phase of the Feature-Driven Development model
- ◆ Understand the role of the WBS in defining project increments
- ◆ Scope the Incremental plan

The first variation from the Linear SDPM strategy is the Incremental SDPM strategy, which is discussed in this part of the book. Incremental models arise out of the customer's need to deliver partial functionality at intermediate points along the systems development time line. For a variety of business reasons, the customer cannot wait until the end of the development cycle to get their glimpse of the product and begin to derive business value. Market forces have put them in a position where they need to generate business value early. In many cases it may simply be a positioning strategy. They want to get to the market first and establish an early position for themselves.

The Incremental SDPM strategy is accomplished by "chunking" the functionality and features into meaningful parts so that each part offers marketable business value. Several increments might be defined so that the released product grows in functionality over time.

The Scoping Phase of an Incremental SDPM Strategy

Basically there is no difference between a Linear and an Incremental SDPM strategy except for the way the deliverables are deployed. Both strategies require a completely documented requirements specification. Given that condition, both strategies are somewhat intolerant of scope change. Unfortunately, they know it will happen, but they proceed on the assumption that it won't.

As you know, in a Linear SDPM strategy the deliverables are first deployed after all integration testing has been successfully completed and the customer signs off on the acceptance test procedure. The deliverables then move to the implementation stage and are put into production status. The project is completed. The customer doesn't see any of the solution until they see all of the solution. There is no chance to "try it out" before they buy it. Their only hope is that the developers understood their needs and delivered according to those needs. The customer isn't looking for any surprises.

In the Incremental SDPM strategy, things are quite different. You still have the same degree of confidence that the requirements are completely defined and documented. The Incremental strategy is scope change–intolerant just like the Linear strategy. The only changes expected are those that emanate from outside the project itself. For example, market changes that compromise the business value of the current scope must be addressed, and change is necessary in order to counter those market changes. Changes that arise because of some shortfall on the part of the customer or project team during requirements gathering should not occur. These conditions are the same for both Linear and Incremental SDPM strategies.

NOTE

Despite the fact that the Incremental SDPM strategy is scope-change intolerant, it does have a way of accommodating scope change that the Linear SDPM strategy does not. More on that issue can be found in Part II, in which the Linear SDPM strategy is discussed.

The differences between Linear SDPM strategy and an Incremental SDPM strategy begin in the Scope Phase. The differences are generated out of the need for the customer to release partial solutions to the market to gain an early market advantage. "The early deployer catches the customer"—to adapt a well-known aphorism to the situation at hand. Getting to market in this fashion is not without its problems, however. The early feedback from the market will undoubtedly bring with it suggestions for change to the solution. This situation cannot occur in the Linear SDPM strategy, because there is only one deployment. That is not to say that this is wrong; it is just a fact of business life. When employing an Incremental SDPM strategy, knowing that change is a likely result of the early deployment, the project team needs to be ready for whatever countermeasures make sense. The project plan will have to have some way of accommodating change without completely upsetting the project plan for later increments.

The Scoping Phase of the Incremental SDPM Strategy for the Staged Delivery Waterfall Model

Figure 11-1 (which is the same as Figure 10-3) illustrates the project management process superimposed on the Staged Delivery Waterfall Model. Note that the project management Scoping Phase includes both the Idea Generation and the Requirements Gathering Phases of the Staged Delivery Waterfall Model.

In this section, you will see exactly how those phases integrate to form the Incremental SDPM strategy for the Staged Waterfall Model. The activities that take place in the Scoping Phase of an Incremental SDPM strategy are:

- Developing the Project Overview Statement (POS) of the project
- Defining the number and duration of each increment
- Identifying the functionality that will be released in each increment
- Planning to build a deliverables-based Work Breakdown Structure (WBS) that supports the release strategy
- Assuring the integrity of the dependency structure between deliverables
- Allocating management reserve in each increment after the first to accommodate processing and incorporating change requests

These topics are discussed in the subsections that follow.

Developing the Project Overview Statement of the Project

The initial meeting of the customer and the project manager is one where the project is defined at a very high level. At this high level, the customer and the project manager come to closure on what the project constitutes. It is documented and signed by them as the first official statement of what the project involves. (Refer to Appendix C for a refresher on what the POS contains.) The same exercise will be part of every SDPM strategy.

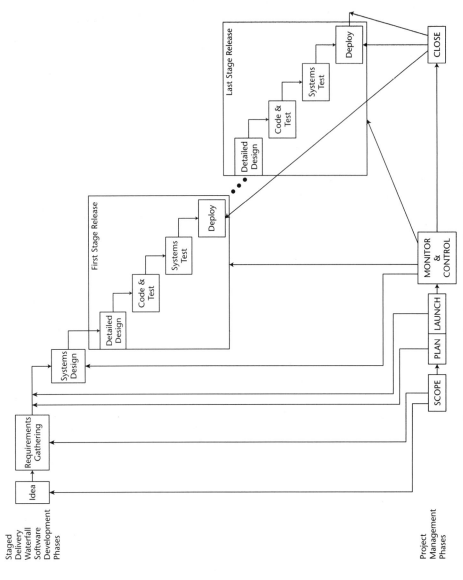

Figure 11-1: Incremental SDPM strategy for the Staged Delivery Waterfall model

Defining the Number and Duration of Each Increment

This will be more market-driven than technology-driven. The customer will have certain objectives in mind that led to the choice of an Incremental SDPM strategy. These must be supported by the decision as to the number and duration of each increment. The project team should let the customer take the lead on the initial determination of number and length. As the project plan unfolds, these numbers will probably change as the realities of function and feature dependency is accounted for.

A number of companies will operate with a quarterly, semi-annual, or even annual release schedule. To the extent possible, the increments may have to conform to this structure. The difficulty arises where there are several systems dependent upon the one system following an Incremental SDPM strategy. The solution is to appoint a person who will be responsible for ensuring the integrity of the interface of each system dependent upon the incremental project. The case study provides a good example of this dependency (see Figure 11-2).

If the Order Entry sub-system is developed following an Incremental approach, there will be some parts of it that are needed by the Order Submit, Logistics, and Inventory Management sub-systems for their development to begin. The scheduling of the Order Entry sub-systems development increments should take these dependencies into account.

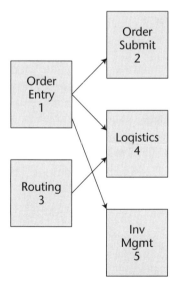

Figure 11-2: An example of system dependencies

Identifying the Functionality to Be Released in Each Increment

This is a very high-level look at the project scope. Using the Requirements Breakdown Structure (RBS), the customer in collaboration with the project team can allocate functionality to increments. Each increment must contain sufficient functionality to have enough business value to justify the increment. At the same time, each increment must preserve the dependency structure, which will usually result in more functionality being placed in an increment than was originally identified. A good practice is to be conservative in what you allocate to an increment until the dependency structure is accounted for. A high-level dependency chart can help in the allocation exercise. The next two topics support this activity.

Planning to Build a Deliverables-Based Work Breakdown Structure

A deliverables-based WBS is the only approach that makes sense for an Incremental SDPM strategy. The reason is that the deliverables will be the very functionality that the customer expects to see in each Incremental release. Since the WBS was built from the RBS the deliverables will be easily attached to the RBS. Refer to Appendix E for a more detailed description of the deliverables-based WBS.

Assuring the Integrity of the Dependency Structure Between Deliverables

This is most important. One of the major schedule risks in an Incremental SDPM strategy is discovering a function or feature dependency that is not accounted for in the incremental structure and sequencing. That happens more often than you might think. For example, this happens if you are developing the functions and features assigned to the second increment only to discover that the first increment did not include functions or features needed to develop and release functions or features assigned to the second increment. That obviously has major scheduling impacts.

Allocating Management Reserve

Despite all your efforts to protect the integrity of the plan, you will have scope changes. Allocating management reserve at the end of each increment schedule will buy protection against schedule risks. That management reserve could be some percentage of the total duration planned for this increment. A percentage in the range of 5–15 is common. Your management objective is to not spend that reserve but have it on hand for scope changes that are justified for that increment.

The Scoping Phase of the Incremental SDPM Strategy for the Feature-Driven Development Model

Figure 11-3 illustrates the project management process superimposed on the Feature-Driven Development Model. The resulting Incremental SDPM strategy for the Feature-Driven Development Scoping Phase is quite different from the Staged Delivery Waterfall Scoping Phase. Staged Delivery is more focused on the customer's need to get to market early, whereas Feature-Driven Development is more focused on the technical architecture of the solution. The Scoping Phase of a Feature-Driven Development SDPM strategy consists primarily of collaborative sessions with the customer to model the solution and the solution approach.

In addition to preparing the Project Overview Statement, you perform seven other tasks in sequence to produce an acceptable model of the solution. These are drawn from Stephen R. Palmer and John M. Felsing's *A Practical Guide to Feature-Driven Development* (Prentice Hall PTR, 2002). They are briefly described in the subsections that follow.

Forming the Modeling Team

The project manager assembles a team comprised of a number domain experts who know and understand the business area being modeled and programmers who understand the development environment in which the project will be done. The membership of the modeling team may change as needs dictate. The domain experts represent the customer. They may be from the customer areas, or they may be business process analysts assigned to a customer area but reporting through an IT unit.

Conducting a Domain Walkthrough

This is a high-level overview of the business being modeled. It is conducted by one or more domain experts who have the broadest understanding of the business area. This places the business units in a leadership position in the process and also creates ownership on their part. Furthermore, it helps establish a language for communications. Any opportunity for the customer to talk about the project from their perspective or the developer to do the same will increase the level of understanding that each has of the other's area. That helps not only in gaining a better understanding of the other's area but also in establishing a common language for communicating. This is definitely a win-win situation, so don't miss an opportunity to engage the other in such conversations.

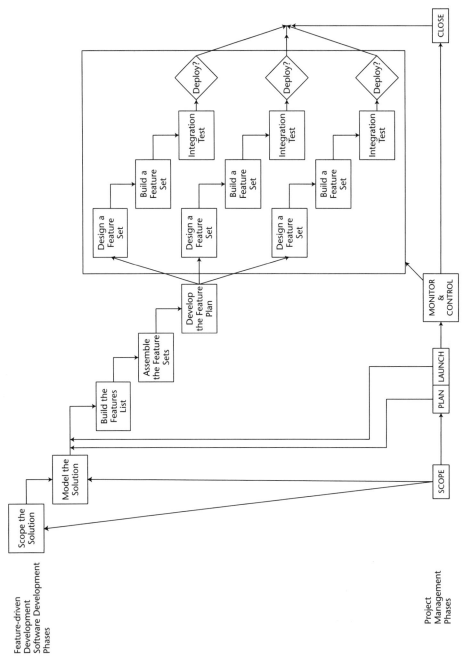

Feature-driven
Development
Software Development
Phases

Project
Management
Phases

Figure 11-3: Incremental SDPM strategy for the Feature-Driven Development model

NOTE

One of the major problems in the business/technical interface is the language barrier. Throughout this book and for every strategy discussed, I make every effort to suggest ways to solidify the customer/technical relationship.

Studying Documents

All of the relevant documents that describe and document the business area provide the foundation elements for the project. These may be business process flow documents, requirements documents, and the RBS for the system to be developed. If a Conditions of Satisfaction was conducted, the documentation from that exchange and the deliverable (the POS) are part of the study documents.

Developing Small Group Models

Depending on the size of the development effort, this step may be integrated into the team model activity. If this step is done, it will produce a number of domain models that are presented to the whole team for consideration and selection. The purpose of the small groups is to generate models. These models will serve to identify alternative solutions from which a final model, that is, solution, will be crafted by the modeling team.

Developing a Team Model

The team model is developed from the domain models presented. A single model may be chosen or a hybrid formed from iterations on the presented models. In any event, a single model emerges from this activity. If the small group modeling exercise was done, the team model should represent the collective thinking of the modeling team and be the best solution they could devise.

Refining the Overall Object Model

This step may be used to improve on the selected model through an iterative process. Like it or not, the initial model will not be the final model. Each increment adds another opportunity for the development team and especially the customer to find and recommend improvements. As long as there is a good business case for the change, it should be accommodated in some future increment.

Writing Model Notes

The documentation consists of notes on models considered but not used as well as technical documentation on the object model chosen. This documentation will often consist of object classes, constraints on those classes, and business process diagrams.

The Role of the RBS

The architecture of the RBS is the key to successful increment development and deployment for an Incremental SDPM strategy. The RBS is a deliverables-based structure of the requirements, functions, and features (see Figure 11-4). The focus will obviously be on the features that are defined by the RBS. The RBS is assumed to be a complete accounting of all features that define the solution. This is important because the balance of the systems development life cycle depends on that completeness. The requirements, the roots of the RBS, are seldom completely identified, and many would argue that they can never be completely defined because that would require a crystal ball (to predict market changes) and perfect solution knowledge on the part of the customer. Neither of those conditions exists. Still, in any case, you have to proceed on an assumption of completeness if you are to use an Incremental SDPM strategy.

The RBS can be generated from a series of Use Cases that define the solution or from some other approach to generating requirements. In either case, to use the Incremental SDPM strategy you must complete the RBS.

In the Staged Delivery Waterfall Model

For the Staged Delivery Waterfall model, the RBS is used as input to making an initial pass at defining the contents of each increment in the development effort. Each increment must have sufficient business value to be a valid increment in the eyes of the customer. The number of increments as well as their durations will be determined based on the RBS and later on by the precedence diagram.

The RBS should be viewed as any other WBS. It must be a complete WBS. Therefore the completeness criteria apply (see Appendix E for a discussion of the completeness criteria). That means that the feature-level decomposition may need to be further decomposed to reach the task level. The schedule for each increment will be built from this level of detail.

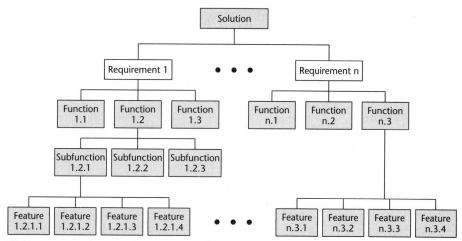

Figure 11-4: The Requirements Breakdown Structure

In the Feature-Driven Development Model

For the Feature-Driven Development model, the lowest level of decomposition in the RBS identifies all of the features that will define the complete solution to the development project. These are known in the Scoping Phase and will guide the scoping of the project plan.

The Role of the Precedence Diagram

From the RBS, the team can develop the precedence diagram at the function or at the feature level. This shows how functions or features are dependent upon one another as either predecessors or successors. The objective here is to decide on groupings of functions/features in the successive increments of the Staged Delivery approach or the Feature-Driven Development approach. The next two subsections take a quick look at each approach and how the precedence diagrams can be used.

In the Staged Delivery Waterfall Model

Because each successive stage is dependent upon all previous stages, it is necessary that all precedence relationships be preserved. That is, whatever functions/features are needed to build the current stage deliverables will have been built in some preceding stage. In practice this is easier said than done, especially in larger projects, where some dependencies are so elusive that they can be discovered only during testing.

In the Feature-Driven Development Model

For this approach you find the precedence diagram serving another role. Feature sets are groupings of features based on technical relationships. Furthermore, the feature sets should be defined with minimal coupling and maximum cohesion in mind. This is critical because the building and testing of feature sets can occur concurrently as well as sequentially. Ideally each feature set would be independent of any other feature set, and the problem would go away. But that does not happen, which means that feature sets need to be scheduled in increments to preserve any cross feature set dependencies.

Discussion Questions

1. The major weakness of Incremental approaches is that they encourage the customer to submit scope change requests. Many of these will be legitimate because of external factors, but many will simply result because customers have seen a partial solution working and now have an idea about how it might be improved. Any scope change request can have significant impact on the resource schedule of future increments. What might you do to reduce unfavorable impact?

2. The Scoping Phase of the Incremental SDPM strategy is a critically important part of the project life cycle. If you were asked to plan a three-day scoping exercise, what would your plan include? Prepare a detailed and timed agenda. Be sure to include the customer as a major player in that scoping exercise.

CHAPTER 12

The Incremental SDPM Planning Phase

The cautious seldom err.

Confucius
Chinese philosopher and teacher

Chapter Learning Objectives

After reading this chapter, you will:

♦ **Understand why you should use a deliverables form of the WBS**

♦ **Be able to decompose a deliverables-based WBS for the Rapid Development Waterfall model**

♦ **Understand the planning phase of an Incremental SDPM strategy for the Staged Delivery Waterfall model**

♦ **Understand the planning phase of an Incremental SDPM strategy for the Feature-Driven Development model**

There is a great deal of similarity between the Linear and Incremental SDPM Strategies in the Scoping Phase. Here in the Planning Phase, you begin to see the differences between the two. Everything that is done in the Planning Phase for the Linear SDPM strategy is done in the Planning Phase for the Incremental SDPM strategy. Those differences relate to the deployment of functionality, and that is a major difference between the two. The deployment of functionality is a planning function and is governed by two variables:

- The first is the grouping of functionality and the assignment of those groups to increments. The groups are formed so as to have business value. Also, the groups must have internal cohesion and minimal coupling to other groups.

- The second is the sequencing of those increments.

The sequencing output from the Scope Phase is a Project Overview Statement (POS) and a clearly defined requirements document. Using these documents as input to the Planning Phase, you develop a plan that follows accepted principles and practices of traditional project management. With the design, build, and test phases as the highest level of decomposition in the Work Breakdown Structure (WBS), you perform a complete decomposition down to the task level. To complete the Planning Phase, you make estimates of task duration and resource requirements and put together an initial project schedule.

Once the requirements have been specified, you make the choice whether or not to follow the Incremental SDPM strategy.

The Planning Phase of an Incremental SDPM Strategy

In addition to having all of the activities associated with planning a Linear SDPM strategy, an Incremental SDPM strategy also includes the definition of what development work will take place in each increment. This is significant task, for it involves two concurrent and dependent activities:

- Decomposing the Requirements Breakdown Structure (RBS) into minimally coupled and maximally cohesive sets of requirements, functions, and features

- Sequencing the development work in order to preserve the dependency relationships between the requirements, functions, and features in each increment

In addition, it would be useful if each increment had sufficient business content to warrant its deployment. If not, the completion of the next increment would be the next opportunity to deploy the then partial solution. The customer would probably prefer to have deployable content at the completion of each increment.

Decomposing the Requirements Breakdown Structure

Figure 11-4 is reproduced here as Figure 12-1 for ease in understanding the further decomposition and gathering of functions and features into deployable increments.

There are three ways to proceed with the decomposition and gathering activity: by requirements, by functions, or by features. For example, you could build an example using the requirements approach. Suppose there are 12 requirements and they have been grouped as shown in the right-hand panel of Figure 12-2.

Requirements are first gathered using any of the approaches described in Appendix D. As indicated, in this case you have gathered 12 requirements. In the second step, the customer prioritizes the requirements with respect to their business value. In the third step the customer groups the prioritized requirements so that each group has sufficient business value to be deployed. In this example, you could have as many as four increments. The actual number of increments may change as a result of imposing the dependency relationships. Determining the actual number of increments is the topic of the next section.

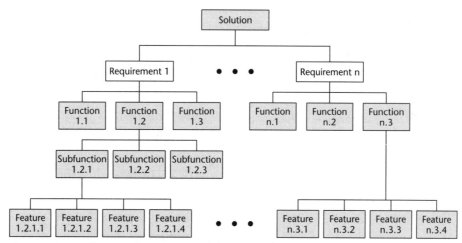

Figure 12-1: The Requirements Breakdown Structure

	PRIORITIZED	GROUPED	
Requirement #01	Requirement #04	Group A	Requirement #04
Requirement #02	Requirement #07		Requirement #07
Requirement #03	Requirement #10		Requirement #10
Requirement #04	Requirement #01		Requirement #01
Requirement #05	Requirement #05		
Requirement #06	Requirement #09	Group B	Requirement #05
Requirement #07	Requirement #12		Requirement #09
Requirement #08	Requirement #03		
Requirement #09	Requirement #08	Group C	Requirement #12
Requirement #10	Requirement #11		Requirement #03
Requirement #11	Requirement #06		Requirement #08
Requirement #12	Requirement #02		
		Group D	Requirement #11
			Requirement #06
			Requirement #02

Figure 12-2: Requirements prioritization and grouping

Sequencing the Development Work

Continuing with the example illustrated in Figure 12-2, your next step would be to build the dependency diagram for the 12 requirements. That is shown in Figure 12-3.

In order to honor the dependency diagram and hold to the requirements prioritizations, you will have two increments.

- The first consists of building Group B initially and then following it with Group A. The first deployment will be the Group B and A requirements.

- The second increment consists of building Group D and then Group C. The second deployment will be the Group D and C requirements.

If you define the increments based only on the dependencies between requirements, you would have no fewer than four increments:

- **First increment**—Requirements 4, 5, 10, and 11

- **Second increment**—Requirements 7, 1, 9, and 6

- **Third increment**—Requirements 8, 3, and 2.

- **Fourth increment**—Requirement 12.

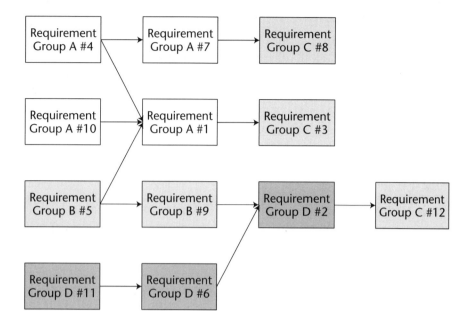

Sequence:
    Increment #1: Group B then Group A
    Increment #2: Group D then Group C

Figure 12-3: Requirements dependency diagram

This approach to decomposition and sequencing scales very well so that, if you choose to decompose to the function or feature level, the same steps work just fine. The one constant through any of these three approaches is to proceed based on customer priorities rather than dependencies. That way you ensure business value as soon as possible. Using the dependency approach by itself does not necessarily result in deployable increments. Increments may have to be piggybacked to ensure business value in a deployment.

The Planning Phase of an Incremental SDPM Strategy for the Staged Delivery Waterfall Model

Figure 12-4 is the Planning Phase of the Incremental SDPM strategy for the Staged Delivery Waterfall model.

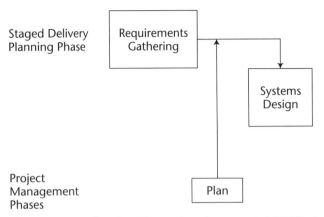

Staged Delivery
Planning Phase

Project
Management
Phases

Figure 12-4: Planning Phase of an Incremental SDPM strategy for the Staged Delivery Waterfall model

For planning the Incremental SDPM strategy for the Staged Delivery Waterfall model, you would know all of the planning input. The RBS would have been generated during the Scoping Phase and is all of the input needed to build a complete project plan. There are six major tasks that you need to do to generate the project plan. They are:

- Building the complete WBS
- Estimating task duration
- Estimating resource requirements
- Building the precedence diagram
- Allocating functions and features to determine number of stages
- Creating the initial project schedule

Each of these tasks is briefly described in the following subsections.

Building the Complete WBS

The RBS is the only input needed here. The RBS is a deliverables-based WBS and needs only to be further decomposed to the task level. Each feature is therefore decomposed until it satisfies the completion criteria. See Appendix E for details.

Estimating Task Duration

Features are rather primitive deliverables and the clock time needed to build them should be easy to estimate. Features are likely to have been defined for other projects. If they are not exactly the same, they will be fairly similar and so estimation of duration should be rather straightforward.

Estimating Resource Requirements

This will be a relatively simple task because the estimate is covering a single feature. The required skill sets by position title is sufficient.

Building the Precedence Diagram

This task and the next are where the planning team and the customer will earn their wages. The precedence diagram should be built at the feature level. In some cases the function level may work, but the risk is that the stages will not be as easily defined and may end up containing far more features than a feature-level approach would have generated. The extra work of generating a feature-level precedence diagram will result in a more effective and efficient project plan.

Allocating Functions and Features to Determine Number of Stages

The precedence diagram is the only input needed for this task. A close inspection of the precedence diagram will highlight streams of dependent tasks that should be allocated to the same stage. While not necessary, allocating dependent tasks to the same stage increases the cohesion within the stage to which they are assigned. Figure 12-5 gives a generic example of what you might expect to see in a typical dependency diagram.

Figure 12-5 is the dependency diagram for the case study. The tasks are defined as follows:

S0 Start

S1 RBS for the Order Entry Sub-system

S2 RBS for the Order Routing Sub-system

S3 RBS for the Order Fulfillment Sub-system

S4 Design the Customer Profile Sub-system

S5 Design the Order Taking Sub-system

S6 Design Order Routing Sub-system

S7 Design Order Fulfillment Sub-system

S9 Design Integration

S10 Coding of the Order Entry Sub-system

S11 Coding of the Order Routing Sub-system

S12 Coding of the Order Fulfillment Sub-system

S13 Integration Testing

S14 System Testing

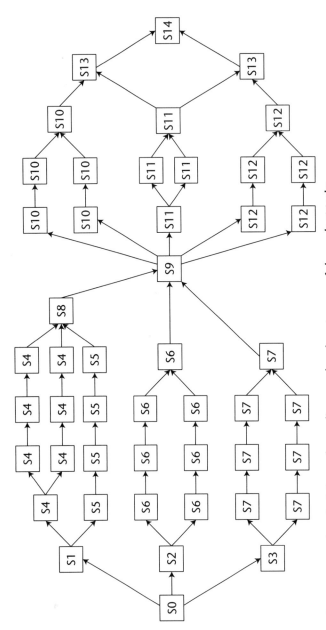

Figure 12-5: A typical dependency diagram showing streams of dependent tasks

When you consider the dependency diagram, you have several ways to allocate these development streams to stages. For example:

- Stage 1—S4, S5, and S8
- Stage 2—S6 and S7
- Stage 3—S9
- Stage 4—S10 (deploy Order Entry Sub-system)
- Stage 5—S11 and S13 (deploy Order Routing Sub-system)
- Stage 6—S12, S13, and S14 (deploy Order Fulfillment Sub-system)

Creating the Initial Project Schedule

Once you have the stages laid out, you have a plan for scheduling the design team in sequence. For instance, the example stages at the end of the previous section lay out schedule the design team in sequence for the project—once a design team has finished the design of say the Order Entry Sub-system, they can move to the Order Routing Sub-system and then to the Order Fulfillment Sub-system. If the systems design bench strength is sufficient, you might choose to approach all three design streams concurrently.

CROSS-REFERENCE

The option of working on streams concurrently is discussed in Chapter 19.

In the Incremental SDPM strategy for the Staged Delivery Waterfall model the major scheduling problem is to keep the dependency relationships consistent between stages. By first examining the dependency diagrams for the entire project, you can allocate tasks to stages to preserve those relationships. That will be fairly straightforward. The only other consideration will be to allocate enough tasks to a stage so that a deployable partial solution can be generated from the stage. If that is not a consideration, there should be no other issues to deal with.

The Planning Phase of an Incremental SDPM Strategy for the Feature-Driven Development Model

Figure 12-6 is the Planning Phase of the Incremental SDPM strategy for the Feature-Driven Development model.

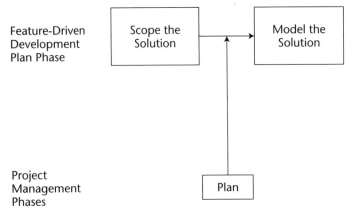

Figure 12-6: Planning Phase of an Incremental SDPM strategy for the Feature-Driven Development model

Four major activities make up the SDPM Planning Phase of an Incremental SDPM strategy for the Feature-Driven Development model:

- Modeling the solution
- Building the feature list
- Assembling the feature sets
- Develop the feature plan

They are briefly described in the following subsections.

Modeling the Solution

The project manager assembles the modeling team, which comprises domain experts (customers) and developers. Under the direction of a Chief Architect (who is an experienced object modeler) a walkthrough of the project scope is conducted. Domain areas to be included in the final solution are identified, and small subteams are commissioned to model each domain in turn. From among the models submitted for each domain, a single model is chosen; it might be one of the suggested models or a hybrid of the submitted models. After a model of each domain is developed, a consolidation produces the overall model solution. This model may be updated later in the life cycle of the project.

Building the Feature List and Assembling Feature Sets

The RBS is the recommended approach to building the feature list. The domains identified in the modeling activity are the starting point. Each domain is decomposed into the functionality needed to satisfy the overall solution. Functionality can then be decomposed into major feature sets and each feature set further decomposed into the minor features that compose that set.

Developing the Feature Plan

The deliverable here is the sequencing of features sets based on the technical dependency relationships between feature sets. You need to consider two separate scenarios: Feature sets built sequentially and feature sets built concurrently and sequentially.

Feature Sets Built Sequentially

The only issue here is to make sure that, for a given feature set, all of the predecessor features have already been built in a previous increment. For relatively large projects this is not a trivial task. The downside is to reach a spot in one increment only to realize that a feature that is needed has not been previously built. Err on the side of giving due consideration to this sequencing task.

Feature Sets Built Concurrently and Sequentially

Sequencing is done as discussed previously. To that complexity you have to factor in concurrent feature set design and build activities. It will usually happen that concurrent feature sets will not be technically independent of one another. Therefore there will be some degree of coupling between feature sets that are being concurrently designed and built. The schedules of each of these parallel swim lanes will have to account for those dependencies.

Discussion Questions

1. You are Pepe Ronee and are planning an Incremental SDPM strategy for the Staged Delivery model. You have this gnawing feeling that the customer will discover scope changes as a result of working with the solution delivered from an earlier increment. Is there a strategy that you might adopt in the planning phases to minimize the adverse impacts of scope changes? What about after the project has started and scope change requests arise? How would you deal with that eventuality?

CHAPTER 13

The Incremental SDPM Launching Phase

Efficiency and economy imply employment of the right instrument and material as well as their right use in the right manner.

Louis Dembitz Brandeis
U.S. Supreme Court Justice

Chapter Learning Objectives

After reading this chapter, you will be able to:

- ◆ **Understand the complications added to the Launch Phase when using an Incremental SDPM strategy**
- ◆ **Plan for scope change requests**
- ◆ **Anticipate and mitigate resource scheduling situations**
- ◆ **Anticipate and mitigate increment scheduling changes**
- ◆ **Understand the launch activities of the Incremental SDPM strategy for the Staged Delivery Waterfall model**
- ◆ **Understand the launch activities of the Incremental SDPM strategy for the Feature-Driven Development model**

All of the Launching Phase discussion for the Linear SDPM strategy situation applies to the Incremental SDPM strategy and will not be repeated here (you can read more about the Launching Phase for a Linear SDPM strategy in Part II). Incremental SDPM strategy projects follow the same procedures as by-the-book projects, except they repeat those procedures several times over the life of the project. Within a single repetition, all of the launching activities done in the Linear SDPM strategy are done in the Incremental SDPM strategy. However, you do have some additional considerations, and they arise out of the repetitive nature of the Incremental project. This chapter identifies those additional considerations and discusses how they are handled in the Launching Phase of Incremental SDPM Strategies for both the Staged Waterfall model and the Feature-Driven Development model.

The Launching Phase of an Incremental SDPM Strategy

Four tasks must be done in the Launch Phase of an Incremental project that are not done in the Launch Phase of a Linear project. They are as follows:

- Handling scope change
- Handling increment handoffs
- Scheduling resources
- Scheduling increments

These are discussed in the subsections that follow.

Handling Scope Change

This is not a discussion of the scope change management process. That has already been defined. Rather, this is a discussion of how to handle a scope change request. You no doubt recall that an Incremental SDPM strategy project is one in which all of the requirements have been defined and minimal changes are expected. In fact, the Incremental SDPM strategy is rather change-intolerant, as you know from earlier discussion in this book. Yet, at the same time, choosing an Incremental approach brings with it the encouragement of scope change. The customer works with and experiences the functionality in each increment, and they will undoubtedly find other things they would have liked in the release if they had only realized it. The current increment gives them the boost they needed to realize the improvement and to make the scope change request to have it implemented in a future increment. This behavior is not unexpected. The fragile nature of requirements gathering will undoubtedly leave some gaps. The customer simply cannot envision everything they need in the solution. It is probably a reasonable request, so what do you do with it?

First of all, don't change the current increment plan to accommodate the scope change request. Instead, complete the project impact statement. Leave the implementation of the scope change request for the next or some later increment. As you look forward to the Iterative, Adaptive, and Extreme SDPM strategies, this same logic will apply. All scope change requests are put in the priority list for consideration in a future increment or iteration. Increments are too short to consider changing once they have begun. Leave change integration for a later cycle.

The solution to handling scope change requests lies back in the Planning Phase. There are two planning situations to consider: a comprehensive increment plan and an increment-by-increment plan.

Comprehensive Increment Plan

The comprehensive increment plan includes the scheduling and resource loading of every increment. In anticipation of scope change requests from the just-completed increment, include a scope bank in the next increment to accommodate scope change requests so that each increment has a scope bank to handle scope change requests from the previous increments. For example, the scope bank for Increment 2 would be some percentage of the total labor estimated for Increment 1. Something like 10–15 percent would be sufficient. That allows some tine in Increment 2 to process scope change requests that arise from the customer as they experience Increment 1 functionality. If that time is not used to process scope change requests it can be used to give the customer some time to work with the just released increment in preparation for the next increment.

Increment by Increment Plan

This project plan schedules only one increment at a time. The schedule for Increment 2 is built at the completion of Increment 1. The customer has a narrow window of time within which to exercise the Increment 1 functionality before they have to commit to any scope change requests to be accommodated in Increment 2 or some later increment.

You need to be aware of four risks to this approach. They are listed in the subsections that follow and briefly described.

Customer Delays

The customer may not be as responsive to the increment release as you would like them to be. They need time to digest what you have given them. They may have questions for clarification, or they may want to get feedback from others in their organization. All of this adds to the quality of the final solution, but it does insert delays into the project and the start of the next increment.

Unavailability of Resources

In a resource-constrained organization, the increment-by-increment plan risks the loss of one or more resources that could have been committed had a comprehensive increment plan been used. This may cause delays in getting the next increment launched.

Loss of Priority

Some other project may be given a higher priority than yours and have first choice on resources. That will bring further delays to the planning and starting of your next increment.

Senior Management Delays

In the time between increments, when the customer is getting familiar with the just released functionality and you are beginning to plan for the next increment, senior management might have a change of heart with respect to your project. You could find yourself working on some other short-term project or task with the promise that once finished you can return to your current project.

Increment Handoffs

There is no guarantee that the team who worked on the just completed increment will work on the next or any other increment for this project. This is especially true if you are using the increment-by-increment plan approach. Priorities of other projects and resource availability determine whether or not you can retain the same team from increment to increment. Because of the likelihood of staffing changes between increments you must have clear documentation describing the just completed increment so that the new team members can pick up where their predecessors left off. In effect what is needed is an "increment notebook." This is not much different than a project notebook except it applies only to an increment of a project that is not yet complete. It should also be a cumulative notebook. All previous increments will be documented for all teams to follow.

Scheduling Resources

Scheduling a resource for a continuous effort on a task is far less complicated than scheduling a resource for several discontinuous efforts on the same or different tasks. In the case of an incremental project, that resource will work on a task in increment 1 and then work on a same-skill task in increment 2 and so on. The resource manager will prefer to know when the resource will be needed over the entire project rather than just one increment at a time.

Scheduling Increments

The project plan for the Incremental SDPM strategy probably includes the complete schedule of all increments and the resources as well. That is certainly one approach and the one that would seem to make the most sense. Resource managers want to know when they have to commit their staff to projects.

Alternatively, the project plan might include commitments only for the first increment. It has to do with the volatility of the organization, the length of the increment, and the depth and breadth of the resource pool.

The Launching Phase of an Incremental SDPM Strategy for the Staged Waterfall Model

The Launching Phase of an Incremental SDPM strategy for the Staged Waterfall model deals with all four of the considerations stated previously for the generic Incremental situation.

Handling Scope Change

First, you have to assume that scope change requests are inevitable. No matter how much effort was spent on requirements gathering and documentation, you will face changes. For projects that affect infrastructure only, you may have fewer scope change requests. For those that have an external impact on markets, customers, and competition, many scope change requests are possible. For infrastructure projects, the requirements are generally the result of internal business processes and, hence, are better defined. They tend to be stable in comparison to projects that are externally focused. The externally focused projects are subject to the whims of the market, which are constantly changing. That tells you something about which planning approach you should choose. In other words, infrastructure projects respond well to Linear approaches, whereas externally facing projects should follow an approach that offers more flexibility, that is, Incremental approaches.

Comprehensive Increment Plan

The comprehensive plan schedules all increments. What is to be built in each increment, the resource schedule, and expected completion date of the increment are put in place for all increments. If accommodations have been made via a scope bank, the impact of unexpected scope change requests can be held to a minimum. With infrastructure projects there will be more stability in the requirements and, hence, less change through discovery. That certainty means that little time will be wasted in building the complete and comprehensive plan. If there is some doubt about that stability, an increment-by-increment plan might be the better choice.

Increment by Increment Plan

For those projects that affect or are affected by external factors, the increment-by-increment plan may be the better choice. That follows from the fact that between increments adjustments can be made and accommodated into the plan going forward. By building that plan on an increment-by-increment basis there is less wasted time (the result of plans that are never followed because of scope changes). The risk is that in between increments the priorities of the organization can change and resources could get reassigned. That puts the continuation of the project to the next increment at great risk. The organization might decide that the functionality in the just completed increment is sufficient and the business can get along for a while with the current solution.

Increment Handoffs

The safe assumption to make is that a new team will continue with the next increment. Because availability is often treated as a skill, you might also assume that the new team will not be up to speed on the project and may not be the best mix of skills to take on the next increment. Anything that can be passed on to them is helpful. These situations obviously put the project at great risk.

This is one of the major weaknesses of the Incremental SDPM strategy as compared to the Linear SDPM strategy. The Incremental SDPM strategy requires considerably more documentation than does the Linear SDPM strategy, regardless of the model being used.

Scheduling Resources

The project manager needs to work closely with all resource providers to make sure that the resources committed to each increment are in fact committed. That means having a strong communications plan in place with periodic reminders of those commitments. Any change in the project plan resulting from slippages should be communicated to the resource managers. Manage expectations to the best of your ability. Keep the resource managers and customers fully aware of any compromises to the plan. If you have chosen to use a comprehensive plan, this is critical. If you have chosen to use an increment-by-increment plan, keep those involved in the current increment fully aware of your status. There should be no surprises. This advice is particularly important for any project that is done in cycles but applies equally well to all projects.

Scheduling Increments

The major drawback to the comprehensive plan is the amount of rework that the plan must undergo. Any schedule change in the current increment will most likely affect all future increments. That translates into non-value-added work for all of the detailed increment planning. Projects are almost always on aggressive schedules, and you should avoid non-value-added work whenever possible. That is certainly the case with the Staged Delivery Waterfall model using the Incremental SDPM strategy. Choose your approach carefully; both have advantages and disadvantages, and only you can determine which approach might help you avoid the waste of non-value-added work.

The Launching Phase of an Incremental SDPM Strategy for the Feature-Driven Development Model

The Launching Phase of the Incremental SDPM strategy for the Feature-Driven Development model has all of the issues of the Staged Delivery Waterfall model and then some. The sequential increments can have concurrent swim lanes within the same increment. That makes life more difficult for the project manager for at least the following reasons:

- Scope changes can be affected by precedence relationships.
- Features not yet developed may render scope change requests unnecessary.

These difficulties are discussed in the subsections that follow.

Scope Changes Can Be Affected by Precedence Relationships

Scope changes do not necessarily align themselves to feature sets. By experiencing a feature set that has been completed, the customer may identify a needed change that has nothing to do with the feature set they experienced. Customers think in terms of functions and the features that support them. They do not think in terms of feature sets. Feature sets are not natural occurrences to customers. Therefore, their scope change request may be unrelated to the feature set from which the request emanated. Instead, it may be related to another feature set not yet developed, and therefore, it cannot be implemented until that feature set on which the change depends is built. The unfortunate thing about this situation is that it may not make any sense to the customer. The burden of an explanation is on the shoulders of the project team and probably the project manager.

Features Not Yet Developed May Render Scope Change Requests Unnecessary

Feature sets are formed of features that are technically related to one another. Often the features in a feature set are related to a single function, but that is not a requirement. Furthermore, those features may not represent all of the features for the specific piece of functionality. What that means is a scope change based on the customer's experience could be based on an incomplete function whose feature set is not representative of all the features associated with that specific piece of functionality. Later feature sets might complete the functionality and might also contain the very scope change request that the customer has submitted. The customer wasted their time, but didn't realize it at the time because they did not have all the necessary information they needed. Further, the project team wasted their time completing the project impact statement for the scope change request. The situation is confusing and should not have happened, but it is unavoidable.

Discussion Questions

1. You are Pepe Ronee, and you have run the Incremental SDPM strategy by the book. But you have this gnawing feeling that what Dee wants is not what she needs. Within the context of the Incremental SDPM strategy what could you do?

CHAPTER 14

The Incremental SDPM Monitoring and Controlling Phase

My experience of the world is that things left to themselves don't get right.

Thomas Henry Huxley
English biologist

Chapter Learning Objectives

After reading this chapter, you will be able to:

- ◆ Understand the Incremental SDPM strategy
- ◆ Discuss the role of project reviews in the Incremental SDPM strategy
- ◆ Implement strategies to handle the Incremental project from scope change requests
- ◆ Understand the role of the Scope Bank and management reserve and when to use them
- ◆ Adapt milestone trend charts to the Incremental SDPM strategy
- ◆ Understand the Incremental SDPM strategy for the Staged Delivery Waterfall model
- ◆ Understand the Incremental SDPM strategy for the Feature-Driven Development model

---

Like the Linear SDPM strategy, the Incremental SDPM strategy is plan-driven. Conformance to plan, schedule, and budget is of the utmost importance. That calls for a structured project performance reporting system, mostly electronic or hardcopy reports distributed on a scheduled basis to a targeted group of stakeholders. You will have versions for immediate managers, senior managers, customers, and other stakeholders. Reports within the team are usually electronic, especially as the team size grows and the team is dispersed around the country or the world. A higher level reporting takes place at milestone events, which typically line up at the completion of each of the increments. These reporting venues may be formal presentations to the stakeholders and customers. Most should contain a formal project review, as discussed in the Linear SDPM strategy models. For larger projects, the milestone events may be the completion of the design, build, and test phases within each increment. This chapter spends some time discussing reporting at all levels.

The Monitoring and Controlling Phase of an Incremental SDPM Strategy

Figure 14-1 illustrates the Monitoring and Controlling Phase of an Incremental SDPM strategy.

Note first that the Monitoring and Controlling Phase of an Incremental SDPM strategy is two-pronged. The first prong focuses on the Design Phase, which is a one-time phase. Design was scheduled and resourced as part of the Planning Phase and the Monitoring and Controlling Phase reports against that schedule, resource usage, and budget. The second prong focuses on the Build, Test, and Deploy Phases. Here again the focus of the Monitoring and Controlling Phase is to report against that schedule, resource usage, budget, and deliverables.

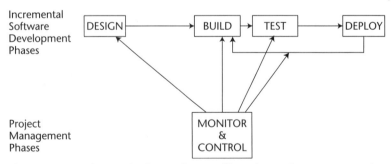

Figure 14-1: The Monitoring and Controlling Phase of an Incremental SDPM strategy

Project Review Sessions

Within each increment there will be a number of milestone events, as was the case for the linear approach, which has only one increment. At each increment's milestone events, a project review should be held. The purpose of these review sessions is to ascertain the performance of the project against the increment's plan. A typical review session will be attended by three or more senior project managers who do not have a vested interest in the project being reviewed, by a manager from the Project Management Office (if there is a PMO), the project manager of the project being reviewed, and any other persons who are associated with the project being reviewed and who the project manager feels would have valid input. Because there will be incremental deliverables in each increment, these are serious sessions. In them the project manager must review the increment plan and the status of the plan. If there are problems, you should have a presentation of them, their cause, and the fix that is in place. Because later increments depend on the successful completion of the present increment, it is critical to the success of the project that delays within an increment do not occur. Just the need to reschedule resources in later increments because of slippages in the present increment is enough to encourage maintenance of the plan. At the next project review it is expected that the project manager will update the reviewers as to the outcome of the fix. The reviewers have three purposes in mind for these sessions.

- **Compliance to the established project management processes**—The project manager must show how that has been achieved or establish a rationale for whatever departure from the process was followed and why it was followed. In the incremental approach there will be more occasions to depart from process than was the case in the linear approach. That follows from the brevity of each increment and its focus on a subset of the deliverables. The needs of an increment will often be a subset of the needs of the entire project.

- **To review status against plan**—They will be looking for variances that might foreshadow problems or continuing trends that need the attention of the project team. The incremental approach is far more complex than the linear approach and hence these variances should have closer scrutiny than in the linear approach. The complexity follows from the series of increments that are dependent upon one another. That situation does not exist in the linear approach.

- **To offer suggestions and strategies to address any issues raised in the previous two paragraphs**—If such are offered, it will be incumbent on the project manager to either reject them with good reason or adopt them and report the outcome at the next project review.

WARNING

Reviews in the Incremental approach, just as in the Linear approach, can often present unexpected problems. It is easy to politicize reviews. They provide a forum for others to jockey for positions of power or set the stage for their own self-serving purposes. In the incremental approach these can generate problems in later increments. Reviews can expose hidden problems in the enterprise that others would just as soon keep hidden. Thus, the review becomes a formality without any real reason for being done. In some organizations reviews are intimidating. The project manager is raked over the coals, many times for problems outside his or her scope of authority and control. Finally and ultimately, a review can and should present a significant opportunity to share lessons learned. Don't miss the opportunity.

Incremental SDPM Strategy for the Staged Delivery Waterfall Model

When you are using the Incremental SDPM strategy for the Staged Delivery Waterfall model (see Figure 14-2), the project reviews should come at the completion of each major phase in the software development process.

That would mean project reviews should come at the milestone events within each increment where sign-off has been obtained for Detailed Design, Code and Test, and Systems Test.

Incremental SDPM Strategy for the Feature-Driven Development Model

When you are using the Incremental SDPM strategy for the Feature-Driven Development model (see Figure 14-3), the project reviews should come at the completion of each phase in the software development process.

That would mean project reviews should come at the milestone events within each feature set development where sign-off has been obtained for Feature Set Design, Build, and Integration Test. Other reviews may be scheduled for the concurrent swim lanes to ensure those efforts are moving along according to the plan.

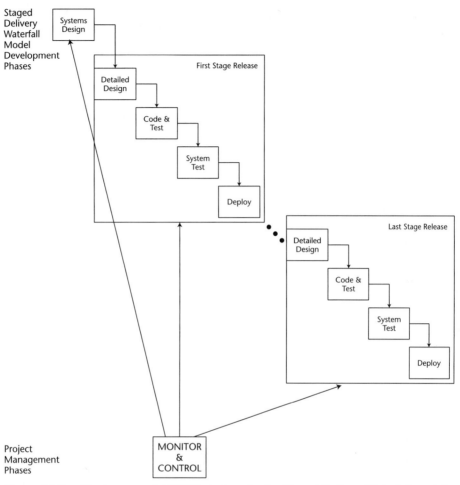

Figure 14-2: The Incremental SDPM strategy for the Staged Delivery Waterfall model

When a project becomes distressed, scheduling additional project reviews with the purpose of correcting the problem and restoring the project is common practice. The target is to bring all the swim lanes to completion on schedule so as not to delay the start of integration testing. The latest-to-complete swim lane drives the start of integration testing.

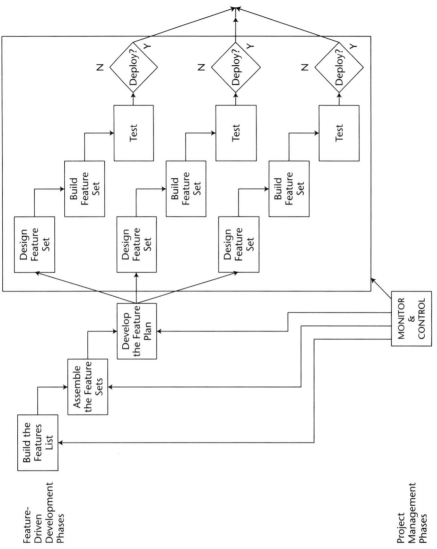

Feature-
Driven
Development
Phases

Project
Management
Phases

Figure 14-3: The Linear SDPM strategy for the Feature-Driven Development model

WARNING

Be prepared to move resources from one swim lane to another to bring the latest swim lane to completion as early as possible. These reassignments are not without their price. Every reassignment adds a bit of transition and ramp-up time to the tasks that are inherited by the resource you have moved. The most talented and adaptive of your team members should be the ones you consider for these reassignments.

Scope Change Management

Why have this section in this chapter given that you assume requirements, functions, and features are completely and clearly defined and documented just as in the case of linear strategies? Well, things aren't always what they seem to be. Even though your assumption holds, the world doesn't stand still for you. The business world changes and some of those changes can affect your project. So despite the fact that you weren't expecting any changes, you shouldn't be overly concerned that they will happen. The material that follows addresses just why this is so.

WARNING

The customer has a very different view of change than does the developer. Customers tend to view change as simpler than the developer. They don't see the system ramifications to what appears to be a very simple request. Developers, on the other hand, see all sorts of ghosts and goblins in even the simplest of requests. The request can indirectly affect all uses of the variables or parameters that are directly affected. The design is compromised and must be revised. The database design and layout is affected because longer character strings result from the change request, and so on.

Protecting the Incremental SDPM Strategy Project Against the Impact of Scope Change

There are two different strategies that I discussed in the Linear approach in Chapter 7 that apply to the incremental approach as well. The first is management reserve. The second is to change to an Iterative SDPM strategy. I want to take a look at each one.

Management Reserve

In the Linear approach, management reserve was a task added to the end of the project to accommodate additional time for contingencies. In the Incremental approach, the same idea applies except the additional time is added at the end of each increment. If it is needed, it is available. If not, it is unspent, and the project moves to the next increment where another management reserve is defined. Management reserve is not cumulative through the project. *It applies only to the increment in which it is defined.* Otherwise, it works exactly as was explained in Chapter 7.

Change to an Iterative SDPM Strategy

Although the Incremental SDPM strategy can accommodate a certain amount of change, there is a limit. At some point you may experience so much change that it begins to negatively affect the plans for future increments. That is a sign that a further change in approach is called for. The preferred change would be an approach that accommodates change. That would be the Iterative SDPM strategy, which is discussed in Chapters 17–23. The Iterative approach expects change as a result of less-than-complete descriptions of the features of the solution. Some are missing, and that is the reason for choosing this approach. As each increment unfolds, the customer discovers something that was missing from the initial requirements gathering exercise. That gives rise to a scope change request. In the Incremental approach, that creates scheduling problems. In the iterative approach, that is expected.

WARNING Pay careful attention to the frequency and trend in scope change requests. If they are increasing in number, you may have chosen the wrong approach. If they are occurring at a constant rate for any period of time, you may have chosen the wrong approach. Consider a change to an Iterative SDPM strategy.

Discussion Questions

1. There are too many scope change requests and they are taking away from project work time to the point where the Incremental schedule is now in jeopardy. You did not include management reserve time or a scope bank at the beginning of any increment. Is it too late to introduce them now? If not, how would you go about introducing these ideas? Be specific. Do you have any other suggestions for protecting the project schedule?

CHAPTER 15

The Incremental SDPM Closing Phase

We cannot afford to forget any experiences, even the most painful.

Dag Hammerskjold
Secretary of the United Nations

Chapter Learning Objectives

After reading this chapter, you will:

- ◆ Understand the Closing Phase of the Incremental SDPM strategy
- ◆ Have a working knowledge of the Closing Phase of the Incremental SDPM strategy for the Staged Delivery Waterfall model
- ◆ Have a working knowledge of the Closing Phase of the Incremental SDPM strategy for the Feature-Driven Development model

Once the customer has signed off that the requirements have been satisfactorily met, the closing phase begins. That sounds like a simple transition but is it?

The Closing Phase of the Incremental SDPM Strategy

Figure 15-1 illustrates the Closing Phase of the Incremental SDPM strategy. First note that there are really two parts to the Closing Phase:

- Closure with respect to each of the increments
- Closure with respect to the completed project

There are some similarities between these two but some important differences as well.

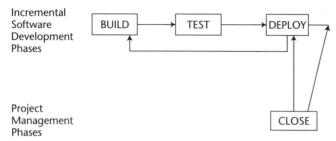

Figure 15-1: The Closing Phase of the Incremental SDPM strategy

The similarities center on requirements satisfaction at the completion of each increment. Remember that the functionality and features allocated to each increment were those that had sufficient business value to the client to be released to the market and its buying public.

Requirements validation should be done on an increment-by-increment basis by comparing the actual features and functions against the planned features and functions. All of this would have been documented in an increment acceptance test procedure developed and approved by the customer and the project manager during the planning phase. As long as that document is kept current, the validation entails nothing more than demonstrating that all items on the acceptance test procedure list for that increment have been checked off. If the document has not been kept current, then validation becomes a shooting contest and the customer usually wins. Because the Incremental SDPM strategy is based on the assumption of clearly defined and documented requirements, validation should be straightforward. But that doesn't mean it should not be a formal process from initial definition through to final acceptance. Regardless of the due diligence with which requirements were gathered and documented, there will be changes. Those changes will be brought on by the customer and the end user using the solution deployed in an earlier increment and suggesting change. That is just a reality that you have to live with and be prepared to have happen.

Incremental SDPM Strategy for the Closing Phase of the Staged Delivery Waterfall Model

Figure 15-2 illustrates the Closing Phase of the SDPM strategy for the Staged Delivery Waterfall model.

Here the dynamics of closing are clearly shown. As you can see, at each increment there is a formal "closing of the increment." The two critical parts of that closing are the acceptance criteria and the lessons learned. These are discussed in the sections that follow.

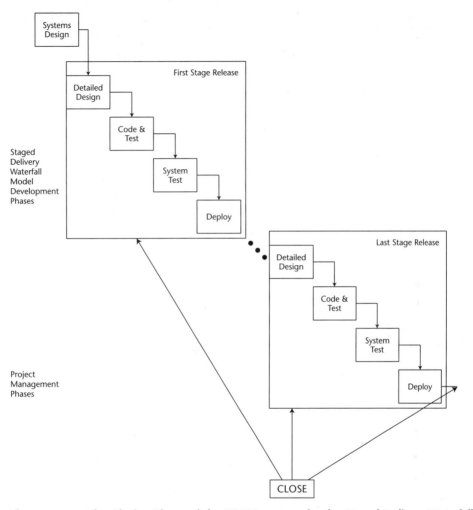

Figure 15-2: The Closing Phase of the SDPM strategy for the Staged Delivery Waterfall model

Acceptance Criteria

There are two types of acceptance criteria: incremental acceptance criteria and project completion acceptance criteria.

Incremental Acceptance Criteria

The closing of the increment involves the validation that the acceptance criteria have been met for that increment and the integration of the new functionality with the then deployed solution completed. Also, the original acceptance criteria for the just completed increment may have been modified with scope change requests coming from earlier increments that were added to the just completed increment. That may be a lot to take in, but it highlights the fact that there are a lot of moving parts in these increments and that good process management is required to stay on top of the situation.

Project Completion Acceptance Criteria

Project completion acceptance criteria include the same considerations applicable to incremental acceptance criteria, so the preceding discussion applies here equally as well. This increment just happens to be the last increment. All of the approved scope change requests should have been reflected in the updated acceptance criteria from all previous increments. This requires a good tracking system for submitted and approved scope change requests. Depending on the volume of such requests, tracking and resolving all such requests could prove challenging.

Lessons Learned

Just as there are two types of acceptance criteria, there are also two types of lessons learned to discuss: increment lessons learned and project completion lessons learned.

Increment Lessons Learned

Some typical examples of lessons learned that I have experienced in increments from completed projects include:

- Don't get too aggressive in the features and functions you will include in the increment. Err on the side of too little rather than too much.
- Make sure that the customer will be satisfied deploying the functions and features included in an increment before committing to deliver it.
- Double check that the features and functions included in the coming increment have all of their predecessor functions and features already deployed or built.

The project benefits from these increment lessons learned. At the completion of each increment, the customer and the developers should take stock of what happened in terms of process and how it could be improved for the next increment. This is entirely separate from any discussion about the deliverables from the increment. Process improvement between increments is vital to the long-term prospects for the project. For teams that are newly formed, this is critical. A team composed of members who have not worked together before has a lot to learn to be effective. The possibility of using the just completed increment as a learning opportunity should not be overlooked. The just-completed increment has considerable learning opportunities if you just look for them. These lessons learned will be a reference of the working relationship with your customer, giving you an opportunity to tailor your processes to match the practices and culture of your customer. That opportunity doesn't come along every day. Take advantage of the situation to improve your relationship with your customer as you go.

Project Completion Lessons Learned

Some typical examples of lessons learned that I have experienced in increments from completed projects include:

- Plan for more increments rather than fewer increments.
- Increments should be kept short (4–6 weeks is a good choice).
- Make sure the customer has sufficient time between increments to evaluate the solution to date. Changes may be needed and rushing into the next increment is not advisable.

The next project benefits from these project completion lessons learned. Again the focus of the lessons learned is on process not product. For example, the process that resulted in your choice of an Incremental SDPM strategy for the project may have been flawed. Maybe there were some signals that you ignored that turned out to be significant data for your decision. What were those signals and how should they be documented? How should they be recognized? The project completion lessons learned are what help you to make better decisions about what strategies to apply to future projects (future projects with the same customer, let's hope).

Incremental SDPM Strategy for the Closing Phase of the Feature-Driven Development Model

Figure 15-3 illustrates the Closing Phase of the SDPM strategy for the Feature-Driven Development model.

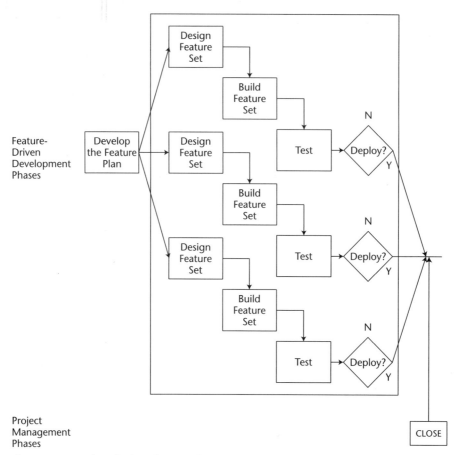

Feature-Driven Development Phases

Project Management Phases

Figure 15-3: The Closing Phase of the SDPM strategy for the Feature-Driven Development model

The Feature-Driven Development model and the Staged Delivery Waterfall model have some similarities, but they have some key differences as well, differences that do affect the acceptance criteria and lessons learned in the Closing Phase. Two key differences are as follows:

- Deployment doesn't necessarily happen with the completion of each feature set.

- Customers will not necessarily relate to feature sets as enthusiastically as they do with increments from the previous strategy.

Both of these change how you approach both acceptance criteria and the lessons learned when working within the Feature-Driven Development model, as is discussed in the next sections.

Acceptance Criteria

As was the case with the Staged Delivery Waterfall model, there are two types of acceptance criteria: incremental acceptance criteria and project completion acceptance criteria. Incremental acceptance criteria focus on the expected look and feel of the feature set deliverables rather than any perceived business value. The project completion acceptance criteria, on the other hand, focus on delivered business value. And although the two types of acceptance criteria may be named the same under each model, how each manifests in process is different.

Incremental Acceptance Criteria

The Incremental SDPM strategy for the Staged Delivery Waterfall produces a partial solution deployment at the completion of each increment. The customer, who chose the functionality in each increment, can see and feel what they got and comment on its acceptability from a business perspective. That is not necessarily the case with the Incremental SDPM strategy for the Feature-Driven Development model. Feature sets are defined based on the technical affinity of the features and not on any consideration of the business value of the feature set. The customer may not be able to judge the acceptability of a feature set simply because it doesn't relate to anything that has meaning to them. In those cases it is not advisable to deploy such feature sets. Rather, a combination of feature sets may show business value that the customer can relate to and use to decide on deployment or not. The acceptance criteria for each increment then become far more subjective in this strategy than in the previous one because the customer cannot relate the feature set deliverables to any specific business value. The acceptance criteria are based more on how a feature or function appears in the application than it does in any business context that the customer could envision.

Project Completion Acceptance Criteria

This looks and feels just like the Closing Phase of the Linear SDPM strategy, and it should. They are identical. An acceptance criterion would have been documented during planning and revised as change requests are submitted and approved. While in the Incremental SDPM strategy for the Feature-Driven Development model individual feature sets may not be deployed, the customer can still identify scope changes they wish to see implemented. As those are approved, the acceptance criteria will be updated accordingly.

Lessons Learned

As was the case with the Incremental SDPM strategy for the Staged Delivery Waterfall, when you use the Incremental SDPM strategy for the Feature-Driven Development model, you have two types of lessons learned to discuss. But the lessons learned in the Feature-Driven Development model are applicable in different ways from those you might learn using the Stage Delivery Waterfall.

Increment Lessons Learned

While the Incremental SDPM strategy for the Staged Delivery Waterfall model is very customer-centric and customer-facing, the same cannot be said for the Incremental SDPM strategy for Feature-Driven Development. This is neither good nor bad, but it does mean that lessons learned in the Incremental SDPM strategy for Feature-Driven Development will be focused on the processes used by the developers and how those might be improved rather than focused on improving the customer relationship. Lessons learned from one increment can be passed forward to the next and subsequent increments to improve the overall process. New teams will find this a meaningful benefit if approached with an open mind. If the new teams can position themselves to be very open to new ideas, their learning experiences from increment to increment are the best form of training and development they can expect. The learning is in the context of an actual project rather than some theoretical construct in the classroom.

Project Completion Lessons Learned

Future projects that follow the Incremental SDPM strategy for Feature-Driven Development model will benefit from your project having documented the lessons learned across the entire project. But take note: for some organizations, the gap between the business side and the technology side is wide, and the Incremental SDPM strategy for the Feature-Driven Development model does little to reduce that gap. The increments are technology-driven, whereas the increments for the Incremental SDPM strategy for the Staged Delivery Waterfall model are customer-driven. Therefore, the lessons that are learned using the Incremental SDPM strategy for Feature-Driven Development model are most important, and anything that happened during the just completed project that can help reduce that gap between the business and technology sides of an organization should be taken seriously and concerted attempts made to implement those lessons in future projects.

Discussion Questions

1. You have completed the first of five increments and the customer is requesting all manner of scope changes. Some changes are minor word-smithing, but other requests are for changes in features. You will be able to absorb these in later increments, but what would you do with future such requests in later increments?

CHAPTER 16

The Incremental SDPM Strategy Summary

People who produce good results feel good about themselves.

Kenneth H. Blanchard
Chairman, Blanchard Training and Development

Chapter Learning Objectives

After reading this chapter, you will:

- ◆ **Understand risk and how it affects the Incremental SDPM strategies**
- ◆ **Understand scope change and how it affects the Incremental SDPM strategies**
- ◆ **Understand team structure and how it affects the Incremental SDPM strategies**
- ◆ **Know why there is a communications gap built into the Incremental SDPM strategy**

You've spent the last five chapters getting to know the Incremental SDPM strategy and in particular looking at variations around the Staged Delivery Waterfall model and the Feature-Driven Development model. In this summary chapter, I'll discuss a few major points regarding both models and draw some conclusions about their further use and adaptation.

Comparing and Contrasting the SDPM Models

The two models (Staged Delivery Waterfall model and the Feature-Driven Development model) are the same in that both the goal and solution are clearly defined and documented. That is the necessary criteria for using either of these two Incremental models. Where the two approaches differ relates to the need to get deliverables into the users' hands. Whether the user is internal to the company or external, there are business reasons to get intermediate solutions into their hands. That is the sole motivation for using an Incremental model instead of a Linear model—to get those intermediate solutions. That is on the positive side of the ledger. On the negative side is the fact that by deploying intermediate solutions you encourage the customer and the end users to suggest changes. These cannot be ignored even though they send disruptive waves coursing through the project schedule and resource plan.

Points to Remember

Looking back at the chapters in this part, I want to drive home a few messages that you need to consider as you deliberate on the strategy to use in your project.

Risk Situations

As you move into projects that are more complex and less certain, you will see that risk takes on more importance. Risk in the Incremental SDPM strategy is slightly more pronounced than in the Linear SDPM strategy. First of all, the same risks that apply in the Linear SDPM strategy also apply in the Incremental SDPM strategy, but there are some new ones as well. There are six that deserve some discussion. They are briefly described in the following subsections.

Risk of Project Closure

The time between the end of one increment and the beginning of the next can seem like an eternity if your organization is in any state of unrest. You have just completed an increment and deployed its deliverables. Everybody is thrilled with your accomplishments. In fact, they have become so enamored with what you have delivered that future increments are at risk. Senior managers are toying with the idea of ending your project on the high note and moving the resources to other ventures. Too bad.

Risk of Team Changes

The time between two successive increments can seem like an eternity for another reason somewhat related to the first but not as drastic. Your team has excelled. They have done such a great job in a difficult situation that others up the food chain have taken notice. There is another project (perhaps of higher priority) that is in trouble and could use someone with exactly the skills and competencies of one or more of your team members. I don't have to tell you what happens. That gap between increments is just the opportunity that a senior manager can grasp onto. Your prized team member(s) are moved and replaced with less skilled developers.

Risk of Changing Priority

This is a good news/bad news situation. On the good news side, you get a higher priority, and now those resources that you have fought so valiantly for are a bit easier to come by and to hold onto once you have them. You now enjoy some leverage in negotiations that you didn't have before the priority change came along. Don't get too comfortable with your newfound power. It can go the other way just as easily. On the bad news side, you get a lower priority. Now all of the great things that you enjoyed with the higher priority vanish, and you are left with the need for more diplomacy and tact as you negotiate with others of more power and leverage.

Risk of Schedule Slippages

Have you ever encountered the situation where one or more of your team members are assigned to a small task between increments? I have, and I'm always fearful of the word "small." Somehow my definition and the other party's aren't the same. Now all resource scheduling that I had worked so hard to put in place is at risk. Furthermore, all of the other risk probabilities are now heightened. My project is now exposed.

Risk of Rework

Now that you have given your customer and end users a look at an intermediate solution, they want changes. It is inevitable so be ready for it. You can always build some contingency time into your schedule as a partial mitigation for new work, but accounting for rework in that contingency is a different matter. I often put aside 10 percent of the total labor of the planned work as a contingency for the time I will need for approved scope change requests. Should there be another percentage put aside for rework? I don't do that, but perhaps it is worth considering. The deal with your customer is that if you don't spend it, you give it back. I'm very cautious about holding something out there that encourages change, so I tend to play it close to the vest. In any case, it is worth discussing with the customer and the development team.

Risk of Resource Contention

As I said in an earlier chapter, this problem seems to plague every project, with the exception of the simplest ones, regardless of how you approach it.

- For the Incremental SDPM strategy for the Staged Delivery Waterfall model, the problem of resource contention isn't of significance except for that which occurs between projects. But that is nothing new. You deal with that all the time, and the fact that you are engaged in an Incremental SDPM strategy with the Staged Delivery model doesn't change the situation at all.

- For the Incremental SDPM strategy for the Feature-Driven Development model, resource contention is exactly the same as in the case of the Linear SDPM strategy for the Rapid Development Waterfall model. Parallel swim lanes of feature set development invariably require concurrent use of a scarce resource. Staggered scheduling is the only strategy worth considering. Even then, you have to prioritize the swim lanes when there is contention for those scarce resources. If there are dependencies across feature sets, then you have yet another contention to work around. Nothing is simple when there are concurrent swim lanes, so just get used to the challenges.

Change Intolerance

I have discussed how the Linear and Incremental SDPM strategies are change intolerant. You chose them as your strategy because requirements were assumed complete and clearly documented. Change requests were not expected to be much of an issue. You don't need to repeat those arguments, but it is instructive to put that foremost on your mind as you go about planning the increments in your project. I religiously put a task called "management reserve" in my project plan. It is a task that ends the project. Its duration is equal to 10 percent of the total labor estimated for the project. I make it visible to the customer. I manage it. I don't want to spend it if I can help it. It's just good commonsense project management. Management reserve is time. Contingencies in your budget are dollar reserves for the unexpected. Dollars or time, it makes no difference. You treat them both the same.

Team Structure

It seems like all I have to summarize with are cautions and warnings about pending disaster. Well, I've saved the positive news for last. As is the case with Linear SDPM strategies, Incremental SDPM strategies are the least demanding on team strength and capacity. Incremental SDPM strategies can work quite well with junior technical staff. As in the Linear SDPM strategies, case co-location is not a requirement. About the only difference between Linear and Incremental models is that Incremental models should strive for continuity across increments. If you suspect that that will be a problem, your risk response plan should include more documentation for the handoff than you would entertain if there were to be team continuity across increments.

WARNING

Communications across the team members has always been a problem with Incremental SDPM strategies. "Throw it over the wall" to the team working on the next increment is just asking for trouble. The handoff between increments should have some overlap if that is at all possible. Bringing new team members into the project at some mid-increment point is risky if it hasn't been planned for.

Discussion Questions

1. Despite your best efforts at discouraging scope change requests for your Incremental project, the customer continues to submit them. Some are well thought out; some are not. Consider postponing action until the last increment. What are the advantages and disadvantages of such a strategy? Would you do it? If not, what alternative would you recommend?

PART FOUR

Iterative ESPM

The Iterative approach is your first departure from the comfortable world of the Linear and Incremental approaches. Here you step out into the unknown. For the first time you encounter a project whose goal is known and clearly documented, but whose solution is not. The desired functionality is known and documented but some of the features behind that functionality are only vaguely known and may not even all be identified. They must be discovered, and it is only by doing the project that that discovery will take place. While this may seem like a minor difference and not worthy of a new approach, such is not the case. These types of projects bring to the project manager quite a number of risks and issues. How to handle them in the most effective and efficient way is the subject of this part.

CHAPTER 17

Iterative SDPM Strategy

I never did anything worth doing by accident, nor did any of my inventions come by accident; they came by work.

Thomas Alva Edison
American inventor and entrepreneur

Chapter Learning Objectives

After reading this chapter, you will be able to:

- ◆ Explain the Iterative SDPM strategy
- ◆ Have a high-level understanding of the Evolutionary Development Waterfall model, SCRUM, Rational Unified Process, and the Dynamic Systems Development Method

---

On the certainty/uncertainty line, the models that lie to the right of the incremental models are those that we have defined as iterative models. These models have been proposed to address the difficulty many project managers face when they try to clearly define requirements. There are four such models, and they all are similar in that the requirements are not fully explored and it is the project itself that helps in that further exploration.

Iterative approaches are used when you have an initial version of the solution but they are known to fall short in terms of features and perhaps functions. The iterative cycles are designed to uncover the missing pieces of the solution. Think of the Iterative SDPM strategy as a variant of production prototyping. The intermediate solutions are production ready, but they might not be released to the end user until the final version is ready. The intermediate versions give the customer something to work with as they attempt to learn and discover additional needed features.

The Iterative SDPM Strategy

The definition of the Iterative SDPM strategy allows for several types of iteration. Iteration can be on requirements, functionality, features, design, development, solutions, and others. Figure 17-1 is the generic model of the Iterative SDPM strategy. There are several models that I discuss that follow this generic framework.

The Iterative SDPM strategy kicks in when not all of the solution is clearly known. This strategy requires a solution that broadly covers the requirements but might be missing some of the details. In other words, the functions are known and will be built into the solution through a number of iterations but the details (the features) are not completely known at the beginning of the project. The missing or detailed features will come to light as the customer works with the most current solution in a prototyping sense. As is true of other Quadrant 2 strategies (goal is clearly defined but solution is not), the Iterative SDPM strategy is a learn-by-doing strategy. The use of intermediate solutions is the pathway to discovering the intimate details of the complete solution.

Scope Phase

The Scope Phase takes on a bit more complexity than in the previous strategies. In the Iterative SDPM Strategy, you move into waters where the complete solution is not known. In this book, iterative strategies deal with cases where you are reasonably certain that you have completely defined functionality but not necessarily the features that accompany that functionality. Each iteration is going to discover additional functionality by having the customer and end user spend some time working with the then solution. Presumably those new-found features are then prioritized and added to one of the future iterations. That game plan suggests that iterations be kept short.

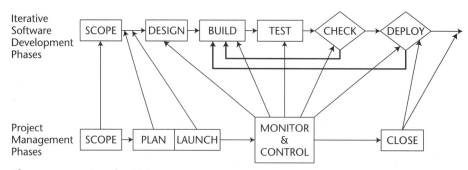

Figure 17-1: Iterative SDPM strategy

Plan and Launch Phases

Planning is done at two levels in the Iterative SDPM strategy. The initial Plan Phase develops a high-level plan without much detail. The reason is that the full detail is not known at the initial stage. The functionality is known, and its design and development can be planned across any number of iterations. In some cases all the functionality will be designed and developed in the first iteration. Later iterations then drill down to possible areas for further identification and development of features. This is probably the most efficient of all the design develop alternatives you might consider. Yet another strategy would be to develop the high-risk parts of the system first. That removes one of the major variables that could adversely affect the project if left to a later iteration.

Within each iteration you might have concurrent swim lanes—each developing a different piece of functionality or expanding on its features. The determining factor is the resource pool from which you are drawing your team members. If you need to compress the development timeframe, you can structure the project much like you would in the Linear SDPM strategy when you moved from the Standard Waterfall model to the Rapid Development Waterfall by adding concurrent swim lanes, each developing a different part of the solution.

Monitor and Control Phases

In the Iterative SDPM strategy, the Monitor and Control Phase begins to change. Because of the speculative nature of the iterative strategy, much of the heavy documentation and status reporting gives way to more informal reporting. Much of that formalism becomes non-value-added work and begins to burden the team with tasks that do not bring them any closer to the final solution. You will want to be careful to not overload the architects and developers with those types of tasks. Let them remain relatively free to pursue the creative parts of the project.

Close Phase

The Close Phase for the Iterative SDPM strategy is similar to the Close Phase for the preceding strategies in that there are customer-specified criteria that must be met in order for the project deliverables to be considered complete. Those criteria were specified during the planning phase and updated as scope change requests were approved and integrated into the solution. The only difference is that the project might end (time and or money used) and there might still be features not integrated into the solution. These are noted in the final report and are to be considered whenever the next version of the solution will be commissioned.

Lessons learned take on an additional dimension. What did the team and the customer learn about doing projects following the Iterative SDPM strategy? How can the approach be improved for the next such project?

Types of Iterative SDPM Strategies

Several models fit into my strict definition of the Iterative class. However, most interpretations would have a broader membership in the Iterative class than I have here. Those models that are iterative by my definition are Evolutionary Waterfall model, SCRUM, Rational Unified Process (RUP), and Dynamic Systems Development Method (DSDM). Each of these models and methods has tight or loose definitions depending on who provides the definition. If the definition is loose, then these models range over more than just the Iterative class. Some of them will take on the characteristics of the Adaptive class, which is the subject of later chapters in this book.

Evolutionary Development Waterfall Model

In this approach, the project begins much like the Standard Waterfall model. A complete systems design is developed based on clearly defined requirements. The systems design component reflects the requirements in the design. As the features and functions needed to deliver the requirements are developed, they will change. Few changes are expected to the original requirements. The WBS for the current version is created along with duration, cost, and resource requirements. This model closely resembles the production prototype approach that was quite popular in the past.

It should be obvious that the meaningful involvement of the client is critical to the success of this model. The client works with a version of the system and provides feedback to the project team as further enhancements and changes to features and functions are discovered. This process continues as version after version is put in place. At some point, the client is satisfied that all requirements have been met. Also note that this model always presents the client with a production-ready version of the system. Succeeding versions merely add to the features and functions.

Iterative SDPM strategies definitely fall in the class of learn and discover. In the Evolutionary Development Waterfall model the learning and discovering experience is obvious from Figure 17-2. With each iteration, more and more of the depth of the solution is revealed. That follows from the customer and developers having an opportunity to play with the then solution.

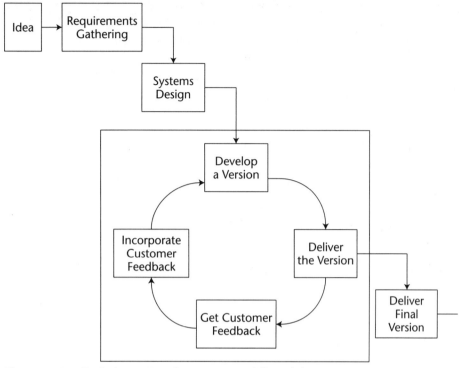

Figure 17-2: Evolutionary Development Waterfall model

Figure 17-2 illustrates the Evolutionary Development Waterfall model, the final variation of the Waterfall models. It handles those cases where the solution is known to a certain level of detail. The final features that completely define the solution are what are missing. Through a sequence of partial solutions the complete solution is discovered.

The discovery of additional features is a process that fully engages the customer in meaningful exchanges with the developers. Both customer and developers work with the prototypes—sometimes independently and sometimes in collaboration. Collaboration usually follows periods where they work independently. The collaboration would be done in an effort to decide how to go forward with new or redefined features in the next and subsequent iterations.

Figure 17-3 illustrates the Iterative SDPM strategy for the Evolutionary Development Waterfall model.

The Evolutionary Development Waterfall model reaches some distance into Quadrant 2 because it can embrace learning and discovery as a way to uncover the complete solution. Its integration with the project management life cycle is rather straightforward, as you will see in Chapters 18 through 23.

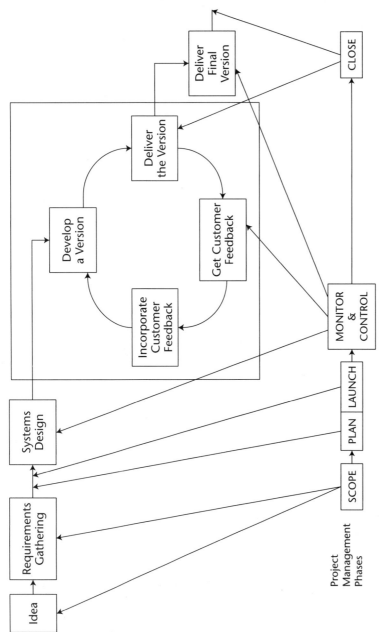

Figure 17-3: Iterative SDPM strategy for the Evolutionary Development Waterfall model

SCRUM

SCRUM is a term taken from rugby. A scrum involves the team as a unit moving the ball down field in what would appear to be an ad hoc manner. Of all the iterative approaches, SCRUM would seem to define a chaotic development environment. The SCRUM software development team is self-directed, operates in successive one-month iterations, holds daily team meetings, continuously offers the client demos of the current solution, and adapts its development plan at the end of each iteration. For a complete discussion on SCRUM and software development, refer to Ken Schwaber and Mike Beedle's *Agile Software Development with SCRUM* (Prentice Hall, 2001).

Of all the development models discussed in this book, SCRUM is clearly the most customer-driven approach. It is the customer who defines the functions and features that the team prioritizes into phases and builds a phase at a time. The process allows the customer to change functions and features as more of the solution depth is uncovered through the previous iterations. Depending on the working definition you are using for SCRUM, SCRUM might be a strict application of the Iterative class as defined herein or it might border on the adaptive class discussed later in the book.

The SCRUM process flow is shown in Figure 17-4, while the sections that follow explain the parts of the flow.

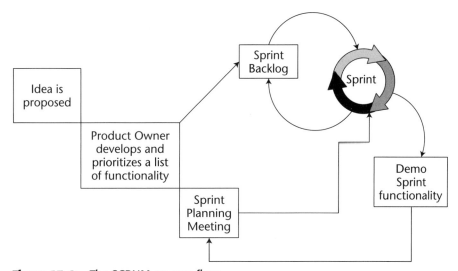

Figure 17-4: The SCRUM process flow

Idea Is Proposed

The original idea for the system might be vague. It might be expressed in the form of business terms. A function level description can be developed as part of the scooping phase but not to the depth of detail that the customer requires. It is not likely to be expressed in system terms.

Developing and Prioritizing a List of Functionality

The Product Owner is responsible for developing this list, which is called the Product Backlog. It helps the team understand more detail about the idea and helps them form some ideas about how to approach the project.

Sprint Planning Meeting

This is an 8-hour meeting with two distinct 4-hour parts. In the first part, the Product Owner presents the prioritized Product Backlog to the team. This is the opportunity for the team to ask questions to clarify each piece of functionality. In the second part, the team commits to the functionality it will try to deliver in the first Sprint. The team then spends the remaining 4 hours developing the high-level plan as to how it will accomplish the Sprint. The work to be done is captured in the Sprint Backlog. The Sprint Backlog is the current list of functionality that is not yet completed for the current Sprint.

Demo Sprint Functionality

At the end of the Sprint, the team demos the solution to the client; functionality is added or changed, and the Product Backlog is updated and reprioritized for the next Sprint. This entire process continues until the Product Backlog is empty or the client is otherwise satisfied that the current Sprint version is the final solution.

SCRUM has often been characterized as a methodology that does not require a project manager. In fact, the position of project manager does not exist, but the role does. It is subsumed primarily into the team with some responsibility resting on the shoulders of the SCRUM Master. Figure 17-5 illustrates the Iterative SDPM strategy for SCRUM.

SCRUM has been characterized as organized chaos and it does seem quite disorganized at first glance. There really doesn't need to be a person with the title of "project manager." The entire team, which is self-managed and self-directed, fills the role of project manager, but not in an overt manner. You will see that the role of project manager is shared across the team members as we explore this integration in Chapters 18–23.

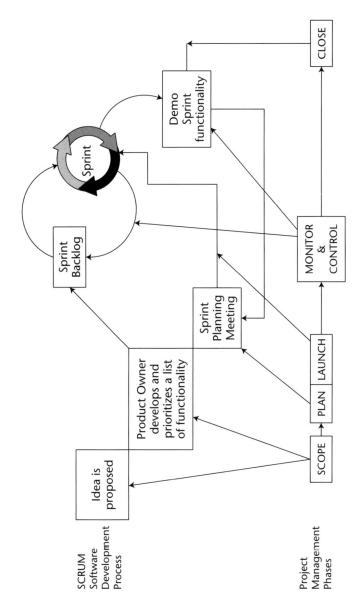

Figure 17-5: Iterative SDPM strategy for SCRUM

Rational Unified Process

The Rational Unified Process (RUP) is a completely documented process for building a software system in an iterative fashion. An extensive library of books and Internet resources is available on the topic. A good starting point is the book by Stefan Bergstrom and Lotta Raberg entitled *Adopting the Rational Unified Process: Success with the RUP* (Addison-Wesley, 2004).

The essential concepts of RUP are:

- Inception
- Elaboration
- Construction
- Transition

Inception

The Inception Phase has as its objective the definition and concurrence of all the stakeholders as to the scope of the software development project. The scope is bounded by a number of use cases that define the functions that the software system must perform. An initial systems architecture is developed using these critical use cases. Cost, schedule, and risk are also estimated as a preparation for the Elaboration Phase.

Elaboration

The Elaboration Phase is the engineering phase of a RUP project. It is here that the details of the problem and its solution are formed and an architecture is finalized. That permits more refined estimates of time, cost, and risk. Prototypes are often built as an aid to the design considerations, more detailed functionality, and features.

Construction

The current design is turned into a working system. If this phase has been repeated, the most recent designs are integrated into the current solution and a more enhanced solution is turned over to the client.

Transition

The Transition Phase turns over a solution that the customer can put into production. It need not be a complete solution, but it does have sufficient business value to be released to the end user. Later minor enhancements will be made to integrate features defined but not integrated.

All four of these phases are embedded within each of the stages and not explicitly shown in Figure 17-6. I'll expand on these in Chapters 18–23.

RUP is probably the most well known of the iterative software development processes. It adapts quite well to a process approach that is documentation-heavy or to one that is documentation-light. The foundation of RUP lies in the library of reusable code, requirements, designs, and so on. That library will have been built from previous project experiences, which means that RUP can have a long payback period. The library must be sufficiently populated to be useful from a Return on Investment (ROI) perspective. Four to five completed projects might be enough to begin to see some payback.

Figure 17-7 illustrates the Iterative SDPM strategy for RUP.

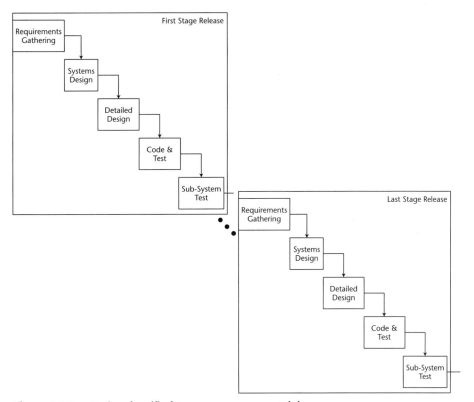

Figure 17-6: Rational Unified Process—process model

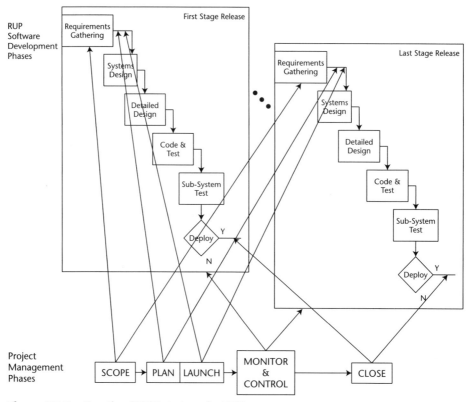

Figure 17-7: Iterative SDPM strategy for RUP

RUP ranges widely over the project landscape. When complexity and uncertainty are low but the solution is not fully defined, RUP is a heavy process. It requires considerable documentation especially for code reuse. On the other hand, an organization that has considerable RUP experiences behind it can deploy a lighter version of RUP. You'll see the flexibility of RUP in the discussions in Chapters 18–23.

Dynamic Systems Development Method

Dynamic Systems Development Method (DSDM) is what the Standard Waterfall model would look like in a zero-gravity world. Feedback loops are the defining features that separate DSDM from the Standard Waterfall model. DSDM is an iterative model, but it can be used in situations where even less of the solution is specified. The feedback loops help guide the client and the project team to a complete solution. The business case is included as a feedback loop so that even the fundamental basis and justification of the project can be revisited.

Figure 17-8 highlights the DSDM method and the following lists the nine key principles of DSDM as indicated in Jennifer Stapleton's *DSDM: Dynamic Systems Development Method* (Addison-Wesley, 1997).

- Active client involvement is imperative.
- DSDM teams must be empowered to make decisions.
- The focus is on frequent delivery of products.
- Fitness for business purpose is the essential criterion for acceptance of deliverables.
- Iterative and incremental development is necessary to converge on an acceptable business solution.
- All changes during development are reversible.
- Requirements are baselined at a high level.
- Testing is integrated throughout the life cycle.
- A collaborative and cooperative approach between all stakeholders is essential.

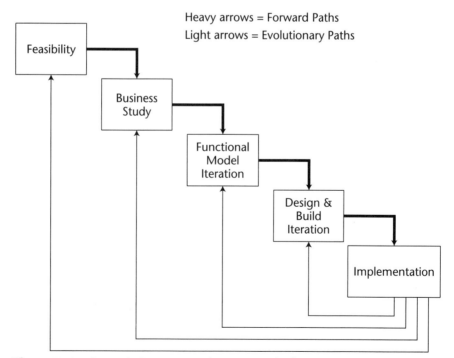

Figure 17-8: Dynamic Systems Development Method

Note that the characteristics in the list are quite similar to those I have identified as good practices throughout the book.

The distinguishing feature of the DSDM is the incremental release and implementation of a production system at the end of each cycle (see Figure 17-9). Note that iterations around Design and Build and Functional Model iterations all follow an implementation phase. DSDM delivers business value to the client as part of its overall process design. Other approaches might do the same as a variation, but DSDM does it as part of the design of the approach itself.

WARNING

Iterative approaches have often been misused. However, the Iterative approaches are suffering more from an informal use of terminology than from misuse. That's why in this book the Iterative class includes models that work effectively in discovering small parts of the solution (features for the most part) rather than in discovering major gaps in functionality. Those projects are better served with one of the adaptive models.

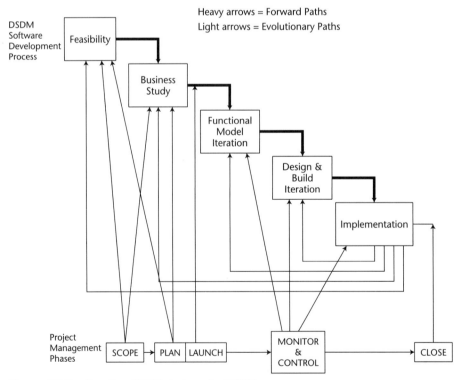

Figure 17-9: Iterative SDPM strategy for DSDM

Discussion Questions

1. What sort of Iterative approach would you take if your customer isn't willing or able to participate? What are the strengths and/or weaknesses of your choice?

2. What sort of Iterative approach would you take if your customer gets so involved with the project that it is adversely affecting the team's productivity? What are the strengths and/or weaknesses of your choice?

CHAPTER 18

The Iterative SDPM Scoping Phase

To improve is to change, to be perfect is to change often.

Winston Churchill
British Prime Minister, writer, and soldier

Chapter Learning Objectives

After reading this chapter, you will be able to:

- ◆ Explain the Scoping Phase of the Iterative SDPM strategy
- ◆ Conduct the Scoping Phase of the Evolutionary Waterfall model
- ◆ Conduct the Scoping Phase of the SCRUM model
- ◆ Conduct the Scoping Phase of the Rational Unified Process (RUP) model
- ◆ Conduct the Scoping of the Dynamic Systems Development Method

---

The Scoping Phase of the Iterative SDPM strategy is the beginning of the project life cycle for these types of systems development projects. In this phase, you establish the parameters for the project and prepare a high-level plan for how you are going to approach the project. While you did the same for the Incremental SDPM strategy, you'll find significant differences for the Iterative project. Project uncertainty has increased as a result of gaps between what you know to be the solution and what actually is the solution. Those gaps have to be discovered and removed through the conduct of the project itself. Therein lies the increase in complexity that comes with Iterative SDPM projects.

The Scoping Phase of an Iterative SDPM Strategy

On the surface, Iterative strategies appear quite similar to Incremental strategies. Both have sequentially released pieces of the solution, but a fundamental difference exists between the strategies.

- In the Incremental SDPM strategy, a part of the known solution is released in each increment.

- In the Iterative SDPM strategy, the known solution is released in each increment.

So, at the end of an iteration in the Iterative SDPM strategy, the complete solution as you know it at the time is released. The customer decides whether or not that release adds enough business value since the last release and should be released to the end user. The customer may find a number of business reasons for either releasing or not releasing. They are discussed in Chapter 22.

The Scoping Phase of the Iterative SDPM Strategy for the Evolutionary Development Waterfall Model

Figure 18-1 illustrates the project management Scoping Phase integrated with the Idea and Requirements Gathering Phases of the Iterative SDPM strategy of the Evolutionary Development Waterfall model. This is the last variation of the Standard Waterfall Model I discuss. The Scoping Phase here is quite similar to the Scoping Phase of the Linear SDPM strategy for the Standard Waterfall model and the Scoping Phase of the Incremental SDPM strategy for the Staged Delivery Waterfall model. All three strategies begin with an idea that is further described and documented through a requirements gathering exercise. The major difference with the Iterative SDPM strategy for the Evolutionary Development Waterfall is that the features list is not complete, and so the strategy requires a number of iterations around the known solution to discover those missing features.

In addition to preparing the Project Overview Statement (POS), you perform four other scoping tasks once you are in the Scoping Phase for the entire project. They are as follows:

- Gathering requirements
- Generating the Requirements Breakdown Structure (RBS)
- Defining the functions and features of the initial solution
- Determining the number and time box for the iterations

These are discussed in the following subsections.

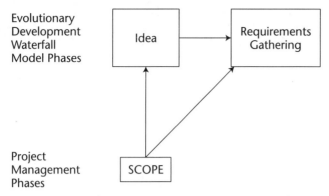

Evolutionary
Development
Waterfall
Model Phases

Project
Management
Phases

Figure 18-1: The Project Management Scoping Phase integrated with the Idea and Requirements Gathering Phases of the Evolutionary Development Waterfall model

Gathering Requirements

Requirements gathering can follow any one of the approaches discussed in Appendix D. The choice of which to use is a subjective call of the project manager based on the comfort level of the customer. In any case, a list of requirements is gathered. At the completion of that exercise, the assessment of the attributes of the requirements list may lead the team to choose the Iterative SDPM strategy for this project. They reach this decision based on the fact that they are able to generate a complete function list but not a complete features list. In other words, some of the functions are completely defined through the features that describe them. In other cases some of the functions are only partially defined through the feature lists that accompany them. The project will have to be planned so as to discover the missing features.

As you may have realized by now, the milestone event defined by the completion of requirements gathering brings the customer and the team to a decision point. They must decide which SDPM strategy makes the most sense at this point in the life cycle of the project. Depending on the status of the features list as the project commences, that decision could be changed. For example, if the team and customer should reach a point where all features have been identified, they may change their strategy to one that better supports the now changed characteristics of the project. In this chapter, I discuss what happens when not all the features have been defined.

Generating the RBS

The trick here is to pay attention to the customer as this exercise is underway. Their comfort level with each function and then each feature of each function is a clue to where there may be holes in the features list. Those potential holes will be your guide to structuring the iterations. For example, you might look for some of the following specific signs or behaviors on the part of the customer as indicators of incompleteness:

- They have taken a passive role rather than an active role in discussing some of the details of a function or feature.
- They do not offer any feature details for an identified function.
- You have suggested a function or feature and they are not contributing any further discussion.
- They are not excited about a function or feature you have suggested.
- They continually need you to clarify a point you have made.

Any of these behaviors would suggest that the associated function or feature is not complete.

On the other hand, you might look for some of the following specific signs or behaviors on the part of the customer as indicators of completeness:

- They display an excitement and constant stream of ideas as to what the solution should contain.
- They always add to your thoughts with added functions or features.
- They have a high level of interest in the discussion of a specific function or feature.
- They contribute a number of "what if" suggestions for discussion.

You will want to expose those holes in the current solution so that the customer has a chance to fill them. The customer will not respond if those holes are buried in the solution. Make them visible for discussion and resolution.

Defining the Functions and Features of the Initial Solution

The requirements should be complete, as should the function list.

- For the functions deemed completely defined, plan to build those into the initial solution. These are not likely to change over later iterations.
- For the functions that are not likely to be complete, plan on building an intermediate solution that exposes the missing features.

Keep in mind that you are building a solution that contains all of the known features and functions. Also keep in mind that your major objective in this initial solution and all later solutions is to discover what is missing.

On the other hand, you might want to consider an alternative approach. Those functions that have missing features along with any predecessor functions might define the initial solution. In this approach you have decided to focus directly on those areas where further solution definition is needed. This is an aggressive approach to finding the complete solution but it helps keep the customer focused on the gaps. This approach has some drawbacks, however. Having the complete solution to review may cause you to identify other areas that were not identified as missing from the function/features list. Keep in mind that anything you present to the customer for review and consideration will almost always result in their discovering other features and even functions that they would like to see in the solution.

Determining the Number and Time Box for the Iterations

The architecture of the plan includes a number of iterations and time boxes. If possible, estimate how many iterations and what their duration will be. This is not necessary, but it does help with resource scheduling and testing. The first iteration is likely to be longer if you are building the known solution. And it is likely to be shorter if you focus on the functions whose features are not completely defined. In either case, preplanning the number and duration of the iterations can be an aid to better management control over the project.

The Scoping Phase of the Iterative SDPM Strategy for the SCRUM Model

Figure 18-2 illustrates the project management Scoping Phase integrated with the Idea and Functionality List Phases of the Iterative SDPM strategy of the SCRUM model. The resulting Iterative SDPM strategy for the SCRUM Scoping Phase is quite different than that of other Iterative SDPM Scoping Phases. The primary difference is in the role of the customer. In this model, called the "Product Owner," the customer is the lead individual in defining requirements, functions, and features. The customer takes a more proactive role in the development life cycle. Before launching into SCRUM you should verify that the customer can fill this role. Many cannot, and the last thing you want to do is take them out of their comfort zone and place them in a threatening position. If you are fixed on using the SCRUM model, you may need to support the Product Owner in fulfilling their tasks.

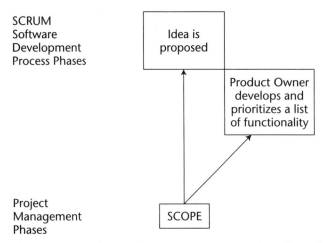

SCRUM
Software
Development
Process Phases

Idea is
proposed

Product Owner
develops and
prioritizes a list
of functionality

Project
Management
Phases

SCOPE

Figure 18-2: The Project Management Scoping Phase integrated with the Idea and Functionality List Phases of the SCRUM model

In addition to preparing the Project Overview Statement, four other tasks are part of the SCRUM scoping phase. They are:

- Idea creation
- Gathering requirements
- Defining the required functions
- Prioritizing functions

These are each described in the following subsections.

Idea Creation

The Product Owner (customer) initiates the process of defining a new or enhanced system. The high-level description takes the form of a POS, which the Product Owner initiates. As needed, a Conditions of Satisfaction (COS) might be done in conjunction with the Product Owner to ensure a well-defined project statement is delivered and agreed to by both parties.

Gathering Requirements

Any one of the approaches defined in Appendix D may be used. Because the customer will take a more proactive role, one or more of the approaches may be preferred. My choices in priority order would be user stories, business process design, and use cases.

Defining the Required Functions

The RBS is the deliverable from this activity. These functions (or sub-functions for larger projects) define the Product Backlog, the prioritized list of functions and features previously identified by the customer that have not yet been integrated into the solution. The contents of the Product Backlog evolve as functionality is released and the learning and discovery of additional functions takes place.

Prioritizing Functions

Creating a prioritized list of functions is generally done on the basis of business value. This metric may be as simple as MoSCoW (an acronym that defines the following prioritization schema: M = must have, S = should have, C = could have, W = wouldn't it be nice if we could have) or be based on a weighted criteria model. Your preference should be for customer-driven approaches.

The Scoping Phase of the Iterative SDPM Strategy for the Rational Unified Process Model

Figure 18-3 illustrates the project management Scoping Phase integrated with the Business Modeling and Requirements Gathering Phases of the Iterative SDPM strategy of the RUP model. The RUP model is essentially an Incremental type approach where each increment includes a complete Standard Waterfall model, but that is where the similarity ends. The purpose, content, and characteristics of each increment are what establish RUP as an Iterative rather than an Incremental approach.

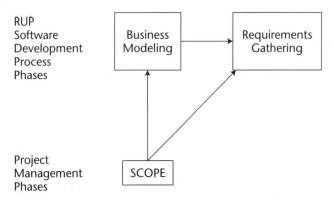

Figure 18-3: The Project Management Scoping Phase integrated with the Business Modeling and Requirements Gathering Phases of the Rational Unified Process model

The Scoping Phase is embedded in the RUP Inception and consists of the following tasks:

- Establishing a business model
- Describing the core requirements through a function and feature list
- Gathering a documented list of all use cases that flow from the functions and features list
- Crafting a high-level outline of the phases and iterations

The following is a description of each task that makes up the Inception Phase.

Establishing a Business Model

This is a bounding task; in it you define the "as is" business model and if appropriate the "to be" business model. Either or both of these become the framework within which the project is further defined and executed. From the business model, the functions and features are defined.

Describing the Core Requirements Through a Function and Feature List

Each business process step is the source of functions and features. These may be existing functions and features or those that are being added to the "as is" model to create the "to be" model. See Appendix D for examples.

Gathering a Documented List of All Use Cases That Flow from the Functions and Features List

Use cases are the primary driver of RUP. See Appendix D for a discussion of requirements gathering using use cases. The use cases are assigned to iterations on the basis of priorities and dependencies and become the basis on which the detailed plan and schedule for each iteration are developed.

Crafting a High-Level Outline of the Phases and Iterations

This outline, once crafted, is a scope of the plan. Obviously, it will change as you go, but for now it is the intended approach to this project.

The Scoping Phase of the Iterative SDPM Strategy for the Dynamic Systems Development Method

Figure 18-4 illustrates the project management Scoping Phase integrated with the Feasibility and Business Study Phases of the Iterative SDPM strategy of the DSDM. Note that the Scoping Phase incorporates both the Feasibility and Business Study Phases of DSDM and that it is iterative, as was shown in the last chapter in Figure 17-9.

The activities that take place in the Scoping Phase of an Iterative SDPM strategy for the DSDM Feasibility Study and the Business Study are as follows:

- Feasibility Study
    - Outlining the plan to build a deliverables-based WBS
    - Building a quick prototype
- Business Study
    - Defining business processes affected by this project
    - Prioritizing the functionality
    - Developing the dependency structure between functionality

These topics are discussed in the following subsections.

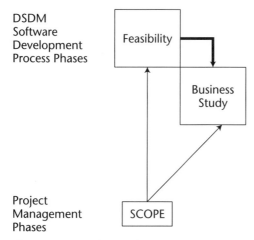

Figure 18-4: The Project Management Scoping Phase integrated with the Idea and Requirements Gathering Phases of the Dynamic Systems Development Method

Outlining the Plan to Build a Deliverables-Based WBS

This is a high-level plan that outlines the approach to be taken. It is a validation that what is needed can actually be built.

Building a Quick Prototype

This is optional and should be used at the discretion of the project manager. Its value to the project is to determine technical feasibility. In those cases where the business processes are well defined and understood, a prototype may not add any value to the feasibility study. On the other hand, if the purpose of the project is to develop a new business process, the prototype may be needed to put forth a visible rendition of the solution as further validation of feasibility and understanding. Customers often find this invaluable.

Defining Business Processes Affected by This Project

Sessions facilitated by an experienced business process expert are called for here. This both bounds the project and provides a graphical depiction of the project boundary expressed in the form of business processes. For the purposes of both new business process design and business process improvement, an "as is" version and a "to be" version should be described.

Prioritizing the Functionality

A deliverable from the facilitated sessions should also be a prioritization of the functions and features to be built. The prioritization should take into account both the business value of each function and feature and the technical relationships between them.

Developing the Dependency Structure Between Functionality

As part of the prioritization exercise, the technical dependencies between functions and features must also be preserved. So if the build activities are sequenced on the basis of prioritizations, they should also be sequenced on the basis of dependencies.

Discussion Questions

1. What criteria would you use to determine whether you should introduce the known solution at each iteration or introduce only that part of the solution where there are suspected gaps in features? Be specific.

CHAPTER 19

The Iterative SDPM Planning Phase

You can never plan the future by the past.
Edmund Burke
English statesman, orator, and writer

Chapter Learning Objectives

After reading this chapter, you will:

- ◆ **Understand the Planning Phase of the Iterative SDPM strategy for the Evolutionary Development Waterfall model**
- ◆ **Understand the Planning Phase of the Iterative SDPM strategy for the SCRUM model**
- ◆ **Understand the Planning Phase of the Iterative SDPM strategy for the Rational Unified Process model**
- ◆ **Understand the Planning Phase of the Iterative SDPM strategy for the Dynamic Systems Development Method**

This is the first of three SDPM Strategies where the planning phase focuses on projects for which the features are not completely known (Iterative SDPM strategy); or the features and functions are not completely known (Adaptive SDPM strategy); or the features, functions, and goal are not completely known (Extreme SDPM strategy). You can take several approaches to these three situations. In this chapter, I discuss the Planning Phase of four different iterative models: the Evolutionary Development Waterfall model, SCRUM, the Rational Unified Process, and the Dynamic Systems Development Method.

The Planning Phase of an Iterative SDPM Strategy

The primary focus of any Iterative, Adaptive, or Extreme SDPM strategy is to discover a complete and acceptable solution beginning with a partial solution. The indication that this is the situation you find yourself in comes when you and/or the customer know that functions or features are missing because the current solution just doesn't feel right to the customer. Working together with the customer, the project team will plan the iterations to discover those missing features. The Iterative SDPM strategy has two variations: Iterate on the complete solution or iterate on those parts of the solution requiring additional features.

Figure 19-1 illustrates the parts of the project management Planning Phase and the iterative planning phase.

Suppose that based on the results of the requirements gathering phase, you reach the conclusion that the solution that suggests itself is not going to meet customer needs. There is something missing from the requirements documentation. It could be any number of things. The most likely scenario is that the requirements list is not complete. Second, the requirements may not be completely defined. That points you to missing features, and that is the focus of the four iterative SDPM Strategies discussed in this chapter. The challenge is to plan a project where you do not know the complete solution but must discover it during through the iterative nature of the four strategies that make up the Iterative SDPM strategy.

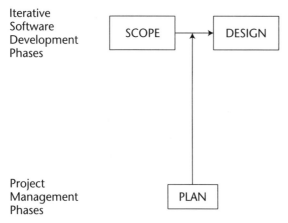

Figure 19-1: The Planning Phase for the Iterative SDPM strategy

The Planning Phase of an Iterative SDPM Strategy for the Evolutionary Development Waterfall Model

Figure 19-2 is the Planning Phase of the Incremental SDPM strategy for the Evolutionary Development Waterfall model.

For planning the Iterative SDPM strategy for the Evolutionary Development Waterfall model, the Requirements Breakdown Structure (RBS) is not complete. There are some features missing from the current solution. The objective of this strategy is to plan each iteration so that the missing features can be discovered and integrated into the solution finally producing a complete solution. There are four major tasks that need to be done to generate the project plan for this strategy. They are:

- Identifying those functions where features may be missing
- Prioritizing the functions that are missing features
- Allocating functions to iterations consistent with the features dependency structure
- Creating the project schedule for this iteration

While this is the more organized approach to Evolutionary Development, it is not the only one. As an alternative, you may simply build the solution with the core features and functions that you know will be in the final solution, let the customer interact with that solution, take suggestions for improvement, integrate them into the solution, and start the process over again. This continues until the customer is happy, you run out of time, or you exhaust the budget. While this may get to the final and acceptable solution, it can lead to scope creep and ineffective use of programmer time. A more structured approach, which offers some time-saving alternatives and is my recommendation, is to follow the four tasks identified in the preceding list. Each of these tasks is briefly described in the following subsections.

Identifying Those Functions Where Features May Be Missing

Using the solution with the core functions and features, have the customer identify those functions that do not produce an acceptable solution. Have the customer tell you what features are acceptable, which are not, and what might be done to correct the anomaly. Do this for every function in the core system.

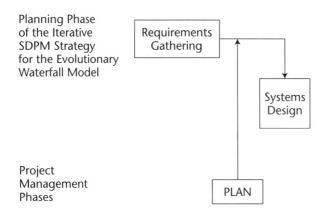

Planning Phase
of the Iterative
SDPM Strategy
for the Evolutionary
Waterfall Model

Project
Management
Phases

Figure 19-2: Planning Phase of an Iterative SDPM strategy for the Evolutionary Development Waterfall model

Prioritizing the Functions That Are Missing Features

Ask the customer to prioritize those functions needing improvement based on their importance in the final solution. This is a business decision that the customer should be making under the advice of the development team. The MoSCoW model might work here.

Allocating Functions to Iterations

There are two approaches that will do the job:

- **Iteration on the whole solution**—This is the most common approach. It works well as it does not overlook any areas of functionality. Even those that were not targeted for improvement are included. That's the upside.

  But there is a downside. The downside is that it encourages scope creep. Customers invariably find something that escaped their notice during requirements gathering that needs to be integrated into the solution. That's okay, but it does divert the developers from their primary mission— find an acceptable and complete solution.

- **Iteration on the targeted functions**—This approach is typically faster than the iteration on the whole solution approach. The reason is that the code for the targeted functions can be isolated from the rest of the code, worked on concurrently, and then integrated to produce the next version of the solution. This keeps the team and the customer focused on the high-priority functions and reduces the likelihood of scope creep. That's the upside. But there is a downside. The downside is that the concurrent swim lanes (one for each function) require a deeper bench of developers. If that is not a binding constraint, the recommendation is to use this approach.

Creating the Project Schedule for This Iteration

Once the deliverables have been identified for the coming iteration, you can develop a schedule. If the iteration is on the whole solution, the task is not any different than building a project schedule for a Linear or Incremental strategy. If the iteration is on the targeted functions, the task is a bit more complex. For skill sets that are used across the functions, a scheduling problem and a resource dependency is created across swim lanes. That dependency arises from the need to not double schedule a resource for work in two different swim lanes at the same time.

The Planning Phase of an Iterative SDPM Strategy for the SCRUM Model

Figure 19-3 is the Planning Phase of the Iterative SDPM strategy for the SCRUM model.

The Planning Phase of an Iterative SDPM strategy for the SCRUM model is iterative itself. After a demo of each solution, the planning process repeats itself. The Sprint Planning Meeting is an 8-hour meeting with a specific set of deliverables. There are three deliverables from this meeting. They are:

- Current Product Backlog
- Prioritized Backlog
- Sprint Backlog

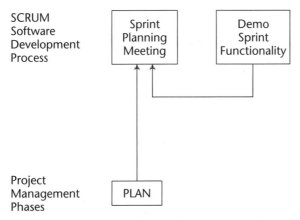

Figure 19-3: Planning Phase of an Iterative SDPM strategy for the SCRUM model

The first two deliverables are produced by the Product Owner and the SCRUM Team in the first 4 hours of the Sprint Planning Meeting. The last deliverable is produced by the SCRUM Team in the second 4 hours of the Sprint Planning Meeting. All three deliverables are briefly described in the following subsections.

Current Product Backlog

The customer (the Product Owner in SCRUM terminology) is responsible for creating the list of functions and features the final solution should contain. This list may change in future iterations as a result of the Product Owner participating in a demo of the solution.

Prioritized Backlog

The Product Owner with the collaboration of the SCRUM team prioritizes the functions and features in the current Product Backlog. There is no prescribed method for completing this prioritization, but it is based on criteria supplied by the Product Owner. MoSCoW would do just fine. The SCRUM Team identifies the features and functions it believes could be implemented in the 30-day Sprint to follow.

Sprint Backlog

The SCRUM Team has a prioritized list of the functions and features they have estimated can be built in the coming Sprint. For the last half of the Sprint Planning Meeting they put a high-level plan together as to how they intend to complete the work that has been assigned to the coming Sprint. That plan contains a list of the tasks that have to be done in order for the Sprint Backlog to be completed. The RBS is helpful to this planning task. By further decomposing the functions and features in the Sprint Backlog they can define specific tasks that can be taken as work assignments by the SCRUM Team. Any sequencing of appropriate tasks can be denoted in the plan.

The Planning Phase of an Iterative SDPM Strategy for the Rational Unified Process Model

Figure 19-4 is the Planning Phase of the Incremental SDPM strategy for the Rational Unified Process model.

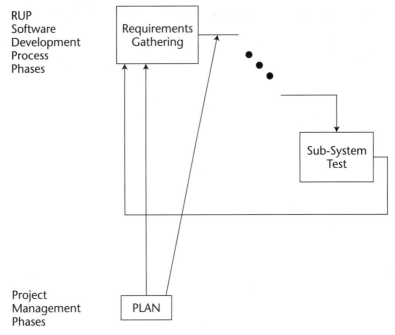

RUP
Software
Development
Process
Phases

Requirements
Gathering

Sub-System
Test

Project
Management
Phases

PLAN

Figure 19-4: Planning Phase of an Iterative SDPM strategy for the Rational Unified Process model

There are two levels of plan that need to be constructed for the Iterative SDPM strategy for the Rational Unified Process model.

- An overall plan, a high-level phase plan that covers all iterations
- A low-level iteration plan that looks inside each iteration

The overall plan is done once at the beginning of the project as part of the initial requirements gathering phase. The iteration plan is done right after the completion of the requirements gathering phase in each iteration.

Overall Plan

The overall plan is a brief description of the framework of the project. It specifies the duration and number of iterations, how to choose the deliverables for each iteration, and how to track project performance (all of which are described in the following subsections). The best time to prepare this plan is at the end of the initial requirements gathering phase.

Iteration Duration and Number

For most cases, an iteration will last from 2–6 weeks. As project size and team size increase, the length of an iteration also increases. The important thing to keep in mind is to maintain the meaningful involvement of the customer. That is difficult to do if the iterations are 3 months long. In the early stages of a project, it is best to keep the iterations as short as possible while building customer involvement. Once you are confident that the customer is committed and involved, you can begin to lengthen the iterations. Whatever duration you decide on, you must be able to fit them into the overall project time box. For example, if iteration duration has been set at 4 weeks and the project time box is 1 year, then you can plan to have 13 iterations. As the project work commences you will find reason to lengthen or shorten the next iteration. Later iterations will have to be adjusted to make up the slack or the deficit.

Assigning Deliverables to Iterations

In the overall plan, you should assign deliverables to the first iteration only. The choice is usually one made by the customer with the advice of the team. The choice is usually one of creating (or adding) the most business value possible within the duration of the coming iteration.

Tracking Project Performance

Any number of metrics can be tracked.

- The percentage of identified requirements that have been successfully implemented. (Keep in mind that the total number of requirements identified changes with each iteration as a result of learning and discovery in previous iterations.)
- The number of requirements/functions/features completed in an iteration divided by the number of requirements/functions/features planned.
- The number of scope change requests submitted per iteration.
- The trend over time of any of the preceding metrics.

Iteration Plan

Each iteration begins with an updating of the requirements list from all previous iterations. This means that the list of unfulfilled requirements grows and its priorities realign. That is why any detailed planning beyond the next iteration doesn't make sense. Armed with the updated and prioritized list of unfulfilled requirements, the customer and the project team will plan the next iteration. This plan is not unlike the detailed plan you create for a Linear SDPM strategy.

There will be a Work Breakdown Structure (WBS) (an updated RBS would be good to have for this exercise), task duration estimates, precedence diagrams, and a project schedule.

The Planning Phase of an Iterative SDPM Strategy for the Dynamic Systems Development Method

Figure 19-5 is the Planning Phase of the Iterative SDPM strategy for the Dynamic Systems Development Method.

Planning is done in two separate phases of the Iterative SDPM strategy for the Dynamic Systems Development Method.

- In the Feasibility Study Phase, there is a one-time planning activity to outline the project plan at a high level.

- During the Business Study Phase, additional information was gathered and used to update the Outline Plan.

    The Business Study Phase can be repeated a number of times. That comes about when additional business functionality is discovered during the Implementation Phase that could not be handled in the current iteration and will have to be handled in a later iteration.

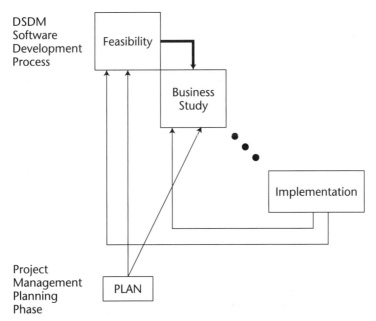

Figure 19-5: Planning Phase of an Iterative SDPM strategy for the Dynamic Systems Development Method

Outlining the Project Plan

The Outline Plan is an additional check on the feasibility of the project. The Outline Plan focuses on the development aspects of the project. The question to be answered is "Is the development of this solution likely to be successful?" or in other words, "Can we do what we say we are going to do?" A further question is, "Is the Dynamic Systems Development Method the appropriate approach for this project?"

Identifying and Prioritizing Functionality

This is the first deliverable from the Business Study Phase. First a business process model is developed. It focuses on the processes to be automated or improved. Usually this is done in facilitated workshops under the leadership of an experienced facilitator. From the processes to be automated or improved, a list of functional development efforts is compiled and prioritized. The prioritization is needed so that the most important functions will be worked on first and the less valuable ones left for later in the project. Function groups may be formed as a first pass at iterative planning. Technical dependencies between functions may alter the grouping and the sequencing. For the most part, the higher priority functions are developed earlier with dependent functions developed scheduled accordingly.

Documenting Architectural Specifications

Using the functionality to be developed, the technical team members begin the design of the architecture that supports the high-priority functionality. This will change based on later discoveries, but at least it gives a starting point for later and more detailed architecture designs.

Discussion Questions

1. Compare and contrast each of the Iterative SDPM strategies with respect to extent of customer involvement, efficient use of time, support of scope change requests, and use of scarce resources. Rank each Iterative model based on each comparative variable. Is any one of the models a clear choice?

2. How might project characteristics affect your choice of an Iterative model?

3. How might customer involvement affect your choice of an Iterative model?

4. Refer back to Figure 11-2. Which sub-systems would you develop using an Iterative approach? Specify which Iterative approach you would use and why.

CHAPTER 20

The Iterative SDPM Launching Phase

The purpose of organizations is to exploit the fact that many decisions require the participation of many individuals for their effectiveness.

Kenneth J. Arrow
Nobel laureate in economics

Chapter Learning Objectives

After reading this chapter, you will be able to:

- ◆ Understand the complications added to the Launching Phase when using an Iterative SDPM strategy
- ◆ Know how to plan for scope change requests
- ◆ Anticipate and mitigate resource scheduling situations
- ◆ Anticipate and mitigate iteration scheduling changes
- ◆ Know how to launch an Iterative SDPM strategy for the Evolutionary Waterfall Development model
- ◆ Know how to launch an Iterative SDPM strategy for the SCRUM model
- ◆ Know how to launch an Iterative SDPM strategy for the Rational Unified Process model
- ◆ Know how to launch an Iterative SDPM strategy for the Dynamic Systems Development Method

All of the Launching Phase discussion for the Linear and Incremental SDPM strategy situations apply to the Iterative SDPM strategy and will not be repeated here (you can see discussions of Linear and Incremental Launching Phases in Parts II and III). Iterative SDPM strategy projects follow the same procedures as by-the-book projects, except they repeat those procedures several times over the life of the project. Within a single repetition all of the launching activities that are done in the Linear and Incremental SDPM strategies are done in the Iterative SDPM strategy. However, you do have some additional considerations, ones that arise because the Iterative approaches all produce the current but incomplete solution at each iteration. Over a series of iterations, the complete solution emerges. This chapter identifies those additional considerations of the Iterative approach and discusses how they are handled in the Launching Phase of Iterative SDPM Strategies for the Evolutionary Waterfall model, the SCRUM model, the Rational Unified Process model, and the Dynamic Systems Development Method.

The Launching Phase of an Iterative SDPM Strategy

Figure 20-1 highlights the Launching Phase of an Iterative SDPM strategy.

An Iterative SDPM strategy differs in principle from an Incremental SDPM strategy in one important way—in the Iterative SDPM strategy each iteration presents the customer with the complete solution. The Incremental SDPM strategy, on the other hand, presents the customer with a portion of the known solution at each increment. While scope change requests are the bane of the Linear or Incremental SDPM strategies, they are the fuel of the Iterative SDPM strategy. You face four tasks that must be done in the Launch Phase of an Iterative project that are not done or are done differently in the Launch Phase of a Linear or Incremental project. They are as follows:

- Processing scope change requests
- Handling solution handoffs
- Handling solution rollout
- Scheduling iterations

These are discussed in the subsections that follow.

Processing Scope Change Requests

The Iterative SDPM strategy is the first of three strategies covered in this book for which scope change requests are vital. The partial solution cannot evolve to a complete and acceptable solution in the absence of scope changes. Scope changes are the redirecting force that keeps the solution converging on the needs of the customer and of the business. Scope change requests come about as the customer responds to the solution; they request added or changed features based on their direct experiences using the solution. Also, some iterations result in a release of a partial solution to the end users, and some scope change requests come about as a response to the true end user experience.

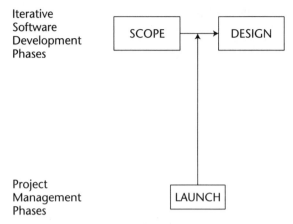

Figure 20-1: The Launching Phase of an Iterative SDPM strategy

Because iterations are of short duration, it is best to integrate scope changes as part of the next iteration's planned functionality. When they are received, the project impact statement can be developed, but any action can be postponed until the appropriate iteration. Interrupting the work flow in the current iteration is too disruptive and that is why a postponement makes the most sense.

Convergence on the final and acceptable solution is an important characteristic of all Iterative strategies. The frequency and number of scope change requests over time is a good measure of the progress of the search for an acceptable solution. The number of scope change requests submitted between each iteration is an easy metric to track. That number may increase for the first few iterations, but then should begin to decrease. If it doesn't, that is a good indicator of trouble. You might want to spend some time with the customer and try to discover the reasons for the anomalies.

Handling Solution Handoffs

As in the Incremental project, you have no guarantee that the team who worked on the just completed iteration can work on the next or any other iteration. Early in the project where the solution is not well-defined or developed, a switch of team members is not too likely. Late in the project, however, the senior management team might decide that the current solution is good enough and further work can be postponed—not good music to the ears of the customer or the project team. They have worked hard to get the solution to where it is and would like to see the project come to a successful and complete conclusion. In any case, documenting the solution is a good strategy. That documentation should also speak to the additional revisions that were planned or identified but not yet implemented. Because the customer and the team may not know when the solution reaches a point where it can be stabilized and further work postponed, they will have to document the solution starting at some iteration where there is sufficient value and the project is at risk of cancellation.

Handling Solution Rollout

Solution rollout occurs for one of two reasons.

- The first is the obvious business value that can accrue for getting a solution, even a partial solution, out to the end user. It means an earlier return on investment for the enterprise—a hard deal to pass up!

- The second reason is to get feedback on the solution with the hopes of discovering missing features and otherwise improving the business value of the final solution. Sounds good, but you have a price to pay. You get feedback from the early adopters of the software solution, and you must pay attention to their input. Because the project is still under development, the only response to the end user has to come from the team that is simultaneously doing development. As the end user experiences the current but incomplete solution, he or she will have a myriad of suggestions to pass on to the development team. All suggestions must be addressed in some manner, which will require the development team to spend time analyzing the suggestions, fitting them into the current solution (if that makes sense), and finally prioritizing them for development and integration into the solution.

Scheduling Iterations

The customer needs some time between iterations to practice with the partial solution produced in the just completed iteration. From that practice come suggestions for additions and changes that are added to the scope change requests already on file. This becomes the input to the planning phase for the next iteration.

The Launching Phase of an Iterative SDPM Strategy for the Evolutionary Development Waterfall Model

The Launching Phase of an Iterative SDPM strategy for the Evolutionary Waterfall model has all four of the considerations stated in the previous section for the generic Iterative situation. Figure 20-2 highlights the Launching Phase of an Iterative SDPM strategy for the Evolutionary Development Waterfall model.

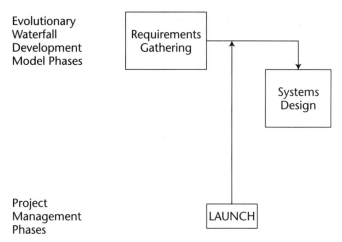

Evolutionary
Waterfall
Development
Model Phases

Project
Management
Phases

Figure 20-2: The Launching Phase of an Iterative SDPM strategy for the Evolutionary Development Waterfall model

Keep in mind that the Evolutionary Development Waterfall model embraces a wide range of situations depending on the extent to which the solution is complete. The more features that are missing from the solution, the more time you will need to allocate to the customer as they work with deliverables from previous iterations. The number and frequency of scope change requests is a function of the degree to which the solution is incomplete. Initially you might expect a higher frequency of scope change requests. As you near the final and complete solution, the number and frequency of scope change requests should begin to diminish. If that is not the pattern, you have a serious problem to contend with—the solution is diverging instead of converging to completeness. The customer should sense this before you do, but it does require some corrective action. Remember, the customer and your team are on a journey of discovery and may need the time to reflect, discuss, and propose additional features or modifications to those already implemented. It is important at Launch time to establish the rules of the engagement. In addition to those tasks established for the Linear and Incremental models, I have previously noted in this chapter that four tasks are unique to an Iterative SDPM strategy; this holds true if you use the Evolutionary model. Those four, which are applicable in the Evolutionary Development Waterfall model, are listed and described in the subsections that follow.

Processing Scope Change Requests

Scope change requests in the Iterative approach, unlike those in the Linear or Incremental approaches, are necessary if a solution is to be found. As the customer experiences the current solution, they will have several suggestions for change and addition to the solution. These are the input that is necessary for that solution to emerge. Treat every one as though it were gold. Give them serious consideration and feedback to the customer about further changes that might improve their request. These scope changes are the foundation on which additional conversations should be held and even more functions and features discovered.

Handling Solution Handoffs

Similar to the Incremental approach, the Iterative approach may be subject to changes in team membership between iterations. For the Iterative approach this is far more serious a change than it was for the Incremental approach. The reason is that the solution is not fully known in the Iterative approach as compared to the Incremental approach. That puts an added burden on the team and especially the project manager to document the solution to date as well as to document ideas not yet integrated into the solution, and to maintain a fluid and seamless handoff to the new team members. The Iterative approach deals with far more complex projects than does the Incremental approach and that also adds to the challenge of affecting a good handoff.

And so you see one of the major weaknesses of the Iterative SDPM strategy as compared to the Incremental SDPM strategy. The Iterative SDPM strategy requires considerably more documentation than does the Incremental SDPM strategy regardless of the model being used.

Handling Solution Rollout

As was the case for the Incremental approach, the Iterative approach requires the project manager to work closely with all resource providers to make sure that the resources committed to each iteration are in fact committed. A strong communications plan is needed with periodic reminders of those commitments. Any change in the project plan due resulting from slippages should be communicated to the resource managers. There should be no surprises.

Scheduling Iterations

The major advantage of the Iterative approach over the Incremental approach is that the Iterative approach is not subject to rework. The solution unfolds as new features and functions are discovered and integrated into the solution. The plan comes together in a just-in-time way rather than developed completely at the beginning of the project. The Iterative approach does not have any re-planning to worry about.

The Launching Phase of an Iterative SDPM Strategy for the SCRUM Model

Figure 20-3 illustrates the Launching Phase of an Iterative SDPM strategy for the SCRUM model.

SCRUM departs from the other models in the Iterative SDPM strategy in that it is a customer-driven model. The Product Owner (the customer) generates the Product Backlog List and participates in a Sprint Planning Meeting at the beginning of each iteration. At that meeting, the updated Product Backlog is discussed and a decision made as to what is to be developed in the next Sprint. The Sprint Team spends the last half of the Sprint Planning Meeting deciding how to produce the agreed upon deliverables.

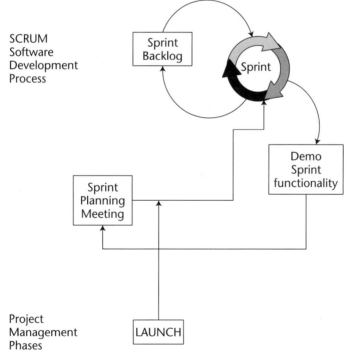

SCRUM Software Development Process

Project Management Phases

Figure 20-3: The Launching Phase of an Iterative SDPM strategy for the SCRUM model

The Launching Phase is a project team activity. They have agreed with the customer as to what is to be built in this Sprint and have put together a preliminary plan as to how they will accomplish it. In the Launching Phase they need to establish (or re-establish) the rules of the engagement. SCRUM teams are typically a small team of subject matter experts (SMEs). If they have worked together before, the rules of the engagement have been crafted in earlier projects and are merely reconfirmed here. If they have not worked together before, their first pass at the rules of the engagement is probably subject to change as they learn each other's work styles and habits. Trust must be built up among the team. Each team member operates pretty much independently of the others. They are self-directed as is the team self-directed. Many would argue that a project manager isn't needed in such a SCRUM team. That is a defensible position to take. In some situations, the SCRUM Master, who is charged with ensuring that the team follows and practices the principles of SCRUM, may act as project manager but only in a coaching or facilitating role.

The Launching Phase of an Iterative SDPM Strategy for the Rational Unified Process Model

The Launching Phase of an Iterative SDPM strategy for the Rational Unified Process model is highlighted in Figure 20-4.

The Iterative SDPM strategy for the Rational Unified Process is a chain of iterations so that each iteration includes the entire project life cycle. Launching is therefore repeated at each new iteration. In some cases, establishing the rules of the engagement may be trivial and nothing more than a validation of the rules of the engagement as defined in the previous iteration. This will happen with teams that are experienced working with one another. In other cases, launching may be a bit more formal. Such would be the case with a team that is new or a team whose members may have changed since the last iteration. New teams can learn from the previous iteration how to improve the rules of the engagement. In other words, they can iterate on how best to conduct the business of the team.

The Launching Phase of an Iterative SDPM Strategy for the Dynamic Systems Development Method

The Launching Phase of an Iterative SDPM strategy for the Dynamic Systems Development Method is highlighted in Figure 20-5.

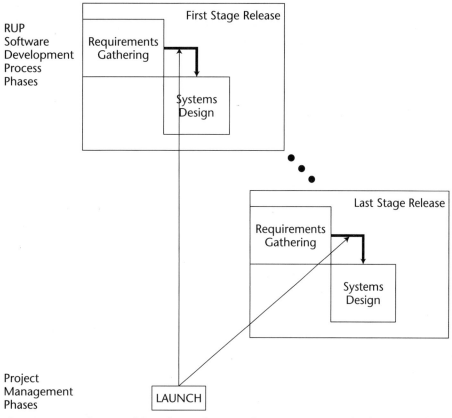

Figure 20-4: The Launching Phase of an Iterative SDPM strategy for the Rational Unified Process model

As you can see, the Launching Phase of an Iterative SDPM strategy for the Dynamic Systems Development Method can be iterative itself. That will happen if the current Implementation Phase concludes that the Business Study Phase must be repeated. That can dramatically alter the project going forward. The current solution might be scrapped, and a new one might take its place. That means a new team, or at least some new team members, so the Launching Phase must be repeated. As in the case of the Rational Unified Process, that Launching Phase might just consist of a re-validation of the previous iteration's rules of the engagement. However, with a new team, the Launching Phase is a definition of the rules of the engagement.

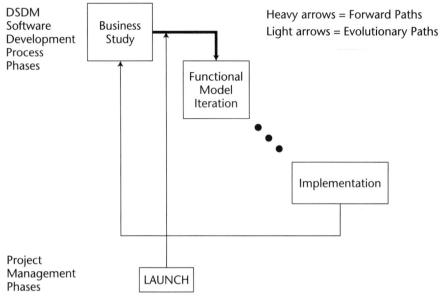

Figure 20-5: The Launching Phase of an Iterative SDPM strategy for the Dynamic Systems Development Method

Discussion Questions

1. You are Pepe Ronee and you have run the Iterative SDPM strategy by the book. But you have this gnawing feeling that what Dee wants is not what she needs. Within the context of the Iterative SDPM strategy, what could you do?

2. Referring to the case study, how would you prepare your new team to adopt an Iterative approach?

CHAPTER 21

The Iterative SDPM Monitoring and Controlling Phase

Method is much, technique is much, but inspiration is even more.

Benjamin Nathan Cardozo
U.S. Supreme Court Justice

Chapter Learning Objectives

After reading this chapter, you will be able to:

- ◆ **Understand the Monitoring and Controlling Phase of the Iterative SDPM strategy**
- ◆ **Discuss the role of project reviews in the Iterative SDPM strategy**
- ◆ **Implement strategies to handle the Iterative project scope change requests**
- ◆ **Understand the Iterative SDPM strategy for the Evolutionary Waterfall Development model**
- ◆ **Understand the Iterative SDPM strategy for the SCRUM model**
- ◆ **Understand the Iterative SDPM strategy for the Rational Unified Process model**
- ◆ **Understand the Iterative SDPM strategy for the Dynamic Systems Development model**

All of the Monitoring and Controlling discussion for the Linear and Incremental SDPM strategy situations apply to the Iterative SDPM strategy and will not be repeated here. Iterative SDPM strategy projects follow the same procedures as by-the-book projects, except they repeat those procedures several times over the life of the project. Within a single repetition, all of the Monitoring and Controlling activities done in the Linear and Incremental SDPM strategies are done in the Iterative SDPM strategy. But you do face some additional considerations. They arise because the Iterative approaches all produce the current but incomplete solution at each iteration. Over a series of iterations, the complete solution emerges. In this chapter, I identify those additional considerations and discuss how they are handled in the Monitoring and Controlling Phase of Iterative SDPM strategies for the Evolutionary Waterfall model, the SCRUM model, the Rational Unified Process model, and the Dynamic Systems Development Method

The Monitoring and Controlling Phase of an Iterative SDPM Strategy

Figure 21-1 highlights the Monitoring and Controlling Phase of an Iterative SDPM strategy.

As noted in a previous chapter, the Iterative SDPM strategy differs in principle from an Incremental SDPM strategy in one important way. In the Iterative SDPM strategy each iteration presents the customer with the complete solution. The Incremental SDPM strategy, on the other hand, presents the customer with a portion of the known solution at each increment. Monitoring the development of a known solution is quite different from monitoring the development of a partially unknown solution.

- **Known solution**—The monitoring can be based on the degree to which the solution is completely developed. The plan will reflect the complete solution and how it will be developed over time and at what cost. A number of metrics can be used, as can earned value analysis (see Appendix J for the details of earned value analysis). The focus on these metrics will be the extent to which the actual progress aligns with the planned progress—in other words, on the process.

- **Partially unknown solution**—Process metrics will not work. The focus on the deliverables will have to be the basis for the metric. Features planned for the next iteration compared to features delivered would be the basis of most metrics that apply in the Iterative SDPM strategy. There are three topics to discuss relative to those metrics. They are:

  - Project progress reporting
  - Discovery of new/revised features
  - Processing scope change requests

These are discussed in the subsections that follow.

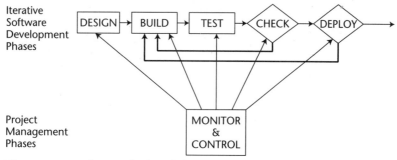

Figure 21-1: The Monitoring and Controlling Phase of an Iterative SDPM strategy

Project Progress Reporting

Iterative SDPM Strategies focus on delivering business value, not on meeting time, cost, and task parameters specified in the project plan. Therefore, progress reporting focuses on the number of deliverables planned versus the number actually delivered as an indicator of iteration success. Progress against the overall solution can be measured by the trend in the cumulative number of scope change requests. A trend that is increasing at an increasing rate indicates a lack of convergence on the final solution. This is depicted in Figure 21-2 by Project A. For this trend, the process of learning and discovery is still active. The final solution may still be some distance off. On the other hand, a trend that is increasing at a decreasing rate is suggestive of an intermediate solution that is converging on the final solution. The final solution may be near. This is depicted in Figure 21-2 by Project B.

Of the two, Project A may be suggestive of a project that is out of control. If the project is one in which the customer is not at all sure of the current solution or if the current solution lacks considerable definition, then the increasing rate of growth may be describing a project that is wandering around and not likely to converge on an acceptable solution. If the behavior persists beyond a reasonable number of iterations, it would be worth doing an analysis to determine whether the project is drifting out of control or whether it can be expected to settle into a converging pattern. It may be drifting out of control because the initial solution was not only missing features, but also had some of its functions poorly defined or implemented. This may indicate that an Adaptive SDPM strategy would have been a better choice for the project. Project B is indicative of a healthy project. Solid learning and discovery are taking place and the customer is gaining in confidence that a final solution is not far off. This should reassure the project team that the Iterative SDPM strategy was the proper choice.

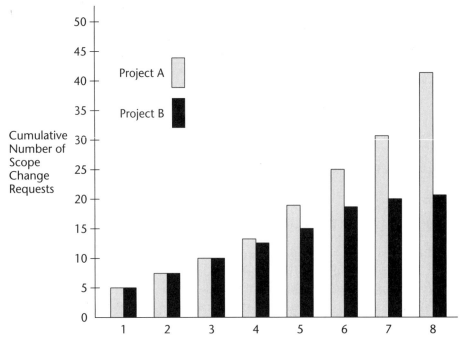

Figure 21-2: Divergent and convergent trends

Discovery of New/Revised Features

Another useful metric for an Iterative SDPM strategy is the number of new/revised features in each iteration. Figure 21-3 shows three typical patterns.

- Project A shows a project whose discovery and learning is growing at a healthy rate for the first several iterations, flattens for a few iterations, and then begins to tail off later in the project indicative of a project nearing its completion.

- Project B displays rather erratic behavior. The number of new/revised features starts at a high level and persists at that level for several iterations. This team is having trouble coming to acceptable closure on most features.

- Project C never really gets its act together. It is possible that only a few minor features need revision and that not much in the way of new features are needed and that the initial solution might be very close to the final solution. Certainly, the customer would know whether or not this is the case. Barring that, however, what is this curve telling us? Most likely there is a problem with customer involvement.

Separately tracking the frequency of new features and revised features may be informative. Figure 21-4 shows some typical patterns.

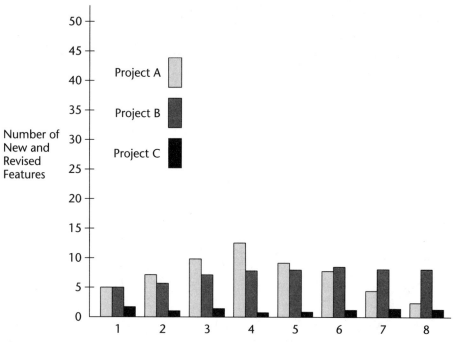

Figure 21-3: Frequency of new/revised features by iteration

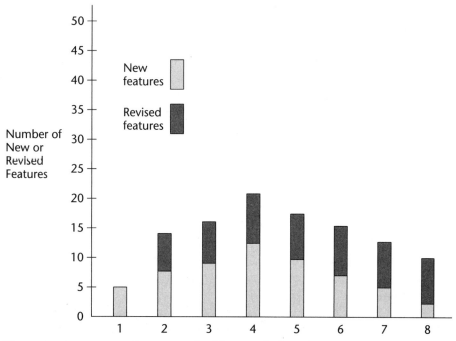

Figure 21-4: Patterns of new or revised features by iteration

Notice that the frequency of total features and new features follows a pattern that has been associated with the healthy project. The frequency increases, plateaus, and then begins to decrease. Such a project looks healthy. But look more closely at the companion pattern for revised features. It holds steady or is increasing. This means that the customers are continually changing their minds about the new features that have been added. Some of the changes are probably for features that have already been changed one or more times. There is no evidence that there is closure on the part of the customer for new features already implemented. While this project is getting close to a final solution as far as new features are concerned, the customer is not at all satisfied with those features. In other words, the project is not healthy. Perhaps the solution lies in doing a better job of specifying the details of new features before they are integrated into the then current solution.

Processing Scope Change Requests

The Iterative SDPM strategy is the first of three for which scope change requests are vital. The partial solution cannot evolve to a complete and acceptable solution in the absence of scope changes. Scope changes are the redirecting force that keeps the solution converging on the needs of the customer and of the business. Scope change requests come about as the customer responds to the solution. They request added or changed features based on their direct experiences using the then solution. Some iterations result in a release of a partial solution to the end users, and some scope change requests come about as a response to the true end user experience. Since iterations are of short duration, it is best to integrate them as part of the next iteration's planned functionality. When they are received, the project impact statement can be developed, but any action should be postponed until the appropriate iteration. Interrupting the work flow in the current iteration is too disruptive and that is why a postponement makes the most sense.

Convergence on the final and acceptable solution is an important characteristic of all Iterative strategies. As discussed earlier in the chapter, the frequency and number of scope change requests over time is a good measure of the progress of the search for an acceptable solution. The number of scope change requests submitted between each iteration is an easy metric to track. That number may increase for the first few iterations but then should begin to decrease. If it doesn't, that is a good indicator of trouble. You might want to spend some time with the customer and try to discover the reasons for the anomalies.

Scope change requests can come at any time during an iteration, and they should. Whenever the customer or a team member identifies a change that they believe will add to the business value of the solution, they should document it with a scope change request. These will be collected and held until the end of the iteration and then prioritized for the build phase of a future iteration along with all other features not yet integrated into the solution.

The Monitoring and Controlling Phase of an Iterative SDPM Strategy for the Evolutionary Development Waterfall Model

The Monitoring and Controlling Phase of an Iterative SDPM strategy for the Evolutionary Waterfall model has all three of the considerations stated in the previous section for the generic Iterative SDPM strategy. Figure 21-5 highlights the Monitoring and Controlling Phase of an Iterative SDPM strategy for the Evolutionary Development Waterfall model.

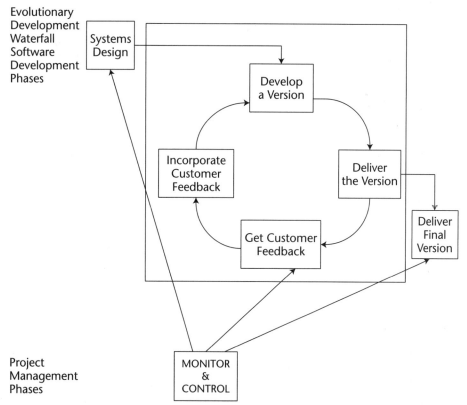

Figure 21-5: The Monitoring and Controlling Phase of an Iterative SDPM strategy for the Evolutionary Development Waterfall model

First note that Systems Design is a systems development phase that is not part of the iterations that define this SDPM strategy. Systems Design is done once with all of the functions having been identified and a number of features also identified for each function. While the systems design may be high level in some aspects, it is relatively complete at the outset. The iterations then focus on further refinement of existing features or the identification of new features. As noted previously in the chapter, the number and frequency of scope change requests is an indicator of the degree to which the solution is incomplete. Tracking the number or cumulative number of scope change requests over time is a recommended metric. Initially you might expect a higher frequency of scope change requests. As you near the final and complete solution, the number and frequency of scope change requests should begin to diminish. If that is not the pattern, you have a serious problem to contend with. The solution is diverging instead of converging to completeness. The customer should sense this before you do, but it does require some corrective action. Remember, the customer and your team are on a journey of discovery and may need the time to reflect, discuss, and propose additional features or modifications to those already implemented.

The Monitoring and Controlling Phase of an Iterative SDPM Strategy for the SCRUM Model

Figure 21-6 illustrates the Monitoring and Controlling Phase of an Iterative SDPM strategy for the SCRUM model.

The focus of monitoring and control here is the status of the Sprint Backlog. When created, the Sprint Backlog contains the features that the team had planned to build and integrate in 30 days. The nature of a SCRUM is to have the team of subject matter experts (SME) focus on development and not be hampered with a lot of non-value-added work—such as formal reporting. In addition to the features metrics introduce earlier in this chapter, one additional, simple metric is of value to those who simply must have some measure of progress. In the Sprint Planning Meeting, the team should have provided individual estimates of the duration (or labor) needed for each feature in the coming Sprint. Compare that to the actual duration (or labor) expended. The ratio of cumulative actual to cumulative estimated gives some measure of efficiency. Additionally, the percentage of the Sprint Backlog completed (as measured by the hours of duration) compared to the percentage of working hours expended gives some measure of the status of the Sprint Backlog. If that metric is too cumbersome to be useful, you might simply take the percentage of features completed divided by the percentage of Sprint days expended. If that ratio is greater than 1, you are ahead of schedule. If that ratio is less than 1, you are behind schedule. This is a crude measure, but it substitutes for more formal and rigorous metrics.

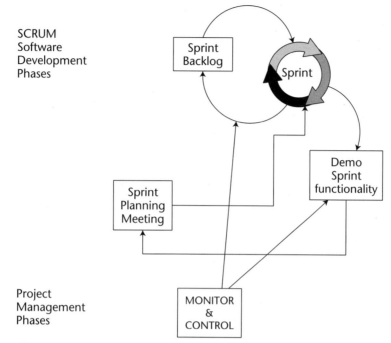

Figure 21-6: The Monitoring Phase of an Iterative SDPM strategy for the SCRUM model

The Monitoring and Controlling Phase of an Iterative SDPM Strategy for the Rational Unified Process Model

The Monitoring and Controlling Phase of an Iterative SDPM strategy for the Rational Unified Process (RUP) model is highlighted in Figure 21-7.

RUP can be a heavy or light process. On the heavy side you have formal use case documentation, formal systems, and detailed design documents. These are revised and updated as each iteration is completed. On the light side, you can take a more tacit approach to use cases with much of the documentation being understood among the team members. Use cases often are the infrastructure on which the solution is built, and the library of use cases can be the documentation depository.

The total number of use cases implemented compared to the total number to be implemented is the simplest metric for measuring status and progress of the SDPM strategy for the Rational Unified Process model. Presumably the use cases have been prioritized and developed in priority order in accordance with the dependency relationships among the use cases.

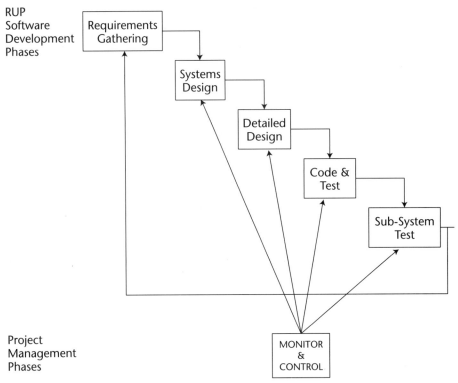

Figure 21-7: The Monitoring Phase of an Iterative SDPM strategy for the Rational Unified Process model

Within an iteration, a use case itself can be used as the metric to measure progress. Each use case has a number of features aligned with it. The number of features implemented as a percentage of the total number of features in the use case is a quick measure.

The Monitoring and Controlling Phase of an Iterative SDPM Strategy for the Dynamic Systems Development Method

The Monitoring and Controlling Phase of an Iterative SDPM strategy for the Dynamic Systems Development method is highlighted in Figure 21-8.

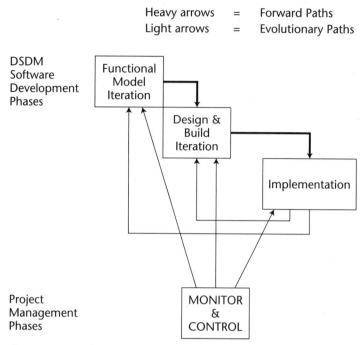

Figure 21-8: The Monitoring and Controlling Phase of an Iterative SDPM strategy for the Dynamic Systems Development Method

As you can see, the Monitoring and Controlling Phase of an Iterative SDPM strategy for the Dynamic Systems Development Method can be iterative itself. That will happen if the current Implementation Phase concludes that the Functional Model Phase must be repeated. That can dramatically alter the project going forward. The current model must be revised; in fact, it might be scrapped and a new one might take its place. That would be a rather drastic turn of events. The more likely result is a partial redesign of the functional model. This comes about as a result of having to eliminate some functionality from the solution in order to meet an aggressive implementation date. If that functionality is deemed necessary for the complete solution, the Functional Model Phase is repeated. Similarly, the Design and Build Iteration Phase is repeated if some of the details of the design had to be left out in order to meet an aggressive implementation date.

The metrics used to track the likelihood of completing both the functional model specifications and the detailed design features can be adapted from the metrics defined previously for the Evolutionary Development Waterfall model.

Discussion Questions

1. Project A in Figure 21-2 reflects the performance of your Iterative approach. Obviously, there are too many scope change requests, and the project is not converging on an acceptable solution. What action might you take to resolve the dilemma?

CHAPTER 22

The Iterative SDPM Closing Phase

We cannot afford to forget any experiences, even the most painful.

Dag Hammerskjold
Secretary of the United Nations

Chapter Learning Objectives

After reading this chapter, you will:

- ◆ Understand the Closing Phase of the Iterative SDPM strategy
- ◆ Have a working knowledge of the Closing Phase of the Iterative SDPM strategy for the Evolutionary Development Waterfall model
- ◆ Have a working knowledge of the Closing Phase of the Iterative SDPM strategy for the SCRUM model
- ◆ Have a working knowledge of the Closing Phase of the Iterative SDPM strategy for the Rational Unified Process model
- ◆ Have a working knowledge of the Iterative SDPM strategy for the Dynamic Systems Development Method

Once the customer has signed off that the requirements have been satisfactorily met, the Closing Phase begins. That sounds like a simple transition, but is it?

The Closing Phase of the Iterative SDPM Strategy

Figure 22-1 illustrates the Closing Phase of the Iterative SDPM strategy. Note that there are really two parts to the Closing Phase just as there were in the Incremental SDPM strategy:

- Closure with respect to each of the iterations
- Closure with respect to the completed project

Of course, there are some similarities between the Closing Phases of an Iterative SDPM strategy and Incremental SDPM strategy, but you find some key differences as well.

The similarities center on requirements satisfaction at the completion of each iteration. In the Incremental SDPM strategy, these closings were pretty much routine because all requirements had been clearly and completed defined and documented up front. That is not so in the Iterative SDPM strategy. Here many of the iterations have integrated new/revised functions and/or features, and their acceptance is not at all assured. Some iterations may close with some functions and/or features excluded from the acceptance only to be reworked in a later iteration. In other words the Closing Phase of an Iterative SDPM strategy contains some unknowns as compared to the Closing Phase of an Incremental SDPM strategy, which has largely been identified much earlier in the project.

When compared, the next iteration in both strategies shows similar differences. In an Incremental SDPM strategy, the deliverables in the next iteration were planned well in advance and, one hopes, have not changed. In an Iterative SDPM strategy, the deliverables for the next iteration are planned at the beginning of the iteration. In other words, it is just-in-time planning. In an Iterative SDPM strategy you have to anticipate changes in direction for the project going forward. Whatever was learned in the just completed iteration may redirect the project for the next iteration. Also keep in mind that that redirection may not be permanent. The next iteration may result in yet another change of direction for the project. That is the nature of the Iterative SDPM strategy. It is a process of continuous learning and discovery. That is also characteristics of the Adaptive and Extreme SDPM strategies, which are discussed in detail in Parts V and VI of this book.

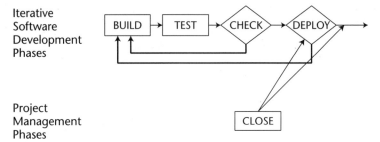

Figure 22-1: The Closing Phase of the Iterative SDPM strategy

Iterative SDPM Strategy for the Closing Phase of the Evolutionary Development Waterfall Model

Figure 22-2 illustrates the Closing Phase of the SDPM strategy for the Evolutionary Development Waterfall model.

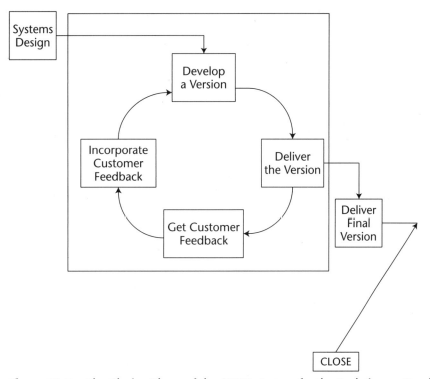

Figure 22-2: The Closing Phase of the SDPM strategy for the Evolutionary Development Waterfall model

The Evolutionary Development Waterfall is not structured to deploy partial solutions at the close of each iteration, although that is not excluded from the model. Formally there is only one close and that is when the customer is satisfied and the final version can be released. That close is identical to the Linear SDPM strategy situation. The customer can opt for an intermediate release but probably only for the purposes of getting outside opinions about functions and features from selected affected groups. The model does not include a formal deployment of intermediate solutions to the end user as in the case of the Incremental SDPM strategy.

For the Iterative SDPM strategy, there are two types of lessons learned to discuss.

Iteration Lessons Learned

Each project that follows the Evolutionary Development Waterfall model presents the development team with a need to learn to work with the customer. Every iteration presents the development team with information to help it to work more effectively and efficiently with their customer team. Even if the development team has worked with the customer team on previous projects, the combination of project type and customer type is still a unique experience. For each project, some customers will naturally take a proactive role in the project while others will be more reactive. Both are acceptable behaviors. The important factor is that the involvement is meaningful. The importance of this behavior grows as you move further out in the agile landscape to the Adaptive and Extreme projects.

At the completion of each iteration, the customer and the developers should take stock of what happened in terms of process and how it could be improved for the next iteration. Here are a few questions that might help that improvement effort:

- Are both parties satisfied that they were able to provide input to the solution?
- Was each party listened to by the other party?
- Did each party feel free to offer new or novel ideas?
- Is there a synergy between the two parties?
- Does each party feel that there is progress toward an acceptable solution?
- Is the entire team working more effectively than earlier in the project?
- What tasks could have been done better? How?
- What tasks are working well and should be retained?

Project Completion Lessons Learned

Two points are worth mentioning here.

Lessons Learned About Working with This Customer

Every customer group is going to be different. What works with one may not with another. Accordingly, for each customer group you should build a file of dos and don'ts. What are the strengths of working with this customer? What are the weaknesses and how were they mitigated? You will find all of this information useful in later projects, but so will other teams that may have an opportunity to work with your customer group.

You might want to give the customer a chance to input into this process. Perhaps a survey by an outside person—the Project Management Office (PMO), for example—would provide valuable information on how the development team could have improved how it worked with the customer. Such a survey can be very simple. The following questions might help improve the process for the next project:

- How did the development team bring us into the project?
- Was our involvement real or contrived? How could it have been improved?
- Did the development team help us understand the alternatives? How?
- Did the development team understand out business problem? How could they have done a better job?

Lessons Learned About the Evolutionary Development Waterfall Model

On a more global basis, the development team should be looking for ways to improve the Evolutionary Development Waterfall model. This would benefit any team that chooses to use this model. As you know, these types of projects require active and meaningful involvement by the customer. Just how to attain and sustain that involvement is valuable information for any team that follows with this customer or any other customer. Record your successes and your failures and find a way to share that information.

Iterative SDPM Strategy for the Closing Phase of the SCRUM Model

Figure 22-3 illustrates the Closing Phase of the SDPM strategy for the SCRUM model.

The SCRUM model is customer-driven. At the completion of each sprint, the customer ("Product Owner" in SCRUM terminology) interacts with the current version of the solution through a demo of it. New features and functions may be identified at that time and added to the Product Backlog to be prioritized by the Product Owner. The deliverables from each iteration are not processed through any formal type of Closing Phase. That is reserved for what becomes the final version of the solution. The final version is the last version completed before either the budget has been expended or the time box for the project has run out. The Closing Phase is formal to the extent that the Product Owner accepts the current solution as the solution that can be released to the end users. There are no formal acceptance criteria for the Closing Phase of the Iterative SDPM strategy for the SCRUM Model. Sprints continue until the product is releasable by the Product Owner. Once deemed releasable, the product then goes through another SCRUM project to turn it into a releasable product.

During the project, there are two types of lessons learned to discuss: the Sprint Planning Meeting and the Sprint itself. At the completion of the project, there are additional lessons learned.

Sprint Planning Meeting Lessons Learned

The Sprint Planning Meeting affords an opportunity for the Product Owner to meet with the Sprint Team. The input to this meeting is the newly prioritized Product Backlog. Together with the Product Owner, the Sprint Team decides how far down that prioritized list they can reasonably be expected to produce deliverables in the next 30-day Sprint. The interaction between the Product Owner and the Sprint Team is the interaction that provides learning opportunities. What might those be? A couple key learning opportunities are as follows:

- How do you negotiate changes in priority to preserve function or feature dependencies?
- How do you avoid over-committing the size of the next Sprint Backlog?

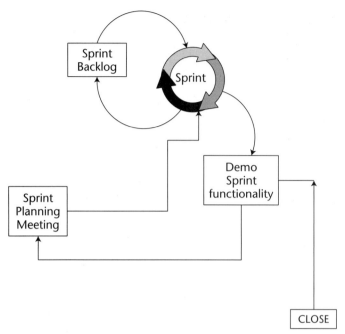

Figure 22-3: The Closing Phase of the SDPM strategy for the SCRUM model

Sprint Lessons Learned

Beginning with the Sprint Planning Meeting, the Sprint Team has to decide how it can accomplish the Sprint Backlog in the allotted 30-day time box. This can range from a formal to an informal plan. As the team moves from sprint to sprint, it learns how best to create their plan. For newly formed teams this can be a painful experience. A good SCRUM Master is invaluable in helping the team reach an acceptable level of proficiency. The major obstacle in gaining that proficiency is for the team to accept the responsibility for its success or failure. Fifteen-minute daily team meetings are a good way to practice becoming a team. Each team member should be encouraged to share exactly where they are in the work that they have taken on. Team members must be encouraged to raise their hands and acknowledge that they are behind and need help. When that begins to happen, it is a sign that the group is morphing into a team. How to make that happen is the lesson learned.

Project Completion Lessons Learned

As discussed earlier in the chapter, future projects that follow the Iterative SDPM strategy for the SCRUM model can benefit from your project having documented the lessons learned across the entire project. Include the Product Owner in gathering data for that documentation. The SCRUM model can be a very effective approach for those projects that meet the criteria for a SCRUM approach. The more experiences that can be shared across the organization, the better for all concerned.

Iterative SDPM Strategy for the Closing Phase of the Rational Unified Process Model

Figure 22-4 illustrates the Closing Phase of the SDPM strategy for the Rational Unified Process model.

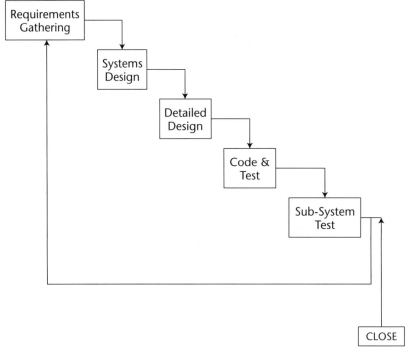

Figure 22-4: The Closing Phase of the SDPM strategy for the Rational Unified Process model

The Rational Unified Process model is a very popular Iterative approach. Its success in the organization depends heavily upon the documentation legacy that has been created from past projects that followed the RUP approach. That legacy commonly includes libraries of reusable code, but it can also contain libraries of reusable Work Breakdown Structures (WBSs) and use cases. Therefore the Closing Phase of the Iterative SDPM strategy for the Rational Unified Process model consists of assuring the appropriate documentation has been added to the reusable libraries. This is no small task. Just wanting to build a reusable library doesn't mean it will happen. Special training is needed to translate project-specific artifacts to reusable library artifacts. That makes the Rational Unified Process model documentation-heavy if the organization intends to realize a return on its investment.

One could successfully argue that a Rational Unified Process project never ends. Technically speaking, they would be correct because implementation is followed by transition to a continuous improvement project. In fact, a Rational Unified Process Project ends when the sponsor is no longer willing to support the project or some hard deadline has been reached.

Iterative SDPM Strategy for the Closing Phase of the Dynamic Systems Development Method

Figure 22-5 illustrates the Closing Phase of the SDPM strategy for the Dynamic Systems Development Method.

The Closing Phase for the SDPM strategy for the Dynamic Systems Development Method is the most inclusive of the Iterative SDPM Strategies presented in this chapter. The complexity arises in deciding which of several alternatives should be undertaken in light of what has happened so far on the development of the solution. As part of the closure on the Implementation Phase, an evaluation of the current solution takes place. The result of that evaluation is to decide how, if at all, the project should go forward. There are four possibilities, as discussed in the following subsections.

Solution Accepted

The evaluation concludes that the acceptance criteria have been satisfactorily met and the project work is complete. No further action is required.

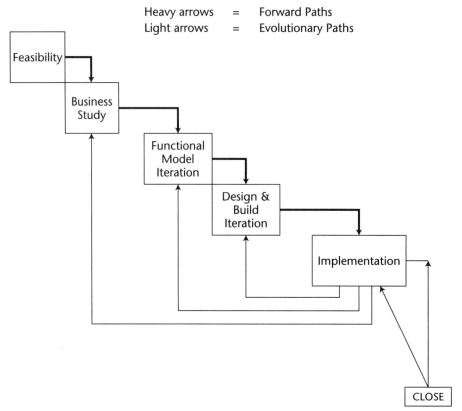

Figure 22-5: The Closing Phase of the SDPM strategy for the Dynamic Systems Development Method

Revise Solution Design

The evaluation concludes that the acceptance criteria have not been successfully met but that modifications to the current design could be made that would make the then revised solution acceptable. Usually this is the result of having to delete some minor feature or function because of time or budget constraints. This feedback loop to the Design and Build Iteration is to simply add in the deleted feature or function, bringing the solution into compliance with the original acceptance criteria. This action is similar to any Iterative deliverables that fails to meet the acceptance criteria and calls for some rework—for example, one or more features or functions may not meet the customer needs as reflected in the acceptance criteria.

Revise Functional Model

This evaluation can have serious consequences. The functional model has failed to meet the acceptance criteria. This is often because of the limits of time or budget that resulted in part of the designed functionality being deleted from the implemented solution. This feedback loop is undertaken to integrate that deleted functionality into the solution, thus meeting the original acceptance criteria. This action could have serious budget and schedule ramifications.

Repeat Business Study

This is usually the result of a discovery during development of some additional functionality that was not part of the original functional model. It could not be included in the current solution because of time and/or budget considerations. Its inclusion after implementation means that the business study would have to be repeated to validate the inclusion of the discovered functionality.

Discussion Questions

1. You have completed the first few iterations and the customer seems very satisfied with the progress to date. Not too much in the way of added features are surfacing. There are two possibilities:

   a. The first is that all business value has already been identified during requirements gathering and there will not be any added features forthcoming. You might as well switch to a Linear SDPM strategy for the remainder of the project.

   b. The customer hasn't really bought into the Iterative approach you are taking and that is the reason there have been few scope change requests. Give them some time and encouragement and they will become more comfortable with the approach.

   What would you do and why?

2. Refer to the Routing sub-system in the case study: How would you deploy a working solution that is acceptable as the initial version but clearly needs to be improved? Are there some functions that should be part of the initial version and other functions that might be better assigned to a later version? Consider the time needed to affect a complete solution versus the time needed to roll out an initial solution.

CHAPTER 23

The Iterative SDPM Strategy Summary

We generally need someone to show us things which should be apparent to the eyes of all.

Francisco Algarotti
Italian writer and scientist

Chapter Learning Objectives

After reading this chapter, you will be able to:

- ◆ Compare traditional versus agile projects
- ◆ Understand the fundamental differences between traditional and agile project managers
- ◆ Understand the fundamental differences between traditional and agile project teams
- ◆ Compare traditional to agile project planning
- ◆ Know the impact of scope change management on traditional and agile projects

The Iterative SDPM strategy is our first entry into the world of the agilist. To the traditionalist, this is a strange world in that many of the basic premises that their project world is based on do not hold true in the agile world. This closing chapter of Part IV discusses some of those differences in an attempt to morph the thinking of the staunch traditionalists.

Traditional Versus Agile Projects

Traditional projects are clearly defined and their requirements, functions, and features well documented and understood. Despite the fact that this specificity is unlikely to happen, this leads the project manager into the development of a complete project plan with all resources scheduled to tasks and tasks scheduled to specific time frames.

Agile projects do not have a complete requirements document in place and can discover it only by doing the project. This leads the project manager to shy away from speculation and develop a plan only for the known requirements. This just-in-time planning approach is driven by the discovery and learning of missing or mis-specified functions and features. The solution unfolds through the iterations that define the agile approaches to projects. Agile projects tend to be high risk compared to traditional projects. The inability of the customer and the development team to completely and clearly define requirements is a clue that something is different and needs to be treated differently. The unknowns are the factors driving the risk higher.

In the end, the traditional and agile approaches converge on the same set of artifacts. They just arise at different points in time along the project life cycle. There is one major difference between the two sets of artifacts. The traditional approach would have identified and planned for a number of deliverables that either changes after being deployed or were never done at all. On the other hand, the agile approaches would have planned only what was finally delivered. There is a distinct absence of waste in the agile project as a result.

Traditional Versus Agile Project Managers

Traditional project managers manage against the budget, schedule, and scope. To the traditionalist, the metrics follow directly from the project plan. A budget and a timeline have been established, and the work needed to deliver against the scope has been determined. The natural approach is to manage against that plan. That means establishing metrics that measure variance from budget and/or timeline, establish trip wires that define out-of-control situations or the presence of distressed projects, initiate the necessary root cause analyses, and implement the necessary corrective action. None of this has anything to do with meeting client needs or the delivery of business value to the customer. It would not be unusual to complete a project that finished within the time frame and budgetary limitations only to find that the customer is not satisfied.

Agile project managers manage against the deliverables and business value. The focus is entirely different. While the budget and timeline are certainly important, they are not the most important. Would you rather satisfy the customer but be a week late or 5 percent over budget. Or would you rather be within budget and timeline but have an unsatisfied customer? Where is the real business value? Probably in the former situation, but definitely not in the latter.

What does all of this say about the project managers of traditional versus agile projects? The traditional project manager is trained to deliver process. They work to reduce risk and preserve the constraints of time and money on the project. The agile project manager is trained to deliver product. To a certain extent, they embrace as the means to discovery and learning how to maximize the value they deliver to their customer.

Traditional Versus Agile Teams

The traditional projects can work with distributed teams of specialists and junior technical staff. The junior technical team members work under the direct supervision of the more senior members of the team. Because of this relationship, it is not necessary for the traditional team members to be co-located. That is always the desirable situation, but in the traditional project it is not a necessity. These teams can be effective if they are dealing with a well-defined project and can proceed on the basis of functional requirements documents.

Agile projects should have co-located teams of senior technical staff. As you move out to the adaptive and extreme projects, the team composition becomes more senior and in less need for supervision. Co-location is an important factor in the success of the agile project. That is not always possible in today's organization but should be sought whenever practical. These teams can be effective if they have really committed to the project and are willing to work in the absence of detailed documentation. They are forced to draw upon their own creativity and interact with their fellow team members. They are called upon to have a commitment to the project that goes beyond any commitment asked of the traditional team members.

The differences between the two types of teams are considerable.

Traditional Versus Agile Project Planning

To the traditionalist, planning is something you do once at the very beginning of the project. For the traditional project manager resources are scheduled and committed against a project plan and then managed to conformance with that plan. Any variances from the plan are corrected as needed.

Having a complete plan sounds great, but is it worth the effort? Every change request that is approved requires some modification to the plan. The modification almost always requires some rescheduling, negotiating with resource managers to adjust commitments, and finally documenting and communicating the changes to all affected parties. If you cost out the changes, you can see that time was spent on parts of the plan that are no longer needed. That time spent was wasted time—non-value-added time to the agilest.

To the agilist, planning is something you do just-in-time and continuously through the project. The agilest does not speculate on the future as does the traditionalist. Change can render that time wasted time and that is a no-no to the agilest. Just-in-time planning is the only thing that makes sense to the agilest. For the agile project manager the only meaningful metric is business value delivered as measured against business value planned, and corrections are made as necessary.

Traditional Versus Agile Scope Change Management

Scope change is the bane of the traditional project manager. Every scope change request brings with it the work needed to generate the project impact statement as the deliverable from having processed the change request. That can be substantial, especially if there is a high frequency of scope change requests. Someone on the team has to process that scope change request, and that takes away from the time they would otherwise spend doing the productive work of the project.

Scope change is a necessary ingredient for the agile project manager to be successful.

WARNING

Spend the time to understand the project, the customer, the business environment, the enterprise, and the resource pool before you make the decision as to the best SDPM strategy.

Discussion Question

1. Your organization has been a staunch promoter of the traditional approaches to project management and systems development. However, senior management is not at all satisfied with the results. Project failure rates are too high and customers never seem to be satisfied with the results. Senior management is open to the contemporary practices of agile project management and has asked you to lead a project to integrate agile approaches into the company's project management processes. What are your concerns, and how would you approach such a project?

PART FIVE

Adaptive ESPM

This is your second step into the unknown. All of the conditions that applied in the Iterative approach apply here, but there is more. Even less of the solution is known in this approach. Not only are features missing or vague, but also are many of the functions that drive the solution. It is fair to say that the Adaptive approach handles software development projects where the solution is just not known. It must be learned and discovered through iterations. This is a common situation. Unfortunately not too many software developers realize that, or they do but they proceed with their tried and true approaches anyways. They are a failure on its way to happen. The Adaptive approaches discussed in this part are designed for exactly the situation where the solution is not known but has to be learned.

CHAPTER 24

Adaptive SDPM Strategy

*It is a mistake to look too far ahead. Only one link of
the chain of destiny can be handled at a time.*
Winston Churchill

There is no data on the future.
Laurel Cutler
Vice Chairman, FCB/Leberf Katz Partners

Chapter Learning Objectives

After reading this chapter, you will be able to:

◆ **Explain the Adaptive SDPM strategy**

◆ **Have a high-level understanding of the Adaptive Project Framework and
Adaptive Software Development models**

The Adaptive models accommodate a higher level of uncertainty and complexity than the Iterative models. In that sense they fill a void between the Iterative and Extreme models. Keep in mind that solution discovery is the focus of these models. Each iteration in the Adaptive models must address not only task completion for newly defined functions and features but also solution definition through function and feature discovery.

The Adaptive SDPM Strategy

This is the first approach you encounter where the solution is not known. It might be totally unknown or partially unknown. Unlike the Iterative approach where some depth of the solution is not known (features, for example), the adaptive approach is missing both depth and breadth of the solution. Figure 24-1 depicts the Adaptive SDPM strategy for those models that meet the conditions of an incomplete solution due to missing features and functions.

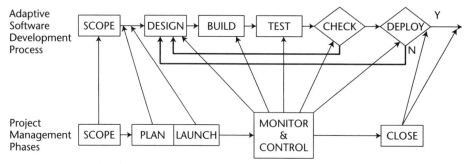

Figure 24-1: Adaptive SDPM strategy

The models that lie between the iterative and extreme models are called adaptive models. The two that you will study here are the Adaptive Project Framework (APF) and the Adaptive Software Development (ASD) models. In both models the goal is clearly defined but the solution to reach that goal is not. These are processes that thrive on learning, discovery, and change. In APF you start from the known and journey into the unknown. In time, and with enough cycles, you hope that a solution will emerge. ASD is a more formal process focusing strictly on software development. In that sense APF is a more robust model.

The Adaptive SDPM strategy, like other adaptive approaches, is best suited to projects whose solution is only partially known. The degree to which the solution is known might vary over a wide range from knowing a lot but not all to knowing very little. The less that is known about the solution, the more risk, uncertainty, and complexity will be present. To remove the uncertainty associated with these projects the solution has to be discovered. That will happen through a continuous change process from iteration to iteration. That change process is supposed to create a convergence on a complete solution. In the absence of that convergence, Adaptive projects are frequently cancelled and restarted in some other promising direction.

The success of Adaptive SDPM strategies is leveraged by accommodating frequent change. Change is the result of learning and discovery by the team and, most important, by the customer. Because change will have a dramatic impact on the project, only a minimalist approach to planning is employed. Planning is actually done just in time. No effort is wasted on planning the future. The future is unknown, and any effort at planning that future will be viewed as non–value-added work. All Quadrant 2 (the goal is clearly defined but the solution is not) approaches minimize non–value-added work.

Adaptive SDPM strategies can also be applied to new product development, process improvement, and research and development projects. This is especially true of APF.

Scope Phase

The Scope Phase in the Adaptive SDPM strategy is a high-level scoping activity because not much is known about the solution (requirements, functions, and features). They have to be discovered and learned through iteration much like the Iterative SDPM strategy. In that strategy, however, you know a lot about the solution; it was just some of the features that you weren't so sure about. For the Adaptive situation, the scoping activities merely set the boundaries and the high-level parameters that will be the foundation on which we proceed to learn and discover. As part of the Scope Phase deliverables, you will document requirements, as you know them; functionality, as you know it; and features, if you know any. In addition, you will specify the number of cycles and cycle length for the first cycle. Compared to the Iterative strategy, the Adaptive strategy requires intimate involvement with the customer. As you will see, customers have more of a directive role in the project than in the three strategies discussed previously in the book. Without their meaningful involvement, the project has little chance of success.

Plan and Launch Phases

Planning at this point in the Adaptive SDPM strategy is high-level planning. Because not too much is known about the solution, planning cannot be done to any level of specificity. Rather, the planning involves structuring what is known about the solution. That will cover prioritizing what little functionality you were able to define in the Scope Phase.

The Launch Phase will be the same as we discussed in the previous strategies. The launch activities will include establishing team operating rules, decision making processes, conflict management strategies, team meetings, and problem solving approaches. The only difference will be defining the approach that will be used to establish subteams to work on concurrent development tasks.

Monitor and Control Phases

As you move from the Iterative SDPM strategies to the Adaptive SDPM strategies, you find a marked shift from formality to informality when it comes to these phases. That move to informality makes room for the marked increase in creativity that the team is called upon to deliver. Creativity and formality are not comfortable bedfellows. You need to give the team and the customer the best opportunity you can to be successful and that means relaxing the need for status reporting and controlling of the schedule. The nature of these projects is that they are focused on delivering value rather than being focused on meeting time and cost criteria.

As Figure 24-1 illustrates, the monitor and control functions pertain to the cycle spanned by design and check. As part of that control function the team collects whatever learning and discovery took place and records it in the Scope Bank. All change requests go into the Scope Bank as well. No changes are implemented within a cycle. All changes and other learning and discovery are reviewed at the check point. The review results in placing newly discovered functions and features into a priority list for consideration at the next or some future cycle.

Close Phase

The Close Phase produces the typical artifacts: lessons learned, validation of success criteria, and so forth. In addition to those, you might have items left in the Scope Bank that were not included in any cycle build. These are to be documented and held for the next version of the solution.

Types of Adaptive SDPM Strategies

The two models included in these strategies cover those situations where the solution is not known. It might be that very little of the solution in terms of functionality and accompanying features can be identified at the outset of the project. The project management methodology that is integrated with the software development life cycle must be capable of discovering the unknowns and transforming them into the known. In other words, the solution will emerge as part of the project work.

Adaptive Project Framework

The Adaptive Project Framework (APF), which I discuss at great length in my book *Effective Project Management: Traditional, Adaptive, Extreme, Third Edition* (Wiley, 2003), unlike most of the approaches in Quadrant 2, is not limited to software development. Although it is beyond the scope of this book to discuss, APF is equally at home with software development, process improvement, product development, and research and development projects.

APF is an approach that spans the gap between Traditional Project Management (TPM), which includes both the Linear and Incremental SDPM strategies, and Extreme Project Management (xPM), which includes the Extreme SDPM strategies. APF and xPM are also called *agile project management*—a term that is more inclusive of the contemporary approaches to software development. APF applies in those cases where what is needed is clearly defined but how to produce it isn't as obvious. Clearly the traditional approach won't work when the solution is not known. For the traditional approach to work you need a detailed plan, and if you don't know how you will get what is needed, you can't generate the Work Breakdown Structure (WBS). So how can you generate a detailed plan? What about the extreme approach? I'm guessing that the "agilists" would argue that any one of the agile approaches would do just fine, and probably you could use one of them and do quite well. Unfortunately, many of them ignore the fact that you know what is needed. It's a given. Why not use an approach that has designed in the fact that you know what is needed? In a number of informal surveys the respondents report that at least 70 percent of their projects met the conditions of the APF project, but they were approaching them using a modified version of a TPM approach. Unfortunately many of these well-meaning attempts ended in failure. The vast majority of their projects are a closer fit with APF than either TPM or xPM.

The Adaptive Scope Triangle

Figure 24-2 helps interpret this for us in the form of a scope triangle. The fundamental concept underlying APF is that scope is variable and within specified time and cost constraints, APF maximizes business value by adjusting scope at each iteration. It does this by making the client the central figure in deciding what constitutes that maximum business value. At each iteration, the client has an opportunity to change the direction of the project based on what was learned from previous iterations. This constant adjustment means that an APF project's course is constantly corrected to ensure the delivery of maximum business value. In other words, change is embraced not avoided. Planning takes on a whole new meaning in APF. Initial planning is done at a high level and is component- or functional-based. TPM planning is activity- and task-based. In APF, planning at the micro level is done within iterations. It begins with a mid-level component or function based WBS and ends with a micro-level activity and task-based WBS. I like to think of it as just-in-time planning. The underlying strategy to APF planning is not to speculate on the future; it's a waste of time. *"When in doubt—leave it out."* At each iteration, plan for what you know to be factual. So, planning is done in chunks where each chunk represents work that requires only a few weeks to complete.

Figure 24-2: The APF Scope Triangle

Definition of an Adaptive Project

Consider the following working definition of an adaptive project:

*An adaptive project consists of a **number of cycles** each comprising a sequence of unique, complex, and connected activities that must be completed within fixed time and budget constraints, and deliver maximum business value.*

Note how the definition differs from how you would define a traditional project. In particular, take note of two significant differences at this time:

- An adaptive project consists of a number of cycles. That is not the case with a traditional project.
- The adaptive project is successfully completed when maximum business value has been delivered. The traditional project would state "according to specification." The burden with the traditional project is clearly on the shoulders of the client. They must define what "specification" means. APF, on the other hand, is a collaborative approach. Both the client and the project team define success.

What Is the Adaptive Project Framework?

For those businesses that have only recently realized the pain of not having a project management process in place and are struggling to adapt traditional practices advocated by the Software Engineering Institute (SEI) and PMI to nontraditional projects, or the extreme practices advocated by the agilists, I say STOP WASTING YOUR TIME! It's time to pay attention to the signals coming from the business environment and discover how projects can succeed given the fast-paced, constantly changing, and high-quality demands of the new business model. The project survival strategy that you are going to explore is what I am calling Adaptive Project Framework (APF). This is definitely not your father's project management. I don't even use the word "management." APF represents a shift in thinking about projects and how they should be run. Consider the following characteristics of APF:

- Thrives on change rather than avoiding it
- Continuously adapts to the project situation
- Adopts traditional and extreme tools and processes
- Based on the principle that you learn by doing
- Seeks to get it right every time
- Client-focused and client-driven
- Grounded in a set of immutable core values
- Ensures maximum business value
- Squeezes out all non–value-added work
- It works—100 percent of the time!

APF Core Values

You might have noticed that one of the characteristics of APF mentioned in the previous section is that APF is grounded in a set of immutable core values. This means that APF is more than just a framework; it represents an entirely new way of thinking about clients, how best to serve them, and how to add significant business value to the enterprise at the same time. Through its core values APF establishes a collaborative environment within which the client and the development team can work effectively to create business value for the enterprise. This way of thinking is embodied in six core values:

- **Client-focused**—The phrases "walk in the shoes of the client" and "always do what is right for the client" express what it means to be client-focused. This is the most important of the core values. The needs of the client must always come first as long as they are within the bounds of ethical business practices. This can never be compromised. More than simply keeping it in mind, being client-focused must be obvious through your interactions with one another and with your clients. And it doesn't mean a passive acceptance of whatever the client might request. Client-focused also means that you have clients' best interests at heart, obligating you to challenge ideas, wishes, and wants whenever you believe challenge is called for. We want to do the right things for the right reasons and to always act with integrity.

- **Client-driven**—Engage the client in every way that you can. You want them to have significant meaningful involvement, to have the sense that they are determining the direction that the project is taking. Remember, it's their money, and they have the right to choose how it will be spent. At the extreme, this would mean having the client take on the role and responsibilities of the project manager. This will not happen very often but look for opportunities to make it happen. More likely is the situation of co-project managers—one from the client and you. In this effective arrangement a clear and established co-ownership exists and you both share equally in the success and failure of the project. Research tells us that this is a key to successful implementation. We say that this is a key factor to successful projects.

- **Incremental results early and often**—Deliver a working application to the client as early as possible, especially in cases where the real solution for the client has not yet surfaced despite all best efforts. The functionality of the first iteration of the application will be very limited but it should deliver business value and give the client an early feel for what the final deliverables will be. Giving the client an opportunity to work with something concrete is always better than asking them to react to some vague concept. If we can put something in front of the client early in the project and repeat it often, they get a sense of belonging and ownership—they become engaged in the project. You should clearly sense their engagement very early in the project. That's important. In later iterations we can lengthen the cycle and not risk losing the client's interest.

- **Continuous questioning and introspection**—When you build a solution iteratively you have more chances for creativity, more opportunity to adjust as better and more valuable features or functions are discovered. The client and the project team should always be looking for improvements in the solution or the functionality offered, both as the cycle build proceeds and as they look back at previous cycles. All of this learning and discovery comes together in the Client Checkpoint Phase, where the client and the project team propose, discuss, and approve changes in a spirit of openness. Neither party should be afraid to offer or challenge an idea or the real value of some present or future deliverable. Teams and clients should understand that if anyone of them has an idea and doesn't share it, it's dereliction of duty.

- **Change is progress to a better solution**—One of my colleagues is often heard saying: "You're always smarter tomorrow than you are today." He is referring to improving estimates over time but his comment applies to

APF as well. APF starts with the client and you coming to a definition of what is needed and what will be delivered. Your efforts will be good and in earnest, but remember all you have done to this point is take the best guess you can as to what will be done. That guess might turn out to be very good but that is not important. What is important is that working with the deliverables from the first cycle gives both parties a better picture of what should be delivered and, because of their experiences with early deliverables, makes them smarter as they move to uncover the solution going forward in the next cycle.

- **Don't speculate on the future**—Someone once said: "If you don't know the future, why waste time planning for it?" APF strips out all non–value-added work. Planning is done just in time. It focuses on what is known about the solution, not on what is not known. It discovers a new function or feature and then plans how to build and integrate it into the solution. When in doubt, leave it out. APF is designed to spend the client's money on business value not on non–value-added work.

An Overview of the APF

Figure 24-3 is a graphic portrayal of how the APF is structured. The next five short sections dig deeper into each of the five phases of APF shown in the figure: Version Scope, Cycle Plan, Cycle Build, Client Checkpoint and Post-Version Review.

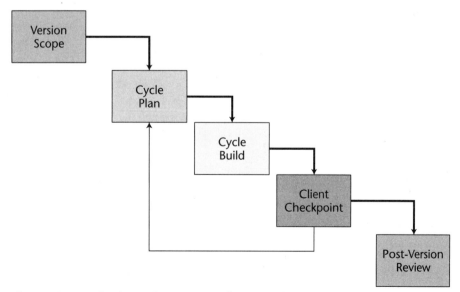

Figure 24-3: Adaptive Project Framework

Version Scope

The Version Scope (see Figure 24-4) is the kick-off of an APF project. A rough idea of the needs is documented, and a high-level plan constructed as to how the project will go forward. The Version Scope might be completed in a matter of hours, or it might take several days. It all depends on the level of complexity and uncertainty present in the project.

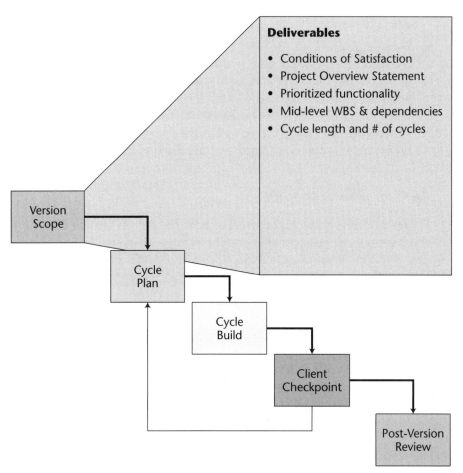

Figure 24-4: Adaptive Project Framework (Version Scope)

Cycle Plan

The Cycle Plan (see Figure 24-5) will be repeated a number of times before this project is complete. Each Cycle Plan begins with a decision as to what functionality from the prioritized list will be developed during the coming cycle. Cycle length generally falls within a 2–6 week period. Many of the planning tools used in a TPM project are used in this phase.

Cycle Build

The functionality to be built in this cycle is input and a detailed plan put together for the cycle. It is usually a whiteboard, sticky note, marking pen type of plan. The Cycle Build ends when the timebox expires, not before and not after. Any tasks not complete are reconsidered and reprioritized in the next cycle plan (see Figure 24-6).

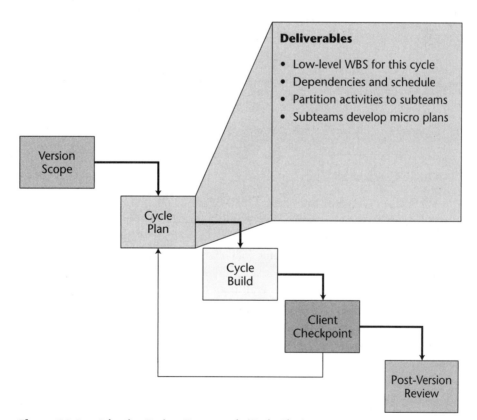

Figure 24-5: Adaptive Project Framework (Cycle Plan)

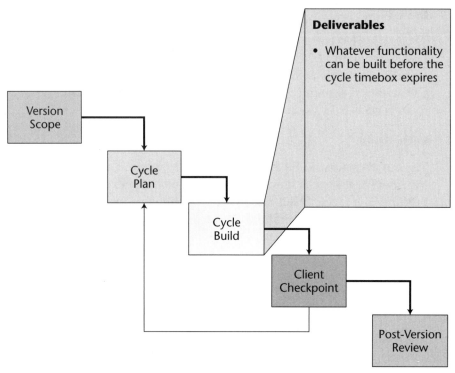

Figure 24-6: Adaptive Project Framework (Cycle Build)

Client Checkpoint

The Client Checkpoint Phase (see Figure 24-7) is a critical review that takes place after every Cycle Build is completed. The client and provider perform a quality review of the functionality produced in the just competed cycle. It is compared against the overall goal of maximum business value, and adjustments are made to the high-level plan and the next cycle work as appropriate. Clients and project teams take all they have learned during the cycle and consider it along with the functionality that had originally been assigned to the coming cycle. The result is a revised prioritization of functionality for the coming cycle.

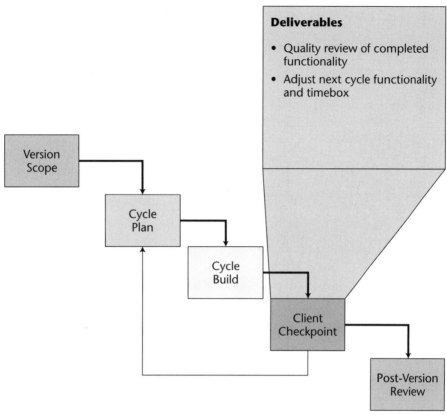

Figure 24-7: Adaptive Project Framework (Client Checkpoint)

Post-Version Review

In the Version Scope Phase, you and the client develop measurable business outcomes that are the rationale on which the project is undertaken in the first place. These outcomes are, in essence, success criteria in that the project is considered a success if, and only if, these outcomes are achieved. Accordingly, the main focus of the Post-Version Review is to check how you did with respect to the success criteria, to document what you learned that will be useful in the next version—how well APR worked on this project, how well the team used APF—and to begin thinking about the functionality for the next version (see Figure 24-8).

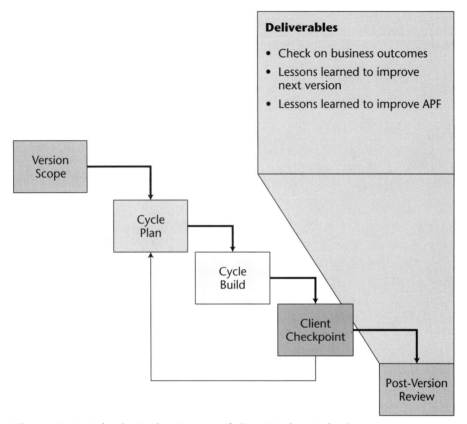

Deliverables

- Check on business outcomes
- Lessons learned to improve next version
- Lessons learned to improve APF

Figure 24-8: Adaptive Project Framework (Post-Version Review)

Figure 24-9 illustrates the Adaptive SDPM strategy for APF.

You might recall that beginning in Quadrant 2 of the software development landscape you are engaged with projects where the solution is not known. This is not the Iterative situation discussed in the previous part of the book where some of the features of the solution were not known. Here the solution itself is not known. That translates into a project management life cycle that is not as directive as the Linear, Incremental, and Iterative classes. The five phases of the project management are still present but not at the level previously encountered. Here more of the formality and documentation gives way to the tacit behavior of the team.

APF Software
Development
Process

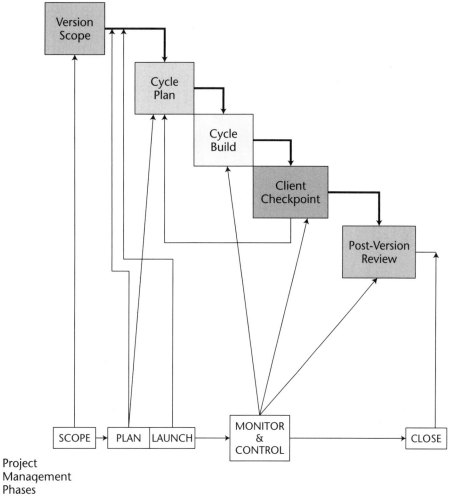

Project
Management
Phases

Figure 24-9: Adaptive SDPM strategy for APF

Adaptive Software Development

The second model I want to take a look at as an Adaptive SDPM strategy is ASD. Adaptive Software Development (ASD) is fully described in a book by James A. Highsmith III titled *Adaptive Software Development: A Collaborative Approach to Managing Complex Systems* (Dorsett House, 2000). ASD has three phases: Speculate, Collaborate, and Learn. The description that follows is a brief adaptation of his presentation.

These three phases are shown in Figure 24-10.

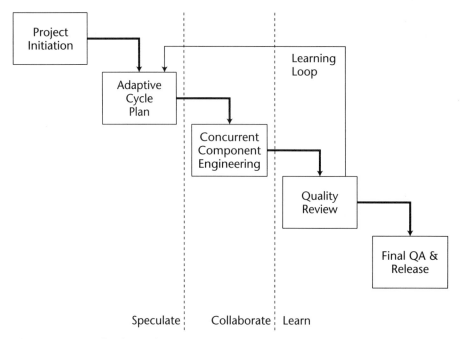

Figure 24-10: The three phases of ASD

Speculate

Unlike the linear TPM, ASD is an adaptive approach. The Speculate Phase is nothing more than a guess at what the final goal and solution might look like. It might be correct, or it might be far from the mark. It really doesn't make much difference in the final analysis because the self-correcting nature of ASD will eventually lead the team to the right solution. "Get it right the last time" is all that matters.

Collaborate

A Speculate Phase has been completed, and it is time to take stock of where the team and client are with respect to a final solution. What great "ahas" did the team and the client discover?

Learn

What was learned from the just completed phase and how might that redirect the team for the next phase?

You might have noticed in Figure 24-10 that each of these three phases encompasses different activities. The following list takes a brief tour inside each of these three phases and explains the activities that go on there.

- **Project Initiation**—The objective of the Project Initiation Phase is to clearly establish project expectations among the sponsor, the client, the core project team, and any other project stakeholders. This would be a good place to discuss, agree upon, and approve the Project Overview Statement (POS). For a project of some size (more than 6 months) it might be a good idea to hold a kick-off meeting, which can last two to three days. During that time requirements can be gathered and documented and the POS written.

- **Adaptive Cycle Plan**—Other deliverables from the kick-off meeting might include the project timebox, the optimal number of cycles and the timebox for each, and objective statements for each cycle.

  Every cycle begins with a plan. These plans are high-level. Functionality is assigned to subteams, and the details are left to them to establish. This is at odds with TPM, which requires organized management oversight against a detailed plan. ASD is light when it comes to management processes.

- **Concurrent Component Engineering**—Several concurrent swim lanes are established for each functionality component. Each subteam is responsible for some part of the functionality.

- **Quality Review**—This is the time for the client to review what has been completed to date and revise accordingly. New functionality might emerge; functionality is reprioritized for consideration in later cycles.

- **Final QA and Release**—At some point the client declares the requirements met and there is a final acceptance test procedure and release of the product.

Unlike APF, ASD focuses exclusively on software development. Figure 24-11 shows the integration of the project management life cycle into the ASD life cycle.

WARNING

Adaptive models can accommodate quite a wide range of situations where some or even all of the solution cannot be defined. While the majority of projects will fall into this class, do not be too quick to make that judgment. Consider the project and what is known about the goal and solution. Perhaps an Adaptive model is the best choice. Even if that is the starting model, continue to ask whether it is the most appropriate model. As the project matures and more of the solution becomes evident, it might make sense to switch to one of the other models in the Linear, Incremental, or Iterative class.

ASD Software
Development
Process Phases

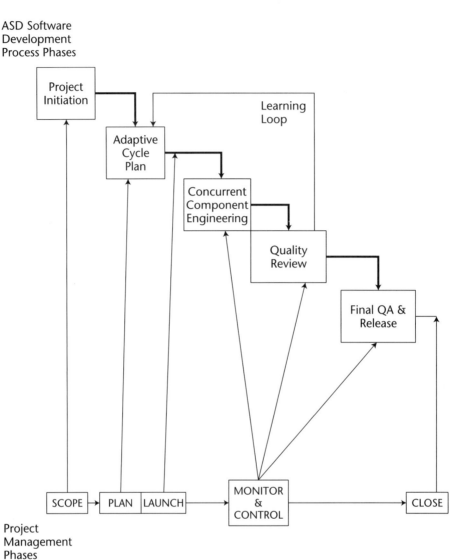

Project
Management
Phases

Figure 24-11: Adaptive SDPM strategy for ASD

Discussion Questions

1. The project has been progressing smoothly and according to plan when the customer manager changes. The new manager isn't willing to have his people participate at the level of the prior manager, and you feel that this will seriously affect the project. What actions would you take and why?

2. All of the ideas that are suggested come from the team and not from the customer. You feel that the final product will not be as good as it could have been because of that. How would you address this situation and why?

3. Refer to the case study: Which sub-systems would you develop using APF and why?

25

The Adaptive SDPM Scoping Phase

"Invention breeds invention."
Ralph Waldo Emerson
American essayist and poet

Chapter Learning Objectives

After reading this chapter, you will be able to:

- ◆ Explain the Scoping Phase of the Adaptive SDPM strategy
- ◆ Conduct the Scoping Phase of the Adaptive Project Framework
- ◆ Conduct the Scoping Phase of the Adaptive Software Development model
- ◆ Understand the role of the WBS in defining Adaptive project iterations
- ◆ Scope the Adaptive plan

The next strategy variation is to move from the Iterative SDPM strategy to the Adaptive SDPM strategy, which is discussed in this part of the book. Adaptive models arise out of the customer's inability to completely define requirements and obviously the features that accompany them. As is the case with the Iterative SDPM strategy, the customer may not be able to identify some of the features associated with known functionality. To find a complete solution, the customer will have to be more intimately involved throughout the entire project life cycle than has been the case in all previous strategies. With few exceptions, the projects that fall into the Adaptive models are new systems development projects.

The Scope Phase of an Adaptive SDPM Strategy

Projects that follow an Adaptive SDPM strategy are those for which a complete Requirements Breakdown Structure (RBS) cannot be defined at the outset and the customer and project team knows it. The situation might be characterized somewhat along the lines of Figure 25-1.

There is a cloud that covers the solution. The objective of the Adaptive SDPM strategy is to move the cloud and discover what lies behind it—in other words, to learn and discover what constitutes the full solution. The Adaptive SDPM strategy must accommodate not only the development of the known parts of the solution but also discovery of the unknown parts of the solution. Implementing the known parts of the solution is much like we discussed in the Incremental and Iterative SDPM strategies. Discovering the unknown parts of the solution will require a tight collaboration of the customer with the project team. It will look much like the pure R&D effort of the Extreme SDPM strategy. Probative ideas will be investigated in one or more cycles. Some will be rejected. Some will open up directions for further probes in later cycles. And some will result in more of the solution being uncovered and then implemented in later cycles. To do this effectively and efficiently is a challenge. The Scoping Phase will lay out the approach at a very high level.

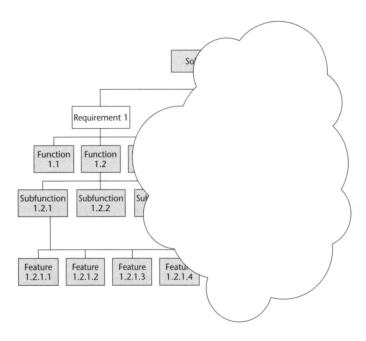

Figure 25-1: The initial RBS for an Adaptive SDPM strategy

Projects that adopt an Adaptive approach are obviously high-risk projects. The fact that there isn't an obvious solution may mean that an acceptable solution might not be found. Therefore, the types of projects that lend themselves to Adaptive approaches would, by nature, be critical mission projects for which a solution must be found if possible. The future of the business may well rest on finding this acceptable solution.

The Scoping Phase of the Adaptive SDPM Strategy for the Adaptive Project Framework Model

Figure 25-2 illustrates the integration of the project management Scoping Phase and the APF Version Scope Phase. This Adaptive SDPM Scoping Phase for the APF model is the beginning of an APF project. It is done once for every APF project. There are two major parts to it: a defining part and a planning part. The defining part can effectively be completed by two parties: a requestor and a provider. These may each be single individuals or small groups that represent the two parties. In either case, the critical factor is that they not only represent their constituency, but they speak for their constituency, and they can make decisions and commitments for their constituency. The defining part uses the Conditions of Satisfaction (COS) (see Appendix D). The planning part is a high-level plan that sets the parameters for the project, that is, cycle length, number of cycles, and high-level WBS. Keep in mind, however, that the high-level WBS may not be the complete high-level decomposition. You can document only what you know to be part of the solution.

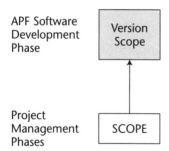

Figure 25-2: Scoping Phase of the Adaptive SDPM Strategy for the Adaptive Project Framework

Overview of the Adaptive SDPM Scoping Phase

An APF project begins with a stated business problem or opportunity. A request has been made to develop a solution to the stated problem or opportunity. A Project Overview Statement (POS) is generated. At this point, you are not at all sure what kind of project that might be or how you might approach it from a methodology perspective. There are four deliverables from the Adaptive SDPM Scoping Phase.

- The first deliverable is a documented conversation COS between the customer and the provider(s) to define more clearly exactly what is needed and what will be done to meet that need. In some cases an RBS will be generated to confirm that an Adaptive approach is appropriate for this project.

- The second deliverable from this phase is a prioritized list of the functionality that has been requested and agreed to in the COS. Both parties recognize that this list will change, but at this point in the project the list reflects the best thinking of both parties based on the information available.

- The third deliverable from this phase is the mid-level Requirements Breakdown Structure (RBS). For our purposes, a mid-level RBS is an RBS that shows a one level decomposition of each known requirement. Generally, such an RBS would have a two- or three-level decomposition. The number of levels is not important. What is important is to have at least one level of decomposition for each known requirement. At this point any more RBS detail would be speculative and not considered useful.

- The fourth deliverable is the setting of the number of cycles and cycle timebox. The first cycle timebox is set to the estimate of the time required to complete the functionality assigned to that timebox. Subsequent timeboxes will be adjusted as well.

Because I use the term *Version Scope*, you have probably guessed by now that more than one version of the deliverables is expected, and if you have, you are correct. This project will develop the first version of the solution. In later projects, a second version may be developed based on the feedback you will have received from users of the first version. However, you are concerned only with this version and will not reference any future versions of the solution. Information will be gathered during this version that will inform management about any further enhancements they might want to consider in future versions. These are the normal releases we see in products, services and systems. While there will be similarities between TPM and APF, one major difference has to do with scope. Scope creep is the bane of the traditionalist. They put up with it because they have no choice. They know it will happen, and they just have to make the best of it. In APF there is no such thing as scope creep. What you do have is change brought about by discovery and learning by the team and by the client. That change is expected and APF is designed to handle it with ease at each Client Checkpoint.

What Is the Version Budget and Timebox?

In APF the budget and timebox are fixed. Try to keep a version timebox to less than 6 months. Any longer and you invite many of the problems that plague the traditionalist. There are no rolling schedules. There is no going back to the well for another budget increase. One of the objectives in an APF project is to maximize business value under fixed time and cost constraints. Period! This is a very different approach to the project than the traditionalist would take. As long as the client is satisfied that the maximum business value has been attained for the time and dollars expended, the project was successfully completed. If the client and the project team pay attention, this result can be achieved every time. No exceptions! Unfortunately the maximum business value they attain may not meet the success criteria, but that is an issue for the client to deal with and should not determine the success or failure of the APF approach. Whatever didn't get done in this version will have to be left for the next version or not at all. Hence, you have another reason for keeping scope to a feasible minimum, and the timebox to less than 6 months. That will reduce the occasion where schedules need to be extended or more dollars are needed. It will also reduce the financial loss to the organization as compared to the traditional approach. With APF you can kill a bad project much earlier than you can with the traditional approach and that accounts for the dollar savings.

The Scoping Phase of the Adaptive SDPM Strategy for the Adaptive Software Development Model

Figure 25-3 illustrates the integration of the project management Scope Phase and the Adaptive Software Development (ASD) Initiation Phase. An ASD project begins much like an APF project. A request has been made to develop a solution to the stated problem or opportunity.

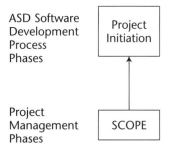

Figure 25-3: Scoping Phase of the Adaptive SDPM strategy for the Adaptive Software Development model

The primary deliverable is the mission statement. The mission statement will establish a sense of direction for the overall project. It will be a motivator for the project team. It will provide a framework for the team and an aid to decision-making. There are three artifacts that a good mission statement will provide:

- A project vision statement
- A project data sheet
- A project specification outline

They are described in the subsections that follow.

Project Vision Statement

The first artifact is the Project Vision Statement. This may take the form of a brief charter statement or a full feasibility study. In either case its purpose is to provide a framework and direction for the project.

Project Data Sheet

The second artifact is the Project Data Sheet (PDS), the document that anyone with an interest in the project would consult for a thumbnail description of the project. In one page the document should describe the following (this information is drawn from *Adaptive Software Development: A Collaborative Approach to Managing Complex Systems* by James Highsmith III (Dorset House, 2000):

- Client
- Brief objective statement of the project
- Product benefits
- Client benefits
- Performance/quality attributes
- Architecture
- Issues/risks
- Major project milestones
- Core team members

Project Mission Profile

The third artifact is the Project Mission Profile. This document profiles the project with respect to four variables: scope, schedule, defects, and resources. The profile is nothing more than a prioritization of these four variables. The reason for this prioritization is to give the project team an aid to decision-making as the project work commences. Whenever the team needs to make a decision, they can use this prioritization to decide which of the project parameters can be compromised. For example, suppose the prioritization lists, from most important to least important, the variables as follows: defects, scope, schedule, and resources. If the choice of alternatives involves compromising on schedule versus compromising on scope, the schedule compromise would be preferred over the scope compromise.

Project Specification Outline

The fourth artifact is the Project Specification Outline (PSO). The PSO is a document that defines the boundary conditions of the project. It will answer questions regarding what is in and what is not in the project. In addition, it serves three other purposes:

- It helps set client expectations as to what the project purports to deliver.

- It helps the team with top-down estimates of project size (time and cost estimates).

- It is the primary input to iteration planning.

Discussion Questions

1. Both APF and ASD are designed for software development projects. APF is also designed for projects that are not just software development–focused but can encompass other types of projects (process improvement and new product development). Is there any reason to prefer either one over the other for a project where the solution is not yet fully identified? Defend your position.

2. The Scoping Phase of the Adaptive SDPM strategy is a critically important part of the project life cycle. If you were asked to plan a three-day scoping exercise, what would your plan include? Prepare a detailed and timed agenda. Be sure to include the customer as a major player in that scoping exercise.

CHAPTER 26

The Adaptive SDPM Planning Phase

Think before you act.

Aesop
Greek fabulist

Chapter Learning Objectives

After reading this chapter, you will:

- ◆ Understand the Planning Phase of the Adaptive SDPM strategy for the Adaptive Project Framework model
- ◆ Understand the Planning Phase of the Adaptive SDPM strategy for the Adaptive Software Development model

---

This the second of three SDPM strategies where the Planning Phase focuses on projects for which the features are not completely known (Iterative SDPM strategy) or the features and functions are not completely known (Adaptive SDPM strategy) or the features, functions, and goal is not completely known (Extreme SDPM strategy). There are several approaches to these three situations. In this chapter we discuss the Planning Phase of two different adaptive models: Adaptive Project Framework and Adaptive Software Development.

The Planning Phase of an Adaptive SDPM Strategy

The primary focus of any Iterative, Adaptive, or Extreme SDPM strategy is to discover a complete and acceptable know these features are missing because the current solution just doesn't feel right to the customer. Working together with the customer, the project team will plan the iterations to discover those missing features. The Adaptive SDPM strategy has but one major purpose: Iterate on the complete solution to add newly discovered functions and features and initiate probative swim lanes to test feasibility of an idea or otherwise attempt to discover otherwise unknown solution characteristics.

Figure 26-1 illustrates the parts of the project management Planning Phase and the Iterative Planning Phase.

The Planning Phase of the Adaptive SDPM strategy occurs in two different phases of the software development life cycle.

■ It occurs at the beginning of the project at a high level. The deliverables in this Planning Phase are the parameters that define the overall approach to the project: the cycle length and number of cycles that are executed for the entire project. These are initial estimates and may change as the project progresses.

■ The deliverables in the second Planning Phase (during Design) are specific to the next cycle. Much of this planning activity looks like the detailed planning that takes place in the Linear SDPM strategy. The tools and processes that you are already familiar with from those earlier projects are used here. The deliverables are a list of functions and features to be delivered in this cycle, the task level schedule and team assignments, and the daily status reports through the cycle.

The next sections take a look at how the Adaptive Project Framework and the Adaptive Software Development model accomplish project planning.

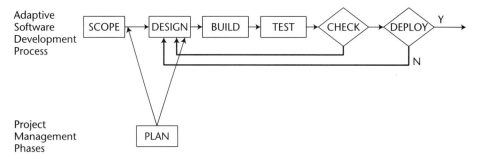

Figure 26-1: The Planning Phase for the Adaptive SDPM strategy

The Planning Phase of an Adaptive SDPM Strategy for the Adaptive Project Framework Model

Figure 26-2 is the Planning Phase of the Adaptive SDPM strategy for the Adaptive Project Framework model.

For planning in the Adaptive SDPM strategy for the Adaptive Project Framework model the Requirements Breakdown Structure (RBS) is not complete. Some functions and features are missing from the current solution and that is what led us to choose an Adaptive approach. In the case of the Iterative SDPM strategy, only features were missing features; that is, the solution was nearly completely defined. Only a few details of the solution had to be worked out. Not so with the Adaptive SDPM strategy. Here parts of the solution are still undefined and must be discovered through iteration. There can in fact be several gaps in the solution as a result of missing functions or the user not knowing how to perform some of those missing functions. The objective of this strategy is to plan each iteration so that the missing features can be discovered and integrated into the solution, finally producing a complete solution. Five major tasks need to be done to outline the project plan for the entire project. They are:

- Completing a Project Overview Statement
- Reviewing the known parts of the RBS
- Determining the cycle length
- Determining the number of cycles
- Prioritizing known functionality

Five major tasks need to be done to outline the project plan for the next cycle. These five tasks are repeated at each Cycle Plan Phase. They are:

- Determining the functionality to be built
- Determining the probative initiatives to be taken
- Creating the WBS for the functionality and probative initiatives to be done
- Estimating task duration
- Creating a resource-managed cycle schedule

All of these deliverables are briefly discussed in the subsections that follow.

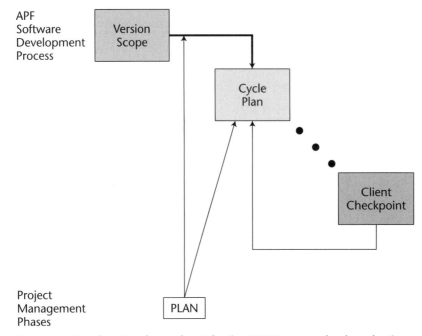

Figure 26-2: Planning Phase of an Adaptive SDPM strategy for the Adaptive Project Framework model

Completing a Project Overview Statement

See Appendix C for a refresher on the five parts of the Project Overview Statement (POS). Figure 26-3 is an example from the case study for one of the initiatives.

Reviewing Known Parts of the RBS

The less that is known about the solution, the more difficult it will be to plan and successfully execute the project. Such projects will call upon all of the creativity and ingenuity that the project team and the customer can muster. You have to progress from the known to the unknown. The less you know, the harder it will be. In any case the known parts of the RBS are the starting point for every APF project. If very little is known, then the first few cycles may be nothing more than prototypes, and their purpose is to create a sensible starting point. Whatever can be built into the solution at the beginning cycles should be built in. These may spur other ideas just as a prototype is designed to accomplish. In fact, you would be correct in calling the solutions at each cycle completion prototypes. The only caveat is that they are working versions of the known solution. So they are production prototypes.

PROJECT OVERVIEW STATEMENT	Project Name Pizza Oven Van	Project No. 2006-02	Project Lead(s) Pepe Ronee

Problem/Opportunity

   PDQ has lost 30% of its sales revenue due primarily to a too long elapsed time from order entry to order delivery.

Goal

   Implement a pizza oven van to minimize the order entry to order delivery time.

Objectives

1. Outfit one or more vans that can assemble, bake, and deliver pizzas.
2. Design and implement a computer system to receive and process phone orders.
3. Design and implement a computer system to dispatch the pizza oven vans in real time.

Success Criteria

1. The time between order entry and home delivery will be less than 45 minutes.
2. The average time between order entry and home delivery will be less than 30 minutes.
3. Home delivery sales will increase by 40% within 3 months of implementation.
4. The revenues from the home delivery business will be double the current level within 12 months of implementation.

Assumptions, Risks, Obstacles

1. At least 90% of current employees will endorse the pizza oven van business.
2. The total development and operations cost of the pizza oven van line of business will be less than $6M for the first three years.

Prepared By Pepe Ronee	Date 4/12/06	Approved By Dee Livery	Date 4/15/06

Figure 26-3: POS example drawn from the case study

Determining Cycle Length

Cycle length should range between 2 and 6 weeks. Early cycles should be shorter in order to fully engage the customer in the project. Once meaningful customer involvement is assured later cycles can be lengthened. Because the early cycles may contain a good dose of probative initiatives, it is good strategy to keep these cycles short. Probative initiatives are designed to discover approaches that will lead to function definition and development. For that reason, you want them short so you can try as many initiatives out as makes sense.

Determining Number of Cycles

This early guess is needed to frame expectations for the team and the customer. As each cycle is planned, its length may be changed—so also might the number of cycles.

Prioritizing Known Functionality

Prioritization is a customer decision. It is based on delivering business value if deployment of partial solutions is in the best interest of the enterprise.

Determining the Functionality to Be Built

The best way to go about this is to have a cycle length in mind, say 2 weeks. Then have the team, armed with the priority list of functions and features, indicate how far down the list they can get in 2 weeks. Keep in mind that there are probative initiatives that are also part of the deliverables from the cycle. Err on the side of having fewer deliverables than might be possible with a Herculean effort. The last thing you want is to fall short of completing the list.

Determining the Probative Initiatives to Be Taken

The best way to get the list of probative initiatives built is with a brainstorming session. Identify as many initiatives as possible, prioritize them, and select the ones that seem most promising. These are to be short excursions, not lengthy projects. All you want to do is narrow the list to added functions and features needed to establish an acceptable solution. You are not out to cure world hunger. Good enough is good enough.

As a result of these probes, you will perhaps modify some and try again. You will find some that hold promise and can be explored to the next level of detail. You might even be lucky and find a few that can be implemented in the next cycle.

Case Study

The case study gives us some examples of initiatives to build functionality. For the Order Entry sub-system the RBS is as follows:

- ◆ **Function 1.1 Identify Customer**
  - ■ **Feature 1.1.1 Identify new customer versus recurring**
  - ■ **Feature 1.1.2 Display customer purchasing history**
  - ■ **Feature 1.1.3 Display Name, Address, Phone Number**
- ◆ **Function 1.2 Get Order**
  - ■ **Feature 1.2.1 Display products customer requests**
  - ■ **Feature 1.2.2 Display size and quantity ordered**
  - ■ **Feature 1.2.3 Display options list**
  - ■ **Feature 1.2.4 Customer requests baked or unbaked**
- ◆ **Function 1.3 Get Delivery Instructions**
  - ■ **Feature 1.3.1 Delivery location**
  - ■ **Feature 1.3.2 Delivery options (home, pick-up, eat-in)**
  - ■ **Feature 1.3.3 Requested delivery time**
- ◆ **Function 1.4 Price Order**
  - ■ **Feature 1.4.1 Promotions**
  - ■ **Feature 1.4.2 Calculate price**
  - ■ **Feature 1.4.3 Maintain pricing table**
- ◆ **Function 1.5 Confirm Order**
  - ■ **Feature 1.5.1 Accept, cancel, modify**
  - ■ **Feature 1.5.2 Payment type**
  - ■ **Feature 1.5.3 Display order with pricing**
- ◆ **Function 1.6 Submit Order**
  - ■ **Feature 1.6.1 Submit order**
  - ■ **Feature 1.6.2 Confirm order accepted**

Functions 1.1 through 1.5 are fundamental to taking orders and must all be done in the first iteration. Function 1.6 is a bit different. Feature 1.6.1 can be very simple or very complex. To submit the order to the closest preparation location is the simplest and might be part of the initial deployment. That would be only a temporary decision until the actual submit order feature was fully developed. To do that would require several iterations. Probative initiatives will be needed to further define the submit order feature. That topic is taken up in the next case study insert.

Case Study

The case study gives some examples of probative initiatives. Take a look at the Submit Order feature. Deciding which preparation location to assign the order to is a complex process. You need to take several variables into account: the length of the order queue at each preparation location, the distance of the preparation location from the delivery address, and how and when to use the mobile pizza vans for preparation and delivery. Each of these variables acting alone must be considered as well as interactions between the variables. The probative initiatives are best investigated by building quick simulation models of the relevant alternatives. Based on the results of those simulations a decision can be made as to which seems most useful. That choice will lead to further probative initiatives regarding the business rules that will govern the approach chosen. Finally, the results of those probative initiatives will lead the development team into the software development part of the project.

Creating the WBS for the Functionality and Probative Initiatives to Be Done

Here is the beginning of familiar territory. These are the tools of the traditional project manager. You already know how to use them from previous projects.

Estimating Task Duration

Remember that the cycle is only a few weeks long. These tasks are hours or even days in duration. You should be able to estimate fairly accurately.

Creating a Resource Managed Cycle Schedule

For this deliverable, create a whiteboard schedule based on the precedence diagram for the tasks to be done. You don't need a software tool to do the schedule. All of this is best done manually.

The Planning Phase of an Adaptive SDPM Strategy for the Adaptive Software Development Model

Figure 26-4 is the Planning Phase of the Adaptive SDPM strategy for the Adaptive Software Development model.

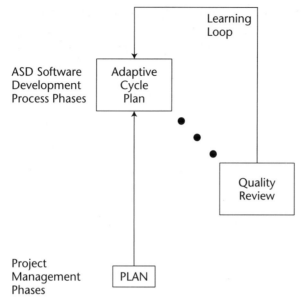

Figure 26-4: Planning Phase of an Adaptive SDPM strategy for the Adaptive Software Development model

The Planning Phase of an Adaptive SDPM strategy for the Adaptive Software Development Model is iterative itself. Each Learning Loop ends with a review of what just happened in the previous development phase. That review identifies what is going to be built in the next cycle. The focus in the Adaptive cycle plan is on improving the components in the current solution and introducing new components into the solution. Unlike the traditional approaches, which focus on tasks, the Adaptive cycle plan focuses on components, that is, on deliverables. There are five characteristics to every Adaptive cycle according to James Highsmith III in his book *Adaptive Software Development* (Dorsett House, 2000). They are:

- **Mission-driven**—There is a specific deliverable that the project must produce.

- **Component-based**—The approach will deliver parts of the solution in each iteration with the entire solution delivered in the final iteration.

- **Iterative**—A number of iterations will be needed in order to create the complete solution.

- **Timeboxed**—Each iteration is limited to a specific time frame (2–4 weeks typical) and the entire project limited to a specific time frame (the sum of all the iteration timeframes).

- **Risk-driven and change-tolerant**—High-risk deliverables are usually produced early in the project and the whole approach expects and accommodates frequent change requests from the customer.

These characteristics pervade all of the Adaptive and Extreme approaches studied in this book. Highsmith defines a seven-step adaptive planning process. The deliverables from each step are defined in the subsections that follow.

The Project Initiation Phase

The purpose of this deliverable is to get as firm a definition of the project and its expectations as is possible given what is currently known about the problem and its solution. To do so effectively requires the attendance and participation of stakeholders, sponsors, line of business managers, the project manager, and at least the core team members. Highsmith recommends a week-long kickoff, which includes Joint Applications Design (JAD) sessions and as much planning as can be put together given what is known about the project.

Project Timebox

As in the case of an Adaptive Project Framework project, a deadline is given. This is called the project timebox, to distinguish it from a cycle timebox. The project timebox is a management-imposed deadline and may have little resemblance to the actual development time required for an acceptable and complete solution. Both dates have to be accommodated in whatever planning is done.

Optimal Number of Cycles and the Timebox for Each

Within the project timebox some number of cycles will be planned. The total duration of the cycles must be within the project timebox constraint. For projects that are overly aggressive, the cycles and their duration may have been exhausted and the complete solution not yet obtained. Perhaps the agreement from the project manager should be to deliver as much of the solution as possible (or equivalently, as much business value as possible) within the project time-box. After all, isn't that the most that could reasonably be expected? Highsmith recommends 4–10 weeks as a function of project length.

Objective Statement for Each Cycle

In addition to the project statement that helps the team focus the overall project goal, each cycle should have its own objective statement. It will help the team and the customer keep focus and stay within scope for each cycle. While these objectives statements can be crafted at the outset, the learning nature of the project causes them to be altered as knowledge of the solution emerges from completed cycles. With that in mind they should be maintained at each Quality Review Phase.

Assign Primary Components to Cycles

Primary components can be thought of as the high-level "whats" of the solution. The lower level "whats" and many of the "hows" may have to be learned. At least this preliminary assignment helps the team with the expectations that senior management has for this project. The rules of the assignment should take into account such factors as business value, dependencies, risk, breadth then depth, resource utilization, skills, and availability.

Assign Technology Support and Components to Cycles

Code development is certainly a necessary component of every software development project, but it isn't a sufficient component. Documentation and infrastructure components are equally as important. The assignment of these components to cycles should parallel their use in the emerging solution.

A Project Task List

In a fully agile-mature organization, this step is optional and in fact not needed. Organizations in transition might use this as a crutch back into the old world from which they are escaping. In a truly agile environment all that is needed is to specify the "what" and leave it up to the team to decide "how." The "how" is an artifact from the traditionalist's world.

Discussion Questions

1. Defend the following statement: The Adaptive Project Framework model is a good transition strategy for traditional organizations that want to fully implement Adaptive project management across the enterprise. The Adaptive Software Development model is a good transition strategy for adaptive organizations wanting to move to a fully Adaptive software development environment.

2. Which of the two Adaptive strategies is a better choice when the solution is almost unknown? Support your choice.

CHAPTER 27

The Adaptive SDPM Launching Phase

Great people don't equal great teams.

Tom Peters
Business writer

Chapter Learning Objectives

After reading this chapter, you will:

- ◆ Understand the complications added to the Launch Phase when using an Adaptive SDPM strategy
- ◆ Know how to launch an Adaptive SDPM strategy for the Adaptive Project Framework model
- ◆ Know how to launch an Adaptive SDPM strategy for the Adaptive Software Development model

---

All of the Launching Phase discussion for the Linear, Incremental, and Iterative SDPM strategy situations apply to the Adaptive SDPM strategy and will not be repeated here (you can see Parts II, III, and IV earlier in the book for those discussions). Adaptive SDPM strategy projects follow the same procedures as by-the-book projects, except they repeat those procedures several times over the life of the project. Within a single repetition, all of the launching activities that are done in the Linear, Incremental, and Iterative SDPM strategies are done in the Adaptive SDPM strategy. But you have to address some additional considerations. Adaptive SDPM strategies focus on projects whose solution is not known or only partially known. Unlike the Iterative SDPM strategies where features are missing for the current solution, the Adaptive SDPM strategies operate without a known solution. Not only are features missing, but functions are also missing. These missing functions give rise to the Adaptive SDPM strategy. It is a learning and discovery approach in much the same way the Iterative SDPM strategy is, but it is much more demanding on the customer and the team. In this category of project all of the creativity that the customer and the team can muster is required to find a solution that at times can be very elusive. Success is no guarantee, and the risk is high.

The Launching Phase of an Adaptive SDPM Strategy

Figure 27-1 highlights the Launching Phase of an Adaptive SDPM strategy.

An Adaptive SDPM strategy differs in principle from an Iterative SDPM strategy in one important way. In the Adaptive SDPM strategy each iteration presents the customer with the complete solution, as well as the results of probes into the missing functions of the solution. The complete solution can be deployed if it is deemed by the customer to have sufficient business value. Most likely that will require several cycles to accomplish. The results of the probes will be to gain further knowledge of the missing pieces and probe again if needed to dig even deeper. Sooner or later the probes in a certain part of the solution stop. The answer may have been found, and the team and customer can rejoice; or the probes may be abandoned because of failure to uncover any additional or useful information.

Four tasks must be done in the Launch Phase of an Adaptive project that are not done or done differently in the Launch Phase of an Iterative project. They are:

- Processing scope change requests
- Handling solution handoffs
- Handling solution rollout
- Scheduling iterations

These are discussed in the subsections that follow.

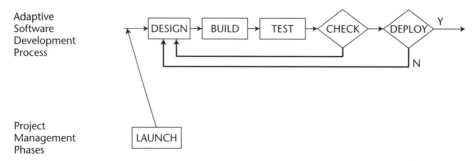

Figure 27-1: The Launching Phase of an Adaptive SDPM strategy

Processing Scope Change Requests

The Adaptive SDPM strategy is the second of three strategies for which scope change requests are a vital artifact.

- As I discuss in Part IV of this book, scope change requests are needed for the Iterative SDPM strategy. In the search for additional features, the customer who knows best, and their review and comment on features helps the team improve what is already in the solution and adds or changes features to come closer to meeting customer needs.

- For the Adaptive SDPM strategy, scope change requests are just as necessary. The solution is not known, and the best way to find it is to engage the customer in the investigation. Feedback from them is the most valued deliverable in that it helps identify and further define functionality and the accompanying features.

- For the Extreme SDPM strategy (the subject of Part VI of this book) scope change requests are essential. These projects are often no different from pure R&D projects. The customer is in the best position for guiding the solution to an acceptable solution. Periods of diverse thinking are followed by periods of convergent thinking, and this is what leads to acceptable solutions. There is no other way, except for blind luck.

The partial solutions for all three strategies cannot evolve to a complete and acceptable solution in the absence of scope changes. For the Iterative SDPM strategy the absence of scope change requests means that a partial solution is all that can be offered. The solution may or may not meet enough business needs to be an acceptable solution. In both the Adaptive and Extreme SDPM strategies, the absence of scope change requests means that no acceptable solution can be developed.

When scope change requests are received in the Adaptive SDPM strategy, the project impact statement is often developed but no action is taken until the Client Checkpoint Phase. Just as the Iterative SDPM strategy interrupting the workflow in the current iteration is too disruptive: A postponement makes the most sense in the Adaptive SDPM strategy as well.

All of this change comes to a head in a scope change request. It is the best way to convey to the team the thinking of the customer. The customer must understand that change requests are expected and embraced. The process should not be cumbersome but should be easy to use.

Handling Solution Handoffs

Contrary to the Incremental and Iterative SDPM strategies, adjusting the team membership between cycles for an Adaptive SDPM strategy doesn't make sense. You may need to make minor adjustments because of unavailability, but the team can orient the new member without the need for extensive cycle documentation.

Handling Solution Rollout

Solution rollout occurs for the same two reasons in the Adaptive situation as it does in the Iterative situation.

- The first is to deliver business value to the enterprise.
- The second is to give the client a chance for feedback of any changes or additions they see.

There are some differences, however. The Adaptive SDPM strategy gives less chance of a solution deployment than the Iterative SDPM strategy because not every Adaptive cycle produces an updated solution. Some cycles may have nothing more than probative initiatives. These are not designed to produce deployable solutions but rather to discover parts of the solution that heretofore have been missing.

Solution rollouts, if they occur in the Adaptive SDPM strategy, occur later in the project life cycle than in the case of the Iterative SDPM strategy. An Adaptive SDPM strategy cycle deliverable may be deployed but not into a production situation. The reason for that deployment is to kick-start the project by getting input from other interested parties. If previous probative initiatives have not met expectations, fresh eyes looking at the current solution may be a springboard to other probative initiatives. In other words, these deployments help get the project moving again.

Scheduling Iterations

The Customer Checkpoint is a more involved phase in the Adaptive SDPM strategy than in the Iterative SDPM strategy. The prioritization of functionality to be added, the consideration of the results of completed probative initiatives, and the analysis of scope change requests are all prerequisites for the next cycle plan.

The Launching Phase of an Iterative SDPM Strategy for the Adaptive Project Framework Model

The Launching Phase of an Adaptive SDPM strategy for the Adaptive Project Framework model has all four of the considerations stated previously for the generic Adaptive situation. Figure 27-2 highlights the Launching Phase of an Adaptive SDPM strategy for the Adaptive Project Framework model.

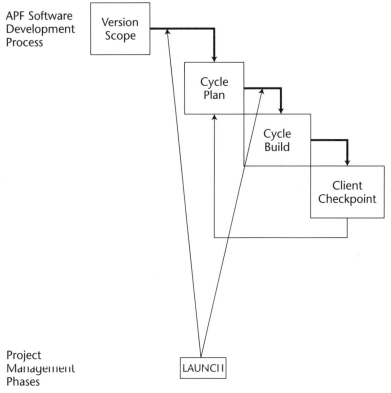

Figure 27-2: The Launching Phase of an Adaptive SDPM strategy for the Adaptive Project Framework model

The Launching Phases of the Adaptive SDPM and Iterative SDPM strategies bear a lot of similarity. However, in the case of the Iterative models, the focus is on discovering missing features, whereas in the Adaptive models the focus is on discovering missing functions. That is a more challenging task. The Iterative models know where they are going as far as defining an acceptable solution.

The Adaptive models do not. That's the challenge of Adaptive projects over the challenge of Iterative projects.

In the search for the missing functionality and the features that further define that functionality, the team and the customer are called upon to be collaborative, open-minded, and creative. Brainstorming sessions are common during the Client Checkpoint as probative initiatives are identified and implemented. Options should be kept open as long as a glimmer of hope that they may uncover something useful in reaching a solution exists.

The Launching Phase of an Adaptive SDPM Strategy for the Adaptive Software Development Model

Figure 27-3 illustrates the Launching Phase of an Adaptive SDPM strategy for the Adaptive Software Development model.

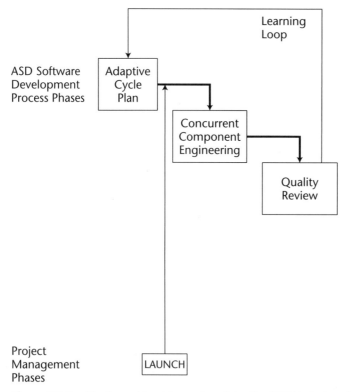

Figure 27-3: The Launching Phase of an Adaptive SDPM strategy for the Adaptive Software Development model

Note that the Launching Phase of an Adaptive SDPM strategy for the Adaptive Software Development model is more involved than in the case of the Launching Phase for the Adaptive Project Framework model. The reason is that the Learning Loop may identify technical changes that require a change of team in preparation for the next cycle. That change is identified during the Adaptive Cycle Plan Phase for the just completed cycle. The new team members go through an orientation program to bring them up to speed with the current solution and past cycle deliverables. They also need to be oriented to the rules of the engagement as previously established by the continuing members of the project team.

In the initial cycle, the team has established the rules of the engagement. At the completion of the initial cycle several questions can be asked about how the cycle went.

- How well did the rules work? New teams may need some adjustments to the rules. They may have been too confining or added too much overhead for the value received. The team will probably have some suggestions to make the rules work for them rather than they work for the rules.

- How effectively did the team work as a team and not just as a group of people? In your daily 15-minute team meetings you can tell a lot about the progress your group has made toward becoming a true team.

- How often do you hear the word *I* or *Me* instead of the word *We*?

- Do team members offer to help others when the situation provides for it?

- Are any of your team members proactive when it comes to working with others?

- How often do team members volunteer for special assignments?

In the absence of these signs, you will have a difficult time bringing an Adaptive project in successfully.

Discussion Question

1. You are Pepe Ronee, and you have run the Adaptive SDPM strategy by the book. But you have just realized that the solution is nearing. You have only a few minor points to flesh out. Should you continue using an Adaptive SDPM strategy or would some other strategy be more appropriate?

CHAPTER 28

The Adaptive SDPM Monitoring and Controlling Phase

Celebrate what you want to see more of.

Tom Peters
Business writer

Chapter Learning Objectives

After reading this chapter, you will:

- ◆ Understand the Monitoring Phase of the Adaptive SDPM strategy
- ◆ Understand the Adaptive SDPM Adaptive strategy for the Project Framework model
- ◆ Understand the Adaptive SDPM strategy for the Adaptive Software Development model

---

The Adaptive SDPM strategy opens a new perspective on systems development where even less is known about requirements than in the case of projects that rightly follow an Iterative SDPM strategy. The differences between projects that follow an Iterative approach versus those that follow an Adaptive approach are staggering and so are the accompanying strategies.

The Monitoring and Controlling Phase of an Adaptive SDPM Strategy

Figure 28-1 highlights the Monitoring and Controlling Phase of an Adaptive SDPM strategy.

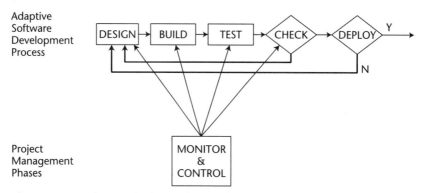

Adaptive
Software
Development
Process

Project
Management
Phases

Figure 28-1: The Monitoring and Controlling Phase of an Adaptive SDPM strategy

First note the inclusion of the Check Phase as a very visible part of the Systems Development Life Cycle. It was part of the Iterative SDPM strategy, but here it takes on a different posture. Here the client is more proactively involved with the development team. The learning and discovery that was generated in the just completed iteration is now used to identify next steps. Those next steps include not only integrating new functions and features but also probing with new initiatives aimed at further learning and discovery. This proactive posture was not as prevalent in the Iterative SDPM strategy because the discovery of new or modified features was not as demanding as the discovery of new or modified functionality. Much more is asked of the development team and the client in an Adaptive SDPM strategy than in the Iterative SDPM strategy. In the most extreme of the adaptive cases very little will be known about the solution from the standpoint of functionality. It has to be discovered. But it isn't going to be discovered just because you want it to be. It's hard work and requires all of the creativity that the client and the development team can muster. That dedication and drive aren't necessary ingredients of the Iterative SDPM strategy.

As far as metrics are concerned, those that were introduced for the Iterative SDPM strategy apply equally as well to the Adaptive SDPM strategy. However, four topics are worth discussing relative to those metrics as they apply to the Adaptive SDPM strategy. They are:

- Project progress reporting
- Discovery of new/revised functions
- Discovery of new/revised features
- Processing scope change requests

These are discussed in the subsections that follow.

Project Progress Reporting

As far as progress reporting, the Adaptive SDPM strategy is no different than the Iterative SDPM strategy. The same types of reports that work for features also work for functions. But there is a difference. The difference is that functions come far less frequently than features. The divergence and convergence trends that are easily seen in features are not as pronounced when reporting the progress of functions discovery and implementation. One function may be worth a hundred features.

One additional report may be useful. Consider the number of probative initiatives that are taken versus the number that yield positive results, that is, that lead to new/revised functions. Track this ratio over time as an indicator of team efficiency. If that trend is decreasing over time, it may indicate that no further function discovery is likely to occur. The focus might then shift totally to feature discovery and enhancement.

Discovery of New/Revised Functions

This is the heart of the Adaptive SDPM strategy, for it is here that the success or failure of the effort is made. The solution is not known. Perhaps very little of the solution is known. It must be discovered. This will be done through a series of probative initiatives. Some will bear fruit; others will be dead ends. The probative initiatives that are proposed may be quite similar to process improvement initiatives that you have undertaken. They are designed to uncover functionality that otherwise might remain undiscovered. Don't underestimate the challenge in these initiatives. They might be the output of a brainstorming session. They might be based on previous successes and failures to uncover them. In any case, the discovery of the solution is limited only by the creativity that the client and the development team can bring to the table.

Discovery of New/Revised Features

Features follow from functions. Once a function has been identified, its features can be found through successive versions shared with the customer. They are in the best position to comment on the suitability of the function and hence the features that should further enhance it.

Processing Scope Change Requests

Scope change requests can come at any time from either the customer or the developers. Probative initiatives that bear fruit should be documented through a scope change request. Enhancements to functions or features are also to be documented through a scope change request. Regardless when they arise, they are held in the scope bank until the checkpoint. This is markedly different from the Linear or Incremental SDPM strategies where scope change requests are handled as they arise. The dynamics that take place within an Adaptive SDPM strategy are so complex and highly charged that interrupting a cycle to process a scope change request will be counterproductive. Save them for the client checkpoint. At that time they can be considered by the customer and the development team, prioritized, and a decision made as to when and if they will be integrated into the solution.

The Monitoring and Controlling Phase of an Adaptive SDPM Strategy for the Adaptive Project Framework Model

The Monitoring and Controlling Phase of an Iterative SDPM strategy for the Adaptive Project Framework model has all four of the considerations stated in the previous section for the generic Adaptive SDPM situation. Figure 28-2 highlights the Monitoring and Controlling Phase of an Adaptive SDPM strategy for the Adaptive Project Framework (APF) model.

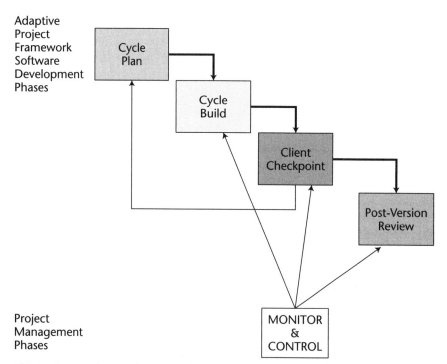

Figure 28-2: The Monitoring and Controlling Phase of an Adaptive SDPM strategy for the Adaptive Project Framework model

In keeping with the spirit of the Adaptive Project Framework, you have a minimum of formal status reporting. Much of it is transmitted in the 15-minute daily team meetings. If there is an out-of-control situation developing, it is discovered early, and the necessary corrective measures are put in place. Except in very unusual situations, a problem will not become too serious in the span of 1 day.

Customer Checkpoint

The Customer Checkpoint Phase is a critical review that takes place after every Cycle Build is completed. During the Cycle Build, both the client and the project team have benefited from several discovery and learning episodes. Variations to the version functionality surface; alternative approaches to delivering certain functionality have been suggested, and the client has learned also through their continuous involvement with the team. All of this is recorded in the Scope Bank and must be considered along with the functionality that had originally been assigned to the coming cycle. The result is a revised prioritization of functionality for the coming cycle. The most important thing to remember is not to speculate on the future. Prioritize for the next cycle only the functionality that you are certain will be in the final solution. And don't dismiss this as an easy exercise. It definitely is not that.

Questions to Be Asked During the Customer Checkpoint

You need to answer several questions during the Customer Checkpoint. These are all in the spirit of monitoring and controlling, but their value is that they improve the solution and the process going forward.

What Was Planned?

There are two lists:

- The first is the list of probative initiatives that were to be undertaken to discover additional functions/features for eventual inclusion in the solution. Some of these will prove useful; some will not.

- The second list is nothing more than the prioritized functions and features that were to be integrated into the solution.

What Was Done?

The results of the probative initiatives are reported. The functions and features actually integrated into the solution are listed. There are often comments accompanying the check-off because some items may not have been completed as planned. Subfunctions may have been left undone, and there may be good reasons for it. In such cases, the Scope Bank should reflect the situation.

Again, the only questions to be answered here are the following: Did the cycle meet its objectives? Did the cycle meet its planned functional specifications? If no, where are the variances? The answers will provide input into planning for the objectives of the next cycle and the functionality to be built in the next cycle. Remember you already specified objectives and functionality for the next cycle in the Version Scope Phase. So you have the original scope and potential revised scope to consider as you consider what the next cycle is to contain. TPM defines a formal change management process that can be invoked at any time in the project. In APF the change process is imbedded in the Client Checkpoint. The only changes accommodated in APF occur between cycles.

What Was Learned?

This is perhaps the most important question of all. The results of the probative initiatives suggest added functions and features or at best further directions for investigation. Here is where the solution is morphed to provide more value to the client. The new ideas that are generated here could not have come about through the Traditional Project Management (TPM) approach. This is where APF—and Extreme Project Management (xPM) in all fairness—really shine. Both APF and xPM take their value from learning by doing.

Is the Version Scope Still Valid?

Armed with the information discussed previously, you now can ask a very basic question: Is the version scope still valid? If yes, terrific—you are on the right track. If not, revise accordingly. Revisions to version scope can be significant. In some cases they may be so significant that the correct business decision is to kill the current project, go back to the drawing board, and start over again. The cost of killing an APF project is always less than the cost of killing a TPM project.

Is the Team Working as Expected?

Real teamwork is a critical success factor in APF. Worker empowerment is threaded throughout APF. One way to gauge—if you count the frequency of the use of the word "I" as compared to the use of the word "We," you will have a pretty good metric for measuring team strength. The formula would be

Team Strength = number of Wes/(number of Is plus number of Wes)

and you want to see this number hovering around 1. The APF team needs to work in an open and honest environment for this to happen. That means that every team member must be forthright in stating the actual status of their project work. To do otherwise would be to violate the trust that must exist between and among team members. The project manager must ensure that the working environment on the project is such that team members are not afraid to raise their hand, say they are having trouble, and ask for help. To do otherwise would be to let your teammates down.

One of the greatest benefits from this approach is the meaningful and continuous involvement of the client. They are the decision maker in all going forward activities, and they are doing it with full knowledge of what has taken place to date. They understand where business value can be achieved by changes in functionality, and they are in a position to take action. APF allows the client to engage in the project even to the level of operating as a co-project manager. They are a constant reminder to the team of the business aspects and value of what they are doing and what changes should be made to protect that business value. This is a very important point to remember. It ensures that what is eventually built meets client needs.

The Customer Checkpoint is the bridge that links two successive cycles. The input to the Customer Checkpoint includes:

- The current solution
- New functions/features identified from the probative initiatives undertaken in the previous cycle
- Functions and features to be revised
- Previously identified functions/features not yet incorporated into the solution

Most of these are documented with a scope change request. These requests are then prioritized and the deliverables for the next cycle identified. All four of these can be monitored through simple metrics.

For example, the metric for assessing the current solution is a simple one: Is the current solution better than the previous solution and is it converging toward an acceptable solution? A sustained pattern of no answers might be the signal that the project is going nowhere and either needs to be killed or significantly redirected. The metric for assessing new functions/features identified from the probative initiatives could simply be the ratio of successful to unsuccessful probative initiatives. This ratio should increase over time as more of the solution comes into focus and the whole team has learned to work together effectively and efficiently. The metric for assessing the functions and features to be revised is simply the trend over time of how that number has changed from cycle to cycle. For a healthy project, you might expect that number to increase for some time and then begin to decrease. Such a pattern is a sign of healthy change as the solution moves through a stage of divergence and then finally begins to converge on the final and acceptable solution. The metric for measuring the number of functions/features not yet incorporated into a cycle will be erratic at first as new functions and features are discovered and not acted upon. But eventually this number should stabilize and then begin to decrease with each cycle. In the end you would hope that the list would be empty—assuming neither time nor budget run out before all functions and features are integrated.

The Scope Bank has been the cumulative depository of all the ideas and proposed changes that were generated during the previous cycles. Some of them were incorporated in later cycles and some were not. In any case, the current contents are all of the items not previously acted upon. There may be cases where any ideas suggested several cycles back that had not been incorporated may now be viable. That is the reason the Scope Bank is cumulative.

Output from the Customer Checkpoint

The output becomes input to the next cycle plan phase. The components of that output are briefly described in the following subsections.

Updated Functionality List

You started this whole process with the Conditions of Satisfaction, and it is to those Conditions of Satisfaction that you now return. The only question to be answered here is this: Are the Conditions of Satisfaction still valid? If yes, continue on. If not, revise accordingly. These revisions are the planned functionality for the next cycle.

The client and the team should spend most of a day in frank and honest conversation considering all of these factors and then agreeing on the functionality that will be planned for the next cycle. Do not underestimate the value that can come from the sharing of learning and discovery. That is your most important information as it really helps both parties understand what this solution is really all about and what should be offered as a final solution. This is no trivial task.

Reprioritized Functionality List

The process that was used in the first cycle to prioritize functionality can be repeated here. The criterion that was used to determine the priority may be the same or different. Again, take advantage of all the learning and discovery from the previous cycles.

Next Cycle Length

The initial estimates of functionality duration for those functions planned for the next cycle may require a change in cycle length. Remember to be true to the overall timebox for the version. That cannot be adjusted.

The Monitoring and Controlling Phase of an Iterative SDPM Strategy for the Adaptive Software Development Model

Figure 28-3 illustrates the Monitoring and Controlling Phase of an Adaptive SDPM strategy for the Adaptive Software Development model.

In these types of software development projects, real progress is hard to measure. So many deliverables are started but few will be complete, at least early in the project life cycle. The development team is close to the action, so they should have a good qualitative feel for progress in the absence of meaningful quantitative metrics. To the extent possible progress should be measured both qualitatively and quantitatively. The quantitative metrics should focus on schedule, cost, defects, scope, and resources.

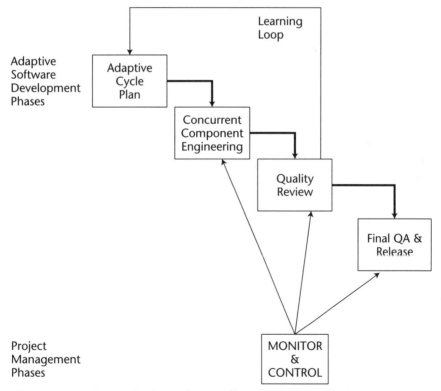

Figure 28-3:   The Monitoring and Controlling Phase of an Adaptive SDPM strategy for the Adaptive Software Development model

At the Quality Review, the following questions should be answered:

- Where are we with this project with respect to the quantitative metrics?
- Where should we be with this project?
- How can we close the gap?
- What is the new estimate of completion?

Discussion Question

1. The probative initiatives in each cycle are discovering new functions and features that add value to the solution and the customer seems satisfied. But you have noticed that the number of revisions to features and functions is growing steadily. In fact, there is very little that you can honestly say has come to closure. Everything seems in a state of flux. That suggests to you that the customer isn't really satisfied. Could there be some other explanation? If not, what should you do?

CHAPTER 29

The Adaptive SDPM Closing Phase

The unfinished is nothing.

Henri Frederic Amiel
Swiss journalist and critic

Chapter Learning Objectives

After reading this chapter, you will:

- ◆ **Understand the Closing Phase of the Iterative SDPM strategy**
- ◆ **Have a working knowledge of the Closing Phase of the Adaptive SDPM strategy for the Adaptive Project Framework model**
- ◆ **Have a working knowledge of the Closing Phase of the Iterative SDPM strategy for the Adaptive Software Development model**

Once the customer has signed off that the requirements have been satisfactorily met, the Closing Phase begins. That sounds like a simple transition but is it?

The Closing Phase of the Adaptive SDPM Strategy

Figure 29-1 illustrates the Closing Phase of the Adaptive SDPM strategy. Note that there are really two parts to the Closing Phase, just as there were in the Iterative SDPM strategy.

- ■ The first is closure with respect to each of the cycles.
- ■ The second is closure with respect to the completed project.

Obviously, there are some similarities between the Closing Phases of Iterative and Adaptive strategies, but there are some key differences as well.

The similarities center on requirements satisfaction at the completion of each cycle. In the Iterative SDPM strategy, these closings were focused on discovering the details of features that had been identified but were not acceptable to the customer. In the Adaptive SDPM strategy, the cycle closings were focused on the discovery of features and functions for later integration into the solution. This highlights the major difference between the two strategies. The Iterative SDPM strategy deals with known features that need change in order to be acceptable to the customer. Each of the proposed changes can be built into the solution and reviewed by the customer for any further changes. The Adaptive SDPM strategy is seeking new features and functionality that can then be built into the solution. So the Iterative SDPM strategy cycles constantly build onto the solution. The Adaptive SDPM strategy uses probative swim lanes as well as swim lanes that integrate changed features into the solution. So the Closing Phase includes not only customer evaluation of the updated solution but also conclusions drawn from the probative swim lane—that is, do the probative swim lanes suggest any new features or functions to be added to the solution in later cycles?

Iterative and Adaptive SDPM strategies share common planning approaches. Both do planning just-in-time, as a follow up to the iteration and cycle Closing Phases. The next iteration has similar properties. In an Iterative SDPM strategy, the deliverables for the next iteration are planned at the beginning of the iteration. In other words, it is just-in-time planning. In an Adaptive SDPM strategy you have to anticipate changes in direction for the project going forward. The changes in direction are the result of learning and discovery from the probative swim lanes. Planning is still done "just-in-time."

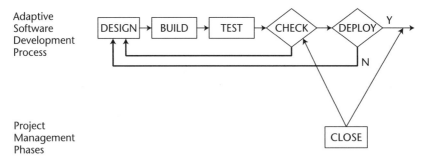

Figure 29-1: The Closing Phase of the Adaptive SDPM strategy

With this as background, the activities in the Closing Phases become obvious. In the Iterative SDPM strategy the Closing Phase assesses the results of the changes to features and functions and whether there was further convergence on an acceptable solution. That leads to the build content of the next iteration. In the Adaptive SDPM strategy, the Closing Phase not only assesses the results of changes to functions and features that were integrated into the solution but also assesses the discovery and learning from the probative initiatives and whether or not that can lead to new or revised features and functions to be integrated into the solution in future cycles or to more probative initiatives for the next cycle. In other words, the Adaptive SDPM strategy includes all of the activities of the Iterative SDPM strategy plus those associated with probative initiatives.

Iterative SDPM Strategy for the Closing Phase of the Adaptive Project Framework Model

Figure 29-2 illustrates the Closing Phase of the SDPM strategy for the Adaptive Project Framework model.

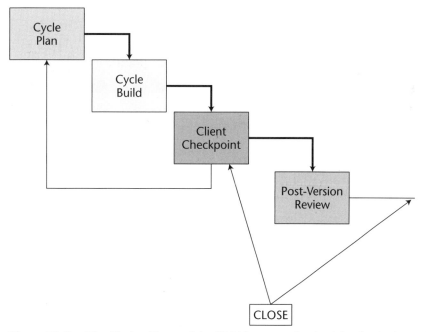

Figure 29-2: The Closing Phase of the SDPM strategy for the Adaptive Project Framework model

The Closing Phase of the Adaptive SDPM strategy for the Adaptive Project Framework is entirely taken up with a Client Checkpoint. Either the Client Checkpoint looks back at the just completed cycle and then looks forward to the coming cycle, or the Client Checkpoint represents the end of the last cycle.

The Just Completed Cycle

Each project that follows an Adaptive Project Framework model presents the development team with a need to learn to work with the customer. Every cycle presents the development team with information to help it to work more effectively and efficiently with their customer team. For the Adaptive SDPM strategy, learning to work with the customer on the probative initiatives is a most critical learning experience. The customer may have no previous experience with the identification, execution, and learning through the use of probative initiatives. Even if the development team has worked with the customer team on previous projects, the combination of project type and customer type is still a unique experience. For each project, some customers naturally take a proactive role in the project while others are more reactive. Both are acceptable behaviors. The important factor is that the involvement is meaningful. The importance of this behavior grows as you move further out from the Adaptive to the Extreme projects.

At the completion of each cycle, the customer and the developers should take stock of what happened in terms of process and how it could be improved for the next cycle. Here are a few questions that might help that improvement effort:

- Did each party offer new or novel ideas?
- Did the probative initiatives suggest new features or functionality?
- Is there a synergy between the two parties?
- Does each party feel that there is progress toward an acceptable solution?
- Is the entire team working more effectively than earlier in the project?
- What tasks could have been done better? How?
- What tasks are working well and should be retained?

The Final Cycle

The final cycle is the final Client Checkpoint. There are two points worth mentioning here. First, the final cycle evaluates the acceptability of the final solution and its worthiness for deployment. Presumably, the final solution can't be far off from whatever ideal solution the customer may have had in mind or else the project would have been terminated in some previous cycle. Second, the project would have taught the developers how to work with this customer and even with any other customer group. The Adaptive SDPM strategy asks more of the customer than the previous strategies. Whereas their involvement could have been passive in the Linear, Incremental, and even in the Iterative SDPM strategies, that is not acceptable in the Adaptive SDPM strategy.

You might want to give the customer a chance to give input into this process. Perhaps a survey by an outside person—the Project Management Office (PMO), for example—would provide valuable information on how the development team could have improved how it worked with the customer. Such a survey can be very simple. The following questions might help improve the process for the next project:

- How did the development team bring us into the project?
- Was our involvement real or contrived? How could it have been improved?
- Did the development team help us understand the alternatives? How?
- Did the development team understand our business problem? How could they have done a better job?

Adaptive SDPM Strategy for the Closing Phase of the Adaptive Software Development Model

Figure 29-3 illustrates the Closing Phase of the Adaptive SDPM strategy for the Adaptive Software Development model.

The same two considerations that were discussed in the Adaptive Project Framework model—those of the just completed cycle and those of the final cycle—are concerns here, too.

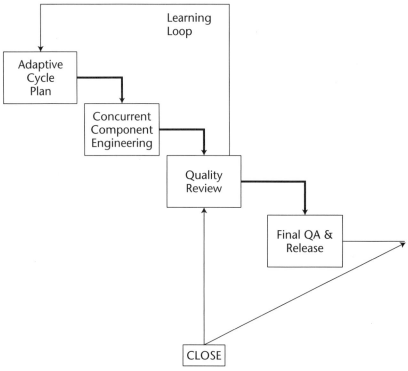

Figure 29-3: The Closing Phase of the Adaptive SDPM strategy for the Adaptive Software Development model

The Just Completed Cycle

The discussion for the Adaptive Project Framework model applies for the Adaptive Software Development model as well. The client role must be as meaningful here as in previous strategies. The difference is that it is more technically focused than in the Adaptive Project Framework model. The reason is that this model focuses on software development only, whereas the Adaptive Project Framework model encompasses software as well as other deliverables.

The Quality Review Phase of the Adaptive Software Development model is the analog of the Client Checkpoint Phase of the Adaptive Project Framework model. Except for the technical focus of the Adaptive Software Development Phase, the two are identical. Neither model is likely to produce a partial solution, although the Adaptive Software Development model is the more likely of the two to produce a partial solution. This will be done for the benefit of the customer when additional input is needed to identify new or revised features and functions on later cycles. These are not production-ready releases.

The Final Cycle

This does not compare directly to the final cycle of the Adaptive Project Framework model. Here the focus is more on the quality of the final solution and its documentation. The Adaptive Project Framework model focuses more on documenting the next version features and functions. Deployment to production is done after the final cycle.

Discussion Question

1. You have completed the first few cycles and the customer seems very satisfied with the progress to date. Not too much in the way of probative initiatives is surfacing from the customer. The solution has only vaguely been defined. There are two possibilities:

   a. The customer is having difficulty thinking outside the box.

   b. The customer hasn't really bought into the Adaptive strategy you are taking.

   Because so little is known about the solution, you are convinced that the Adaptive SDPM strategy is the correct approach. What would you do?

CHAPTER 30

The Adaptive SDPM Strategy Summary

Creative people have much more confidence in their imaginative leaps, in their intuition.

Laurel Cutler
Vice Chairman, FCB/Leber Katz Partners

Chapter Learning Objectives

After reading this chapter, you will be able to:

- ◆ Compare Traditional versus Adaptive projects
- ◆ Understand the fundamental differences between the responsibilities of Traditional and Adaptive project managers
- ◆ Understand the fundamental differences between Traditional and Adaptive project teams
- ◆ Compare Traditional to Adaptive project planning
- ◆ Know the impact of scope change management on Traditional and Adaptive projects

---

The Adaptive SDPM strategy is our second entry into the world of the agilist. The Adaptive world gets its strength from the creative spirit of the customer and the Adaptive team working in collaboration. In fact, creativity may be the only factor that accounts for a successful Adaptive project.

Traditional Versus Adaptive Projects

As you know, the Traditional project has clearly defined requirements, functions, and features. They are completely documented and unlikely to change—despite the fact that reality will prove otherwise and this specificity is unlikely to happen. However, it still leads the project manager to adopt a Linear or Incremental SDPM strategy. A complete project plan with the resource schedule is followed, and the project is completed within budget, time, and scope requirements. The success of the Traditional project hinges on the accuracy of the original requirements document. Small adjustments can be made, but the major direction of the project is determined at the front end. Major adjustments most often result in project termination with a view toward restarting the project with a new scope and requirements specification. That turns into a big wasted effort of time and money resulting from the aborted attempt.

Adaptive projects do not have that degree of specificity. In fact, much of the solution (expressed in terms of requirements, functions, and features specification) may be unknown. The more unknowns there are, the more challenge it will be to the creative energies of the whole team to produce a successful solution. This leads the project manager to shy away from speculation and develop a plan only for the known requirements. That plan is very different from the Traditional plan. For one thing, it is not a process-driven plan.

The Adaptive plan is cycle-based and just-in-time. It has two major thrusts:

- **The plan to add/revise functions or features into the current solution**—These would have come about as part of the original solution that had not yet been added or part of the solution discovered from earlier cycles now ready to be added to the solution. Each cycle plan contains such additions.

- **Learning and discovery**—Here the customer and the development team brainstorm and otherwise suggest probative initiatives to find out about the missing parts of the solution or about feasibility of certain ideas relative to adding/revising features and functions to the solution. Some of these initiatives will prove successful; others will not. But even those that do not still provide additional guidance as to which directions may prove successful. This is nothing more than a hunting expedition and should be viewed from that perspective.

Traditional Versus Adaptive Project Managers

I have already discussed the fact that Traditional project managers manage against the budget, schedule, and scope, and I don't need to repeat that discussion here. Simply recall that their approach is formal and based on status meetings, performance reviews, reports, and metric tracking.

Adaptive project managers manage against the deliverables and business value. Formality gives way to informality. With few exceptions, reports give way to the passing of tacit knowledge between the customer and all of the team members. Anything that does not contribute directly to the learning and discovery process is avoided as much as possible. There will, of course, be some reports that senior management requires. These cannot be avoided. That allows the focus to be solely on creating deliverables and the related business values. Anything else falls in the category of non–value-added work and is to be avoided. Only those artifacts that lead to that discovery are relevant. It is really at the discretion of the team as to which artifacts will be used. Bottom line—if it doesn't add value to your ability to manage the project, don't use it. Period.

What does all of this say about the project managers of Traditional versus Adaptive projects? The Traditional project manager is trained to follow process, and success is measured against their ability to meet budget, time, and scope constraints. Their consistency is a strong asset. They tend to be risk-averse. They work to reduce risk and preserve the constraints of time and money on the project.

The Adaptive project manager, on the other hand, is trained to deliver product and business value. They don't worry about meeting budget and time constraints, as does the Traditional project manager. Time and budget are fixed and scope is the variable. Whenever the timebox elapses or the budget runs out, the project is finished. At that point in time, they have collaboratively produced the best business value that the two constraints permitted.

The Adaptive project manager tends to be a risk-taker as is evidenced by the probative initiatives that they support. They depend heavily on the collaborative involvement of the customer and the development team. This is obviously based on the project manager having established a trusting relationship with the customer and the developers. The project manager will depend on their honest input and their willingness to push back if the probative initiatives just don't make good sense. The project manager has to make the call as to what eventually will be in the next cycle and that call will be difficult if the customer and the developers haven't spoken their mind and shared their real beliefs. Decisions are based on the extent to which they maximize the value they deliver to their customer, and the project manager will want all the assurance the customer and the development team can give.

Traditional Versus Adaptive Teams

As I discussed earlier, the Traditional projects can work with distributed teams of specialists and junior technical staff. The details will not be repeated. Recall, however, that the junior technical team members work under the direct supervision of the more senior members of the team. It is not necessary for the Traditional team members to be co-located. The requirements specification document and project schedule are their guides.

Ideally, Adaptive projects should have co-located teams of senior technical staff. When that is possible, the team should have its own team "war room." It is an area that they own for the duration of the project. They work side by side. They share ideas in real time rather than by e-mail or voice mail. The walls of their war room are covered in risks, issues, solution ideas, the updated project schedule, and other relevant information. They hold daily 15-minute team meetings in the war room. This is ideal but not always or often possible. When this is not possible, adjustments have to be made. Real-time meetings are still possible, but now some of the members are conferenced in from remote locations. The walls of the team war room are replaced by e-mails, chat rooms, instant messaging, and shared files of status, problems, risks, and so on. Time zones present a particular challenge. Some team members will be inconvenienced but even that can be rotated around by adjusting meeting times.

Little or no supervision of an Adaptive team is required or wanted for that matter. That is important because the team needs the freedom to pursue what they believe is in the best interest of discovery and learning and delivering business value.

Traditional Versus Adaptive Project Planning

To the traditionalist, planning is something you do once at the very beginning of the project. For the Traditional project manager, resources are scheduled and committed against a project plan and then managed to conformance with that plan. Any variances from the plan are corrected as needed. Having a complete plan sounds great, but is it worth the effort? Every change request that is approved requires some modification to the plan. The modification almost always requires some rescheduling, negotiating with resource managers to adjust commitments, and finally documenting and communicating the changes to all affected parties. If you cost out the changes, you can see that time was spent on parts of the plan that will no longer be needed. That time spent was wasted time—non–value-added time to the Adaptive project manager.

To the Adaptive project manager, planning is something you do just-in-time and continuously through the project. There is no speculation of the future, and therefore the cycle plan deals only with the coming cycle. Part of the plan deals with integrating new or revised functions and features and part deals with identifying probative initiatives for the next cycle. All of these are known, and there is no speculation about what could be or might be. Time is spent on planning those things that are known to be part of the solution.

Traditional Versus Adaptive Scope Change Management

You already know that scope change is the bane of the Traditional project manager. Every scope change request brings with it the work needed to generate the project impact statement as the deliverable from having processed the change request. This is non–value-added time. Depending on the extent of the scope change request, it can render many parts of the project plan obsolete or incorrect. The time and effort spent building those parts of the plan that are no longer relevant was time wasted. None of this is found in the Adaptive approaches.

You already know that scope change is the lifeblood of the Adaptive project manager. Scope change is a necessary ingredient for the Adaptive project team to converge on a successful solution that delivers maximum business value for the time and money invested. The frequency of scope change requests over the cycles can be a good bellwether for the effectiveness of the project. The frequency should increase at an increasing rate over consecutive early cycles, level off to a constant rate during the middle cycles, and finally increase at a decreasing rate over the later cycles. As the project nears completion, scope change requests should disappear. Any pattern significantly different from this one is a signal of problems. Too few scope change requests means that meaningful involvement is probably lacking. Too many scope change requests in later cycles is probably an indicator that the solution is not converging.

WARNING The Adaptive SDPM strategy is a high-risk strategy. The team must comprise seasoned professionals to undertake such a venture. No rookies allowed.

Discussion Question

1. Your organization has been a staunch promoter of the Adaptive approaches to project management and systems development. However, they are not at all satisfied with the results. Customers never seem to be satisfied with the results either. What are your concerns, and what positive steps might you take to mitigate them?

PART SIX

Extreme ESPM

In the Extreme approach you are at the edge of the uncertainty and complexity. Not only is there no solution, but also the goal is not even clearly known. There may be a goal—cure world hunger—but no one knows for sure if it is even attainable. Surely something is attainable that is related to the goal, but what is it? That has to be discovered through some Extreme approach. These projects are unique. They are the only types of projects where the goal and the solution are developed in parallel. One informs the other until an end is reached. That end is either acceptable or not. Pure research and development projects are often of this type.

CHAPTER 31

Extreme SDPM Strategy

An extreme project is a complex, self-correcting venture in search of a desired result.

Doug DeCarlo
Author and Senior Consultant
Cutter Consortium

Chapter Learning Objectives

After reading this chapter, you will:

- ◆ **Be able to explain the Extreme SDPM strategy**
- ◆ **Have a high-level understanding of INSPIRE and the Flexible model**

At first glance, you might wonder what the difference is between an Adaptive SDPM strategy and an Extreme SDPM strategy. First and foremost, the difference lies in goal clarity. Adaptive SDPM strategies require a clearly defined goal while the Extreme SDPM strategies do not. That places Extreme SDPM strategies in a research and development mode. Translated into application I would expect to see a number of parallel investigative swim lanes in the early stages of an Extreme SDPM strategy. The number of those parallel swim lanes decreases as the project moves forward. The decrease occurs because several swim lanes are eliminated as feasible directions for goal and solution discovery.

This final SDPM model type applies to those projects whose solution and goal are not known or not clearly defined. Here you are in the world of pure research and development, new product development, and process improvement projects.

The Extreme SDPM Strategy

What do you do if what is needed is not clearly defined? What if it isn't defined at all? As I just indicated, when you enter the world of the Extreme SDPM strategy, you enter the world of research and development—a world where goals are not clearly defined and, of course, the solution is not clearly defined either. In fact, the solution might be quite elusive. The bottom line, however, is that the project is critically important to the enterprise. The goal must be clarified and a solution must be found. Perhaps, you have tried to force fit the traditional approach into these situations and found it flat out doesn't work. Extreme SDPM strategies are designed to handle projects whose goal can be only fuzzily defined or really not defined at all. Figure 31-1 illustrates the generic relationship between the Extreme software development process phases and the project management phases.

Building a business-to-business (B2B) Web site with no further specification is an excellent example of a project in need of an Extreme SDPM strategy. Much like the early stages of an R&D project, building the B2B Web site starts out with a guess, or maybe several guesses. As the project commences, the client reflects upon the alternatives chosen and gives some direction to the development team. This process repeats itself over and over again. Either the partial solution converges on a satisfactory solution or is killed along the way. In most cases, there is no fixed budget or timeline. Obviously, the client wants it completed ASAP for as little as possible. Furthermore, the lack of a clear goal and solution opens the project to a lot of change. Unfortunately, the nature of this project does not lend itself to fixed time and cost constraints.

The Extreme SDPM strategy lies at the outpost of the software development landscape. It serves the needs of those development projects where very little is known about the details of the development effort. This section gives a high-level overview of what constitutes Extreme SDPM strategies. As such, it is a good starting point for the executive or manager who simply needs to become familiar with Extreme SDPM.

Scope Phase

The Scope Phase for the Extreme SDPM strategy closely resembles the Scope Phase of the Adaptive SDPM strategy. The difference is that much less is known about the typical Extreme project than about the typical Adaptive project. Keep in mind that you are in the realm of projects that look much like research and development projects. The Scope Phase should include a brainstorming session where all possible avenues for exploration are identified. Many of these will become concurrent swim lanes in the early cycles of the project. The best strategy here is to leave all options open. Do not prematurely discard an idea if it has any possibility of providing fruitful results. Some ideas, no matter how avante garde, might lead to other ideas that do produce results.

Plan and Launch Phases

These two phases are essentially the same as in the Adaptive SDPM strategy. However, because the Extreme project is far more speculative than the Adaptive project, you can expect to have far more concurrent swim lanes early in the project with a high mortality rate. In the case of the Adaptive project the swim lanes are based on established requirements, functions, and features with only a modicum of speculation in some of the swim lanes. For the Adaptive project these are the probing swim lanes. They are trying to uncover unknown functions and features. The Extreme project, on the other hand, might be nothing more than probing swim lanes, at least at the start.

Monitor and Control Phases

Because of the highly speculative nature of Extreme projects, be prepared to cancel swim lanes that don't seem to be leading to any productive results. You are basically on a fishing expedition. If something isn't working, move on to something that holds promise. The plan should reflect a beginning strategy that is divergent with later cycles starting to show signs of convergence. In the absence of that, the project might not be appropriate and should be cancelled.

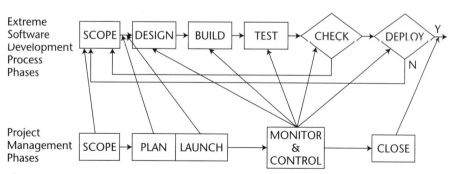

Figure 31-1: Extreme SDPM strategy

Close Phase

Closing the Extreme SDPM strategy project can occur in two ways. Because it is a very speculative project, it might not be heading in a productive direction, and it is cancelled. The funding source is not seeing any convergence and isn't willing to spend any more money on the direction chosen. The project might still be worked on but from a different direction altogether. On a positive note, the project might end because the money has run out and at least a partial solution has been achieved. The project might continue but with new funding.

Types of Extreme SDPM Strategies

The literature doesn't have much to offer here. I have been promoting a model that I call INSPIRE (**IN**itiate, **SP**eculate, **I**nnovate, **RE**view) as one approach. Another approach, the Flexible model, is documented in a recent book by my colleague and friend Doug DeCarlo, *eXtreme Project Management: Using Leadership, Principles, and Tools to Deliver Value in the Face of Volatility*" (Jossey-Bass, 2004), and a brief description of it is also presented in this section.

These two strategies are discussed from the perspective of software development but their application is more far reaching than that. Both strategies can be applied in other areas. Pure research and development, process improvement, and new product development are three areas where they both have been applied with great success. That sets these two approaches apart from the other approaches discussed earlier. They are all defined with software development as their focus.

INSPIRE

By its very nature, as a form of Extreme Project Management (xPM), INSPIRE is unstructured. It is designed to handle projects with "fuzzy goals" or goals that cannot be defined because of the exploratory nature of the Extreme project. By way of example, consider the Routing sub-system in the case study. It is truly an exploratory venture. No one has yet to build a delivery system where the sources are moving entities. The sources are always stationary. Then how about the goal? Exactly what is it? Delivering the pizza on time would seem to be the goal, but could the goal also include delivery by the most efficient route or maximizing the number of deliveries in a period of time? Just as in the Adaptive SDPM strategy, the theme is that the learning and discovery takes place between the client and the project team in each iteration and moves the project forward toward an acceptable solution. But that solution unfolds in parallel with the clarification of the goal.

The first model I am going to discuss is called INSPIRE. As Figure 31-2 illustrates, INSPIRE consists of four phases that I am calling **IN**itiate, **SP**eculate, Incubate, and **RE**view.

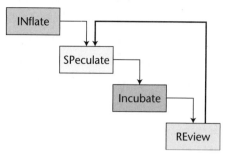

Figure 31-2: INSPIRE

INSPIRE is an iterative approach. INSPIRE iterates in an unspecified number of short cycles (1- to 4-week cycle lengths are typical) in search of the solution to a poorly specified goal. It might find an acceptable solution, or it might be cancelled before any solution is reached. But at the start, the goal is unknown, or at best, someone has a vague, but unspecified, notion of what the goal consists of. It may be nothing more than a desired end state with no idea of how to accomplish it or even whether it can be accomplished. As the search for a solution unfolds, so does a clarification of the goal.

Let's consider an example that's not specifically software development–related, such as an example might be to state the original goal as "Cure world hunger." As the project work commences, it becomes obvious that the original goal is not feasible but curing hunger in Botswana is and so that becomes the goal. A software development example might be to build a sub-system that minimizes the cost of home delivery of pizza. As the project unfolds it becomes obvious that no such closed form solution exists and some heuristic solution may be the only possibility. All that can be expected is to reduce the cost of home delivery by successively modifying the solution through experience.

Also, INSPIRE requires the client to be more involved within and between cycles, whereas Adaptive SDPM strategies require client involvement between cycles. The project team begins by choosing some investigative direction(s) and hopes that intermediate findings and results will do two things:

- Provide a more informed and productive direction for the next and future cycles
- Convince the funding agent the learning and discovery is potentially rewarding so that they continue the funding support

INSPIRE does have stopping rules, but they are very different than any found in Traditional Project Management (TPM) or even in Adaptive SDPM strategies. INSPIRE has two stopping rules:

- **Success!**—The project is over when an acceptable solution is found.

- **Failure!**—The project is over when the sponsor is not willing to continue the funding because the project is not making any meaningful progress or it is not converging on an acceptable solution. In other words, the project is killed.

The next sections take a high-level look at the four phases of INSPIRE.

INitiate

The INitiate Phase is a mixture of selling the idea, establishing the business value of the project, brainstorming possible approaches, forming the team, and getting everyone on board and excited about what they are about to undertake. It is definitely a time for team building and creating a strong working relationship with the client. During this phase, you will perform the following activities that you know from more traditional projects, but will approach them in a new way:

- **Defining the project goal**—Unlike the goal of an Adaptive project, the goal of an Extreme project is not much more than a vision of some future state. It is not something that you can plan to achieve; it is only something that you and the client discover along the way. That process of discovery is exciting. It will call upon all of the creative juices that the team and the client can muster.

    At this early stage, any definition of the project goal should be that vision of the future. It would be good at this point to discuss how the user or client of the deliverables will use the software product. Don't be too restrictive, either. Forming a vision of the end state is as much a brainstorming exercise as it is anything else. Don't close out any ideas that may prove useful later on.

- **Establishing a project timebox and cost**—An Extreme project is not usually constrained by a fixed timeframe or cost limit. It is best to think of the INSPIRE time and cost parameters as something to give the project team guidance on what the client expectations are. It is much like having the client say: "I would like to see some results within X months, and I am willing to invest as much as $Y to have you deliver." The reality is that at each REview phase, the decision to continue or abort is made. That decision isn't necessarily tied to the time and cost parameters given earlier by the client. In fact, if there is exceptional progress toward a solution, the client might relax either or both of the time and cost parameters. Put another way, if the progress to date is promising, more time and/or money might be put at the team's disposal.

■ **Establishing the number of cycles and cycle length**—In the beginning, short cycles are advisable as new ideas are tested, and many are rejected; proof of concept might be part of the first few cycles. Don't commit to complex activities and tasks early on. As the team gains a better sense of direction, cycle length can be increased. Specifying cycle length and the number of cycles up front merely sets expectations as to when and how frequently the REview phase will take place. At each occurrence of a REview phase, cycle length and perhaps the number of cycles remaining can be changed to suit the situation. Flexibility is the key to a successful xPM project.

■ **Prioritizing trade-offs in the scope triangle**—Despite the fact that INSPIRE is unstructured, it is important that the priorities of the variables in the scope triangle (see Figure 31-3) be set. As project work commences and problems arise, which variable or variables are the client and the team willing to compromise? The five variables in a project are as follows:

 ■ Scope

 ■ Quality

 ■ Cost

 ■ Time

 ■ Resource availability

Which of these is least likely to be compromised? Which would you choose to compromise first, if the situation warranted it? The answer depends on the type of project.

Figure 31-3: Scope triangle

SPeculate

This phase defines the beginning of a new cycle and always starts with a brainstorming session. The input will either be a blank slate or output from the previous SPeculate-Incubate-REview cycle. In any case, the project team, client, and final user of the software product should participate in the brainstorming session. The objective of this session is to explore ideas and identify alternative directions for the next Incubate phase. Because an Extreme project has a strong exploratory nature about it, no idea should be neglected. Cycle length, deliverables, and other planning artifacts are defined in the SPeculate phase as well.

Defining How the Project Will Be Done

The initial sense of direction for the team to take in the first cycle of an Extreme project can vary considerably. A good approach is to use a Project Overview Statement (POS) as a guide. (See Appendix C for details on the POS.) The POS can continuously be updated to reflect the current view of the project, and its objective statements can serve as a guide to what will be done. In later cycles, the team and the client will have the benefit of learning and discovery from the prior cycles.

Scenarios, Stories, and Use Cases

For your purposes, these three terms are synonymous because all can be defined as descriptions of how a person might use the application. Because the application may be feature-rich, there can be, and usually will be, several such descriptions. If done correctly, these descriptions will be exhaustive of how the application can be used and can then be prioritized and assigned to the appropriate development cycles. There is no practical limit to the number of such situations that are documented, but be careful not to get too aggressive with them. Many will be speculative and not worth spending much time on. Remember that after every iteration you and the client will be reviewing what happened and deciding on the next ones to integrate into the solution. In the case of technology projects, such as Web site development, the client may be more comfortable telling you how they envision someone using the deliverable and what they can do at the Web site than they would be in trying to help you write a functional specification. The advantage in using scenarios, stories, and use cases is that the view you are building is from the user side, not from the technology side.

Prioritizing Requirements

The collection of scenarios, stories, and use cases provides insight into the requirements that the deliverable should meet. For the client, it is far easier to prioritize the collection than it is to prioritize the requirements. Prioritization is the next step in the SPeculate phase.

Identifying the First Cycle Deliverables

Once the prioritization is done, it is time to decide how much of that prioritized list to bite off for the initial cycle. Remembering that you want shorter cycles in the early part of the project suggests that you limit the first cycle deliverables to what you can reasonably accomplish in a week or two.

NOTE By taking this approach, you are keeping the client's interest up. That is important. Once the client has been fully engaged in the project, later cycles can be lengthened.

Because your team resources are limited, it might be better to extend the breadth to accommodate more functions by not delving deeply into any one function. Produce enough detail in each function in this initial cycle to get a sense of further direction for the function. You might learn from only a shallow look at a function that it isn't going to be part of the final solution, which saves you the labor that might have been spent on that function.

Go/No Go Decision

Because the initial cycle can be exploratory, the sponsor must have an opportunity to judge the soundness of the initial cycle plan and decide whether it makes sense to proceed. It is entirely possible that the original idea of the client cannot be delivered with the approach taken in the first cycle, and the first cycle leads the client to the decision that the idea doesn't make any sense after all. The go/no go decision points will occur at the end of each cycle. Decisions to stop a project are more likely to occur in the early cycles than in the later cycles. One should expect later cycles to have the benefit of earlier results that suggest that the project direction is feasible and should be continued.

Planning for Later Cycles

Later cycles will have the benefit of output from a REview phase to inform the planning activities that will take place in the SPeculate phase that will follow. Each REview phase will produce a clearer vision and definition of the goal. That clearer vision translates into a redirection of the project and that translates into a new prioritized list of deliverables for the coming Incubate phase. The revised prioritized deliverables list is taken into consideration as the team plans what it will do in the coming Incubate phase. It is now in the same position as it was in the very first SPeculate phase. What follows then is the assignment of deliverables to subteams and the scheduling of the work that will be done and who will do it.

Incubate

The Incubate Phase is the INSPIRE's version of the Cycle Build Phase in APF. However, an important distinction exists between the INSPIRE approach and that in APF. Although the Incubate Phase has a prioritized list of deliverables that are to be produced in this cycle, INSPIRE still maintains the spirit of exploration, a learning and discovery experience that might result in mid-cycle corrections that arise from that exploration. APF, on the other hand, does benefit from learning and discovery as it proceeds with the cycle plan, but it does not vary from the plan. The learning and discovery are input to the Client Checkpoint and that is where plan revisions take place.

The Incubate Phase proceeds as follows:

- **Assigning resources**—The Incubate Phase begins with an assignment of team members to each of the deliverables that have been prioritized for this cycle. This should be a team exercise; because of the exploratory nature of INSPIRE cycles, team members need to express their interest in one or more deliverables and also share their ideas with their fellow team members. It's a great opportunity for project managers to create a synergy among team members with similar interests, as well as between subteams that will be working in parallel on different deliverables.

- **Establishing the cycle plan**—With the subteams in place and with their assignments made, the subteams can plan how they will produce the deliverables assigned to them. A whiteboard layout can be used to show a day-by-day schedule of what is going to be done and who is going to do it.

NOTE

Never forget that there are some differences to a cycle plan in INSPIRE. In INSPIRE, you have to be ready for changes at any time, ready to move when you come to a point where a change of direction makes sense. In these situations, the team needs to collaborate with the client and decide how to go forward.

- **Collaboratively producing deliverables**—Collaboration among subteams must occur. Because of the exploratory nature of an INSPIRE project, no one has a lock on the solution. Even the goal is somewhat elusive. The goal and the solution can be attained only through a solid team effort—a collaborative effort, much like brainstorming. As Estill I. Green, VP of Bell Telephone Laboratories, has said: "Clearly no group can as an entity create ideas. Only individuals can do this. A group of individuals may, however, stimulate one another in the creation of ideas."

REview

The REview phase is very similar to the Client Checkpoint Phase in APF. All of the learning and discovery from the just-completed Incubate phase is brought together in another brainstorming session. Answers to questions such as the following will be shared:

- What did we learn?
- What can we do to enhance goal attainment?
- What new ideas arose and should be pursued?
- What should we do in the next cycle?
- Have the results to date met client expectations?
- Is the project converging on an acceptable solution?
- Should the project continue?

These answers determine whether or not the project continues to the next cycle or is cancelled (the go/no go decision point). Be prepared; INSPIRE is so exploratory and research-based that cancellations are likely.

Revising the Project Goal

The first order of business is for the client and the project team to revisit the goal statement that was produced during the prior REview phase. That review is best facilitated by asking the following questions:

- What new information do you have from the just-completed Incubate Phase?
- What approaches can you eliminate?
- What new discoveries suggest a change in the goal definition?
- Are you converging on a more clearly defined and acceptable goal statement?

This revision of the project goal is an important step and must not be treated lightly. The client and the team need to be very objective and open and come to a consensus on that new goal statement. Updating the POS with the new goal statement would be good closure to this exercise.

Reprioritizing Requirements

The second order of business is for the client and the project team to revisit deliverables and requirements. The following questions should be asked here:

- How does the new goal statement impact the deliverables list?
- Should some items be removed?
- Should new items be added?
- How is the functionality already embedded in the solution affected by the revised goal statement?

The answers to these questions allow the client and the project team to reprioritize the new requirements. Updating the POS to reflect the changes in the objective statements would be good closure to this exercise.

Making the Go/No Go Decision for Next Cycle

Will there be a next SPeculate-Incubate-REview cycle? Equivalently, the question could be this: Are we converging at an acceptable rate on a clearly defined goal and acceptable solution? The client will consider this question in the face of the money and time already spent. Does it make business sense to continue this project? The updated POS is the input to this decision.

Complexity and uncertainty are at their highest points in Extreme project management. The goal and obviously the solution are not clearly known at the outset of the project. The approach you must take is one of learning and discovery. As such, the project management life cycle will be very light. Figure 31-4 shows the integration of the INSPIRE and project management life cycles.

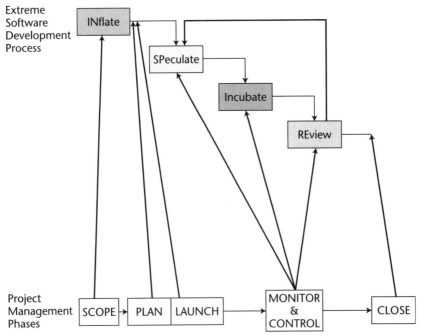

Figure 31-4: Extreme SDPM strategy for INSPIRE

Many of the artifacts visible in earlier approaches are present in an Extreme project, but they are not as visible. There is less dependence on formal documentation and more dependence on tacit knowledge. You'll see that as you further explore INSPIRE in Chapters 32–37.

The Flexible Model

This model was recently defined in a comprehensive book by Doug DeCarlo, *eXtreme Project Management: Using Leadership, Principles, and Tools to Deliver Value in the Face of Volatility"* (Jossey-Bass, 2004). DeCarlo calls his model "The Flexible model." It is illustrated in Figure 31-5.

Note that the Flexible model is a five-phase model whereas INSPIRE was represented in four phases. The difference is the Disseminate Phase that DeCarlo has added. The first three phases of the Flexible model are iterative, as is the Speculate-Innovate-Reevaluate sequence. The next sections take a look at each phase in some detail.

Visionate

This beginning phase is purposed to define what is needed, who needs it, and why they need it. It is a collaborative and iterative exercise involving the project manager and the sponsor. The vision that is captured by their collaboration is put to later scrutiny and a collective vision emerges. The collective version is the output from consideration by critical stakeholders, the sponsor, and the project manager. That collective version becomes the basis for launching the project.

Speculate

Having agreed on the what, who, and why of the project, the Speculate Phase looks into the question of what it will take to achieve the vision of the project. This is basically a planning meeting to identify the infrastructure that will be needed—tools, templates, resources, financial support, communications, and so on. Again, this is an iterative and collaborative exercise. Stakeholders, the customer, the project manager, and the core project team are all involved in defining the environment in which the project will operate. The Speculate Phase considers the business value that will result and answers the question: "Is it worth it?"

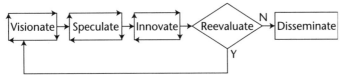

Figure 31-5: The Flexible model

Innovate

Here is where the real work of the project takes place. Think of it as the equivalent of design, build, and test, and you won't be far off the mark. The major difference is that time is not spent on planning the last detail. Rather, the focus is on doing and learning by doing. You will have several false starts and many failures along the way. The goal is to get it right the last time. APF, on the other hand, seeks to get it right every time. You never know when the plug will be pulled and funding cut off.

Reevaluate

This is the stage-gate where the team and the customer do a quality check on what has happened so far. The big question here is: "What is the future of the project?" Either success or failure can be claimed here. Success might mean you are done or that more work will be done in future cycles. Failure might mean that the result was not worth it and the project will be killed. However, that is not to say that a new effort, in a different direction, will not be commissioned.

Disseminate

If the project is a success, and the result worth it, the product will be deployed to the end users. Future versions might be undertaken to add more business value, but at least there is an acceptable product at this point.

Figure 31-6 illustrates the Extreme SDPM strategy for the Flexible model.

The details and application of this strategy will be discussed in Chapters 32–37.

WARNING Extreme strategies are self-correcting, as mentioned in the quote that introduced this chapter. That means that what little planning is done is done just in time. That often leaves senior managers in a rather unsettled condition. Taking an Extreme approach means that you are entering the world of research and development project management. The risk is high, but the importance of the project dictates that such an approach must be taken. Good strong sponsorship will be required.

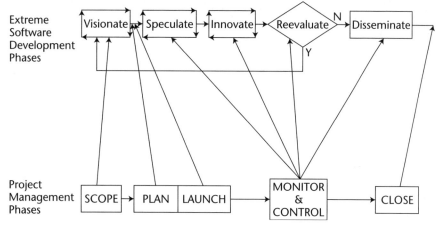

Figure 31-6: Extreme SDPM strategy for the Flexible model

Discussion Questions

1. The customer is heavily involved in the project but keeps introducing new directions that are preventing you from converging on a solution. You feel like the team is spinning its wheels and morale is suffering as a result. What would you do and why?

2. Early cycles are not converging on a solution and the project seems to be drifting out of control. How would you address this situation?

The Extreme SDPM Scoping Phase

"Never kill an idea, just deflect it."
3M Company saying

Chapter Learning Objectives

After reading this chapter, you will be able to:

- ◆ **Explain the Scoping Phase of the Extreme SDPM strategy**
- ◆ **Conduct the Scoping Phase of the INSPIRE model**
- ◆ **Conduct the Scoping Phase of the Flexible model**

The final strategy variation is to move from the Adaptive SDPM strategy to the Extreme SDPM strategy, which is discussed in this part of the book. Adaptive models arise out of the customer's inability to completely define requirements and obviously the features that accompany them. As is the case when the Iterative SDPM strategy is used, the customer may not be able to identify some of the features associated with known functionality. To find a complete solution, the customer will have to be more intimately involved throughout the entire project life cycle than has been the case in all previous strategies. With few exceptions, in most cases the projects that fall into the Extreme SDPM strategy are new systems development projects. Often these will be standalone projects rather than highly integrated into other software systems.

The Scoping Phase of an Extreme SDPM Strategy

In the Extreme SDPM strategy the Requirements Breakdown Structure (RBS) from the Adaptive SDPM strategy is modified to look like Figure 32-1. You have very little knowledge of the goal (the solution) and very little knowledge of the requirements, functions, or features. Hence, you have a project that is not much different than a pure R&D project. Projects that follow an Extreme SDPM strategy are those for which both a complete RBS cannot be defined at the outset, and the customer and project team know it.

Figure 32-1 characterizes this by illustrating a cloud that covers the goal. So in this case, the goal and solution are both hidden by the cloud cover. The solution is represented by the requirements, functions, and features decomposition. The objective of the Extreme SDPM strategy is to move the cloud and discover what lies behind it—in other words, to learn and discover through iteration what the goal really is and how it can be reached. The Extreme SDPM strategy follows a path quite similar to the Adaptive SDPM strategy in that it must accommodate not only the development of the known parts of the solution but also discovery of the unknown parts of the solution, while, at the same time, defining the goal that the solution will attain. Discovering the goal and the solution in parallel requires even a tighter collaboration of the customer and the project team, as was the case in the Adaptive SDPM strategy. Purely probative ideas are investigated in one or more cycles. Some are rejected. Some open up directions for further probes in later cycles. And some result in more of the solution being uncovered and then implemented in later cycles. To do this effectively and efficiently is a challenge. The Scoping Phase lays out the approach at a very high level.

Projects that follow an Extreme approach are the highest risk projects in the project landscape. Their successful completion is critically important to the enterprise. Like the Adaptive projects, the future of the business may well rest on finding this acceptable solution. At the same time, they are high-reward projects. Their successful completion may result in the introduction of a major innovation in the product or service marketplace. The financial rewards will be worth the effort.

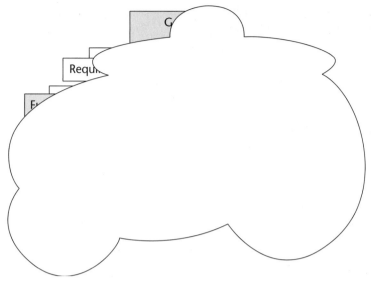

Figure 32-1: The initial RBS for an Extreme SDPM strategy

The Scoping Phase of the Extreme SDPM Strategy for the INSPIRE Model

Figure 32-2 illustrates the integration of the project management Scope Phase and the INSPIRE Initiate Phase. This Extreme SDPM Scoping Phase for the INSPIRE Model is the beginning of the project. As you can see, the initial Scoping Phase is done once for the INSPIRE project. There are two major parts to it: a defining part and a planning part. The defining can effectively be completed by two parties: a requestor and a provider. These may each be single individuals or small groups that represent the two parties. In either case the critical factor is that they not only represent their constituency but also speak for their constituency and can make decisions and commitments for their constituency.

Figure 32-2: Scoping Phase of the Extreme SDPM strategy for the INSPIRE model

An INSPIRE project begins with a business-critical need. There are five artifacts that are produced in the Scoping Phase of the Extreme SDPM strategy for the INSPIRE model. They are as follows:

- **The Project Overview Statement (POS)**—The POS, which you have encountered in all previous SDPM strategies, is the documentation you use to sell the idea.

- **A definition of the project goal**—Because you know so little about the goal, this definition will not be much more than a desired end state. As the project proceeds, you will get more clarity on that end state and may change it based on our findings. That can come about because the initial vision of the end state turns out to not be feasible. Some compromises might have to be made. On the other hand, you may discover that much more than the initial end state can be done within the time and cost constraints. In either case, you must be flexible and open to new ideas as to the real targeted end state. The realities of an Extreme project are that the problem (the goal) and its solution (requirements, functions, and features) are discovered in parallel.

- **The timebox and cost**—The specification of these is not needed for the project to commence, but they do give the project team some boundaries to shoot for. The customer is paying the bill, and their criteria results in a continuance or cancellation of the project. As long as their expectations are being met, they continue to fund the project. At any time they may decide to cancel. That decision usually results from a lack of convergence on a meaningful solution. They will tolerate some divergence of thinking as a number of alternative ideas are investigated, but sooner or later they expect to see convergence on a meaningful business solution.

- **The establishment of the number of cycles and length of each cycle**—In the beginning, cycle length should be short—the shorter the better. That allows for a large number of potential solution areas to be quickly investigated for their feasibility. Once a candidate list of feasible solution areas has been identified, the areas can be prioritized and worked on in more detail to accept, reject, or modify for future cycle investigation. It's important not to reject ideas prematurely. In other words, keep your options open as long as possible.

- **Prioritization of the five variables (scope, quality, cost, time, and resource availability) that define the scope triangle**—The goal is to give the team a sense of direction and a tool for decision-making as team members complete their work within the cycles.

The Scoping Phase of the Extreme SDPM Strategy for the Flexible Model

Figure 32-3 illustrates the integration of the project management Scoping Phase and the Flexible model Visionate Phase. This Extreme SDPM Scoping Phase for the Flexible model is the beginning of the project. As you can see, the Visionate Phase is iterative and is repeated a number of times throughout the cycles of an INSPIRE project.

There are two parts to the Visionate Phase:

- The Sponsor's Vision
- The Collective Vision

As Figure 32-3 shows, this is an iterative process. The Visionate Phase is focused on answering two business questions:

- What is needed?
- Why is it needed?

Sponsor's Vision

To get the Sponsor's Vision you need to have a face-to-face meeting with the sponsor. At that meeting your questions should be guided by the first three parts of the POS. In order, you need to document:

- **Problem/opportunity statement**—What is the problem or opportunity that has given rise to this project?
- **Goal and objectives**—What are your goals and objectives for this project; that is, what do you expect to deliver?
- **Success criteria**—What is the quantitative business value that will result from the successful completion of this project?

The POS would be a good way to communicate, in written document form, the high-level description of the project. The sponsor should have an opportunity in a second meeting to review and approve the POS.

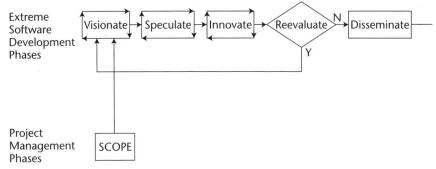

Figure 32-3: Scoping Phase of the Extreme SDPM strategy for the Flexible model

Collective Vision

The purpose of the collective vision is to come to closure on how the project will commence. It is not a planning document, but merely another view of the Sponsor's Vision. Doug DeCarlo's *eXtreme Project Management: Using Leadership, Principles, and Tools to Deliver Value in the Face of Volatility* (Jossey-Bass, 2004) lists the following as the steps that lead to the Collective Vision effort:

1. Scoping meeting held
2. Probable future scenarios identified
3. Three-sentence project skinny agreed to
4. Project boundaries agreed to
5. Program breakdown structure agreed to
6. Project imperatives agreed to
7. Product vision agreed to
8. Project win conditions agreed to
9. Benefits map drafted
10. Wow! Factor identified
11. Project uncertainty profile updated

These are briefly described in the following subsections.

Scoping Meeting Held

This will be the second or third meeting with the sponsor, but in this meeting the core team will be included for the first time. The purpose is to come to closure on the scope of the project.

Probable Future Scenarios Identified

The entire team should spend some time describing the end state. It may not be achievable, but at least the stake is put in the ground. It also gives a sense of direction to the early stages of the project even though it may change as new discoveries are made.

Three-Sentence Project Skinny Agreed To

The *project skinny* is a short and precise description of the project.

- The first sentence states who is doing what and for whom.
- The second sentence defines what the end of the project will look like. In other words, it is the doneness criteria that must be met in order for the project to be deemed complete.
- The third sentence states why the project is being done. It relates the project to the enterprise strategy and establishes the expected business value.

Project Boundaries Agreed To

To the extent possible the boundary conditions are defined by what is within the scope of the project and what is outside the scope of the project. Because of the lack of clarity on what form the final solution will take, these boundary conditions are expected to change.

Program Breakdown Structure Agreed To

Many, if not all, Extreme projects will really be a combination of several dependent projects. They are collected together as a project. The Program Breakdown Structure is a graphic depiction of how those projects are related to one another as a program.

Project Imperatives Agreed To

Among all of the requirements, which few must be part of the final solution for the project to be deemed a success? Without these requirements the project could not succeed.

Product Vision Agreed To

The collective understanding and agreement among sponsor and core team of what the final solution will be is the critical deliverable from the scoping meeting. Both parties agree that it will probably change, but based on their current knowledge of the situation, this vision statement represents their best effort.

Project Win Conditions Agreed To

DeCarlo (2004) identifies seven generic "win conditions" that are inclusive of the win conditions for any Extreme project. They are:

- Quality
- Schedule
- Scope: Functions and features
- Resources
- Return on investment
- Customer satisfaction
- Team satisfaction

For a given project specific, values are assigned to each win condition. As appropriate, they should each have quantitative and measurable values.

Benefits Map Drafted

The purpose of the benefits map is to show how the project deliverables are related to the expected business outcome. Figure 32-4 shows an example Benefits map for the PDQ case study.

Wow! Factor Identified

The term "Wow Project" speaks of a project that is so exciting and revolutionary that it "gets you out of bed in the morning." You can hardly wait to get to the office and continue working on it, which is why it is important to establish your project as a "Wow Project." Rather than have team members think that they are just working on another project, wouldn't you rather have them thinking they are working on a groundbreaking project? That's a no brainer!

Project Uncertainty Profile Updated

There are four primary areas of project risk: business, product, project, and organizational. Assessing these areas early on is of great use when making the decision to go forward with a project or not. Beyond the early assessment there should be periodic updates of the risk assessments for each of these areas. As more is learned about the solution, more will be known about the project uncertainties. This update will support or not the decision to continue the project to the next milestone event.

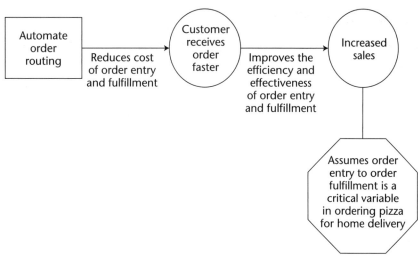

Figure 32-4: Benefits map for the PDQ case study

Discussion Question

1. We have seen the scoping phase of five different SDPM strategies. Based on that information how will you decide which strategy to adopt? Will you ever encounter a situation during the project that will cause you to change your mind and switch to a different strategy? Be specific.

CHAPTER 33

The Extreme SDPM Planning Phase

Tis best to build no castles in the air.

Fanny Burney
English novelist

Chapter Learning Objectives

After reading this chapter, you will:

- ◆ **Understand the planning phase of the Extreme SDPM strategy for the INSPIRE model**

- ◆ **Understand the planning phase of the Extreme SDPM strategy for the Flexible model**

This is the last of the three SDPM strategies that apply to situations where some or all of the solution cannot be known at the outset of the project but must be discovered through the iterations of the project. In this chapter, you face projects where the goal isn't even clearly definable. You think you have a statement for the goal except you do not know if it is attainable. The fallback position is what goal is attainable or to what degree can we solve this problem? Given that the problem is critical, how can we plan such endeavors? Such projects are not for the faint of heart. They are high-risk and high-reward projects, and you have no choice but to attack them. In this chapter, I discuss the planning of such projects.

The Planning Phase of an Extreme SDPM strategy is truly a just-in-time planning event.

The Planning Phase of an Extreme SDPM Strategy

Simply put, you are in a project situation where you don't know where you are going but somehow you have to figure out how to get there as you simultaneously define where it is that you are going. The situation is not unlike the one depicted in Figure 33-1.

You start out on Path 1 toward a desired goal (the solution). Along the way you adjust the path as you gain some information that suggests the goal is not where you thought it was. Continuing in this fashion you either kill the project or eventually arrive at an acceptable goal—a goal that may be very different than the one that launched the project. This is the typical Extreme project.

Now, how do you plan such a project? Most would say that it is impossible. If you don't really know where you are going, how could you possibly know when you get there? That is a good question and the Extreme project manager has an answer. As long as the customer is happy with the interim results and is willing to continue supporting the project, you continue. At some point, the customer either cancels the project (because of unacceptable progress or lack of convergence on an acceptable solution) or congratulations, you are done. The current solution is acceptable. Whatever goal is attached to that end state, it is the true goal. And as the diagram shows, the attained goal is very different than the desired goal but within the range of acceptable solutions.

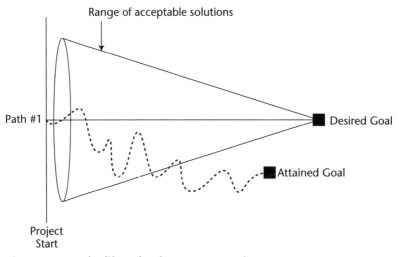

Figure 33-1: The life cycle of an Extreme project

If you look at this life cycle from another perspective, you can define the problem and the solution in concurrent swim lanes. The current solution helped you define the current problem. As soon as you reached a point where you solved a meaningful problem, you were done. You could have just as easily come up with a solution outside the range of acceptable solutions or not come up with any solution at all, in which case the project would have been deemed a failure.

To get back to discussing just how you might plan such a project, Figure 33-2 illustrates the parts of the project management Planning Phase and the Extreme Planning Phase.

First of all, note that the Planning Phase of the Extreme SDPM strategy is an iterative Planning Phase. It is repeated after every checkpoint in which the customer agrees that the project should continue. Planning, therefore, is focused on the next cycle only. You don't speculate and plan for the future because the future is unknown. So planning is restricted to the next cycle, which will typically be 2–6 weeks in length.

The next sections take a look at how the INSPIRE model and the Flexible model conduct Extreme project planning.

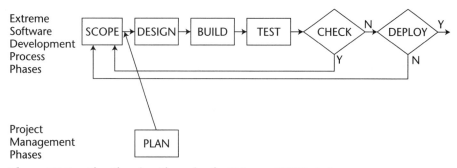

Figure 33-2: The Planning Phase for the Extreme SDPM strategy

The Planning Phase of an Extreme SDPM Strategy for the INSPIRE Model

Figure 33-3 is the Planning Phase of the Extreme SDPM strategy for the INSPIRE model.

Note that planning is an iterative activity in the Extreme SDPM strategy for the INSPIRE model. Planning takes place at the beginning of the SPeculate Phase. The input to the Planning Phase is the current solution produced in the previous cycle and any new learning or discoveries from the last iteration. Three deliverables are produced in the Planning Phase:

■ The functionality to be developed in the next cycle

■ New probative initiatives for the next cycle

■ Validation of the next cycle length

They are described in the subsections that follow.

Next Cycle Functionality

The prioritized list of functionality is updated with the discoveries and learning from the just completed cycle. A probative initiative may have uncovered another piece of the solution in the form of new functionality or new features for existing functionality. Functionality planned for the just completed cycle may not have actually been completed and has to be returned to the prioritized list for consideration in the next cycle. In either case this new information must be integrated into the prioritized list of functionality. The project team identifies the functionality that it can complete in the next cycle. Some consideration must be given to the business value to be created. If there is to be a deployment of a partial solution, it must have sufficient business value, so other functionality may be added to the next cycle list. That will probably lengthen the cycle.

Next Cycle Probative Initiatives

The search for the unknown parts of the solution continues with the specification of probative initiatives for the next cycle. These will be parallel swim lanes to accompany the solution development swim lanes. Brainstorming these initiatives is the best approach I can recommend.

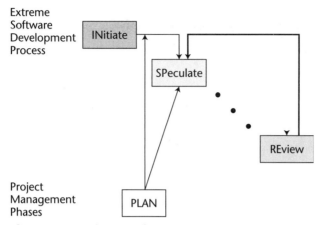

Extreme
Software
Development
Process

Project
Management
Phases

Figure 33-3:   Planning Phase of an Extreme SDPM strategy for the INSPIRE model

Validation of Next Cycle Length

Taking into consideration the new functionality to be built and the probative initiatives, the project team either validates the cycle length or requests a change. A very high-level plan might be required, but avoid planning the "how." That is left up to the team as the initial tasks in the Innovate Phase.

The Planning Phase of an Extreme SDPM Strategy for the Flexible Model

Figure 33-4 is the Planning Phase of the Extreme SDPM strategy for the Flexible model.

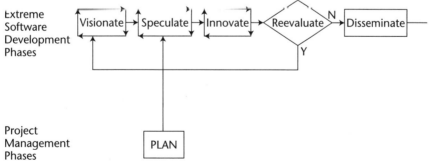

Extreme
Software
Development
Phases

Project
Management
Phases

Figure 33-4:   Planning Phase of an Extreme SDPM strategy for the Flexible model

The Planning Phase of an Extreme SDPM strategy for the Flexible model is also an iterative process. Each Development Cycle ends with a review of what just happened in the previous cycle. The customer and the project team have learned and discovered more details on the functions and features and suggested several changes during that cycle. The customer and the project team return to another round of Visionate and Speculate Phases as prerequisite to the next round of solution development. In his book *Extreme Project Management: Using Leadership, Principles, and Tools to Deliver Value in the Face of Volatility"* (Jossey-Bass, 2004), Doug DeCarlo defines a 12-step planning process briefly described in the following subsections.

Step 1: Review and Update the Collective Vision

This is just a check to make sure that the collective vision has not changed and that all parties present at the planning session are on the same page regarding the direction the project should take.

Step 2: Review the Project Uncertainty Profile

DeCarlo has developed a Project Uncertainty Profile (PUP). It is a multipart assessment of the risk profile of the project. It measures risk in four areas: business, product, project, and organizational.

Step 3: Decompose the Project into a Set of Deliverables

Through iteration, the customer and the project team are expected to converge on a solution to a goal that also comes into focus with each iteration. The decomposition is therefore based on what the team has defined as the current solution. The decomposition and the steps that follow it closely align with the traditional approach to project planning. The decomposition is a deliverables-based Work Breakdown Structure (WBS). The approach to decomposition can follow the approach described in Appendix E.

Step 4: Estimate the Size of Each Deliverable

In this case, "size" refers to a metric that measures "bigness." For software development projects this could be lines of code, or function or feature point estimates.

Step 5: Estimate the Effort to Produce Each Deliverable in Person Days

Duration is estimated in terms of elapsed time to complete. Any one of the six approaches described in Appendix F would be appropriate. Because of the lack of clarity on many of the deliverables, range estimates rather than point estimates should be preferred. The three-point technique would be one such choice.

Step 6: Select a Development Life Cycle

Depending on the characteristics of the project, a development life cycle model is chosen. Several are described in this book. The Extreme project is an iterative project. Therefore, a development life cycle, such as those described in the Iterative and Adaptive SDPM strategies would be the ones from which a life cycle is chosen.

Step 7: Schedule the Deliverables

A precedence diagram showing the dependency structure among the deliverables is generated as input to the project schedule. The schedule covers only what is to be developed during the coming cycle.

Step 8: Agree on Timeboxes

These are the durations of each iteration, with 2–6 weeks being typical. The project team decides what deliverables can be generated in the allotted cycle time for each cycle. These are tentative because ultimately the decision is firmed up for the next cycle during the Planning Phase for that cycle.

Step 9: Assess Technical and Support Requirements

This is a sanity check on whether the team will have the support it needs at the time it needs it. It is a partial answer to the question "Can you do it?" One often overlooked support requirement is the testing facilities and capacity available. Can they support the testing phase when it is needed?

Step 10: Assess Team Requirements

The skills of the core team already assigned to the project need to be compared against the skills that are needed based on the deliverables that have been identified. The critical question is this: "What is the gap between what you have on the team versus what you need on the team?" The answer leads you to the more significant question: "Can you do it?" The next question is this: "When do you need it?" That may leave some time for skills development or recruiting of additional team members.

Step 11: Identify Development Tools

What are the hardware, software, telecommunications, physical facility, and so on needs that are required to support the project? What is available and what has to be acquired? Again, this provides answers to the question: "Can you do it?"

Step 12: Produce a Risk Management Grid

The customer and the team now have all of the information needed to assess the "doability" of the project and the attendant risks. A detailed risk management plan is generated. It identifies the risks, assesses their impact and likelihood of occurrence, and establishes the appropriate risk mitigation actions.

Discussion Questions

1. Defend the following statement: The Flexible model is a good transition strategy for traditional organizations that want to fully implement Extreme project management across the enterprise. The INSPIRE model is a good transition strategy for Adaptive organizations wanting to implement an Extreme software development environment.

2. Which of the two Extreme SDPM strategies discussed in this chapter would be a better choice when very little is known about the solution? Support your decision.

CHAPTER 34

The Extreme SDPM Launching Phase

A community is like a ship, every one ought to be prepared to take the helm.

Henrik Ibsen
Norwegian playwright

Chapter Learning Objectives

After reading this chapter, you will:

- ◆ Understand the complications added to the Launching Phase when using an Extreme SDPM strategy
- ◆ Know how to launch an Extreme SDPM strategy for the INSPIRE model
- ◆ Know how to launch an Extreme SDPM strategy for the Flexible model

---

All of the Launching Phase discussion for the Linear, Incremental, Iterative, and Adaptive SDPM strategy situations apply to the Extreme SDPM strategy and will not be repeated here. (You can see Parts II, III, IV, and V earlier in the book for those discussions.) Extreme SDPM strategy projects follow the same procedures as by-the-book projects, except they repeat those procedures several times over the life of the project. Within a single repetition all of the launching activities that are done in the Linear, Incremental, Iterative, and Adaptive SDPM strategies are done in the Extreme SDPM strategy. But you do face some additional considerations. Extreme SDPM strategies focus on projects whose goal is not clearly specified and obviously whose solution is not known. The goal or solution that can be obtained is discovered in parallel.

In fact, your initial statement of the goal may not be attainable. For example, the goal is to cure cancer. That is an admirable goal, but it may not be realistic. However, you are still going to work on this project because just what is realistic will be discovered as you attempt to do what you can to cure cancer. What you will do and how you will do it will be discovered at the same time—for example, the progress that has been made to date on finding a cure for cancer. The more researchers investigate and learn about the disease, the more they learn of its complexity and likewise the more they learn about the varied cures for some types of cancer. One informs the other in an iterative fashion. Think of an Extreme project as a pure R&D project, and you won't be far off the mark. Success is no guarantee, and the risk is very high.

The Launching Phase of an Extreme SDPM Strategy

Figure 34-1 highlights the Launching Phase of an Extreme SDPM strategy.

The interesting difference between the Extreme SDPM strategy and all other strategies is the multiple occurrences of the Launching Phase. That does not occur in any other strategy. The reason is that changes that result from the Check Phase can be so extensive as to require a completely different approach and perhaps team structure to continue to project. The Launch Phase is the appropriate place for those revisions to be implemented.

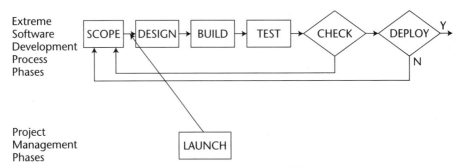

Figure 34-1: The Launching Phase of an Extreme SDPM strategy

The Launching Phase of an Extreme SDPM Strategy for the INSPIRE Model

The Launching Phase of an Extreme SDPM strategy for the INSPIRE model occurs once after the INitiate Phase and then after each SPeculate Phase, as illustrated in Figure 34-2.

The Launching Phase of the Extreme SDPM strategy for the INSPIRE model and the Adaptive SDPM strategy for the Adaptive Project Framework model bear a lot of similarity. In the case of the Adaptive model the focus is on discovering missing functions and features and hence the complete solution, whereas in the Extreme model the focus is on discovering the goal, missing functions, missing features, and hence the complete goal and solution. For the INSPIRE model, that is a challenging task. The Adaptive models know where they are going as far as defining an acceptable solution. The Extreme models do not. That's the challenge of Extreme projects—setting out on a journey to solve a problem that is not clearly specified. Obviously, launching such projects requires a team that thinks outside of the box and is not afraid to take risks.

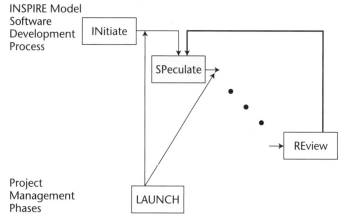

Figure 34-2:   The Launching Phase of an Extreme SDPM strategy for the INSPIRE model

The first part of the Launching Phase focuses on establishing the rules of the engagement for the entire project. These are not unlike previous rules establishment for problem solving, change management, brainstorming, conflict resolution styles, and so on, and won't be repeated here. The one difference that deserves some discussion is the assignment of roles and responsibilities. This assignment task means knowing your team members and what they like to do, don't like to do, and what competencies and skills they bring to the table. For example, some may relish the thought of being able to work with customers in speculative ventures—solving problems in a collaborative way. Others may not have the same proclivity and would rather work apart from the customer—solving problems in their own manner. Both types are valuable and needed. The project manager just has to have the insight and specific knowledge of each team member to make the proper assignments.

The second part of the Launching Phase focuses on each single cycle. The project changes as it moves from cycle to cycle. Different tasks may have a low priority in one cycle and a high priority in another. Assignments aren't fixed for the duration of the project either. Depending on the situation with the project, the assignments might need to change to take advantage of a team member's particular skills, competencies, and preferences.

Roles need to be assigned, but this doesn't have to be a permanent assignment either. Managing the intake and resolution of scope change requests is one such area. One team member can be the designated intake for all scope change requests whether they come from the customer or from another team member. Once logged in, the scope change request might be assigned to another team member who will conduct the project impact statement preparation. Time in the form of a scope bank should have been reserved for writing the project impact statement. Once completed, the project impact statement is simply held with other project impact statements until the Review Phase, at which time all scope change requests are prioritized along with other functionality or features to decide on what will be done in the next cycle.

The Launching Phase of an Extreme SDPM Strategy for the Flexible Project Model

Figure 34-3 illustrates the Launching Phase of an Extreme SDPM strategy for the Flexible Project model.

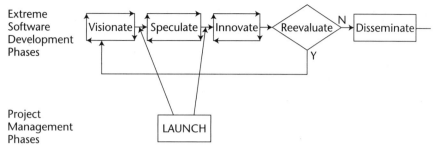

Figure 34-3: The Launching Phase of an Extreme SDPM strategy for the Flexible Project model

The Launching Phase of an Extreme SDPM strategy for the Flexible Project model is a bit more structured than in the case of the INSPIRE model. It is a two-part Launching Phase, just as the INSPIRE model has a two-part Launching Phase. The two Launching Phases are quite similar.

- The first part of the Launching Phase of the Extreme SDPM strategy for the Flexible Project model consists of establishing the rules of the engagement and of parameter setting decisions. This is the same as several models discussed in earlier chapters.

- The second part of the Launching Phase of an Extreme SDPM strategy for the Flexible model is somewhat different than you might expect. Even though the goal is not well defined and the solution is not known, this model advocates a traditional planning activity as part of the Speculate Phase. That translates into a Launching Phase that resembles the Linear and Incremental SDPM strategies. The planning activities that take place in the Linear, Incremental, and Flexible model are identical. The only difference is that a complete solution is known for the Linear and Incremental SDPM strategies and perhaps almost unknown in the Flexible model situation. The tools, templates, and processes of the Linear and Incremental SDPM strategies are the same as for the Flexible model situation. While that might seem like adding a burden of non–value-added work, it does keep the Flexible project on a repeatable path.

Discussion Question

1. You are Pepe Ronee, and you have run the Initiating and Planning Phases of the Extreme SDPM strategy for the INSPIRE model by the book. But you have just realized that the team is not as confident as you in the approach. What might you say to them to assure them of the soundness of your approach?

CHAPTER 35

The Extreme SDPM Monitoring and Controlling Phase

Nothing is more dangerous than an idea when it is the only one you have.

Emile Chartier (Alain)
French philosopher and essayist

Chapter Learning Objectives

After reading this chapter, you will:

- ◆ **Understand the Monitoring and Controlling Phase of the Extreme SDPM strategy**
- ◆ **Understand the Extreme SDPM strategy for the INSPIRE model**
- ◆ **Understand the Extreme SDPM strategy for the Flexible model**

The Extreme SDPM strategy opens yet another new perspective on systems development where even less is known about requirements than for those projects that follow an Adaptive SDPM strategy. The typical Extreme project will not have a clearly defined goal or may have a goal whose feasibility is not known. For example, curing world hunger is an admirable goal, but can it be done? Maybe not as stated, but perhaps it can be done in certain parts of the world. Can you do it? It's a fair question to ask. Obviously these are high risk projects. The difference between projects that follow an Extreme versus an Adaptive approach is staggering and so are the accompanying strategies. Monitoring and controlling such projects is a true challenge. You are in the world of research and development, and in that world the monitoring of progress is difficult at best. Some might rather say, "Let's not get in their way. Leave them alone so they can focus on the daunting task before them. If they come up with anything useful, we'll be the first to know." While the "leave them alone" approach might find favor with the development team, that is not the approach that I advocate. Still, I do advocate an approach that is minimally invasive of the team's work time.

The Monitoring and Controlling Phase of an Extreme SDPM Strategy

Figure 35-1 highlights the Monitoring and Controlling Phase of an Extreme SDPM strategy.

First note the inclusion of the Check Phase as a very visible part of the Systems Development Life Cycle. It was part of the Adaptive and Iterative SDPM strategies, but here it takes on a different posture. Here the client and the development team are challenged to the limits of their creative abilities. The learning and discovery that was generated in the just completed iteration is used to identify next steps. Those next steps include not only a revalidation and redirection of the project scope and the integration of new functions and features, but also new initiatives aimed at further learning and discovery. In other words, the scope and its achievement are defined in parallel. One feeds on and clarifies the other. This proactive posture was not as prevalent in the Adaptive SDPM strategy. Much more is asked of the development team and the client in an Extreme SDPM strategy than is in the Adaptive SDPM strategy. In the Extreme case very little will be known about the solution from the standpoint of functionality and its accompanying features. It all has to be discovered. But it isn't going to be discovered just because you want it to be. It will be hard work and will require all of the creativity that the client and the development team can muster. That dedication and drive isn't necessarily a required characteristic of the Adaptive SDPM strategy.

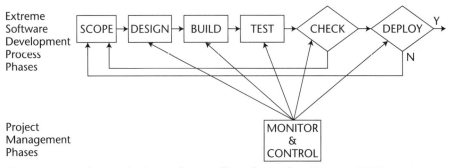

Figure 35-1: The Monitoring and Controlling Phase of an Extreme SDPM strategy

As far as metrics are concerned, those that were introduced for the Iterative and Adaptive SDPM strategies apply equally as well to the Extreme SDPM strategy. The discovery of new/revised functions and features is much like that reported for the Adaptive SDPM strategy and won't be repeated here. However, two topics discussed in the Monitoring and Controlling Phase of the Adaptive SDPM strategy are different in the Monitoring and Controlling Phase of the Extreme SDPM strategy. They are:

- Project progress reporting
- Processing scope change requests

These are discussed in the subsections that follow.

Project Progress Reporting

In the beginning of a typical Extreme project is a period of divergence as several probative initiatives are undertaken in an attempt to bound the solution. At some point in time, the divergence shifts to a more convergent pattern as the solution comes into focus. Figure 35-2 illustrates the dynamics of the typical Extreme project.

This divergence-convergence pattern is present in both the Adaptive and Extreme SDPM strategies. In the Extreme project it is more pronounced. Because so little is known about the goal and the solution in an Extreme project, you would expect to see more probative initiatives in the Extreme project. Figure 35-2 illustrates this pattern. In the first cycle, five probative initiatives are undertaken. Two of them (B1 and C1) do not yield any favorable results and are discontinued. The learning that took place with those two discontinued initiatives is merged with A1, D1, and E1 and gives rise to six probative initiatives in Cycle #2. At this point you have six undertakings, any one of which may provide further clarification as to the solution. The Cycle #2 initiatives may contain the complete solution as defined so far or some part of the solution that has been defined so far. The point of each of the initiatives is to further push the boundaries of the known solution or to investigate in a "what if" style other ideas that may result in meaningful additions or clarification of the solution. Cycle #2 results in three initiatives being discontinued (A2, D2, and F2). Combining all of the learning and discovery from Cycle #2 results in seven probative initiatives undertaken in Cycle #3. This process repeats itself for as many cycles as budget, time, or the client's interest in continuing the project are maintained. Finally, a single solution emerges (A6). Along with this solution is a restatement of the scope (or goal) of the project.

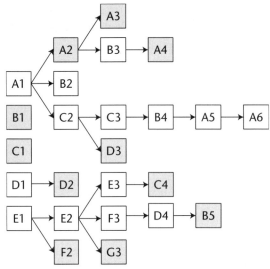

Figure 35-2: The divergence/convergence patterns of a typical Extreme project

The question now becomes this: "How would you monitor and control such a project?" The last thing you would want to do is burden the team with so much reporting that it hampers their productivity or stifles their creativity. That says stay out of their way. On the other hand, you do want to know if progress is being made. Depending on the nature of the project you might need to know what percentage of the budget and/or timeline has been consumed and whether there seems to be progress toward an acceptable solution. In some cases, all you want is as much functionality as possible out of the time and budget available for this project. The criteria may be very subjective. As long as the sponsor feels that value is being delivered and an acceptable solution is emerging, they will continue funding. If not, the project will be abandoned and perhaps an entirely different approach launched.

Processing Scope Change Requests

For the Extreme project scope change becomes more of a formality than in the case of the Adaptive or Iterative project. Scope change in an Extreme project is more like change in a process improvement project. If the current direction is not bearing results, kill it and move in a direction that the learning and discovery suggests will be more rewarding. Cycles, or rather swim lanes in cycles, can come and go for any valid reason. You are on a fishing expedition, and don't keep throwing your line in an empty hole. Continuously redirect your resources where there is the promise of results. Extreme teams tend to move spontaneously based on tacit knowledge rather than on any documentation.

The Monitoring and Control Phase of an Extreme SDPM Strategy for the INSPIRE Model

The Monitoring and Controlling Phase of an Extreme SDPM strategy for the INSPIRE model has all of the considerations stated previously for the generic Extreme SDPM situation. Figure 35-3 highlights the Monitoring Phase of an Extreme SDPM strategy for the INSPIRE model.

As is the case with the Adaptive Project Framework, there is a minimum of formal status reporting in the Extreme SDPM strategy for the INSPIRE model. The team is in constant communication with one another. Any need to change direction or take advantage of a newly learned or discovered function or feature is immediately communicated and action taken when appropriate. Swim lanes come and go as learning and discovery take place. This is the team at its most agile and adaptive form.

SPeculate Phase

This is the creative piece that starts the team thinking about what to do in the coming cycle. A review has been completed of what was done, learned, and discovered in the just completed cycle. It's now time for the team to put on their thinking caps and identify what will be done in the next cycle. Think of it as similar to the Cycle Plan Phase of the Adaptive SDPM strategy for the Adaptive Project Framework model. The difference is that you are proceeding on far less information about the goal and solution. You should be discussing what you can do rather than what you should do. Depending on where you are in the life cycle of the project, you might still be in the diverging part of the project rather than the converging part of the project. If divergent thinking is dominant, brainstorming is the norm. If convergent thinking dominates, then validation should be the norm. The initiatives being considered should be aligned with the thinking style of the times.

As for the metrics to monitor this activity, I have already discussed several in the Iterative and Adaptive SDPM strategies. If any of them are useful in the Extreme SDPM strategy, by all means use them. Just be careful not to overburden the team with reporting requirements that do not add value to the project. Keep the team focused on the problem, not on the history of what has been accomplished to date.

INSPIRE
Software
Development
Phases

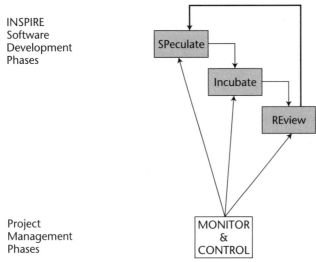

Project
Management
Phases

Figure 35-3: The Monitoring Phase of an Extreme SDPM strategy for the INSPIRE model

Incubate Phase

You've decided what you are going to do in this cycle in the SPeculate Phase. Now you have to decide how to do it and then do it. It would be good to periodically check for alignment and progress toward what you have planned to do in this cycle. Because of the highly speculative nature of the Extreme project, it is easy to get diverted off the planned path into efforts that have little to do with the project but are enticing in their own right. Ventures into the great unknown can be very mesmerizing. Stay the course as long as there is visible progress toward the cycle objectives. Abandon any initiative that does not meet muster. Don't waste time fishing in an empty hole.

REview Phase

The cycle is finished, and it's time to evaluate what has been accomplished in the cycle and what has been learned or discovered about the solution. This is the time to be objective about the just completed cycle. What probative initiatives hold the promise of adding to what is known about the solution? What probative initiatives didn't? What did you learn from these dead-end initiatives to something like the next or final solution? What new probative initiatives are suggested by those just completed? These are the types of monitoring and control questions that should be answered.

The Monitoring and Controlling Phase of an Extreme SDPM Strategy for the Flexible Model

Figure 35-4 illustrates the Monitoring and Controlling Phase of an Extreme SDPM strategy for the Flexible model.

In these types of projects, real progress is hard to measure. As stated earlier in the chapter, many deliverables will have been started but few will be complete, at least early in the project life cycle. The important parts of monitoring and controlling are imbedded in the Reevaluate Phase. Here the discussion with the sponsors and other stakeholders focuses on answering a few pertinent management-related questions, as indicated in the subsections that follow.

What Are the Results to Date Versus Your Original Goal?

The original goal was a statement made with little or no information as to its feasibility. Now that you have one or more cycles completed, is the original goal still your current goal? In many cases, the learning and discovery that have taken place will give good reason to reconsider the goal. Perhaps you have learned something that extends (or retracts) some of the scope in the original goal statement. With these revisions, management has to decide whether or not the project still makes sense and should be continued, killed, or redirected.

Has the Project Priority Changed?

The business world doesn't stand still just because you are working on an Extreme project. Other priorities arise that couldn't have been imagined when the goal was first stated and a priority assigned. Perhaps the project has become even higher priority than when first defined. However the priority of the project has changed, it affects the project going forward, if it is to go forward at all.

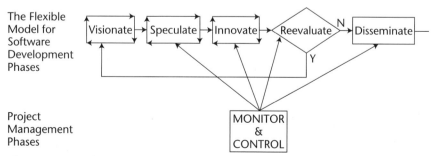

Figure 35-4: The Monitoring Phase of an Extreme SDPM strategy for the Flexible model

How Do You Intend to Realign with the Original Goal?

If the original goal is fixed and for whatever reason cannot be changed, then the team has to produce a revised project plan that demonstrates how the realignment will take place. If the original goal changes because of what has been learned, then the new goal with a revised plan will be expected.

The answers to the preceding three questions provide management with the information it needs to decide on the future of the project.

Discussion Question

1. The project seems to have migrated into a permanent divergent state. Every cycle brings with it a whole new panorama of ideas to integrate into the solution. The scope is growing in proportion. The client is the major factor behind this seemingly uncontrolled scope expansion. What would you do?

CHAPTER 36

The Extreme SDPM Closing Phase

*The most beautiful thing in the world is, precisely,
the conjunction of learning and inspiration. Oh, the
passion for research and the joy of discovery.*
Wanda Landowska
Polish harpsichordist and music critic

Chapter Learning Objectives

After reading this chapter, you will:

- **Understand the Closing Phase of the Extreme SDPM strategy**
- **Have a working knowledge of the Closing Phase of the Extreme SDPM strategy for the INSPIRE model**
- **Have a working knowledge of the Closing Phase of the Extreme SDPM strategy for the Flexible model**

The Extreme project ends when one of two things happens. Either the customer is no longer willing to support the project and the project is terminated, or the project reaches an acceptable solution. We'll explore both of these in this chapter and discuss the Closing Phase for the INSPIRE and Flexible models.

The Closing Phase of the Extreme SDPM Strategy

Figure 36-1 illustrates the Closing Phase of the Extreme SDPM strategy.

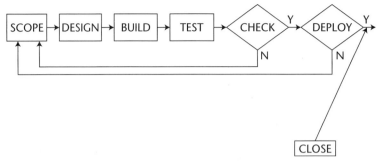

Figure 36-1: The Closing Phase of the Extreme SDPM strategy

Note, first of all, that there is only one place where deployment of the solution can take place and that is after the final check. The final check results in either project completion or termination. Project completion occurs when the customer is satisfied that the project has converged on an acceptable solution and no further cycles will be launched. Solution and goal are now aligned and clearly defined. The final goal may be very different than the original goal. For example, the original goal might have been to cure cancer but the solution converged on a cure for colon cancer—still acceptable but not the initial vision. For another example, consider the case study.

Adaptive and Extreme SDPM strategies have very similar planning approaches. Both do planning just-in-time as a follow up to the cycle Closing Phases that lead to another cycle. In an Extreme SDPM strategy the deliverables for the next cycle are planned at the beginning of the cycle. In other words, it is just-in-time planning. In an Extreme SDPM strategy, you have to anticipate changes in direction for the project going forward. While this also happens in an Adaptive SDPM strategy the changes of direction are not as dramatic. The reason for that is the goal statement that is known in an Adaptive SDPM strategy but not in an Extreme SDPM strategy. In both strategies the changes in direction are the result of learning and discovery from the probative swim lanes of the just completed cycle. Planning is still done just in time.

The second way that an Extreme Project can end is by termination. In these cases, the project cycles have not been converging on an acceptable solution, and the customer finally decides that to continue the project along the present course would just be a waste of money and time. They pull the plug on this approach to the project. That doesn't change the fact that the project must be done and be done successfully. Another approach is needed. Consider the goal to cure cancer. The project may have been following a preventative attack with no apparent convergence on a solution. The project might be restarted but with another approach—perhaps an intervention attack would prove fruitful. That is an entirely different project than the initial approach. It will require a different team with different skills and competencies than the initial project.

PDQ Case Study

The original goal was to reduce order entry to order delivery time to 30 minutes maximum. A number of changes were made both to the systems and processes. Five subsystems were designed and implemented in order to leverage technology into the processes. The processes were changed: Two new pizza factories were opened, and delivery trucks were equipped with ovens and GPS technology. All of this was intended to reduce order entry to order delivery time to less than 30 minutes. What if it didn't? Was the reduction acceptable? PDQ will use the results even if the initial goal was not achieved. It would probably launch into a process improvement program to drive out the excess delivery time but that is another case study.

With this as background, the activities in the Closing Phase become obvious. In the Extreme SDPM strategy, the Closing Phase assesses the results of the just completed cycle to assess the degree of divergence or convergence to an acceptable solution. That leads to the specification of the content of the next cycle. Measuring convergence or divergence can be done in several ways. Here are just a few.

New Probative Initiatives

In the early cycles, the team should experience a number of new probative initiatives. In the first few cycles, these may be the result of brainstorming sessions with the customer and the development team. In later cycles these are the result of learning and discovery that sets the project off in an entirely different probative direction. If the project is converging on an acceptable solution, the frequency of new probative initiatives decreases and drops to zero as the project nears its end. If this pattern is not observed, the customer will likely terminate the project.

Extended Probative Initiatives

After a few cycles are complete, the customer and the development team should begin to see potentially rewarding directions emerging from earlier probative initiatives. Those probative initiatives (the parent initiatives) that look promising suggest further exploration in the same directions. One probative initiative may suggest several variations to pursue with other probative initiatives (the children) related to their parent initiative. If the project is converging on an acceptable solution, the frequency of extended probative initiatives would increase early in the project and decrease as the project nears its end. But remember that an acceptable solution is going to come from some trail of extended probative initiatives. If this pattern is not observed and instead the number of probative initiatives continues to extend with few being abandoned, the project is most likely in a continual diverging state and should be terminated.

Abandoned Probative Initiatives

Sooner or later, the new or extended probative initiatives will be abandoned. This means that further investigation of these initiatives will not be productive. At some point in the project, the number of abandoned probative initiatives must exceed the combined number of new and extended probative initiatives. That is an indication of convergence.

Iterative SDPM Strategy for the Closing Phase of the INSPIRE Model

Figure 36-2 illustrates the Closing Phase of the SDPM strategy for the INSPIRE model.

The Closing Phase of the Extreme SDPM strategy for the INSPIRE model is entirely taken up with the decision as to how to proceed with the now completed solution. The solution may be acceptable and may then be deployed, or it may be unacceptable and some further action may be specified. I explore those alternatives later in this section. First, take a look at lessons learned.

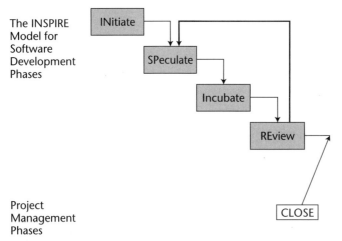

Figure 36-2: The Closing Phase of the Extreme SDPM strategy for the INSPIRE model

Lessons Learned

The Extreme SDPM strategy for the INSPIRE model takes meaningful customer involvement to the extreme (pardon the pun). Both parties must be open and honest in offering and reacting to ideas, no matter how outlandish they may seem. Brainstorming is a critical skill in every Extreme project. At the completion of the project, the customer and the developers should take stock of how well they did with respect to creativity, openness, and honesty. Here are a few questions that might help that improvement effort:

- Did each party offer new or novel ideas?
- Is there a synergy between the two parties?
- Is the entire team working more effectively later in the project compared to earlier in the project?

Solution Types

The final cycle produces a solution. As indicated earlier in the chapter, that solution may be acceptable, requiring a decision to be made on deployment, or the solution may be unacceptable, requiring a decision to be made on how to go forward, if at all, with another approach.

Acceptable Solution

The entire team should be overjoyed at having reached an acceptable solution. Remember that this was a previously undefined solution. Finding the solution was a challenge, and the team has risen to that challenge. There is surely reason for celebration.

The decision to deploy the solution must be a considered decision. If the solution is independent of other existing systems, the decision to deploy is not as complex as the case where there are other dependent systems at stake. Best practices would suggest that another project be commissioned. This project's goal would be to integrate the newly found solution into the dependent systems. This would not have been feasible with the just completed project because the discovery of an acceptable solution was not at all assured. You might argue that the just completed project should have taken dependencies into account, but that is not recommended because it would divert the team's thinking away from its primary goal—to find an acceptable solution. The dependent systems may have to be modified to accommodate the newly found solution and that is work for the follow-on project.

Unacceptable Solution

You might be tempted to conclude that this project failed, but that might be a rush to judgment. As Thomas Alva Edison put it so clearly: "I never did anything worth doing by accident, nor did any of my inventions come by accident; they came by work." So what is he saying? I think the underlying meaning here is to persevere. View the just completed experience as one more step on your journey to find an acceptable solution. No matter how brief or extended the project was, it carries with it a message that will inform the next project. What might you do? What shouldn't you do? What new and creative directions does it suggest? Here you will face the real challenge of finding a way to reach the goal. Reexamine the evidence in the completed project. Draw upon all of your creative energies. Open your mind to the possibilities. Take a chance.

Extreme SDPM Strategy for the Closing Phase of the Flexible Model

Figure 36-3 illustrates the Closing Phase of the Extreme SDPM strategy for the Flexible model.

The Closing Phase of the Extreme SDPM for the Flexible model is embodied in its Disseminate Phase. This phase is entered when the previous Reevaluate Phase results in the decision that the project is now complete. There are four artifacts in the Disseminate Phase:

- Deployment of the solution
- Lesson learned
- Benefits and recognition
- Benefits tracked and harvested

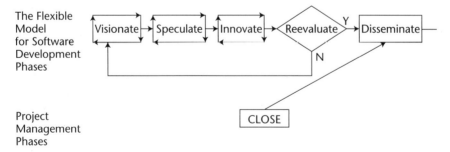

Figure 36-3: The Closing Phase of the Extreme SDPM strategy for the Flexible model

Deployment of the Solution

This artifact is the official launch of the solution. The two major questions that need to be answered are:

- Is the customer satisfied with the deliverables?
- Are the benefits realized?

Benefits realization ties back to the original business validation and justification studies done at the beginning of the project. The project was commissioned based on the value to be delivered. Now it's time to pay the piper and verify that those benefits will be achieved.

Lessons Learned

This has been an important artifact in every model studied in this book. Because this is the most challenging and difficult of all the strategies, lessons learned deserves the most attention and due diligence you can give it. You want to take an honest and open look at what worked, what didn't work, and what would be done differently the next time. The Extreme project is out on the frontiers of project management. At this time, there are no real experts. You are all students of the game and should be open to one another about that. Don't treat the post-implementation review artifact as a blaming session. It should be a learning session. That is how you add value to the enterprise and to your next venture into the world of the Extreme project.

Benefits and Recognition

This artifact focuses on how the team and the enterprise ensure that benefits are realized. A plan may need to be developed and even a project launched. The effort to get to this point and deliver an acceptable solution was enormous, so to fail in benefits realization would be truly unfortunate.

Benefits Tracked and Harvested

If you don't measure it, you can't manage it, and if you can't manage it, it won't happen. We've all heard this many times over. There is no denying the truth to the statement. So establish and track one or more metrics to make sure benefits are realized.

Discussion Question

1. You have completed the first few cycles of an Extreme SDPM strategy for the INSPIRE model and the customer seems very satisfied with the progress to date. Not too much in the way of probative initiatives is surfacing from the development team, however. There are two possibilities:

   a. The team is having difficulty thinking outside the box.

   b. The development team hasn't really bought into the INSPIRE model.

   Because so little is known about the goal and the solution, you are convinced that the INSPIRE model is the correct approach. What would you do?

CHAPTER 37

The Extreme SDPM Strategy Summary

If I understood too clearly what I was doing, where I was going, then I probably wasn't working on anything very interesting.

Peter Carruthers
Physicist

Chapter Learning Objectives

After reading this chapter, you will be able to:

- ◆ Compare Traditional versus Extreme projects
- ◆ Understand the fundamental differences between Traditional and Extreme project managers
- ◆ Understand the fundamental differences between Traditional and Extreme project teams
- ◆ Compare Traditional to Extreme project planning
- ◆ Know the impact of scope change management on Traditional and Extreme projects

The Extreme SDPM strategy is our third and final entry into the world of the agilist. As is the case in the Adaptive world, the Extreme world gets its strength from the creative spirit of the customer and the Extreme team working in harmony and collaboration. Similar to the structure of the previous summary chapters, this chapter compares and contrasts the Traditional and the Extreme project along several lines.

Traditional Versus Extreme Projects

These two project types are at opposite ends of the landscape you have been studying in this book. For that reason, they are as different as any two projects could be. You know that the Traditional project is completely defined and specified. You also know that the Extreme project will usually have very little of this to base itself on. That translates into differences between project managers, teams, planning, and scope change management, as discussed in this chapter.

Extreme projects do not have the degree of specificity of even the Adaptive projects. Not only will much of the solution (expressed in terms of requirements, functions, and features specification) be unknown, but also the goal itself is often somewhat of a mystery. While a goal may be stated, it is not known whether it is feasible or can be attained. If it can be attained, how will it be attained and will it be different than originally stated? That translates into the goal and the solution being discovered at the same time with one another. That is remarkably different from what any Traditional project might envision.

Traditional Versus Extreme Project Managers

You have already read about the fact that Traditional project managers manage against the budget, schedule, and scope so I won't repeat that discussion here. Simply recall that their approach is formal and based on status meetings, performance reviews, reports, and metric tracking.

Extreme project managers manage against goal and solution discovery. Again, think of their projects as research and development projects, and you will not be far off the mark at understanding this unique and challenging management environment. Formality has no place in their world. They view it as a nuisance. And indeed they have a point. Creativity and risk-taking are the hallmark of their world. Unfortunately, formality and creativity are not compatible. The more you have of formality, the less room there will be for creativity. And so it is important that the Extreme project manager not be fettered with producing an endless stream of reports and attending meetings that do not add value to the team's efforts. The best thing a project manager's supervisor can do is keep the rest of the organization off the project manager's back. Let them be free to manage and lead the Extreme project in ways that make sense to them. They are in a high-risk situation, and all of the help and support they can get from their management will go a long way toward a successful outcome.

Traditional Versus Extreme Teams

As I discussed earlier, the Traditional projects can work with distributed teams of specialists and junior technical staff. The details will not be repeated here. Recall, however, that the junior technical team members work under the direct supervision of the more senior members of the team. It is not necessary for the traditional team members to be co-located. The requirements specification document and project schedule are their guides.

Almost without exception, Extreme projects should have co-located teams of senior technical staff. The project is so encompassing that they should be assigned 100 percent. You don't want to have conflicting priorities getting in the way. The team members must be single-purposed for the entire project. A constant exchange of ideas is needed to fuel the Extreme engine.

Distance and time are the enemies and must be minimized wherever possible. About the only concession is to use Instant Messaging or some equivalent for members that are not within eyesight of one another. Like the Adaptive project team, the Extreme project team should have a team "war room." This is the space where they work together and that they own for the duration of the project. The walls of their war room are covered with the same information as in the Adaptive project team war room, as well as additional information such as the results of brainstorming sessions and any other ideas that have been proposed. A parking lot is a good tool to use. Here would be posted any ideas that a team member feels the team should discuss at some later point in time—like the time between cycles.

Little or no supervision of an Extreme team is required, or wanted for that matter. They should be free to self-organize. That is important because the team needs the freedom to pursue what they believe is in the best interest of discovery and learning and delivering business value.

Traditional Versus Extreme Project Planning

Planning the Extreme project is certainly different from planning the Traditional project, and it is even different from planning the Adaptive project. I like to think of the Extreme project plan as a high-level plan for the next cycle, which contains a number of parallel swim lanes each defining a probative initiative. The time spent on planning for the next cycle should be minimal. Once the deliverables for the coming cycle are identified and assigned to team members, they may wish to do some lower-level planning for the work they are about to undertake. Even that plan should not be too detailed. The reason is simple. Change is very likely. Swim lanes come and go on a moment's notice. Time is not wasted pursuing probative initiatives that don't seem fruitful. Even in mid-cycle, a probative initiative can be cancelled and written off as a dead end. Effort is refocused on new or promising initiatives. The daily 15-minute team meetings are the place for team members to discuss their progress against any plan or schedule they may have put in place for their work.

As discussed earlier, the Traditionalist planning is something you do once at the very beginning of the project. The project plan specifies tasks, durations, resource requirements, task dependencies, and a schedule. The project manager, customer, and development team collaborate on the development of the plan, and now the project manager is expected to deliver against that plan. Variances are to be reported and corrected before they get out of control.

To the Extreme project manager, planning is something you do just in time and continuously throughout the project. There is no speculation of the future, and therefore the cycle plan deals only with the coming cycle. Part of the plan deals with integrating new or revised probative initiatives for the next cycle. All of these are known, and there is no speculation about what could be or might be. Time is spent on planning those things that are known to be part of the solution. Most reporting is within the whole team where new initiatives are introduced, discussed, and integrated into the existing initiatives. In some cases, reporting does and should go outside the team to the project manager's manager or customer's manager for resolution. However, the ability to adjust the direction of the project must be the responsibility and authority of the whole team.

Traditional Versus Extreme Scope Change Management

You already know that scope change is the bane of the Traditional project manager. Every scope change request brings with it the work needed to generate the project impact statement as the deliverable from having processed the change request. Schedules need to be revised—sometimes creating significant problems if they cannot be rescheduled to meet the new requirements within the constraints of time and money. Negotiating the changes into the schedule often requires numerous meetings and additional replanning. Think of all the time that was wasted planning parts of the project that are now changed or even eliminated from the project altogether. Think of all the time that was wasted building out parts of the solution that are no longer needed. It is no wonder that there's such a high probability of failure.

You already know that scope change is the lifeblood of the Adaptive project manager. If possible, it is even more important to the Extreme project manager. The Extreme project calls upon the customer, the project manager, and the development team to be fully engaged and committed to the project.

WARNING
The Extreme SDPM strategy is high-risk. Ideally the team must be 100 percent assigned to the project and co-located.

Discussion Question

1. Your organization has been a staunch promoter of Incremental and Iterative approaches to project management and systems development. You have been assigned a project that is clearly an Extreme project. How would you go about convincing your customer and management that that is the best choice of approaches? Be specific.

PART SEVEN

In Summary

The journey is complete. A new discipline has been defined. In these two closing chapters, I look at implementation of the SDPM Strategy. That implementation is cast on the form of a continuous process improvement program. Both process maturity and practice maturity are the foundations on which the improvement program is based.

CHAPTER 38

Where Are You?

It doesn't matter if the cat is black or white, so long as it catches mice.

Deng Xiaoping
Premier of China

Chapter Learning Objectives

After reading this chapter, you will be able to:

- ◆ Understand projects from the perspective of the enterprise, the customer, the project manager, and the development team
- ◆ Compare and contrast the five SDPM strategies
- ◆ Define metrics for assessing where you are

The previous 35 chapters set out 5 different SDPM strategies for the integration of project management and systems development approaches. To my knowledge this is the first book to attempt such a treatment. By no means will this be my last attempt. I believe there is a discipline to be developed around these five strategies and expect to add to this humble beginning with additional writings and editions of this book over the next few years. I further believe that a new collaborative must be formed if significant inroads into achieving success with projects is to be made. That collaborative is made up of customer, project manager, project team, and the enterprise. These thoughts are explored in this chapter and the next.

This chapter is basically an assessment of the status of systems development project management in the contemporary business world.

The Perspective of the Enterprise

Whether the enterprise is publicly traded or privately owned, it is in business for one reason and one reason only—to make money for its stockholders or for its owners. When you come down to basics, they have no other reason for their existence. The alternative is to go out of business. In making money the enterprise must decide how to invest its resources across the lines of business. They can do that in a variety of ways.

An enterprise may have several portfolios: strategic, tactical, operational, infrastructure, maintenance, and others. The focus here is on the strategic portfolio, but much of the discussion applies similarly to the other portfolios as well. To reach its goals and objectives for the planning horizon the enterprise will define a number of strategic initiatives mapped to each of its goals or objectives. Each strategy will have a certain amount of resources (money or people) assigned depending on the priority or importance of the strategy to the enterprise. The more resources as a percentage of the total that are allocated to a particular strategy, the more important it is to the strategies of the enterprise. These resources will be distributed to projects requesting those resources based on some evaluation criteria. That criterion is often related to the bottom line impact of the proposed projects. For example, the enterprise allocates $15M to a particular strategy, and there is a total of $20M of project proposals seeking to be funded from the $15M allocation. The enterprise awards monies to those projects based on some criteria such as Return On Investment (ROI). The objective of the enterprise is to maximize its return to the business for the monies expended. All senior management cares about is the return to the portfolio. They really don't care about any individual project. Projects that are distressed or are not delivering business value as promised may be terminated or reduced in scope and some or all of the resources moved to more promising alternatives.

All projects, whether strategic, tactical, operational, maintenance, or infrastructure are funded on some basis like that described in the preceding paragraph. For example, a department may be allocated funds for infrastructure projects. It prepares a list of possible projects and based on some criteria decides how to allocate its funds across the infrastructure projects proposed. Some projects will be totally funded, others partially funded, and others postponed to a later time.

A good strategy for the project manager is to build a project plan that delivers value early rather than late in the project life cycle. That offers some protection against arbitrary decisions to terminate the project when it seems to be drifting and not producing business value. Projects that seem to be trending towards the distressed category are also vulnerable to budget cuts. Because of this, those projects would support an approach other than the Linear SDPM strategies that deliver value at the end of the project rather than in increments through the project life cycle.

From the Perspective of the Customer

Your customer wants to and expects to be number one on your list of priorities. Many also expect to tell you what they want and then have you deliver it at some later point in time with minimal involvement on their part. How often have you heard, "Oh, that's a technology project, and we don't know much about technology. Just do what we have asked." That's a signal that trouble is just waiting to happen. The biggest challenge to many project managers and their development teams is to engage the customer in a meaningful way over the entire course of the project life cycle.

The more your customer has been involved with you and your team on past projects, the more likely you are to be successful with the full spectrum of strategies. From those previous projects, both you and the customer have learned how to work effectively with each another. A certain level of trust, honesty, and openness has been established. That will have a direct payoff to the next project.

Your ability to speak the language of the customer rather than dazzling them with your technical brilliance is the key. Keep your focus on the business not on the technology.

As previously discussed, that level of customer involvement varies with the adopted strategy. For Linear and Incremental SDPM strategies that involvement is minimal because of the assumption that requirements, functions, and features have been identified and fully documented. As you change adopted strategies to the Iterative, Adaptive, and Extreme, that involvement increases. Your actual choice of strategy depends on a number of factors, which are discussed in the next chapter. The point here is that you should avoid choosing a strategy that requires a level of involvement of your customer that they are not comfortable entertaining. If you know the customer from previous projects, you should have this information. If that is not the case, my recommendation is that you spend time up front discussing how the project should go forward. Don't surprise the customer with an 11th hour announcement of your approach.

From the Perspective of the Project Manager

You want to do whatever you can to not waste time—your time, the time of your team, and even the time of your customer. To do that you will do whatever you can to make sure you and the team understand what the customer needs and that the customer understands what you will deliver. The less certain either party is of what will be delivered, the more your strategy should tend towards the agile approaches (Iterative, Adaptive, or Extreme). Each of these choices minimizes guessing as to future undefined requirements, functions, or features. With guessing minimized, it minimizes wasted time due to incorrect assumptions on the part of anyone. The project environment is characterized by aggressive schedules, tight resources, and limited budgets. Any waste that can be prevented must be prevented. And that means no guessing.

Project managers don't want any surprises. Surprises can come from the enterprise, the customer, resource managers, or the development team itself.

■ Change in the financial position of the enterprise often plays itself out in the form of budget adjustments. Projects are an easy target because they are not part of the operational budget of the enterprise. Budgets can be cut by reducing project scope, extending the time line, or canceling altogether. In anticipation of these developments, the project manager should be prepared. That preparation could simply be a collaborative prioritization of the deliverables with the customer. Supposedly, then, unexpected budget cuts would compromise only lower priority deliverables and hence minimize the negative impact on the needs of the customer.

■ Surprises from the customer are many. You demo interim deliverables, and they comment, "That's not what I thought it was going to look like." Or, "That's not what I wanted." Or, "I forgot to tell you that we also need . . ." You no doubt all heard these, so you should take steps to prevent this from happening.

■ Surprises from the resource managers are always bad news. It usually comes in the form of not having a particular resource available as the schedule expects. Often you don't know this until it is too late to make adjustments. A good risk management plan would have triggers, mitigations, and contingencies in place in expectation of that resource contention situation. You can't do that for all team members, but you can do it for the critical and scarce skills or for critical tasks that cannot sustain any delays. This is not an unusual situation and should be expected in every good project plan.

■ Surprises from the development team are varied and numerous. Most frequent is the news that they are behind schedule and can't meet a deliverables deadline. That situation is very common and should be expected.

But fortunately the project manager can do something to minimize the likelihood and the problems that result from it. That means creating a team environment that is open, honest, and trusting. Team members should not hesitate to raise their hand and say, "I have a problem and I need some help." I discuss more about how to create this team environment in the next chapter.

From the Perspective of the Development Team

Developers come in all sizes, shapes, and descriptions. At the one extreme are those who want others to do the thinking for them. They want a clear and complete specification that they can work with without fear that changes will come forth from the customer. Many of them have no interest in even talking with the customer. At the opposite extreme are those who relate well with the customer and want to engage collaboratively with them in crafting the best solution that money and time can buy. They don't mind working on a complex ill-defined project. In fact, many thrive on just such projects. In between these two extremes is a vast gulf of variations.

As project manager you certainly know your team members and where they are between the two extremes. The team is certain to be distributed across this spectrum. Those who prefer to be given their assignments and minimize interactions with the customer should be given roles and responsibilities that honor their wishes. The roles and responsibilities that involve customer interaction should be assigned to those who favor that type of relationship.

If the project strategy is either the Linear SDPM strategy or the Incremental SDPM strategy, you can deal with teams whose members are mostly customer averse. You should avoid choosing and agile strategy, if that is the type of team membership you have. My past experiences in systems development are with teams of customer averse members. That was the nature of the business. Customer interaction was left in the hands of, first, the systems analyst and later the business analyst. The contemporary business analyst is supposed to know the customer's business, perhaps even more so than the customer themselves. They work with the customer to develop requirements and pass those requirements to the developers. There is no direct contact between developers and customers in this scenario. That has been made to work effectively in a number of companies, especially when a Linear or Incremental SDPM strategy is chosen. As you move into the agile approaches, this model loses its effectiveness, and direct real-time customer contact becomes essential.

WARNING
The Extreme SDPM strategy is a high-risk strategy. Ideally the team must be 100 percent assigned to the proejct and co-located.

Tracking Where You Are

To quantify where you are you need to define and track several metrics. In this section I identify several types of metrics that are in common use. This section discusses two perspectives with respect to tracking.

- The first is process tracking, that is, how good is the process we are following?

- The second is practice tracking. That is how well are the project teams practicing the process?

Both of these are discussed in the subsections that follow, along with a discussion of some key individual project tracking tools.

Process Tracking

The effectiveness of your project management process is assessed using a project management maturity assessment measure. A few such assessment tools are available. I have developed my own and used it on several client engagements. It is called the Project Management Maturity Assessment (PMMA). It consists of a number of questions that are categorized by process and maturity level. There are 39 processes and 5 maturity levels, which generates 195 cells in which are found 2–10 yes/no questions. A trained interviewer will usually have to ask about 200–250 questions in order to establish the maturity level for each of the 39 processes. A new instrument is under development that will incorporate the most recent release of the Project Management Body of Knowledge (PMBOK) Standards. Figure 38-1 is a typical report from a recent client assessment.

The vertical scale is the maturity level as defined by the Software Engineering Institute (SEI) in their Capability Maturity Model (CMM). The levels are:

- **Level 1**—There are some processes in place, but everyone does projects their own way.

- **Level 2**—There is a fully documented process in place, and some teams are using it.

- **Level 3**—There is a fully documented process in place, and all teams are using it.
- **Level 4**—The project management process is integrated into business processes.
- **Level 5**—There is an active continuous process improvement effort in place.

As the organization moves up to higher maturity levels, it is assumed that higher level translates into a higher percentage of successfully completed projects. That causal relationship makes sense because project teams are following a repeatable process and have the benefit of the learning from other teams' experiences and from the translation of their best practices into process improvements that all teams can benefit from. Repeatability lies at the heart of great project management. Without it little in the way of increasing project success can be expected to happen. Attaining Level 3 assures that repeatability.

The data is taken from a recent engagement. This client exhibits a high level of maturity for the documentation of the beginning processes but is very weak in many of the related processes. A look at the data from the process group perspective is even more illuminating. Figure 38-2 is the same data as given in Figure 38-1 but grouped by process group.

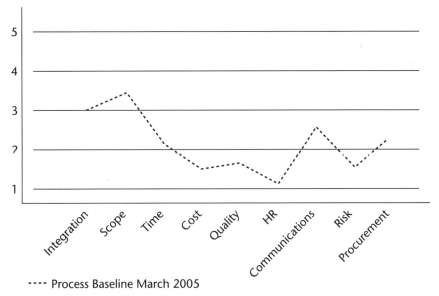

---- Process Baseline March 2005

Figure 38-1: Project Management Maturity Assessment report

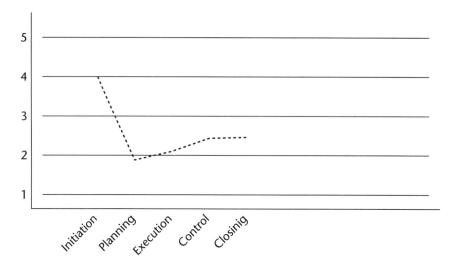

---- Process Group Baseline March 2005

Figure 38-2: Process Group Maturity Assessment report.

The client does fairly well at initiating projects and that is not unusual. The Planning and Execution groups are sadly lacking. Next, I want to take a look inside the Planning group at the processes that make up the group and how their relative maturity levels are distributed.

- Project Plan Development—3.00
- Scope Planning—4.00
- Scope Definition —3.00
- Activity Definition—2.67
- Activity Sequencing—2.00
- Activity Duration Estimating—2.00
- Schedule Development—2.06
- Resource Planning—1.50
- Cost Estimating—1.38
- Cost Budgeting—2.00
- Quality Planning—1.00
- Organizational Planning—1.14
- Staff Acquisition—1.22
- Communication Planning—2.00

- Risk Management Planning—1.33
- Risk Identification—1.00
- Qualitative Risk Analysis—2.00
- Quantitative Risk Analysis—2.00
- Risk response Planning—1.33
- Procurement Planning—3.00
- Solicitation Planning—2.30

This is the lowest level of maturity data aggregation that you have to work with. It gives you the clues to where you should focus your process improvement efforts, however. Anything at 2.00 or below is a good candidate for process improvement efforts. Here, the majority of processes are below that threshold value.

Returning to Figure 38-1 once more, you should note that along the horizontal axis are listed the nine Knowledge Areas that comprise the Project Management Institute (PMI) Project Management Body of Knowledge (PMBOK). In practice the client would establish target maturity levels for each of the Knowledge Areas and put a process improvement program in place to attain those levels. The assumption is that there is a causal relationship between process maturity levels and project success.

Practice Tracking

Having an effective process is only one side of the equation. The practice of that process is the other side. Figure 38-3 shows the results of several interviews of project managers as to how they use the process. The data displayed in the figure is the compilation for 20 interviews.

The icon, which represents the summary of all the practice maturity data, needs some explanation. It is a statistical tool that has been in use for many years to summarize and graphically report data. It is called a box and whisker plot. It is interpreted as follows.

The end points of the heavy vertical line plots the range, the lowest to the highest assessed practice maturity for all project managers interviewed. The further apart those two end points are, the more variation there is in the data points—that is, the more differences there are in the way project managers use the process. So, for example, the Scope Knowledge Area practice maturity levels calculated from the interviews ranged from 1.2 to 4.2. That is a very wide range.

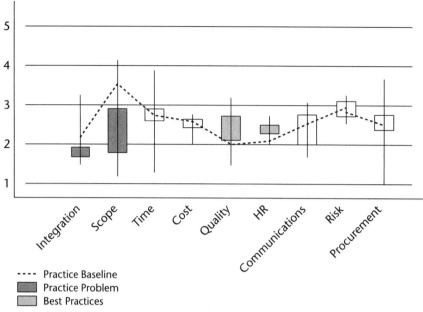

Figure 38-3: The Practice Maturity Level report

The rectangle represents the inter-quartile range. In English that is the middle half of the data. So one quarter of the data points lie below the lower limit of the inter-quartile range and one quarter of the data points lie above the upper limit of the inter-quartile range. The remainder, half of the data points, lie between the lower and upper limits of the inter-quartile range. The width of the range is an indicator of how closely distributed are the data points or how widely varied they are. When that inter-quartile variance is small, you have more assurance that the project managers are doing pretty much the same thing in the practice of that process. For the Scope Knowledge Area half of the practice maturity levels fall between 1.8 and 2.9. That is a pretty wide variance, which indicates that the project managers are doing many different things in the practice of that process.

The shading identifies those practices that either lie entirely below or entirely above the process maturity levels. If the inter-quartile range lies entirely below the process maturity level, it suggests a problem with that practice area, and practice improvement initiatives are in order. Those might take the form of selected on- or off-the-job training, mentoring, coaching, or consulting. If the inter-quartile range lies entirely above the process maturity level, it suggests that best practices may be behind that increased maturity level. Again, improvement initiatives to identify those best practices and integrate them into the process are in order. If the inter-quartile range spans the process maturity level, it is interpreted as the normal distribution of the practice maturity level around the process maturity level, and no action is suggested. For this data both the Integration and Scope Knowledge Areas display serious practice maturity levels below the process levels. For the Quality and HR Knowledge Areas further investigation might uncover best practices that can be incorporated into the process. The remaining Knowledge Areas display a typical distribution around the process level maturity values and no further action is suggested at this time.

A few spurious data points are worth checking out. Regardless of the shape and position of the icon relative to the process maturity level, if data points lie above the process maturity level, they should be investigated for possible best practices. That is the case for all of the nine Knowledge Areas.

One would think that the process maturity level would act as a glass ceiling for the practice. You would defend that position by arguing that the practice cannot have a maturity level higher than the process because the process defines what the practice should be. Fortunately that is not the case. For the client depicted in Figure 38-3 the HR Knowledge Area process maturity is about 2.1. However, the practice area reports an average of about 2.6 except almost every project manager interviewed reported a maturity level above the process maturity level. As a group, they had independently changed the processes they were using. They each might have been implementing their own processes, but at least what they did was in excess of the process level maturity. If this were a process improvement program, you would want to investigate what these project managers were doing. There might be a best practice just waiting to be discovered.

Another view of the data in Figure 38-3 proves very useful in process improvement programs. Each of the Knowledge Areas can be exploded to the process level. As one example, see Figure 38-4.

Each of the processes that make up the Scope Knowledge Area is shown with its process and practice maturity level plotted. You already knew that the Scope Knowledge Area was a problem from Figure 38-3, but now you can look inside the Scope Knowledge Area at the processes that make it up and see exactly where those problems reside. This is useful information for your process improvement program.

You have yet one other way to look at the maturity data, and that is by process group. When using this metric in a process improvement program, you would prefer to see the data as shown in Figure 38-5. Here the process and practice maturity data is grouped by process group.

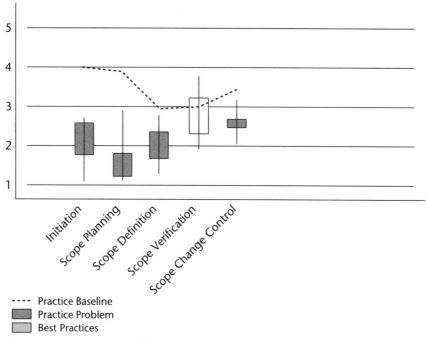

```
---- Practice Baseline
[Practice Problem]
[Best Practices]
```

Figure 38-4: Process and practice maturity levels for the Scope processes

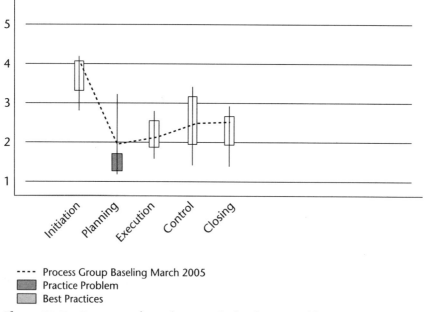

```
---- Process Group Baseling March 2005
[Practice Problem]
[Best Practices]
```

Figure 38-5: Process and practice maturity levels grouped by process group

This is an interesting report. It tells you that the Planning Process Group should be the focus of your process improvement efforts. The other four process groups are all operating within a nominal range of the process group maturity level.

All of these maturity level reports are produced from a Project Management Maturity Assessment tool that I developed for my consulting practice. The process maturity data is generated by reviewing the documentation that supports the organization's project management processes. The practice data is collected through one-on-one interviews with project managers. For the interview data to produce any reliable conclusions, you need about 20 project managers involved. Each interview lasts about 2½ hours. Interview data is collected at the process level and aggregated to knowledge areas and process groups. Both of these aggregations are designed to support the design and monitoring of process improvement programs.

Project Tracking

While a bit off the topic of process and the practice of the process, it is useful to take a quick look at some of the metrics you might want to use to determine your performance on a single project. This becomes important when there is a process improvement program in place and you want to measure the impact of process changes on actual project performance. This is not intended to be a complete treatment of the topic but rather a brief presentation of some tools that I have found particularly useful in measuring how well you and the team are doing on a specific project as you try to implement the enterprise project management processes.

Only a limited number of performance reporting tools can be used to assess the past and future performance of projects. They are milestone trend charts and earned value analyses. The material that follows takes a look at both of those tools as early warning indicators of practice problems and then creates a hybrid of the two for additional early warning indicators.

Milestone Trend Charts

Milestone trend charts are of more recent vintage having been introduced by me in 1995 and more recently discussed in my book *Effective Project Management: Traditional, Adaptive, Extreme, Third Edition* (John Wiley & Sons, 2003).

Milestones are significant events in the life of the project that you wish to track. These significant events are zero-duration activities and merely represent that a certain condition exists in the project. For example, a milestone event might be that the approval of several different component designs has been given.

This event consumes no time in the project schedule. It simply reflects the fact that those approvals have all been granted. The completion of this milestone event may be the predecessor of several build-type activities in the project plan. Milestone events are planned into the project in the same way that activities are planned into the project. They typically have Finish-to-Start relationships with the activities that are their predecessors and their successors.

Look at the milestone trend chart in Figure 38-6 for a hypothetical project. The trend chart plots the difference between the planned and estimated date of a project milestone at each project report period. In the original project plan the milestone is planned to occur at the ninth month of the project. That is the last project month on this milestone chart. The horizontal lines represent one, two, and three standard deviations above or below the forecasted milestone date. In the examples that follow, one standard deviation is about one month.

Any activity in the project has an expected completion date that is approximately normally distributed. The mean and variance of its completion date are a function of the longest path to the activity from the report date. In this example, the units of measure are one month. For this project the first project report (at month 1) shows that the new forecasted milestone date will be 1 week later than planned. At the second project report date (month 2 of the project) the milestone date is forecasted on target. The next four project reports indicate a slippage to 2 weeks late, then 3 weeks late, then 4 weeks late, and finally 6 weeks late (at month 6 of the project). In other words, the milestone is forecasted to occur 6 weeks late, and there are only 3 more project months in which to recover the slippage. Obviously, the project is in trouble. The project appears to be drifting out of control. Some remedial action is required of the project manager.

Certain patterns signal an out-of-control situation. These are given in Figures 38-6 through 38-10 and are described in the following subsections.

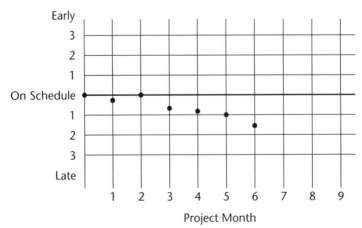

Figure 38-6: A Run up or down of four or more successive data points

Successive Slippages

Figure 38-6 depicts a project that is drifting out of control. Each report period shows additional slippage since the last report period. If you have decomposed activities down to 2 week or shorter duration tasks, then each month there will be different tasks that are worked on. Those that are on the critical path to the milestone event are cumulating slippages that put the milestone event further and further out in the time line, thus creating the downward trend. Four such successive occurrences, however minor they may seem, require special corrective action on the part of the project manager.

Radical Change

Figure 38-7, while it does show the milestone to be ahead of schedule, reports a radical change between two successive report periods. Activity duration may have been grossly overestimated. You may be a data error. One other explanation would be a scope change or technology change that resulted in several future tasks being removed from the project. These tasks affected the critical path leading to the milestone event and hence the wild aberration in forecasted delivery date of the milestone event. In any case, the situation requires further investigation.

Successive Runs above the Planned Milestone Date

Figure 38-8 is an interesting pattern. In the first month, something caused the milestone event to be forecasted to come in 6 weeks ahead of schedule. Subsequent months maintained that early date but only because the project manager was able to re-negotiate the resource schedule for each of the succeeding months. The task duration estimates and the project plan look solid. All dates were hit because resources were re-scheduled to the earlier dates. Barring any radical shifts and the availability of resources over the next 2 months, the milestone will probably come in 1 month early. Remember that you have negotiated for a resource schedule into these 2 months and now you will be trying to renegotiate an accelerated schedule.

Successive Runs below the Planned Milestone Date

Figure 38-9 depicts the opposite situation shown in Figure 38-8. Here the project gets behind schedule in the first month and then stays there for the next 6 months. The project plan is good just as it was in the previous example. But the project remains behind with no apparent attempt being made to get the milestone back on schedule. The project manager has some explaining to do.

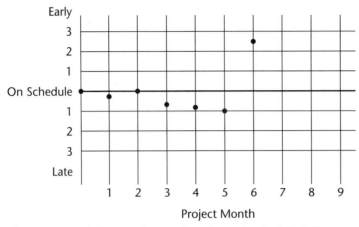

Figure 38-7: A change of more than three standard deviations

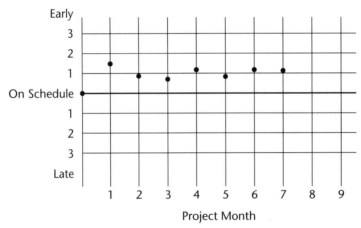

Figure 38-8: Seven+ successive data points above the planned milestone date

Schedule Shift

Figure 38-10 depicts a major shift in the milestone schedule. The cause must be isolated and the appropriate corrective measures taken. One possibility is the discovery that a downstream activity will not be required. Perhaps the project manager can buy a deliverable rather than build it and remove the associated build activities from the project plan.

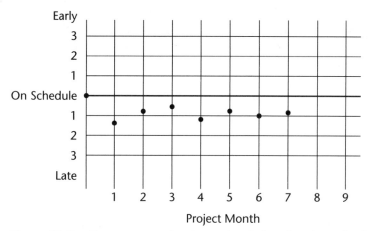

Figure 38-9: Seven+ successive data points below the planned milestone date

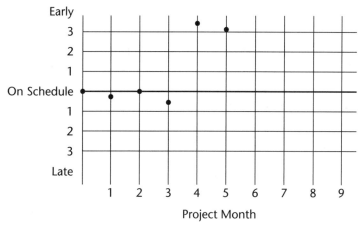

Figure 38-10: Two successive data points outside three standard deviations from the planned milestone date

Earned Value Analysis

Earned value (a.k.a., cost/schedule control) has been used in the federal government for nearly 50 years. Only recently has it been adopted by commercial enterprises

Earned value analysis is used to measure project performance and, by tradition, uses the dollar value of work as the metric. As an alternative, resource person hours/day can be used in cases where the project manager does not directly manage the project budget. Actual work performed is compared against planned and budgeted work expressed in these equivalents. These metrics are used to determine schedule and cost variances for both the current period and cumulative to date. Cost or resource person hours/day are not good objective indicators with which to measure performance or progress, but while this is true, there are no other good objective indicators. Given this, we are left with dollars or person hours/day, which we are at least familiar working with in other contexts. Either one by itself does not tell the whole story. You need to relate them to one another.

The Standard S-Curve

One drawback that these metrics have is that they report history. Although they can be used to make extrapolated predictions for the future, they primarily provide a measure of the general health of the project, which the project manager can correct as needed to restore the project to good health. These metrics can be used as the measure of practice success in a process and practice improvement program

Figure 38-11 shows a standard S-curve, which represents the baseline progress curve for the original project plan. The curve can be constructed using cumulative budget data or cumulative person hours/day as reflected in the project plan. It can be used as a reference point. You can compare your actual progress to date against the curve and determine how well the project is doing. Again, progress can be expressed as either dollars or person hours/day.

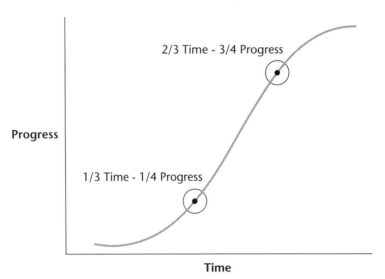

Figure 38-11: The standard S-curve

While the curve given here is a standard, it is a good idea to plot this curve for your project plan. Comparing the standard curve with your curve can be illuminating, as I discuss later in this section. Simply record dollars spent over time or labor hours spent over time. Two plots to be cautious of are shown in the next two figures.

The Aggressive Curve

This situation (Figure 38-12) occurs when too much work is loaded in the front end of the project. Usually this indicates a lack of proper planning up front and a "rush to code." This increases the risk in the project. For teams that have worked together before this may work. For a newly formed team, this rarely works. The team needs time to learn to be a team and that is not the time to load them up with heavy work schedules.

The Curve to Avoid

This situation (Figure 38-13) is the reverse of the previous one. Here a lot of up front time is spent deciding what to do, who does what, when will it be done, how will progress be reported. In other words, no actual work is being done. If your process is such that it forces the project team into this pattern, you might want to go back to the drawing board and lighten the process so the team can log in progress earlier in the project life cycle.

Measuring Earned Value

There are four popular ways to measure earned value (Figure 38-14).

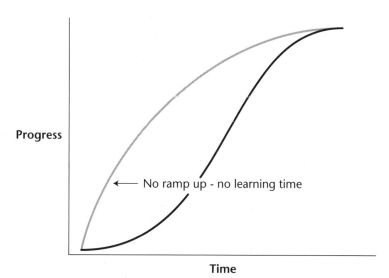

Figure 38-12: The aggressive curve

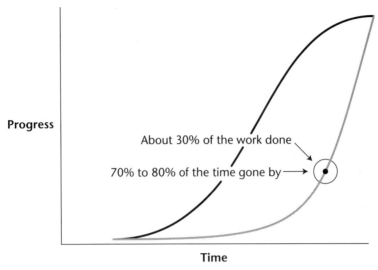

Figure 38-13: The curve to avoid

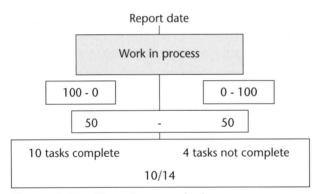

Figure 38-14: Measuring earned value

Tasks that are completed before the report date have accrued their full. Tasks that are not scheduled to begin until some time after the report date do not affect this report. It is only for the tasks that have passed their start date and have not yet been completed by the report date. In other words, they are a work in process. The four popular ways to measure earned value (and represented in Figure 38-14) are as follows:

- **100 percent when work begins on the task and 0 percent when the task is complete**—All the value is accrued when the task has been opened for work.

- **0 percent when work begins on the task and 100 percent when the task is complete**—No value is accrued until the task has been successfully completed.

- **50 percent when work begins and 50 percent when work is completed**—When the task is open for work, half of the value is accrued. When the task has been successfully completed, the other 50 percent is accrued.

- **Proportional to the number of subtasks completed**—Each task has one or more subtasks. The proportion of subtasks that have been successfully completed is the basis for accruing value. In the example, the task has a total of 14 subtasks, and 10 have been completed before the report date. Therefore 10/14 of the value is accrued on the report date.

Cost Variance

By superimposing the actual progress curve to the baseline curve, you can now see the current status versus the planned status. Figure 38-15 shows the actual progress curve to be below the planned curve. If this represented dollars, you might be tempted to believe the project is running under budget. Is that really true?

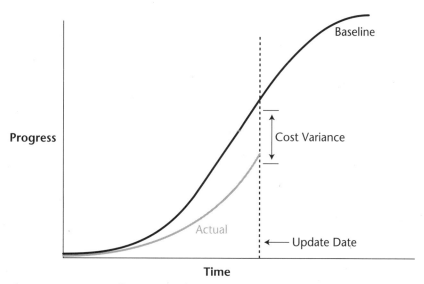

Figure 38-15: Baseline vs. actual cost curve illustrating cost variance

As it turns out, you cannot draw any conclusions about being over or under budget from just this data. You might be over budget for the work that you did do but under budget for the cumulative total that should have been spent by the report date. On the other hand you might be on budget for the work that you did, but you didn't do all of the work that was budgeted by the report date. Obviously you need more information before any logical conclusions can be reached about over or under budget on the report date.

Schedule Variance

Projects rarely run significantly under budget. A more common reason for the actual curve to be below the baseline is that the activities that should have been done have not been and thus the dollars or person hours/day that were planned to be expended have not been. The possible schedule variance is highlighted in Figure 38-16.

The curves are telling you that you should have reached a certain level of value much earlier than you actually have. That could be indicative of a schedule variance. But you still do not know the real situation. One curve is missing from this picture that when added will tell the whole story.

The Whole Story

Management might react positively to the news shown in Figure 38-16, but they might also be misled by such a conclusion. The full story is told by comparing both budget variance and schedule variance, shown in Figure 38-17.

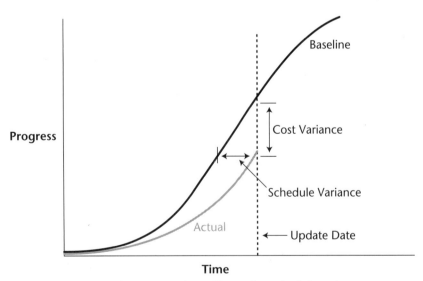

Figure 38-16: Baseline vs. actual cost illustrating schedule variance

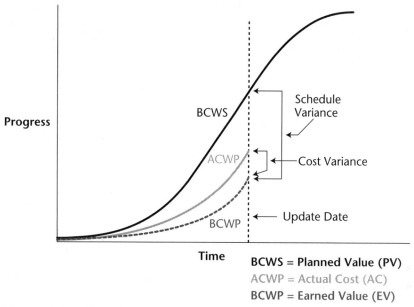

Figure 38-17: The whole story

To correctly interpret the data shown in Figure 38-17, you need to add the earned value (EV) data that was given in Figure 38-16 to produce Figure 38-17. Comparing the EV curve with the planned value (PV) curve, you see that you have under spent because all of the work that was scheduled has not been completed. Comparing the EV curve to the actual cost (AC) curve also indicates that you overspent for the work that was done. Clearly, management would have been misled by Figure 38-15 had they ignored the data in Figure 38-16. Either one by itself may be telling a half-truth. In addition to measuring and reporting history, EV can be used to predict the future status of a project.

Performance Indices

The three basic indicators (PV, AC, and EV) yield one additional level of analysis for you. Schedule Performance Index (SPI) and Cost Performance Index (CPI) are a further refinement. They are computed as shown in Figure 38-18.

Many people find these indices to be more intuitive than the three cost curves in Figure 38-17. When tracked over time, they do reveal good insight into the past performance of the project and provide indicators of the likely future if trends continue.

- Cost Performance Index
  CPI = EV/AC = BCWP/ACWP

- Schedule Performance Index
  SPI = EV/PV = BCWP/BCWS

INDEX VALUES
<1: over expended or behind schedule
>1: under budget or ahead of schedule

Figure 38-18: Earned value–performance indices

Cost Performance Index

CPI is a measure of how close the project is to spending on the work performed what was planned to have been spent. If you are spending less on the work performed than was budgeted, the CPI will be greater than 1. If not, and you are spending more than was budgeted for he work performed, then the CPI will be less than 1.

Some managers prefer this type of analysis because it is intuitive and quite simple to equate each index to a baseline of 1. Any value less than 1 is undesirable; any value over 1 is good. These indices are displayed graphically as trends compared against the baseline value of 1.

Schedule Performance Index

SPI is a measure of how close the project is to performing work as it was actually scheduled. If you are ahead of schedule, EV will be greater than PV, and therefore the SPI will be greater than 1. Obviously this is desirable. On the other hand, an SPI below 1 would indicate that the work performed was less than the work scheduled. Not a good thing.

Adapting to Accommodate Milestone Trend Charts and Earned Value

Both milestone trend charts and earned value can easily be accommodated within the project life cycle. All of these metrics can be used to track practice level improvements resulting from a process improvement program. After all, they are where the rubber meets the road.

Accommodating Earned Value

At each report date, tasks that are open for work or were scheduled to be open for work can be in one of three situations:

- They are complete and hence have accrued 100 percent value.

- They are still open for work and hence have accrued a percentage equal to the proportion of subtasks completed.

- They are still open for work, and no subtasks are completed; hence, they have accrued 0 percent value.

Add all of the accrued value since the last report date and add that to the cumulative project total. Display that data on the baseline S curve.

Accommodating Milestone Trend Data

At each report date, the task managers of tasks that are open for work or were scheduled to be open for work should update the project file. The update information will be:

- The task is reported as complete as of a certain date.

- A certain percentage of the task work is complete (same as earned value report mentioned previously) and an updated estimate to completion is also given.

- No progress is reported.

The software produces an updated project file with new forecasted dates for the milestones you are tracking.

The presentation of the SPI and CPI data over time can be represented using the same format as was used to report milestone trend data. Three examples are shown below.

Figure 38-19 is a common situation. Here the project has gotten behind schedule (denoted by the "S: in the figure) while at the same time being under budget (denoted by the "C" in the figure). That is probably due to the fact that work that was scheduled has not been done and hence the labor costs associated with those tasks has not incurred.

Project: ALPHA

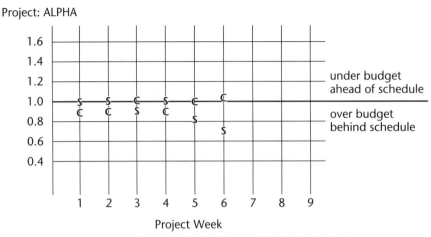

Figure 38-19:   A project that is under budget and behind schedule

On rare occasions you might experience the situation in Figure 38-20. The project is ahead of schedule and under budget. Less costly ways were found to complete the work, and the work was completed in less time than was planned. If this should ever happen to you, relish the moment. Take whatever kudos your customer or management care to heap on you. You deserve their accolades. They don't happen often.

Figure 38-21 is the worst of the worst. Nothing more need be said.

Project: BETA

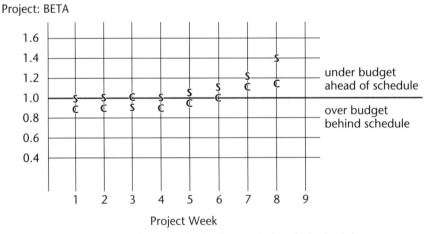

Figure 38-20:   A project that is under budget and ahead of schedule

Project: GAMMA

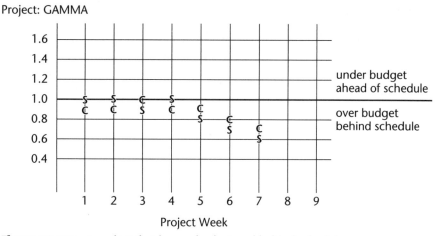

Figure 38-21: A project that is over budget and behind schedule

The same approach can be used to track a project portfolio over time, as shown in Figure 38-22.

The graph shows the SPI values of the individual projects that comprise the portfolio. This will also be a useful graphic for summarizing the practice changes from your process improvement program. If there is a clear trend at the portfolio level, it is indicative of a successful transition from process to practice.

Project: DELTA Program

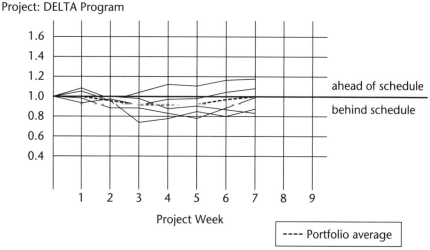

Figure 38-22: Adapting the Life Cycle for a Project Portfolio Schedule

Other Warning Signs

In addition to milestone trend charts and earned value, you have several other metrics that can be defined to identify project performance trends and, hence, can be used as a trigger for identifying distressed projects. Figure 38-23 lists some of the more popular choices.

Figure 38-24 shows a few examples of what those warning signs might look like.

- Resource deviations
  - Cumulative # of days late/absent by team member
  - Cumulative # of mistakes/misunderstandings
- Performance metrics
  - Cumulative # of scope change requests
  - Cumulative # of outstanding bugs over time

SITUATIONS...

Increasing at an increasing rate:	a problem
Increasing at a decreasing rate:	normal

Figure 38-23: Other warning signs

- Project is > 50% behind schedule
- Project is > 33% over budget
- # of days late/absent per week by any team member has increased for 4 consecutive weeks
- # of mistakes/misunderstandings has increased for 4 consecutive weeks
- # of scope change requests has increased for 4 consecutive weeks
- # of outstanding bugs has increased for 4 consecutive weeks
- Meeting attendance has been decreasing for 4 consecutive weeks

CUMULATIVE PERFORMANCE METRICS...

Increasing at an increasing rate:	a problem
Increasing at a decreasing rate:	normal

Figure 38-24: Examples of warning signs

Discussion Question

1. The project is clearly suited to an Adaptive strategy, but your team does not have the skills/competencies/customer relationship that you would need. What would you do? Be specific.

CHAPTER 39

Where Do You Want To Go and How Can You Get There?

First, I believed it could be done. Second, I believed that it could be done within the time period that had been set. Third, I was consumed with accomplishing the task. Fourth, I told all with whom I came into contact of my goal and asked for their help.

James E. Buerger
Publisher, *Travelhost National*

Chapter Learning Objectives

After reading this chapter, you will be able to:

- ◆ Understand the ideal SDPM end state
- ◆ Know the steps to follow to achieve the ideal end state

You've now come to the end of this journey through the contemporary systems development project management landscape. Much has been accomplished in the understanding of that landscape. You can now understand its strengths and its weaknesses. You know that it has a significant potential for contributing business value to the enterprise. You know how important it is that you who are from the project management discipline and the systems development discipline contribute to that business value, and you know how to do that, too.

In this chapter I intend to paint a picture of the ideal end state for software project management that I see for us and then spend some time discussing how that future state might come about.

Where Do You Want To Go?

My goal is for 100 percent project success. Your goal should be very similar or exactly the same. Since the latest reports give estimates of around 30 percent IT project success, most organizations have a long ways to go to reach their goal. In Chapter 38 you set targets for several metrics that are tracked with your projects. These become the baseline against which all improvements are measured. A target goal of 100 percent project success is a sight to set for your enterprise, but the metrics will give you a more useful improvement measure. Set target values for those metrics consistent with the target goal.

One hundred percent project success means that the enterprise fully embraces and is willing to support the five SDPM strategies that have been discussed in this book.

The ideal end state is just that—ideal—a zero defect goal that is probably not attainable. But that shouldn't diminish your enthusiasm or dedication to trying to reach that goal. My bias is that you establish a process improvement program where improvement is measured directly by increased levels of process and practice maturity and indirectly by project success rates. That is not the only way, but that is the way that I have found most effective. So think of the journey as nothing more than a *continuous* process improvement program, with the obvious emphasis on continuous. How it will end up is anybody's guess. But at least you will have the satisfaction of knowing that you, your customer, and your team gave it their best effort.

There are other goals that my clients have set for their process improvement program, and this discussion would not be complete without some mention of them. In the first scenario the client sets a maturity level that all processes must meet. Maturity Level 3 is often chosen as the first goal level. For them it is an intermediate goal and may be followed by another process improvement program to take all processes to Level 4. At Level 4 all processes are fully integrated into the business processes. Attaining this level for an enterprise means that project management has really become a bottom line contributor. Attainment of that level is very difficult, however, and that is the main reason many enterprises choose a two-step process improvement program. That is a major step for an enterprise at Level 3. At Level 3 all projects are following the completely documented project management process. This establishes repeatable practices in project management. That is a precondition to further project success.

The other scenario is to establish separate maturity level goals for each process. This approach positions each process in terms of its overall contribution to project success and business value. From past practice data the enterprise knows where its pain points are with respect to project failure. By targeting on those processes the enterprise hopes to raise the likelihood of project success thus making a significant contribution to the enterprise. It may view some processes as not broken and hence not in need of fixing.

Figure 39-1 is a high-level schematic of the end state software development management environment that I envision regardless of the maturity level of the enterprise.

Despite its simple form this end state is rich in content and structure. The sections that follow examine each of the steps.

Review POS

The Project Overview Statement (POS) is the document that marks the early beginnings of the project. It was written and approved by the customer and the project manager. It is time to enter the planning stage, and the review of the POS is the first collaborative task that you will engage the customer and the development team in. You and the customer should have that alignment, but the development team would not have had the opportunity to engage with the customer for the purposes of extending that alignment. Regardless of the process you followed to generate the POS you must ensure that all parties have the same understanding of its meaning. The same word doesn't mean the same thing to different people. What you intend by what you say isn't necessarily what the receiving party understands you to have said. The only way to ensure complete alignment is to talk through the document. Ask questions about what is in and what is not in the project. Make sure the goal and objectives are commonly understood. Again this happens only with face-to-face discussion of each part of the POS. This is your best chance to establish a foundation on which your team will be built. Having the customer, the project manager, and the development team all on the same page and pulling in the same direction is invaluable. The discussion of the initial POS is a great place to experiment with other ideas about the project. Are there some considerations that the developers see that maybe the customer or the project manager did not see? Explore these as a prerequisite to requirements gathering. The information you gather here will be critical input to your decision as to choice of SDPM strategy later in the planning process.

I can't stress enough the importance of this step. How many times have you come to some intermediate point in a project only to find out that the customer has a slightly different understanding about what the project will deliver? What if that discovery is made during integration testing? These are the things that project failures are made of, and we don't tolerate project failures in our ideal end state.

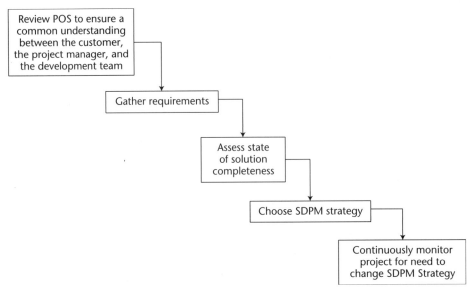

Figure 39-1: The ideal end state of the SDPM environment

Gather Requirements

Regardless of how you are going to approach the project, the Requirements Breakdown Structure (RBS) is the tool of choice to deciding on the best fit approach. How you choose to gather requirements is largely a matter of personal preference and what has worked well for your enterprise in the past. The resulting RBS is not only a customer-facing artifact, but it is the best way to understand the completeness and confidence you have that all of the requirements, functions, and features have been identified and clearly documented. The RBS is your primary input to the process of deciding which SDPM strategy you will choose for the project. No other project management artifact has that level of importance in getting your project off to the correct start and assuring its success. Your ideal end state will have the RBS as the pivotal artifact.

There are two variables of concern here:

- Completeness
- Clarity

Either one of them and usually both can be used as the criterion for choosing the best fit SDPM strategy.

Completeness

Completeness is a necessary condition if you choose to follow a Linear or Incremental SDPM strategy. Easily said but difficult to know if you have met that condition. As you go through the requirements gathering process with your customer, try to read their body language and be observant of any verbal clues. If you are satisfied that you have achieved completeness, that is probably the best sign that you have. If you have any doubts whatsoever, assume you haven't met that condition. That will lead you to choose an SDPM strategy towards the agile side. It is better to take the safe ground than to put the project at risk needlessly. Unless you know the customer from previous projects, it would be risky to depend on their saying that all requirements have been identified to conclude that the requirements are complete.

Clarity

Clarity has equal weight in your decision to choose one SDPM strategy over another. Clarity can be attained only through extensive Conditions of Satisfaction type discussions between project manager and customer. Don't cut this effort short. It is worth the investment of time to get it as right as you can. Don't rush into the project until you have done your due diligence on the choice of infrastructure for the project. You'll want to be clear what is in and what is not in the solution. This may mean discussing what is in and what is not down to the function and feature level. But it is worth every minute you spend on clarifying the requirements. Mark any part that does not meet that litmus test. These will be your scorecard for choosing the best fit SDPM strategy later in the planning process.

Assess State of Solution Completeness

If the requirements, functions, and features are complete and clearly documented, the solution is probably complete, and you are safe choosing a Linear or Incremental SDPM strategy. On the other hand, if the requirements, functions, and features are not complete and clearly documented, than neither is the solution. But just how incomplete is the solution? There is no quantitative metric that I know of that will answer that question. It is a judgment call on your part. So assume that you are not convinced that you have a complete definition of the solution. That means your choice of SDPM strategy falls into the agile realm, and you need to choose from among Iterative, Adaptive, and Extreme SDPM strategies. That choice will not be as difficult as you might think. In the next section, you can take a look at several different variables and how they can be used to narrow the choices.

Choose SDPM Strategy

This is where the rubber meets the road and you make a commitment to follow a specific SDPM strategy. It is a critical decision and your best effort at due diligence is required. You must take into account several variables in making this decision. They are listed in the sections that follow and briefly discussed.

The Enterprise Environment

Constant change at the enterprise level will be the biggest obstacle to project success. It generates instability in the project and hence raises the risk of the project being repurposed, changed, terminated, or significantly reduced in scope or budget. Changing priorities (and hence changing budgets), reorganizations (with a likely change of sponsors or reporting managers), and budget cuts that can create all sorts of problems with projects that are underway and not yet complete can all have adverse effects on your project.

If what I have described sounds like your organization, what would you do to protect your project? Maybe the more appropriate question is can you even protect your project? The more likely you are to encounter these situations the more you should look to a strategy that delivers value early and often. If your project lends itself to a Linear SDPM strategy, choose an Incremental SDPM strategy. That will deploy a partial solution early and build on it through successive increments. Choose small increments with clear business value at each increment. If you are going to choose an Adaptive SDPM strategy, alter it to deliver business value at each or, if that is not possible, at most cycles.

The Sponsor

Your sponsor is your defense against the enterprise. They are the ones that protect you from the wiles of the organization. They have a position of power and leverage in the organization and are often your only defense when times go bad. Your sponsor's continuing support of the priorities of your project is a key to project success. If you lose that during the project, your project is now exposed to some risk of cancellation. A new sponsor may not share your enthusiasm for the project or have other priorities to fund. Even without a change of sponsor, a change in enterprise priorities can change your sponsor's priorities regarding your project. These changes may be beyond their control.

If you suspect that a change in sponsor may be in the offing, what would you do? I would still choose the SDPM strategy that I thought was a best fit for the project. But I would do more. Whatever documentation I could produce to sell the benefits of the project or enhance its business case, I would be doing. These are good insurance policies against a change in sponsor, and they are also good briefing papers for that new sponsor. If you do end up with a new sponsor, you need to do two things

- First understand their priorities
- Second, position your project to contribute to their priorities

Your Experience with the Customer

The more your customer has demonstrated a proactive position in prior projects, the more comfortable you can be with choosing one of the agile strategies. On the other hand, if the project clearly calls for an agile approach and your customer is not aligned with such approaches, you might be exposed to some risk if you choose an agile strategy. Spend some time with the customer. Perhaps a workshop on the agile approach you are thinking about using would be a good start. You can use that to gauge the customer's willingness to engage in such an approach. I've had good success with running workshops in parallel with the project. The project becomes the vehicle for learning the approach. In any case, some compromise may be called for, and you will just have to take up the slack. You could be in for rough times in such situations, but that is what they are paying you those big bucks for!

The Skill/Competency/Experience Level of the Project Team

Inexperienced project teams do not do fit well into agile approaches. Distributed teams do not do well when using agile approaches. Junior members of the technical and development staffs need the supervision of the more senior members of their discipline.

The Physical Location of the Project Team

Co-located or distributed are the determining factors in many choice of SDPM strategy. The further out into the outer reaches of the agile landscape, the more you will need an experienced co-located team. In some organizations that is not possible. So what do you do if the project requires an Adaptive SDPM strategy? If at all possible, bring the team together once to meet each other. Having a face to put with a name goes a long way to building a functioning team. The first concern should be communications. Video conferencing is best; audio conferencing is second best; e-mail is a distant last. You'll need to set up a Web site for the project where all project documentation is stored and updated. Having a project administrator keep the project files up-to-date is the safest approach.

The Criticality of the Project

Just how important is this project to the enterprise? The less you know about the solution and the more important it is to the enterprise, the higher the risk. Some problems must have a solution, no matter how complete (or partial) it might be. The more critical the project is to the enterprise the less you will want to compromise on your choice of the best fit strategy. The other variables will need to line up pretty closely with the choice, or the risk may become unmanageable.

Continuously Monitor the Project

You aren't finished with choice of SDPM strategy just because you reached a decision early in the Planning Phase. The project will change, and you may have to revisit your decision about SDPM strategy. There are situations where a change is called for.

For example, you started with an Adaptive SDPM strategy and have reached a point in the project where the remainder of the solution comes into clear focus. There is no need to continue with the Adaptive strategy. You could just as easily switch to a Linear or Incremental SDPM strategy. That affords you the opportunity to deploy a partial solution and then a complete solution in a later increment. Remember that the first priority should be to get business value in the hands of the customer. The Adaptive SDPM strategies do not do that but the Incremental SDPM strategies do.

For another example, suppose you chose a Linear SDPM strategy and the frequency of customer scope change requests is getting out of hand. Switch to an Iterative SDPM strategy and accommodate the scope changes more readily. Staying with the Linear SDPM strategy just wastes the time of the development team and eats away at their value-added work time.

How Will You Get There?

This is your continuous SDPM Process Improvement Program. Plan on spending all of your days with some level of involvement in this program. It will never end. In the beginning there will be lots of improvement initiatives. At some point that will level off and move more into a monitoring program, but it will still be a continuous improvement program. Figure 39-2 is a continuous process improvement process that I have used successfully for several years. It fits very well the Adaptive Project Framework model. In fact, the Adaptive Project Framework model was designed to accommodate process improvement projects and programs.

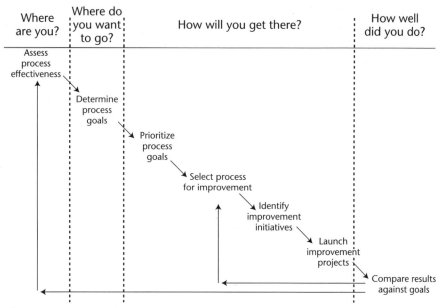

Figure 39-2: A continuous process improvement program process

You can see that this process answers all of the questions posed in the last chapter and this one. Each step in this four-phase process model is discussed in the following sections.

Assess Process Effectiveness

First of all, process in the context of this section may refer to the entire project management process or to just one of the 44 processes that make it up. (A complete description of these processes can be found in the Project Management Institute's publication: *A Guide to the Project Management Body of Knowledge, Third Edition,* 2004.) It will be clear from the context what is being referred to.

My approach is to assess both the process and practice level maturities for the 44 processes of the entire project management process. Use that information in conjunction with the recent history of project success and failure. Try to correlate reasons for failure with the individual processes. That will be the baseline measure of where you are with respect to project success and the root causes as defined by the 44 processes as to project failure.

Determine Process Goals

These goals should be defined with respect to the overall process and practice maturity levels as well as the individual process level maturities (both process ands practice). Express the goals in terms of target maturity levels for each process and its practice as well as target success rates at the project level. These are quantitative measures that can be monitored as part of the overall improvement initiative.

Prioritize Process Goals

You can use any number of criteria to establish these priorities (largest maturity gap, most business value, low hanging fruit, and so on). I'll assume for the sake of this discussion that you will have established that priority order and no more need be said about that.

Select Process for Improvement

And so with that priority list in hand you select the next process on which to focus your improvement initiatives. Note in the diagram that this is the first step in the iterative portion of this improvement process. You reached this step by contributing all of the improvements you could to the then highest process on your list. That process then moves down the list and a new process pops to the top of the priority list. That is the process I focus on as I continue this discussion.

Identify Improvement Initiatives

This is nothing more than a brainstorming session where the process owner and the team come together to identify all of the possible changes that could be made to improve the process under consideration. The longer the list the better. So don't try to short-circuit this exercise. Let everyone express their ideas however outlandish they may be. Once no new ideas are coming forth, consider the list complete (for now at least). The next part of the step is to prioritize the list. There are really only two criteria to consider.

- The first is order the list by easiest to implement.
- The second (and the one I prefer) is to order the list based on maximum likely contribution to improvement.

Launch Improvement Projects

With that list in hand and based on resource availability, start down the list. If your resources are constrained, you might do the improvement projects one at a time is the order of their priority. As you have more and more resources available you might establish parallel swim lanes—one for each improvement project.

Compare Results against Goals

How did you do? Did the just completed improvement projects meet the targeted maturity level goal or not? If so, move to the next process. If not, continue to work the prioritized list of improvement ideas.

WARNING
■■■■ **Above all, flexibility and openness are the critical success factors of successful process impriovement programs leading towards the end state.**

Discussion Questions

1. Your organization has recently embraced the agile approaches in addition to their long time use of traditional models to project management and systems development. You have been assigned a project that is clearly an adaptive project. You have gathered the following information:

   - **The enterprise environment**—While there is not a lot of history in the organization on the use of Adaptive SDPM strategies, you believe the organization will be supportive. The organization is stable, and senior management is informed.

   - **The sponsor**—The sponsor has supported you in the past, and you are reasonably comfortable that they will support you on this project. However, you are not sure of their understanding of an Adaptive SDPM strategy.

   - **The customer**—You have experience with this customer on several traditional projects in the past. They do what is expected of them but are not too enthused about being directly involved in projects. They are a bit gun shy of the Adaptive SDPM strategy. This may be due to their never having been involved in one before and to their lack of knowledge of the Adaptive SDPM strategy.

   - **The skill/competency/experience level of the project team**—Your team is solid. There is no reason for concern here. You have worked with them on all types of projects. They tend to be the more senior members of the development staff.

   - **The physical location of the project team**—The team is co-located.

   - **The criticality of the project**—The project is mission critical and a large part of revenues depends on the success of the effort.

   What SDPM strategy would you choose and why? What are some of the possible issues that may arise, and what might you do to mitigate them?

What's on the Web Site?

He who would search for pearls must dive below.
John Dryden
English poet

Appendix Learning Objectives

After reading this appendix, you will be able to:
- ◆ **Know how to find the Web site**
- ◆ **Describe what is on the Web site**

The Web site has been established to provide a ready source of useful information on the book contents.

It is designed to bring you quickly to some supporting materials for your reference and further study or for your use in presentations and other learning experiences.

The Web site can be accessed at `www.wiley.com/go/espm`

Pizza Delivered Quickly (PDQ) Case Study (MS Word File)

PDQ is a new and comprehensive case study. Throughout the book I draw on the case study for examples of the applications of the tools, templates, and processes discussed.

Figures Master File

This is a file that contains a printable and reproducible file for every figure used in the text. This is made available for those who are teaching a course from our book and for those who might find some use for the figures in their presentations. You have my permission to imbed the figures in your slide presentations. All I ask is that you give the appropriate attributions whenever you use one of the figures.

A Note on the Answer File for Discussion Questions

Each chapter ends with a few discussion questions that might be used by instructors to create some dialog with the class or might be used for written assignments. These are questions that I hope will be thought-provoking. There are no right answers, although there are plenty of wrong answers. An answer file has been created for instructors. Just e-mail me at rkw@eiicorp.com, identify yourself as a legitimate instructor or faculty member, and I'll send you the answer file. I'd love to hear from you and hear how you are using the book and its materials.

Bibliography

Ignorance never settles a question.
Benjamin Disraeli
English Prime Minister

Those who have read of everything are thought to understand everything, too; but it is not always so—reading furnishes the mind only with materials of knowledge; it is thinking that makes what is read ours. We are of the ruminating kind, and it is not enough to cram ourselves with a great load of collections; unless we chew them over again, they will not give us strength and nourishment.

John Locke

Appendix Learning Objectives

After reading this appendix, you will be able to:

- ◆ Conduct further reading and study into SDPM strategies
- ◆ Know the relevant literature in SDPM strategies

The following books are a collection of current publications from my private project management library. I have included only books published in the last 10 years. With a few exceptions there are titles that were published more than 10 years ago. These were written by leaders in our field or have a particularly valuable contribution to the literature. They are classics. All of these books will be of particular interest to professionals who have project management responsibilities, are members of project teams, or simply have a craving to learn about the basics of sound project management. The focus of many of the books is systems and software development because that is our primary interest, although several also treat the basic concepts and principles of project management. I have also included books on closely related topics, which I have found to be of value in researching and writing this book. You might find value in them, too.

For your ease in finding specific sources, I have arranged the bibliography into four sections. The first section corresponds to Part I of the book. The second section corresponds to the Traditional approach to project management and includes references to the Linear and Incremental SDPM strategies. The third section covers the agile landscape and includes references that cover the Iterative, Adaptive, and Extreme SDPM strategies. The fourth part covers references to topics discussed in Part VII.

The Changing SDPM Landscape

Barkley, Bruce T. and James H. Saylor. 1994. *Customer-Driven Project Management: A New Paradigm in Total Quality Implementation.* New York, NY: McGraw-Hill, Inc. (ISBN 0-07-003739-6)

Ibbs, C. William and Young-Hoon Kwak. 1997. *The Benefits of Project Management: Financial and Organizational Rewards to Corporations.* Newtown Square, PA: The Project Management Institute. (ISBN 1-880410-32-X)

Jensen, Bill. 2000. *Simplicity: The New Competitive Advantage in A World of More, Better, Faster.* Cambridge, MA: Perseus Books. (ISBN 0-7382-0210-X)

Kerzner, Harold. 1998. *In Search of Excellence in Project Management.* New York, NY: Van Nostrand Reinhold. (ISBN 0-442-02706-0)

Laufer, Alexander. 1997. *Simultaneous Management: Managing Projects in A Dynamic Environment.* New York, NY: AMACOM. (ISBN 0-8144-0312-3)

Lientz, Bennet P. and Kathryn P. Rea. 1995. *Project Management for the 21st Century.* New York, NY: Academic Press. (ISBN 0-12-449965-5)

Martin, Paula. 1995. *Leading Project Management into the 21st Century: New Dimensions in Project Management and Accountability.* Cincinnati, OH: MartinTate. (ISBN 0-943811-04-X)

Traditional Project Management

Baker, Sunny and Kim Baker. 1998. *The Complete Idiot's Guide to Project Management.* New York, NY: Alpha Books. (ISBN 0-02-861745-2)

Bechtold, Richard. 1999. *Essentials of Software Project Management.* Vienna, VA: Management Concepts. (ISBN 1-56726-085-3)

Blaylock, Jim and Rudd McGary. 2002. *Project Management: Best Practices A to Z.* Columbus, OH: PM Best Practices, Inc. (ISBN 0-9719121-0-6)

Cable, Dwayne P. and John R. Adams. 1997. *Principles of Project Management.* Upper Darby, PA: Project Management Institute. (ISBN 1-880410-30-3)

Chapman, Chris and Stephen Ward. 1997. *Project Risk Management: Processes, Techniques and Insights.* New York, NY: John Wiley & Sons. (ISBN 0-471-95804-2)

Conway, Kieron. 2001. *Software Project Management: From Concept to Deployment.* Scottsdale, AZ: The Coriolis Group. (ISBN 1-57610-807-4)

DeMarco, Tom 1997. *The Deadline: A Novel about Project Management.* New York, NY: Dorset House. (ISBN 0-932633-39-0)

DeMarco, T. and T. Lister. 1999. *Peopleware: Productive Projects and Teams, Second Edition.* New York, NY: Dorset House Publishing. (ISBN 0-932633-43-9)

Goodpasture, John C. 2002. *Managing Projects for Value.* Vienna, VA: Management Concepts. (ISBN 1-56726-138-8)

Greer, Michael. 1996. *The Project Manager's Partner: A Step-by-Step Guide to Project Management.* Amherst, MA: HRD Press, Inc. (ISBN 0-087425-397-7)

Hallows, Jolyon. 1998. *Information Systems Project Management: How to Deliver Function and Value in Information Technology Projects.* New York, NY: AMACOM. (ISBN 0-8144-0368-9)

Harrington, H. James, et al. 2000. *Project Change Management: Applying Change Management to Improvement Projects.* New York, NY: McGraw-Hill. (ISBN 0-07-027104-6)

Haugan, Gregory T. 2002. *Project Planning and Scheduling.* Vienna, VA: Management Concepts. (ISBN 1-56726-136-1)

Haugan, Gregory T. 2002. *Effective Work Breakdown Structures.* Vienna, VA: Management Concepts. (ISBN 1-56726-135-3)

Hill, Peter R. 2001. *Practical Project Estimation: A Toolkit for Estimating Software Development Effort and Duration.* Warrandyte, Victoria, Australia: International Software Benchmarking Standards Group. (ISBN 0-9577201-1-4)

Humphrey, Watts S. 1997. *Managing Technical People.* Reading, MA: Addison-Wesley. (ISBN 0-201-54597-7)

Ireland, Lewis R. 1991. *Quality Management for Projects and Programs.* Upper Darby, PA: Project Management Institute. (ISBN 1-880410-11-7)

Johnston, Andrew K. 1995. *A Hacker's Guide to Project Management.* Oxford, England: Butterworth-Heinemann Ltd. (ISBN 0-7506-2230-X)

Kerzner, Harold. 2001. *Project Management: A Systems Approach to Planning, Scheduling, and Controlling.* Seventh Edition. New York, NY: John Wiley & Sons, Inc. (ISBN0-471-39342-8)

Kliem, Ralph L. and Irwin S. Ludin. 1997. *Reducing Project Risk.* Hampshire, England: Gower Publishing Limited. (ISBN 0-566-07799-X)

Kloppenborg, Timothy J. and Joseph A. Petrick. 2002. *Managing Project Quality.* Vienna, VA: Management Concepts. (ISBN 1-56726-141-8)

Kyle, Mackenzie. 1998. *Making It Happen: A Non-Technical Guide to Project Management.* Toronto, Canada: John Wiley & Sons, Canada Ltds. (ISBN 0-471-64234-7)

Lambert, Lee R. and Erin Lambert. 2000. *Project Management: The CommonSense Approach.* Columbus, OH: LCG Publishing. (ISBN 0-9626397-8-8)

Laufer, Alexander and Edward J. Hoffman. 2000. *Project Management Success Stories: Lessons of Project Leaders.* New York, NY: John Wiley & Sons, Inc. (ISBN 0-471-36007-4)

Levine, Harvey A. 2002. *Practical Project Management: Tips, Tactics, and Tools.* New York, NY: John Wiley & Sons, Inc. (ISBN 0-471-20303-3)

Lewis, James P. 1995. *Project Planning, Scheduling & Control.* Chicago, IL: Irwin. (ISBN 1-55738-869-5)

Lewis, James P. 1998. *Mastering Project Management.* New York, NY: McGraw-Hill. (ISBN 0-7863-1188-6)

Lewis, James P. 2000. *The Project Manager's Desk Reference, 2nd Edition.* New York, NY: McGraw-Hill. (ISBN 0-07-134750-X)

Lientz, Bennet P. and Kathryn P. Rea. 2001. *Breakthrough Technology Project Management, Second Edition.* San Diego, CA: Academic Press. (ISBN 0-12-449968-6)

Michaels, Jack V. 1996. *Technical Risk Management.* Upper Saddle River, NJ: Prentice Hall. (ISBN 0-13-155756-4)

Muller, Robert J. 1998. *Productive Objects: An Applied Software Project Management Framework.* San Francisco, CA: Morgan Kaufmann Publishers, Inc. (ISBN 1-55860-437-5)

Neuendorf, Steve. 2002. *Project Measurement.* Vienna, VA: Management Concepts. (ISBN 1-56726-140-X)

Pinto, Jeffrey K. 1998. *Project Management Handbook.* San Francisco, CA: Jossey-Bass Publishers. (ISBN 0-7879-4013-5)

Pritchard, Carl L. 1998. *How to Build A Work Breakdown Structure: The Cornerstone of Project Management.* Arlington, VA: ESI International. (ISBN 1-890367-12-5)

Pritchard, Carl L. 2001. *Risk Management: Concepts and Guidance.* Arlington, VA: ESI International. (ISBN 1-890367-30-3)

Project Management Institute. 1997. *Principles of Project Management.* Upper Darby, PA: Project Management Institute. (ISBN 1-880410-30-3)

Project Management Institute. 1997. *The PMI Book of Project Management Forms.* Upper Darby, PA: Project Management Institute. (ISBN 1-880410-31-1)

Project Management Institute. 1999. *Project Management Software Survey.* Newton Square, PA: Project Management Institute. (ISBN 1-880410-52-4)

Project Management Institute. 1999. *The Future of Project Management.* Newtown Square, PA: Project Management Institute. (ISBN 1-880410-71-0)

Project Management Institute. 2000. *A Guide to the Project Management Body of Knowledge.* Newtown Square, PA: Project Management Institute.

Project Management Institute. 2000. *Project Management Experience and Knowledge Self-Assessment Manual.* Newtown, PA: Project Management Institute. (ISBN 1-880410-24-9)

Project Management Institute. 2001. *Practice Standards for Work Breakdown Structures.* Newtown Square, PA: Project Management Institute. (ISBN 1-880410-81-8)

Rad, Parviz F. 2002. *Project Estimating and Cost Management.* Vienna, PA: Management Concepts. (ISBN 1-56726-144-2)

Royer, Paul S. 2002. *Project Risk Management: A Proactive Approach.* Vienna, VA: Management Concepts. (ISBN 1-56726-139-6)

Schuyler, John. 2001. *Risk and Decision Analysis in Projects, Second Edition.* Newtown Square, PA: The Project Management Institute. (ISBN 1-880410-28-1)

Schwalbe, Kathy. 2000. *Information Technology Project Management.* Boston, MA: Course Technology. (ISBN 0-7600-1180-X)

Siegel, David. 1997. *Secrets of Successful Web Sites: Project Management on the World Wide Web.* Indianapolis, IN: New Riders. (ISBN 1-56830-382-3)

Sodhi, Jag and Prince Sodhi. 2001. *IT Project Management Handbook.* Vienna, VA: Management Concepts. (ISBN 1-56726-098-5)

TechRepublic. 2001. *IT Professional's Guide to Project Management.* Louisville, KY: TechRepublic. (ISBN 1-931490-16-3)

Toney, Frank and Ray Powers. 1997. *Best Practices of Project Management Groups in Large Functional Organizations.* Upper Darby, PA: Project Management Institute. (ISBN 1-880410-05-2)

Verzuh, Eric. 1999. *The Fast Forward MBA in Project Management.* New York, NY: John Wiley & Sons, Inc. (ISBN 0-471-32546-5)

Ward, J. LeRoy. 2000. *Project Management Terms: A Working Glossary.* Arlington, VA: ESI International. (ISBN 1-890367-25-7)

Whitten, Neal. 1995. *Managing Software Development Projects, Second Edition.* New York, NY: John Wiley & Sons. (ISBN 0-471-07683-X)

Whitten, Neal. 2000. *The EnterPrize Organization.* Newtown Square, PA: The Project Management Institute. (ISBN 1-880410-79-6)

Wysocki, Robert K., Robert Beck, Jr., and David B. Crane. 2000. *Effective Project Management, Second Edition.* New York, NY: John Wiley & Sons. (ISBN 0-471-36028-7)

Yourdon, Edward. 1999. *Death March: The Complete Software Developer's Guide to Surviving "Mission Impossible" Projects.* Upper Saddle River, NJ: Prentice Hall. (ISBN 0-13-014659-5)

Agile Project Management

Ajani, Shaun. 2002. *Extreme Project Management: Unique Methodologies–Resolute Principles–Astounding Results*. San Jose, CA: Writers Club Press. (ISBN 0-595-21335-9)

Ambler, Scott W. 2000. *The Unified Process Elaboration Phase: Best Practices in Implementing the UP*. Lawrence, KS: R&D Books. (ISBN 1-929629-05-2

Ambler, Scott W. 2002. *Agile Modeling: Effective Practices for Extreme Programming and the Unified Process*. New York, NY: John Wiley & Sons, Inc. (ISBN 0-471-20282-7)

Ambler, Scott W. and Larry L. Constantine. 2000. *The Unified Process Inception Phase: Best Practices in Implementing the UP*. Lawrence, KS: CMP Books. (ISBN 1-929629-10-9)

Ambler, Scott W. 2004. *The Object Primer: Agile Model-Driven Development with UML 2.0, Third Edition*. Cambridge, United Kingdom Cambridge University Press. (ISBN 0-521-54018-6)

Anderson, David J. 2004. *Agile Management for Software Engineering: Applying the Theory of Constraints for Business Results*. Upper Saddle River, NJ: Prentice Hall. (ISBN 0-13-142460-2)

Augustine, Sanjiv. 2005. *Managing Agile Projects*. Upper Saddle River, NJ: Prentice Hall. (ISBN 0-13-124071-4)

Beck, Kent. 2000. *Extreme Programming Explained: Embrace Change*. Reading, MA: Addison-Wesley. (ISBN 0-201-61641-6)

Beck, Kent and Martin Fowler. 2001. *Planning Extreme Programming*. Reading, MA: Addison-Wesley. (ISBN 0-201-71091-9)

Bergstrom, Stefan and Lotta Raeberg. 2004. *Adopting the Rational Unified Process: Success with RUP*. Boston, MA: Addison-Wesley (ISBN 0-321-20294-5)

Boehm, Barry and Richard Turner. 2004. *Balancing Agility and Discipline: A Guide for the Perplexed*. Reading, MA: Addison-Wesley (ISBN 0-321-18612-5)

Chin, Gary. 2004. Agile Project Management: How to Succeed in the Face of Changing Project Requirements. New York, NY: AMACOM. (ISBN 0-8144-7176-5)

Cockburn, Alistair. 1998. *Surviving Object-Oriented Projects*. Boston, MA: Addison-Wesley. (ISBN 0-201-49834-0)

Cockburn, Alistair. 2001. *Writing Effective Use Cases*. Boston, MA: Addison-Wesley. (ISBN 0-201-70225-8)

Cockburn, Alistair. 2005. *Crystal Clear: A Human-Powered Methodology for Small Teams*. Boston, MA: Addison-Wesley (ISBN 0-201-69947-8)

Cohn, Mike. 2004. *User Stories Applied: For Agile Software Development*. Boston, MA: Addison-Wesley. (ISBN 0-321-20568-5)

Coplien, James O. and Neil B. Harrison. 2005. *Organizational Patterns of Agile Software Development.* Upper Saddle River, NJ: Prentice Hall (ISBN 0-13-146740-0)

DeCarlo, Doug. 2004. *Extreme Project Management: Using Leadership, Principles, and Tools to Deliver Value in the Face of Volatility.* San Francisco, CA: Jossey Bass. (ISBN 0-7879-7409-9)

DeGrace, Peter and Leslie Hulet Stahl. 1990. *Wicked Problems, Righteous Solutions.* Englewood Cliffs, NJ: Yourdon Press Computing Series. (ISBN 0-13-590126-X)

Eckstein, Jutta. 2004. *Agile Software Development in the Large: Diving into the Deep.* New York, NY: Dorset House. (ISBN 0-932633-57-9)

Fowler, Martin. 2000. *Refactoring: Improving the Design of Existing Code.* Boston, MA: Addison-Wesley. (ISBN 0-201-48567-2)

Highsmith, James A. 2000. *Adaptive Software Development: A Collaborative Approach to Managing Complex Systems.* New York, NY: Dorset House Publishing (ISBN 0-932633-40-4)

Highsmith, Jim. 2002. *Agile Software Development Ecosystems.* Boston, MA: Addison-Wesley. (ISBN 0-201-76043-6)

Jeffries, Ron, Ann Henderson, and Chet Hendrickson. 2001. *Extreme Programming Installed.* Boston, MA: Addison-Wesley. (ISBN 0-201-70842-6)

Kruchten, Philippe. 2000. *The Rational Unified Process: An Introduction, Second Edition.* Boston, MA: Addison-Wesley. (ISBN 0-201-70710-1)

McConnell, Steve. 1996. *Rapid Development.* Redmond, WA: Microsoft Press. (ISBN 1-55615-900-5)

McConnell, Steve. 1998. *Software Project Survival Guide.* Redmond, WA: Microsoft Press. (ISBN 1-57231-621-7)

Newkirk, James and Robert C. Martin. 2001. *Extreme Programming in Practice.* Boston, MA: Addison-Wesley. (ISBN 0-201-70937-6)

Palmer, Stephen R. and John M. Felsing. 2002. *A Practical Guide to Feature-Driven Development.* Upper Saddle River, NJ: Prentice Hall. (ISBN 0-13-067615-2)

Pollice, Gary, et al. 2004. *Software Development for Small Teams: A RUP-Centric Approach.* Boston, MA: Addison-Wesley. (ISBN 0-321-19950-2)

Royce, Walker. 1998. *Software Project Management: A Unified Framework.* Reading, MA: Addison-Wesley. (ISBN 0-201-30958-0)

Schwaber, Ken and Mike Beedle. 2002. *Agile Software Development with SCRUM.* Upper Saddle River, NJ: Prentice Hall. (ISBN 0-13-067634-9)

Stapleton, Jennifer. 2003. *DSDM: Business Focused Development, Second Edition.* Boston, MA: Addison-Wesley. (ISBN 0-321-11224-5)

Succi, Giancarlo and Michele Marchesi. 2001. *Extreme Programming Examined.* Boston, MA: Addison-Wesley. (ISBN 0-201-71040-4)

Thomsett, R. 1993. *Third Wave Project Management*. Englewood Cliffs, NJ: Yourdon Press Computing Series. (ISBN 0-13-915299-7)

Thomsett, Rob. 2002. *Radical Project Management*. Upper Saddle River, NJ: Prentice Hall. (ISBN 0-13-009486-2)

Wake, William C. 2002. *Extreme Programming Explored*. Boston, MA: Addison-Wesley. (ISBN 0-201-73397-8)

Wysocki, Robert K., 2003. *Effective Project Management: Traditional, Adaptive, Extreme, Third Edition*. New York, NY: John Wiley & Sons. (ISBN 0-471-43221-0)

Putting It All Together

Block, Thomas R. and J. Davidson Frame. 1998. *The Project Office*. Upper Darby, PA: Project Management Institute. (ISBN 1-56052-443-X)

Chang, Richard Y. 1994. *Continuous Process Improvement*. Irvine, CA: Richard Chang Associates. (ISBN 1-883553-06-7)

Chang, Richard Y. 1995. *Process Reengineering in Action*. Irvine, CA: Richard Chang Associates. (ISBN 1-883553-16-4)

Chang Richard Y. and P. Keith Kelly. 1994. *Improving Through Benchmarking*. Irvine, CA: Richard Chang Associates. (ISBN 1-883553-08-3)

Chang, Richard Y. and Matthew E. Niedzwiecki. 1993. *Continuous Improvement Tools, Vol I*. Irvine, CA: Richard Chang Associates. (ISBN 1-883553-00-8)

Chang, Richard Y. and Matthew E. Niedzwiecki. 1993. *Continuous Improvement Tools, Vol II*. Irvine, CA: Richard Chang Associates. (ISBN 1-883553-01-6)

Cooper, Robert G., Scott J. Edgett, and Elko J. Kleinschmidt. 1998. *Portfolio Management for New Products*. Reading, MA: Perseus Books. (ISBN 0-201-32814-3)

Crawford, J. Kent. 2002. *The Strategic Project Office: A Guide to Improving Organizational Performance*. New York, NY: Marcel Dekker, Inc. (ISBN 0-8247-0750-8)

Crawford, J. Kent. 2002. *Project Management Maturity Model: Providing a Proven Path to Project Management Excellence*. New York, NY: Marcel Dekker, Inc. (ISBN 0-8247-0754-0)

Dinsmore, Paul C. 1999. *Winning in Business With Enterprise Project Management*. New York, NY: AMACOM. (ISBN 0-8144-0420-0)

Dymond, Kenneth M. 1998. *A Guide to the CMM: Understanding the Capability Maturity Model for Software*. Annapolis, MD: Process Transition International, Inc. (ISBN 0-9646008-0-3)

Dye, Lowell D. and James S. Pennypacker, (editors). 1999. *Project Portfolio Management: Selecting and Prioritizing Projects for Competitive Advantage*. West Chester, PA: Center for Business Practices. (ISBN 1-929576-00-5)

Fuller, Jim. 1997. *Managing Performance Improvement Projects: Preparing, Planning, Implementing.* San Francisco, CA: Jossey Bass. (ISBN 0-7879-0959-9)

Graham, Robert J. and Randall L. Englund. 1997. *Creating an Environment for Successful Projects.* San Francisco, CA: Jossey-Bass Publishers. (ISBN 0-7879-0359-0)

Hallows, Jolyon. 2002. *The Project Management Office Toolkit: A Step-by-Step Guide to Setting Up A Project Management Office.* New York, NY: AMACOM. (ISBN 0-8144-0663-7)

Hunt, V. Daniel. 1996. *Process Mapping: How to Reengineer Your Business Processes.* New York, NY: John Wiley & Sons, Inc. (ISBN 0-471-13281-0)

Kerzner, Harold. 2001. *Strategic Planning for Project Management Using A Project Management Maturity Model.* New York, NY: John Wiley & Sons, Inc. (ISBN 0-471-40039-4)

Phillips, Jack J. et al. 2002. *The Project Management Scorecard: Measuring the Success of Project Management Solutions.* Boston, MA: Butterworth Heinemann. (ISBN 0-7506-7449-0)

Rad, Parviz F. and Ginger Levin. 2002. *The Advanced Project Management Office: A Comprehensive Look at Function and Implementation.* Boca Raton, FL: St Lucie Press. (ISBN 1-57444-340-2)

Raynus, Joseph. 1999. *Software Process Improvement with CMM.* Boston, MA: Artech House. (ISBN 0-89006-644-2)

The Project Overview Statement

Define the problem before you pursue a solution.
Neils Bohr

NOTE Most of the material in this chapter is an abridged version of material discussing the Project Overview Statement (POS) from my earlier book *Effective Project Management: Traditional, Adaptive, Extreme, Third Edition* (Wiley, 2003). It is presented here for completeness so that this book may be used as a text for an introductory course in software project management. For courses requiring more detail the earlier work may be used as a companion text.

There needs to be a high-level description of every project. This will be a document that should get broad distribution across the enterprise. I call that document the Project Overview Statement. It is a one-page non-technical description of the Opportunity/Problem, Goal, Objectives, Success Criteria, Risks and Assumptions of the project.

The Requirements Document provides the input you need to generate the Project Overview Statement (POS). The POS is a short document (ideally one page) that concisely states what is to be done in the project, why it is to be done, and what business value it will provide to the enterprise when completed.

The main purpose of the POS is to secure senior management approval and the resources needed to develop a detailed project plan. It will be reviewed by the managers who are responsible for setting priorities and deciding what projects to support. It is also a general statement that can be read by any interested party in the enterprise. For this reason, the POS cannot contain any technical jargon that generally would not be used across the enterprise. Once approved, the POS becomes the foundation for future planning and execution of the project. It becomes the reference document for questions or conflicts regarding project scope and purpose.

Parts of the POS

The POS has five component parts:

- Problem/opportunity
- Project goal
- Project objectives
- Success criteria
- Assumptions, risks, obstacles

Its structure is designed to lead senior managers from a statement of fact (problem/opportunity) to a statement of what this project will address (project goal). Given that senior management is interested in the project goal and that it addresses a concern of sufficiently high priority, they will read more detail on exactly what the project includes (project objectives). The business value is expressed as quantitative business outcomes (success criteria). Finally, a summary of conditions that may hinder project success is identified (assumptions, risks, obstacles). This appendix takes a look at each of these sections more closely. An example POS is given in Figure C-1.

Stating the Problem/Opportunity

The first part of the POS is a statement of the problem or opportunity that the project addresses. This statement is fact—it does not need to be defined or defended. Everyone in the organization will accept it as true. This is critical because it provides a basis for the rest of the document. The POS may not have the benefit of the project manager's being present to explain what is written or to defend the reason for proposing the project to the management. A problem or opportunity statement that is known and accepted by the organization is the foundation on which to build a rationale for the project. It also sets the priority with which management will view what follows. If you are addressing a high-priority area or high-business-value area, your idea will get more attention and senior management will read on.

Establishing the Project Goal

The second section of the POS states the goal of the project—what you intend, written in the language of the business, to do to address the problem or opportunity identified. The purpose of the goal statement is to get senior management to value the idea enough to read on. In other words, they should think enough of your idea as stated in the goal statement to conclude that it warrants further attention and consideration.

Defining the Project Objectives

The third section of the POS comprises the project objectives. Think of objective statements as a more detailed version of the goal statements. The purpose of the objective statements is to clarify the exact boundaries of the goal statement and define the boundaries or the scope of your project. In fact, the objective statements you write for a specific goal statement are nothing more than a decomposition of the goal statement into a set of necessary and sufficient objective statements. That is, every objective must be accomplished in order to reach the goal, and no objective is superfluous.

Identifying Success Criteria

The fourth section of the POS answers the question, "Why do we want to do this project?" It is the measurable business value that will result from doing this project. It sells the project to senior management. It is essential that the criteria be quantifiable and measurable and, if possible, expressed in terms of business value. Remember that you are trying to sell your idea to the decision makers.

PROJECT OVERVIEW STATEMENT	Project Name **Office Supply Cost Reduction**	Project No.	Project Leads **PAUL BEARER**

Problem/Opportunity

Our cost reduction task force reports that office supply expenses have exceeded budget by an average of 4% for each of the last 3 years. In addition, an across the board budget cut of 2% has been announced and there is an inflation rate of 3% estimated for the year.

Goal

To implement a cost containment strategy that will result in office supply expenses being within budget by the end of the next fiscal year.

Objectives

1. Establish a departmental office supply budgeting and control system.
2. Implement a central store for office and copying supplies.
3. Standardize the types and brands of office supplies used by the company.
4. Increase employee awareness of copying practices that can reduce the cost of meeting their copying needs.

Success Criteria

1. The total project cost is less than 4% of the current year office supply budget.
2. At least 98% of office supply requests are filled on demand.
3. At least 90% of the departments have office supply expenses within budget.
4. No department office supply expense exceeds budget by more than 4%.

Assumptions, Risks, Obstacles

1. Central stores can be operated at or below the breakeven point.
2. Users will be sensitive to and supportive of the cost containment initiatives.
3. Equitable office supply budgets can be established.
4. Management will be supportive and consistent.
5. The existing inventory control system can support the central stores operation.

Path Forward Recommendations

1. Conduct preliminary planning based on the elements contained herein. Planning may uncover issues, which require further clarification in order to reach more definitive conclusions.
2. Schecule a tentative meeting to discuss preliminary planning findings.
3. Incorporate all comments and recommendations from meeting and receive approval to proceed to definitive planning.

Prepared By **Olive Branch**	Date **04/01/04**	Approved By **Del E. Lama**	Date **04/05/04**

Figure C-1: An example POS

There are only three types of success criteria.

■ The results of the project can **increase revenue,** and as a part of the success criteria that increase should be measured in hard dollars or as a percentage of a specific revenue number.

- The second type of success criteria is to **avoid costs**. Again this can be stated as a hard dollar amount or a percentage of some specific cost. Be careful here because oftentimes a cost reduction means staff reductions. Staff reductions do not mean the shifting of resources to other places in the organization. Moving staff from one area to another is not a cost reduction.

- The final type of success criteria is to **improve service**. Here the metric is more difficult to define. It usually is some percentage improvement in customer satisfaction or a reduction in the frequency and/or type of customer complaints.

NOTE

You might be familiar with the term IRACIS. It is formed from the first letter of each of the three types of success criteria.

In some cases, it can take some creativity to identify the success criteria. For example, customer satisfaction may have to be measured by some pre- and post-surveys. In other cases, a surrogate might be acceptable if directly measuring the business value of the project is impossible. Be careful, however, and make sure that the decision maker buys into your surrogate measure. Also be careful of traps such as this one: "We haven't been getting any customer complaint calls; therefore, the customer must be satisfied." Did you ever consider the possibility that the lack of complaint calls may be the direct result of your lack of action responding to complaints? Customers may feel that it does no good to complain because nothing happens to settle their complaint.

Senior management also will look at your success criteria and assign business value to your project. In the absence of other criteria this will be the basis for their decision whether to commit resources to complete the detailed plan. The success criteria are another place to sell the value of your project.

List Assumptions, Risks, and Obstacles

The fifth and final section of the POS identifies any factors that can affect the outcome of the project and that you want to bring to the attention of senior management. Perhaps they can find ways to mitigate them. These factors can affect deliverables, the realization of the success criteria, the ability of the project team to complete the project as planned, or any other environmental or organizational conditions that are relevant to the project. You want to record anything that can go wrong. Be careful, however, to put in the POS only those items that you want senior management to know about and in which they will be interested. This is not the place to conduct a comprehensive risk identification exercise.

The project manager uses the assumptions, risks, and obstacles section to alert management to any factors that may interfere with the project work or compromise the contribution that the project can make to the organization. Management may be able to neutralize their impact. On the other hand, the project manager will include in the project plan whatever contingencies can help reduce the probable impact and its effect on project success.

Attachments

Even though I strongly recommend a one-page POS, in some instances a longer document is necessary. As part of their initial approval of the resources to do detailed project planning, senior management may want some measure of the economic value of the proposed project. They recognize that many of the estimates are little more than a guess, but they will nevertheless ask for this information. In my experience, I have seen two types of analyses requested frequently:

- Risk analysis
- Financial analyses (such as the following):
    - Return on Investment
    - Breakeven Analysis
    - Internal Rate of Return
    - Cost/Benefit Analysis

A discussion of these analyses is outside the scope of this book.

Requirements Gathering

In most management problems there are too many possibilities to expect experience, judgement, or intuition to provide good guesses, even with perfect information.

Russell L. Ackoff
Management Information Systems scientist

Appendix Learning Objectives

After reading this appendix, you will be able to:

◆ Understand the significance of wants versus needs

◆ Describe what managing customer expectations really means

◆ Know what a requirement is and how to gather requirements

◆ Understand the role of the stakeholder in requirements gathering

---

NOTE Most of the material in this chapter is an abridged version of material discussing gathering requirements from my earlier book *Effective Project Management: Traditional, Adaptive, Extreme, Third Edition* (Wiley, 2003). It is presented here for completeness so that this book may be used as a text for an introductory course in software project management. For courses requiring more detail the earlier work may be used as a companion text.

Gathering requirements is one of the first and major places that the project can go wrong. This is the first opportunity to really explore what the customer needs as opposed to what the customer thinks they want. Completeness and clarity are paramount. There will be many cases where one or both of those will not be possible. That situation is discussed at length throughout the book. In this appendix the discussion is limited to the industry best practices for requirements gathering.

Requirements gathering can be simple and straightforward or it can be complex and meandering and anywhere in between. Add to that customers or clients who can't seem to make up their minds or are known to constantly change their minds, and you have a significant problem to deal with.

The approaches this appendix explores for requirements gathering are Conditions of Satisfaction (COS) and the Volere Process.

- COS works well on smaller, simpler projects. It produces a document of understanding, which we call a Project Overview Statement (POS). COS is a dynamic tool in that it is validated at major check points in the project, like during project status meetings or at milestone events.

- COS does not scale well, so for larger more complex projects I use the Volere Process, as outlined in *Mastering the Requirements Process* by Suzanne Robertson and James Robertson (Addison-Wesley, 1999).

Conditions of Satisfaction

The root cause of many problems that come up in the course of doing a project originate in a disconnect between what the client says they want and what they really need. The disconnect may come about because the client is swept up in a euphoria over the technology and is so enamored with what they see on the web, for example, that they have convinced themselves that they have to have it without any further thought of exactly what it is they really need. The disconnect can also come about because the client does not really know what they need. Traditional Project Management (TPM) forces them into specifying what they want when that is the absolute wrong thing to do. If there is any reason to believe that what the client says they want is different from what they need, the project manager has the responsibility of sifting and sorting this out ASAP. That is one of the reasons for the Conditions of Satisfaction (COS).

Many projects run into trouble at the very beginning. For some reason, people have a difficult time understanding what they are saying to one another. How often do you find yourself thinking about what you are going to say while the other party is talking? If you are going to be a successful project manager, you must stop that kind of behavior. An essential skill that project managers need to cultivate is good listening skills.

Good listening skills are important in two critical stages of the project planning phase.

- The first, and the ideal one, occurs when a client makes a request for a project. At this point, two parties are brought together to define exactly what the request is and what kind of response is appropriate. The deliverable from this conversation is a COS.

- The second, and the more likely situation, occurs when you inherit what we call the "watercooler project." As the name suggests, these are the projects that are assigned to you when you accidentally meet your manager at the water cooler. Up to that point, you probably had not heard of such a project, but you now need to find out all about it ASAP.

The COS document is the result of your investigation.

For smaller simpler project situations Conditions of Satisfaction (COS) is an effective approach to understanding what the client wants (or needs, but that's for a later conversation) and having the client understand what you will be able to do for them. Figure D-1 is a simple representation of the process of requirements gathering using COS.

The first thing to realize about COS is that to do it effectively requires good listening skills. Many have the bad habit of planning what they are going to say while the other person is saying their piece. If that is your style, you have to cure that habit.

Referring again to Figure D-1 I want to take a walk through a generic COS session. The requester (the client) and the provider (the project manager) are sitting across the table from one another. The requester begins to explain what they want while the provider is listening attentively. Once the requester has completed their request, the provider begins to explain, in their own words, what it is they heard the requester ask for. A conversation follows in which the provider continues to explain what they heard. The conversation continues until the requester says, "You understand what I am asking for." At that point the tables are turned and the provider begins to explain what it is that can provide. Once the provider has completed that explanation the requestor beings to repeat what they heard will be provided in their own words. That continues until the provider says, "You understand what I can provide."

In this simple scenario, a lot more has been accomplished than you might think at first brush. First, both parties have made their positions known and know that the other party understands. The positions may not be compatible with one another but at least they are known. Secondly, the parties have begun to establish a common language. They can talk to one another in the language of the project they are forming and know what the other person is saying. I consider this to be a critical success factor for any project where the two parties have very different professional and business orientations. Their languages are different. They have their own acronyms and code words that may not be shared by anyone outside of their area of expertise. But now our requester and provider have breached that gap and are talking and understanding one another.

The remaining part of the COS session is to come to an agreement about what will be delivered, when, how, and so on.

Business Outcomes

It is a good idea to specify within the COS what exactly will be the outcome that demonstrates that the COS has been met. The outcomes have been called success criteria, explicit business outcomes, and objectives. Whatever term you use, you are referring to a quantitative metric that signals success. It is a quantitative measure (profit, cost avoidance, improved service levels) that defines success.

Milestone Reviews

The COS is not a static agreement. It is a dynamic agreement that becomes part of the continual project monitoring process. Situations change throughout the project life cycle, and so will the needs of the customer. That means that COS will change. At every major project status review and project milestone, review the COS. Do they still make sense? If not, change them and adjust the project plan accordingly.

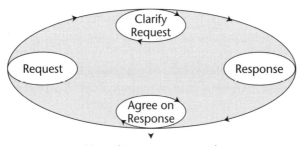

Negotiate agreement and
write Project Overview Statement

Figure D-1: Establishing the Conditions of Satisfaction.

The Volere Process

Perhaps the most documented and complete approach to requirements gathering is found in the Volere Process. You can use it as a base for the process that I recommend to gather requirements.

Gathering Customer Requirements

Simply put, IS teams who make a concerted effort to manage customer requirements do so because they want to satisfy their customer needs by having their projects succeed. Research studies find that the majority of project failures are related in some way to changing customer requirements.

This section is based on a modified Volere Requirements Process and its associated Specification Template. I have found this to be a best practice. Originally designed for use in systems application development, the process is a generic requirements gathering and specification process whose principles can be applied to small and large projects across varied industries. These processes are discussed in detail in the next section. Before I get into those details, I need to put a few definitions in place.

What Are Requirements?

Requirements are the things that you should discover before starting to fully design, build, or execute a project. Discovering the requirements during execution/construction is inefficient and detrimental.

A requirement exists either because the type of product demands certain functions or qualities, or the client wants the requirements to be part of the product/project delivery.

Project requirements start with what the customer really needs and end when those needs are satisfied. In the end-to-end chain of specifications, there is an ongoing danger of misunderstanding and ambiguity. This often leads to nonessential or over specified requirements.

What Kinds of Requirements Are There?

Requirements define the product or service that is the deliverable of the project. These requirements are the basis for changes that a customer is seeking. At this stage, after stakeholder assessment, the project manager and the project team are now tasked with going through the steps to establish the requirements baseline. This process is a systematic step-by-step effort that requires diligence. It is these requirements that will be used for estimating the cost and time for the project. Ultimately, these requirements drive acceptance of the product or service by the customer.

Requirements are separated into four categories and not just considered as one large bucket of information.

Functional Requirements

Functional requirements specify what the product or service must do. They are actions that the product or service must take such as check, calculate, record, and retrieve. For example,

- The product shall accept a scheduling date for service.
- The product shall accept a valid inventory warehouse identifies.
- The product shall confirm that the designated warehouse is the one wanted by the product.

Non-Functional Requirements

Non-functional requirements demonstrate the properties that the product or service should have in order to do what it must do. These requirements are the characteristics or qualities that make the product or service attractive, or usable, or fast, or reliable. Most non-functional requirements are associated with performance criteria and are usually those requirements that will establish the product or service boundary. Non-functional requirements can sometimes be generated by the refinement of a global requirement. Non-functional requirements are usually associated with performance criteria that set the parameters for how a system is to function. For example,

- The product shall be colorfully packaged.
- The product shall have an expensive appearance.
- The product shall be attractive to a senior audience.

Global Requirements

Global requirements describe the highest level of requirements within the system or project. Global requirements will describe properties of the system as a whole. During the initial stages of a project, many requirements end up being global requirements. They require the project manager and the team to refine them through the methods of requirement generation. *Global requirements* is a relatively new term. In the past, these have been called general requirements or product constraints or constraining requirements. The caution with global requirements is that in most cases, they can be turned into a non-functional requirement simply by asking the questions associated with what, why, or how. In fact, it is wise to move a global requirement to a non-functional requirement in order to focus in better on what the requirement really is. For example,

- The system shall have a maximum response time of 4 microseconds regardless of the inquiry.
- The system shall be designed to be intuitive and require no user training.

Product/Project Constraints

Product/project constraints are those requirements that, on the surface, resemble design constraints or project constraints. Design constraints are those pre-existing design decisions that mandate how the final product must look or how it must comply technologically. Project constraints cover the areas of budget and schedule along with deadlines and so on. One important note here is that product constraints can be listed as global requirements, but project constraints are *not*. For example,

- The system shall run on the existing network.
- The total out-of-pocket cost of the system shall not exceed $35M.

It is very important to realize that requirements identification and categorization is critical to understanding the direction of the project. It is now that the framework for the project begins to take shape.

Refining the Product Definition

With an agreed-upon high-level product definition and a well-understood initial scope, it is both possible and economical to invest resources in more refined product definitions. Refining the product definition includes two key considerations:

- Developing more detailed descriptions of the high-level product definition
- Verifying that the product will comply with stakeholder needs and behave as described

The descriptions are often the critical reference materials for project teams. Descriptions are best done with the audience in mind. A common mistake is to represent what is complex to build with a complex definition, particularly when the audience may be unable or unwilling to invest the critical thinking necessary to gain agreement. This leads to difficulties in explaining the purpose of the product to people both inside and outside of the project team. Instead, you may discover the need to produce different kinds of descriptions for different audiences.

Managing Changing Requirements

No matter how carefully you define your requirements, they will change. In fact, some requirement change is desirable! It means that your team is engaging your stakeholders. Accommodating changing requirements is a measure of your team's stakeholder sensitivity and operational flexibility—team attributes that contribute to successful projects. Change is not the enemy; unmanaged change is. A changed requirement means more or less time has to be spent on implementing a particular feature and a change to one requirement may have an impact on other requirements. Managing requirement change includes activities such as establishing a baseline, keeping track of the history of each requirement, determining which dependencies are important to trace, establishing traceable relationships between related items, and maintaining version control. It is also important to establish a change control or approval process, requiring all proposed changes to be reviewed by designated team members. Sometimes this single channel of change control is called a Change Control Board (CCB).

Volere Requirements Process

A graphic of the adapted Volere Requirements Process (Figure D-2) shows the activities and how they are linked by their deliverables. The deliverables are shown as moving from one activity to the next. This represents the concept that the output from one activity is input to the next. This is not a hard and fast rule, as it is usually necessary for activities to iterate and overlap before the final product of the process is achieved.

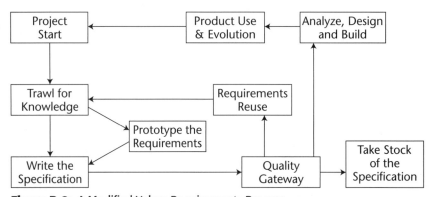

Figure D-2: A Modified Volere Requirements Process

Start

The project start is a joint planning meeting(s) where the project principals work together to define the project's overall objectives. Their goal is to gather enough facts and information to develop a project scope document (Project Overview Statement) and gain commitment for the project from the proper stakeholders.

Trawl for Knowledge

Once the kickoff is completed, the project manager and team (where applicable) start mining for knowledge and data. The initial scope of work and objectives need to be broken down into specific types of work (disciplines and technology areas) for further detailed study. The team must query the users of the product, system or facility in order to achieve the correct balance of functionality, constructability, compliance, operability, reliability and maintainability.

Trawling for knowledge involves three steps.

1. Conduct a Stakeholder Analysis

To get started on the right foot in the requirements identification part of the baselining process, the project manager and the project team must conduct a stakeholder analysis. The process of requirements identification should be just that—identification and only identification. Once there has been a list of requirements created, the team can now assess what category to put them in. This must be done in order to prepare for effective requirements generation.

Project stakeholders are individuals or organizations that are involved in or affected by project activities. When a company makes decisions, they often have major implications for a number of stakeholder groups such as stockholders, environmental groups, government agencies, and others.

Analyzing the project stakeholders can help to identify the effects an action can have on various groups. For example, the decision to cut a company's contribution to health insurance may make financial sense and please the stockholders, but the associates and their families are likely to be upset about it. Smart companies take this into consideration before the decision is made.

Depending upon their level of influence, stakeholders can have a tremendous impact on *project* development. They can help or hinder development time, startup problems, and top management support.

There is an old saying in project management: "Never get the accountant mad." It makes good sense to consider the implication of angering stakeholders before the deed is done. This thought process is inherent to organizations that are truly customer focused.

Project stakeholders may include internal and external groups as shown in Tables D-1 and D-2:

Table D-1 Internal Stakeholders

GROUP	IMPACT
VP/Director level management	Holds tremendous control over project managers. Authorizes the development of projects and protects teams from organizational pressures.
Team managers	Control project managers "regular" responsibilities. Can make it difficult/easy for the project manager to perform on the project team.
Project team members	Focused on the need to get the job done. Look for customers to agree on requirements definition process early so that project direction is more clearly defined.

Table D-2 External Stakeholders

GROUP	IMPACT
Customers	Demand willingness of the project team to be flexible up to the last minute.
Outside Suppliers and Contractors	Can have a large impact on the final cost and completion date of the project. These vendors must be treated as important stakeholders.
Associations and other groups	May include environmental or consumer organizations, or government agencies. By lobbying or rallying other public support, can force their demands on the project team.

Conflict among stakeholders is inevitable. Different variables are important to different stakeholder groups. For example, the accountant may be concerned only with project performance against budget. Top management's concerns include on-time delivery and customer satisfaction. A customer may only care about the final product performing to their specs.

To rationalize and resolve the diverse goals and priorities of various stakeholders, a considerable amount of bargaining and negotiation is necessary. Bargaining and negotiation are two primary methods of resolving conflict in organizational politics. Project implementation success is based on the project manager's ability to successfully bargain and negotiate with the various stakeholders to balance their needs and the realities of the project.

Unfortunately, it is almost impossible to keep every group satisfied. If the accountant is happy that the project is progressing on budget, the customer may be dissatisfied that all of his/her demands have not been met. Top management may be upset by the fact that the project is running slightly behind schedule.

Given the nature of this conflict, it is often appropriate to have all of the stakeholder groups slightly annoyed with the project team. If all groups are minimally upset, the delicate balance between stakeholders will be maintained and no group will be likely to take negative action against the project.

Another aspect of pleasing stakeholders is that not all stakeholders have equal priority. In many cases, the customer is the most important stakeholder. As a result, project managers must consider tradeoffs among the various stakeholder groups. The project team should always consider the importance of the stakeholder when making these tradeoff decisions.

Upon sign off on this document, a detailed planning process can begin with the development of a Work Breakdown Structure (WBS).

2. Identify Requirements

The start of requirements identification—the systematic approach used to develop the details associated with each of the requirements—is prefaced by a discussion that focuses on the readiness of the requirements for the next step. These questions center on the next stakeholder. There is a need here to double check to make sure that nothing (as far as is known at this point) is missing. A key question is: "Is there sufficient detail to move on?" If the answer is yes, then it is on to generation; if no, then it is back to the stakeholders and the source documents for more discovery.

The steps to generate requirements begin by looking at the business function as a whole. This is quickly followed by the selection of a method or methods for generation. This effort must be planned. While in the generation session, be prepared with the appropriate documentation method to ensure that each requirement is documented.

Of all the requirements gathering approaches, I recommend you choose from among the seven discussed below. These seven are widely used methods for generating requirements. Usually more than one method is chosen to generate the requirements on a project. Selection of the best methods to generate potential requirements for the project is the responsibility of the project manager, who must evaluate each method for costs, ease of implementation, and risks. Further, selection of a particular method should be based on specific product and project needs, as well as proven effectiveness. Certain methods have been proven effective for specific industries and products. An example of this would be using physical, three-dimensional modeling in product development and construction.

Table D-3 looks at each method and provides an indication of strengths and risks.

Table D-3 Requirements Gathering Approaches

METHOD	STRENGTHS	RISKS
Facilitated Group Sessions	Excellent for cross-functional processes Detailed requirements can be documented and verified immediately Resolves issues with an impartial facilitator	Use of untrained facilitators can lead to a negative response from users Time and cost of planning/executing session can be high
Prototypes	Innovative ideas can be generated Users clarify what they want Users identify requirements that may be missed Customer focused Early proof of concept Stimulates thought process	Customer may want to implement prototype Difficult to know when to stop Specialized skills required Absence of documentation
Interviews	End user participation High-level description of functions and processes provided	Descriptions may differ from actual detailed activities Without structure, stakeholders may not know what information to provide Real needs ignored if analyst is prejudiced
Observation	Specific/complete descriptions of actions provided Effective when routine activities are difficult to describe	Documenting and videotaping may be time consuming, expensive and have legal overtones Confusing/conflicting information must be clarified Misinterpretation of what is observed
Requirements Reuse	Requirements quickly generated/refined Redundant efforts reduced Customer satisfaction enhanced by previous proof Quality increase Reinventing the wheel minimized	Significant investment to develop archives, maintenance, and library functions May violate intellectual rights of previous owner Similarity may be misunderstood

Table D-3 Requirements Gathering Approaches

METHOD	STRENGTHS	RISKS
Business Process Analysis	Excellent for cross-functional processes Visual communication Verification of "what is/what is not"	Implementation of improvement is dependent on an organization open to changes Good facilitation, data gathering, and interpretation required Time consuming
Use Case Scenarios	State of system described before entering the system Completed scenarios used to describe state of system Normal flow of event/exceptions revealed Improved customer satisfaction and design	Newness has resulted in some inconsistencies Information may still be missing from scenario description Long interaction required Training expensive

The following bulleted list contains additional information about each of these methods.

■ **Facilitated Group Sessions**—A good facilitator can establish momentum with a group and get quite a bit of information in short order. Have someone working with you to take notes or better yet record the conversations for later offline summary.

■ **Prototypes**—Prototyping has been around since the days of the pyramids. There are production prototypes, mock prototypes, and everything in between. They are a visual model of something. Their purpose is to put something tangible in the hands of the customer so they can touch, feel, and play with it. The expectation is that they will discover features and functions that should change, be added, or be deleted. The design of the final product can be efficiently done using this approach. But the approach works equally well for discovering requirements. Many customers will respond positively to prototypes. Consider them as one more tool in your requirements gathering arsenal.

■ **Interviews**—I've gotten the best results from one-on-one interviews and by simply asking people to talk to me about their jobs and the pain points they have to live with. They might also be good sources for prescriptive suggestions. My interviews are very conversational. Questions flow quite naturally in that mode and one leads to another without having to spend a lot of upfront time scripting the interview sessions.

- **Observations**—Gathering requirements by walking around and observing processes being conducted in real time will often be brutally accurate and more reliable than someone's recollection during an interview. You will have to take copious notes because there will undoubtedly be questions to clarify what you are seeing. Talking to the operators will provide candid input that might not be recalled during interviews. Exceptions to the process will note where an interview may skip over them entirely. In order to get a complete picture you will want to choose several different times and days for making those observations.

- **Requirements Reuse**—From previous projects you should have built an inventory of requirements. This inventory will often be used in conjunction with one of the other approaches to gathering requirements. As you are conducting say interviews, you will have this inventory in mind and reach in and pull out a similar requirement. It may turn out to be exactly the same or sufficiently similar to the case in point so that it can be modified and used in the present project.

- **Business Process Analysis**—Books have been written on this topic.

- **Use Cases**—The basis of most adaptive and iterative systems development processes is the use case.

3. Generate Requirements Definitions

At this stage of the requirements process, we would refer to all requirements as "potential requirements." The reason for this designation is that so far the requirements have not been fully scrutinized and/or have not passed the tests that would clear the quality gateway. Prior to inspection at a quality gateway, they need to be documented in a consistent format.

Writing the specification refers to the task of putting together a complete description of the product to be built. It is appropriate to think of this activity as 'building' a specification—you assemble a specification during the requirements process rather than writing it all at once. Writing the requirements is not really a separate activity, but is done partly during trawling when you discover the requirements and partly during the quality checks when you are ensuring that each requirement is complete.

The Shell

In order to proceed with clarity and completeness, the requirements must be formally documented and in a certain structure, and for this purpose, I utilize the shell that was introduced in Robertson and Robertson's text and adapted for our use here.

The shell is a container for an individual requirement. When you write your requirements, it is not sufficient to write natural language statements, as they lack the necessary rigor. There is a collection of components necessary to make a complete requirement. These components have been implemented in what you call a shell.

The shell can be documented on cards (see Figure D-3) or can be automated. Cards are convenient when trawling for requirements, but at some stage, you will want to transfer the requirements to an automated tool. So now, look at how the complete, formalized requirement is constructed.

As you treat each of the items that make up the requirement, consider how you will discover it and how well it applies to your organization. For this activity, I will assume that you are using the Volere shell, or that you are using some mechanism to ensure that you capture all the relevant parts of each requirement.

Start by identifying the requirement. Each requirement has three pieces of identification: its unique number, its type, and the event(s) and/or use case(s) that spawned the requirement.

SHELL CARD		
Requirement #:	Requirement Type:	Event/User Case #:
Description:		
Rationale:		
Source:		
Fit Criteria:		
Customer Satisfaction:		
Customer Dissatisfaction:		
Dependencies:		
Conflicts:		
Supporting Materials:		
History:		

Figure D-3: The Shell card

Requirement Number

Each requirement must be uniquely identified. The reason is straightforward—it must be traceable throughout the development of the product, so it is convenient and logical to give each requirement a unique number. I use the term *number* here to mean any unique identifier, although it can be any kind of identifier you wish. To keep this from being an onerous clerical task, I suggest you use a simple sequential number. It is not important how you uniquely identify the requirements as long as you identify it.

Requirement Type

The requirement type will be one of: functional, non-functional, global, or constraint.

Attaching the type to the requirement is useful in several ways:

- The requirements can be sorted into type. By comparing all requirements of one type, you more readily discover requirements that conflict with one another.

- It is easier to write an appropriate fit criterion when the type of requirement is established.

- By grouping all the known requirements of one type, it becomes more apparent if some of them are missing or duplicated.

Event/Use Case Number

The context of the work is broken into smaller pieces using the business events as the partitioning tool. For each business event, you decide which part of the response to that event will be carried out by the product. It is this part of the response—the part being done by the product—that is referred to as a use case. When you identify each use case, you identify the user or users who will interface with that part of the product. Each business event is given a number for convenient referencing. Similarly, each use case is numbered. For traceability and change control purposes, it is useful to keep track of all requirements that are generated by a business event. Each of your product use cases corresponds to a business event and the product use case. If, however, you choose to cluster your requirements into sub-use cases, then you will need a separate numbering system for your use cases. Whatever your preference, you must tag each requirement so that you can identify which parts of the business it relates to (business events) and which parts of the product it relates to (use cases).

NOTE Business events are interactions with the system that are initiated by an outside entity (for example a customer, an invoice receipt) that causes the system to perform some function or functions. For example, a customer approaches a check out clerk to pay for an item, or a shipment of ordered materials arrives at the warehouse.

During later analysis, you will analyze each business event and use case separately. Thus, it is convenient to be able to collect all the requirements for that part of the work. This will help you to find missing requirements, and to confirm the actions of a use case with its users.

Description

The description is the intent of the requirement. It is an English (or whatever natural language you use) statement in the user's words as to what is required. Do not be too concerned that it may contain ambiguities (but neither should you be sloppy with your language). The objective when you first write the requirement is to capture what the user, or client wishes. So for the moment, a clear statement of the user's intentions will suffice.

Rationale

The rationale is the reason behind the requirement's existence. It tells why the requirement is important, and what contribution it makes to the product's purpose. Adding a rationale to a requirement helps you to clarify and understand it. Having this justification of the requirements helps you to assess its importance when you are testing for gold plating in the Quality Check activity.

Source

The source is the nature of the person who raised the requirement in the first instance, or the person to whom it can be attributed. You should attach the source to your requirements so that you have a referral point if there are questions about the requirement, or if the requirement is rejected by the quality gateway. The person who raises the requirement must have the knowledge and authority appropriate for the type of requirement.

Fit Criteria

The fit criteria are quantified goals that the solution has to meet—they are acceptance criteria. While the description of the requirements is written in the language of the users, the fit criterion is written in a precise quantified manner so that solutions can be tested against the requirement.

The fit criteria set the standard to which the builder constructs the product. While they do not say how the implementation will be tested, they do provide the goals that the tests will use when they determine if each requirement has been met.

Dependencies

Dependencies are other requirements that have an impact on this one. For example, there may be another requirement that will have to be changed if this one changes, or one whose data is linked very closely to the data that this one uses. Alternatively, there may be other requirements whose continued existence depends on the existence of this one.

Conflicts

Conflicts are other requirements that contradict this requirement, or make this one less feasible. For example, there may be a requirement that the product has to calculate the shortest route to the destination. There may be another that states the product is to calculate the quickest route to the destination. There could well be a conflict between these two if they are both considered to be the preferred route and if conditions dictated that the shortest was not always the quickest route.

Similarly, you may discover that a conflict between two or more requirements exist when you design the product and begin to look at solutions. It may be that the solution to one requirement means that the solution to the other is impossible, or severely restricted.

Conflicting requirements are a normal part of development. Don't be concerned that conflicts between requirements appear—as long as you are able to capture the fact that the conflict exists then you can work towards solving it.

Quality Check

This is a single gateway that every requirement must pass through before it can become a part of the specification or scope. Every requirement must be checked for completeness, relevance, coherency, traceability and several other qualities before it can be added to the specification or scope.

Requirements must be completely unambiguous and must be able to be measured against the client's expectation. If it can't be measured, then you can't be sure that the project/product will meet the client's expectations. This measurement is the fit criterion, and the gateway process ensures that a fit criterion is attached to each requirement. This also prohibits "requirements creep." The technology or readiness review is a form of the quality gateway. A peer review serves as a quality gateway for the definitive project scope, schedule, and budget.

Analyzing the Specification

The quality gateway exists to keep inaccurate requirements out of the specification or scope; however, it deals with one requirement at a time. At the point you feel that the specification is complete (or close to being so), you would conduct a specification review to uncover missing requirements, consistency, and any unresolved conflicts between requirements (conflicting requirements).

This is also an opportunity to reassess the cost, schedule, and risk parameters of the product/project. This should continue iteratively until all elements of the specification or scope have been completely reviewed and approved.

At this point, there is confidence that the Requirements Specification (as written) can now become the Requirements Baseline. The most important reason for baselining is so that the project can proceed with the knowledge that the baselined requirements are essentially complete and reasonably stable. When the requirements are baselined, iterations of requirements generation have ceased adding significant value to the product. It is an indication that, with minor exceptions handled through change management, all requirements have been identified. It is now that the project manager can direct the project team to proceed with a trip toward finalization of cost and schedule estimates.

A major precursor to the decision to baseline is running the preliminary specification through a thorough analysis. This is a formal review accompanied by a detailed analysis that focuses on the attributes the requirements have. In a "motherhood-type" statement, good requirements have certain attributes that make them good. Absence of attributes that can be verified and validated can render the product or service useless or at least render it to the point where it cannot be baselined and the project cannot go forward.

In the requirements analysis, the attributes are verified through adequate measuring and testing. This is accomplished as a step-by-step process addressing each attribute. The process is a bit time-consuming, but the value is tremendous.

Table D-4 is a list of attributes and the respective question to ask about each.

Table D-4 Questions to Analyze Requirement Attributes

ATTRIBUTE	QUESTION(S) TO ASK
Completeness	Are the requirements essentially complete? Are some requirements missing?
Clarity	Are the requirements clear? Are they ambiguous or imprecise?
Validity	Do the requirements reflect the customer's intentions?
Measurability	Does the requirement have a fit criterion (measurement)?
Testability	Can the criterion be used to test whether the requirement provides the solution?
Maintainability	Will the implementation be difficult or easy to understand or maintain?
Reliability	Can reliability and availability requirements be met?
Look and Feel	Have all human factors been met (GUI, ergonomics, and so on)?
Feasibility	Can the requirements be implemented?
Precedent	Has a requirement similar to this been implemented before?
Scale	Are the requirements large and/or complex?
Stability	How often and to what degree might the requirements change?
Performance	Can the performance be met on a consistent basis?
Safety	Can the safety requirements be fully demonstrated?
Specifications	Is the documentation adequate to design, implement and test the system?

The actual writing of the specification is to be done using a combination of text and graphics. This provides those who will be the next-in-line users of the requirements with the documentation needed to go into design through to development and test and further to implementation. Once written, the specification must go through a review before final approval.

All requirements need to be approved by the critical stakeholders, for example, senior management, the customer, and the sponsor, before they become a part of the requirements baseline. The project team prepares the official copy of the specification for sign-off. The project manager must use his/her skills to sell the baseline and get approval. It is imperative to move to the next phase.

Reusability

Gathering, documenting, and validating requirements are arduous tasks. Once done however, the requirements can be reused in future projects. Archiving them is a must.

The Work Breakdown Structure

Efficiency and economy imply employment of the right instrument and material as well as their right use in the right manner.

Louis Dembitz Brandeis, 1856-1941
U.S. Supreme Court Justice

Appendix Learning Objectives

After reading this appendix, you will be able to:

- ◆ Recognize the difference between activities and tasks
- ◆ Understand the importance of the completeness criteria to your ability to manage the work of the project
- ◆ Explain the approaches to building the work breakdown structure
- ◆ Generate a complete work breakdown structure

NOTE

Most of the material in this chapter is an abridged version of Chapter 4 from my earlier work *Effective Project Management: Traditional, Adaptive, Extreme, Third Edition* (Wiley, 2003). It is presented here for completeness so that this book may be used as a text for an introductory course in software project management. For courses requiring more detail on these topics the earlier work may be used as a companion text.

The foundation of the traditional approach to project management is the Work Breakdown Structure (WBS). The WBS is a hierarchical description of the work that must be done to complete the project as defined in the Project Overview

Statement (POS). With a WBS in place, the project team can go about the task of creating a comprehensive project plan including the schedule, resource requirements, and budget. As you will see, in many other project situations it is not possible to build a WBS, at least not at the beginning of the project.

There are several approaches to building the WBS. There is no right answer. In fact, the WBS is only as good as the project manager deems it to be. After all, the project manager has to manage the project and so should be the single individual that says the WBS is appropriate. A generic example of the WBS is shown in Figure E-1.

To begin the discussion of the WBS, you need to be familiar with the terms introduced in the figure.

- The first term is **activity**. An activity is simply a chunk of work. Later in this appendix where I discuss "Six Criteria to Test for Completeness in the WBS," I'll expand on this definition.

- The second term is **task**. Note that in Figure E-1, activities turn to tasks at some level in the hierarchy. A task is a smaller chunk of work.

While these definitions seem a bit informal, they are useful for my purposes in this appendix. The terms *activity* and *task* have been used interchangeably among project managers and project management software packages. Some would use the convention that activities are made up of tasks, while others would say that tasks are made up of activities, and still others would use one term to represent both concepts. In this appendix, I refer to higher-level work as activities, which are made up of tasks.

I also use the term *work package*. The term is familiar to most professionals. In this appendix a work package is a complete description of how the tasks that make up an activity will actually be done. It includes a description of the what, who, when, and how of the work.

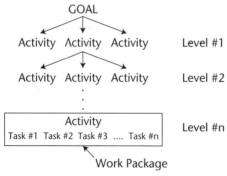

Figure E-1: Hierarchical visualization of the Work Breakdown Structure

Breaking down work into a hierarchy of activities, tasks, and work packages is called decomposition. For example, take a look at the top of the WBS in Figure E-1. Notice that the goal statement from the POS is defined as a Level 0 activity in the WBS. The next level, Level 1, is a decomposition of the Level 0 activity into a set of activities defined as Level 1 activities. These Level 1 activities are major chunks of work. When the work associated with each Level 1 activity is complete, the Level 0 activity is complete. For this example, that means that the project is complete. As a general rule, when an activity at Level n is decomposed into a set of activities at Level n+1 and the work associated with those activities is complete, the activity at Level n, from which they were defined, is complete.

Decomposition is important to the overall project plan because it allows you to estimate the duration of the project, determine the required resources, and schedule the work. The complete decomposition will be developed by using the completeness criteria discussed later. By following those criteria, the activities at the lowest levels of decomposition will possess known properties that allow you to meet planning and scheduling needs. The lowest level activities that meet the six criteria are called tasks. Now you have a working definition of activities, tasks, and work packages.

Those who have experience in software development should see the similarity between the hierarchical decomposition and functional decomposition. In principle, there is no difference between a WBS and a functional decomposition of a system. The approach you will use to generating a WBS departs from the generation of a functional decomposition in that you follow a specific process with a stopping rule for completing the WBS. I am not aware of a similar process being reported for generating the functional decomposition of a system. Veterans of software development might even see some similarity to older techniques like stepwise refinement or pseudo-code. These tools do, in fact, have a great deal in common with the techniques you use to generate the WBS.

Generating the WBS

There are two fundamental approaches that can be used to identify project activities and tasks. The first is the top-down approach; the second is the bottom-up approach.

Top-Down Approach

The top-down approach begins at the goal level and successively partitions work down to lower levels of definition until the participants are satisfied that the work has been sufficiently defined and they have reached the task level as determined by the completion criteria.

In my consulting practice, I have used two variations of the top-down approach: the team approach and the subteam approach.

Team Approach

The team approach, while it requires more time to complete than the subteam approach, is the better of the two. In this approach the entire team works on all parts of the WBS. For each Level 1 activity, appoint the most knowledgeable member of the planning team to facilitate the further decomposition of that part of the WBS. Continue with similar appointments until the WBS is complete. This approach allows all members of the planning team to pay particular attention to the WBS as it is developed, noting discrepancies and commenting on them in real time.

Sub-team Approach

When time is at a premium, the planning facilitator will prefer the subteam approach. The first step is to divide the planning team into as many subteams as there are activities at Level 1 of the WBS. Then follow these steps:

- The planning team agrees on the approach to building the first level of the WBS.
- The planning team creates the Level 1 activities.
- The team is split into subteams with a subject matter expert leading each subteam in further decomposition of the WBS.
- The subteam continues decomposition until each activity within the Level 1 activities meets the WBS completion criteria.
- Re-assemble as a team and report your part of the WBS to the whole team.

Note that the entire planning team decides on the approach for the first-level breakdown. After that the group is partitioned into subteams, with each subteam having some expertise for that part of the WBS. It is hoped that they will have all the expertise they need to develop their part of the WBS. If not, outside help may be brought in as needed. Be careful not to clutter the team with too many people.

When the subteams have reassembled into a whole team pay close attention to each presentation and ask yourself these questions:

- Is there something in the WBS that I did not expect to see?
- Is there something not there that I expected to see?

The focus here is to strive for a complete WBS.

As the discussion continues and activities are added and deleted from the WBS, questions about agreement between the WBS and the POS will occur. Throughout the exercise the POS should be posted on flip chart paper and hung on the walls of the planning room. Each participant should compare the scope of the project as described in the POS with the scope as presented in the WBS. If something in the WBS appears out of scope, challenge it. Either redefine the scope or discard the appropriate WBS activities. Similarly, look for complete coverage of the scope as described in the WBS with the POS. This is the time to be critical and carefully define the scope and work to accomplish it. Mistakes found now, before any work is done, are far less costly and disruptive than they will be if found late in the project.

The dynamic at work here is one of changing project boundaries. Despite all efforts to the contrary, the boundaries of the project are never clearly defined at the outset. There will always be reason to question what is in and what is not in the project. That is all right. Just remember that the project boundaries have not yet been formally set. That will happen once the project has been approved to begin. Until then you are still in the planning mode, and nothing is set in concrete.

Bottom-Up Approach

Another approach to identifying the activities in the project is to take a bottom-up approach. This approach is more like a brainstorming session than an organized approach to building the WBS. I personally don't recommend or use this approach, but I have seen it work successfully in practice so I discuss it here for the sake of completeness.

The bottom-up approach works as follows. The first steps are the same as those for the top-down approach. Namely, the entire planning team agrees to the first-level breakdown. The planning team is then divided into as many subteams as there are first-level activities. Each subteam then makes a list of the activities that must be completed in order to complete the first-level activity. To do this they proceed as follows. Someone in the subteam identifies an activity and describes it to their teammates. If they agree that it is part of the WBS, then the activity is written on a slip of paper and put in the middle of the table. The process repeats itself until no new ideas are forthcoming. The subteam then sorts the slips into activities that seem to be related to one another. This grouping activity should help the subteam add missing activities or remove redundant ones. Once the subteam is satisfied it has completed the activity list for the first-level breakdown, their work is done. Each subteam then reports to the entire team the results of its work. Final critiques are given, missing activities added, and redundant activities removed.

While this approach has worked well in many cases, there is the danger of not defining all activities or defining activities at too high or low a level of granularity. The completeness criteria that we define later in the chapter are not ensured through this process. My caution to you then is that you may not have as manageable a project as you would if you followed the top-down approach. Obviously, risk is associated with the bottom-up approach; if you do not have to take the risk, why expose yourself to it voluntarily? Unless there is a compelling reason to the contrary, I recommend the top-down approach. In my experience there is less danger of missing part of the project work using the top-down approach.

Intermediate WBS for Large Projects

For very large projects you may be tempted to modify the top-down approach. While I prefer to avoid modification, difficulty in scheduling people for the planning meeting may necessitate some modification. As project size increases, it becomes unwieldy to build the entire WBS with the entire planning team assembled. When you are in this situation begin by following the whole team approach and decompose the WBS down to Level 3. Assign Activity Managers to each of the Level 3 activities and adjourn the planning session. The Level 3 Activity Managers are charged with completing the WBS for their part of the project. They will convene a session to complete that work. The planning facilitator will then consolidate these Level 3 WBSs into the WBS for the entire project. The full team can be reassembled and the planning process can continue from that point.

Six Criteria to Test for Completeness in the WBS

Developing the WBS is the most critical part of the project planning activity. If this part is done correctly, the rest is comparatively easy. How do you know that you've done this right? You will if each activity possesses the six characteristics described as follows:

- Status/completion is measurable
- Start/end events are clearly defined
- Activity has a deliverable
- Time and cost are easily estimated
- Activity duration is within acceptable limits
- Work assignments are independent

If an activity does not possess all six of these characteristics, decompose the activity and ask the questions again. As soon as an activity possesses the six characteristics, you have no need to further decompose it. That activity can now be called a task. As soon as every activity in the WBS possesses these six characteristics, the WBS is defined as complete. The following sections look at each of these characteristics in more detail.

Start/Completion Is Measurable

The project manager must be able to ask for the status of an activity at any point in time when the activity is open for work. If the activity has been defined properly, that question is answered easily. The answer should consist of what has been done, how much time was required to complete the work, how much remains, and how long it will take to complete. If that information is not readily available, the activity needs to be further decomposed.

Start/End Events Are Clearly Defined

Each activity should have a clearly defined start and end event. Once the start event has occurred, work can begin on the activity. The deliverable is most likely the end event that signals work is closed on the activity. If those events are not clearly obvious, the activity needs to be further decomposed.

Activity Has a Deliverable

The result of completing the work that makes up the activity is the production of a deliverable. The deliverable is a visible sign that the activity is complete. This could be an approving manager's signature, a physical product or document, the authorization to proceed to the next activity, or some other sign of completion. If the activity does not result in a deliverable, the activity needs to be further decomposed.

Time and Cost Are Easily Estimated

This is a relative characteristic. You may have very little experience or knowledge of the activity in which case "easily estimated" will be very different than the case where the activity is one that has been repeated many times and is well understood. In any case, each activity should have an estimated time and cost of completion. Being able to do this at the lowest level of decomposition in the WBS allows you to aggregate to higher levels and estimate the total project cost and the completion date. By successively decomposing activities to finer levels of granularity, you are likely to encounter primitive activities that you have performed before. This experience at lower levels of definition gives you a stronger base on which to estimate activity cost and duration for similar activities.

Activity Duration Is Within Acceptable Limits

While there is no fixed rule for the duration limitation of an activity, common practice is to set the limit at 2 weeks. Again this is a relative limit. For very long projects some limit greater than 2 weeks will be appropriate. For a project that will only last a few weeks, a much lower limit is appropriate. There will be exceptions when the activity defines process work, such as will occur in many manufacturing situations. There will be exceptions, especially for those activities whose work is repetitive and simple. For example, if you are going to build 500 widgets and it takes 10 weeks to complete this activity, you are not going to decompose the activity into 5 activities with each one building 100 widgets. There is no need to break the 500-widget activity down further. If you can estimate the time to check one document, it does not make much difference if the activity requires 2 months to check 400 documents or 4 two-week periods to check 100 documents per period. The danger you avoid is longer duration activities whose delay can create a serious project-scheduling problem.

Work Assignments Are Independent

At first brush this may seem to be a rather strange criterion, yet it may be the most important one of all. Here's why. It is important that each activity be independent of other activities in the following sense. Once work has begun on the activity, if it is independent of other activities, the work can continue without interruption and without the need of additional input or information until the activity is complete. This allows the project manager to schedule the work contiguously, but it can be scheduled otherwise for a variety of reasons. You can choose to schedule it in parts because of resource availability, but you could have scheduled it as one continuous stream of work.

Approaches to Building the WBS

There are many ways to build the WBS. Hypothetically, if you put each member of the planning team in a different room and ask each one to develop the project WBS, they might all come back with different renditions. That's all right—there is no single best answer. The choice is subjective and based more on the project manager's preference than on any other requirements. However, even though you might like the choice to be a personal one that the project manager makes (after all, he or she is charged with managing the project, so why not allow him or her to choose the architecture that makes that task the easiest), unfortunately that will not work in many cases. The choice of approach must take into consideration the uses to which the WBS will be put.

There are three general approaches to building the WBS:

Noun-Type Approaches

Noun-type approaches define the deliverable of the project work in terms of the components (physical or functional) that make up the deliverable. This is the approach currently recommended by PMI.

Verb-Type Approaches

Verb-type approaches define the deliverable of the project work in terms of the actions that must be done to produce the deliverable. These include the design-build-test-implement and project objectives approaches. This approach was once recommended by PMI.

Organizational Approaches

Organizational approaches define the deliverable of the project work in terms of the organizational units that will work on the project. This type of approach includes the department, process, and geographic location approaches.

I have seen these approaches used in practice to create the WBS. The next sections take a look at each one in more detail.

Noun-Type Approaches

Basically, there are two noun-type approaches:

- **Physical decomposition**—In projects that involve building products, it is tempting to follow the physical decomposition approach. Take a mountain bike, for example. Its physical components include a frame, wheels, suspension, gears, brakes, and so on. If each component is to be manufactured, this approach might produce a simple WBS. This type of WBS is initially attractive because it looks similar and, in fact, could be identical to a company's financial chart of accounts (CoA). CoAs are noun-oriented because they account for the cost of developing things such as gears and brakes.

NOTE
━━━━━ A CoA should not be confused with the WBS. The WBS is a breakdown of work; the CoA is a breakdown of costs.

■ **Functional decomposition**—Using the bicycle example, you can build the WBS using the functional components of the bicycle. The functional components include the steering system, gear-shifting system, braking system, pedaling system, and so on. The same cautions that apply to the physical decomposition approach apply here as well.

Verb-Type Approaches

Basically, there are two verb-type approaches:

■ **Design-build-test-implement**—The design-build-test-implement approach is commonly used in those projects that involve a methodology, such as a software development methodology. Using the bicycle example again, you could use a variation on the classic waterfall categories. The categories are design, build, test, document, and implement. If you were to use this architecture for your WBS, then the bars on the Gantt Chart would all have lengths that correspond to the duration of each of the design, build, test, and implement activities and hence would be shorter than the bar representing the entire project. Most, if not all, would have differing start and end dates. Arranged on the chart, they would cascade in a stair-step manner, hence, the name waterfall. These are just representative categories; yours may be different. The point is that when the detail-level activity schedules are summarized up to them, they present a display of meaningful information to the recipient of the report.

Remember that the WBS tasks, at the lowest levels of granularity, must always be expressed in verb form. After all, you are talking about work, and that implies action, and that implies verbs.

■ **Objectives**—The objectives approach is similar to the design-build-test-implement approach and is used when progress reports at various stages of project completion are prepared for senior management. Reporting project completion by objectives gives a good indication of the deliverables that have been produced by the project team. Objectives will almost always relate to business value and will be well received by senior management and the customer as well. There is a caveat, however. This approach can cause some difficulty because objectives often overlap. Their boundaries can be fuzzy. You'll have to give more attention to eliminating redundancies and discovering gaps in the defined work.

Other Approaches

The deployment of project work across geographic or organizational boundaries often suggests a WBS that parallels the organization. The project manager would not choose to use this approach but rather would use it out of necessity. In other words, the project manager had no other reasonable choice. These approaches offer no real advantages and tend to create more problems than they solve. I list them here only because they are additional approaches to building the WBS.

Geographic

If project work is geographically dispersed (the U.S. space program, for example), it may make sense from a coordination and communications perspective to partition the project work first by geographic location and then by some other approach at each location.

Departmental

On the other hand, departmental boundaries and politics being what they are, you may benefit from partitioning the project first by department and then within department by whatever approach makes sense. You benefit from this structure in that a major portion of the project work is under the organizational control of a single manager. Resource allocation is simplified this way. On the other hand, you add increased needs for communication and coordination across organizational boundaries in this approach.

Business Function

Finally, breaking the project down first by business process and then by some other method for each process may make sense. This has the same advantages and disadvantages as the departmental approach, but the added complication that integration of the deliverables from each process can be more difficult than in the former case.

Again, no single approach can be judged to be best for a given project. Our advice is to consider each at the outset of the planning session and pick the one that seems to bring clarity to defining the project work.

Estimation

Round numbers are always false.
Samuel Johnson
English critic

Appendix Learning Objectives

After reading this appendix, you will be able to:

◆ Explain the relationship between resource loading and activity duration
◆ Use any of the six activity duration estimation methods

NOTE Most of the material in this appendix is an abridged version of Chapter 5 from my earlier work *Effective Project Management: Traditional, Adaptive, Extreme, Third Edition* (Wiley, 2003). It is presented here for completeness so that this book may be used as a text for an introductory course in software project management. For courses requiring more detail on these topics the earlier work may be used as a companion text.

Estimating Time, Cost, and Resource Requirements

Before you can estimate duration, you need to make sure everyone is working from a common definition. The duration of a project is the elapsed time in business working days required to complete the project, activity, or task. Duration is different from effort. Effort is labor hours required to complete a project, activity, or task. Effort is always less than or equal to duration. Labor hours can be consecutive or nonconsecutive hours. It is this elapsed time that you are interested in estimating for each task. It is the true duration of the task. For costing purposes you are interested in the labor time (work) actually spent on the task.

Resource Loading versus Task Duration

The duration of a task is affected by the number of resources scheduled to work on it. I say *affected by* because there is not necessarily a direct linear relationship between the amount of resource assigned to a task and its duration. For example, suppose you are responsible for completing a certain programming task. You estimate that it will take 4 weeks to complete. The project manager says that it must be done in 2 weeks so she will ask another programmer to join you in the task. Will that reduce the task duration to 2 weeks? Absolutely not. There are several reasons why the relationship is not linear. Among the reasons are the need for person-to-person communications, deciding on programming conventions, deciding who will work on what, and a host of other reasons. In fact, the addition of a second programmer could increase the time to write the program.

The point of this simple example is to show that there are diminishing returns for adding more resources. You would probably agree that there is a maximum loading of resources on a task to minimize the task duration, and that by adding another resource you will actually begin to increase the duration. You have reached the crash point of the task. The crash point is where adding more resources will increase task duration. There will be many occasions when the project manager will have to consider the optimum loading of a resource on a task.

Variation in Task Duration

Task duration is a random variable. Because you cannot know what factors will be operative when work is underway on a task, you cannot know exactly how long it will take. There will, of course, be varying estimates with varying precision for each task. One of your goals in estimating task duration is to define the task to a level of granularity so that your estimates have a narrow variance—that is, the estimate is as good as you can get it at the planning stages of the project. As project work is completed, you will be able to improve the earlier estimates of tasks scheduled later in the project. There are several causes of variation in the actual task duration, discussed in the following subsections.

Varying Skill Levels

Your strategy is to estimate activity duration based on using people of average skills assigned to work on the activity. In actuality, this may not happen. You may get a higher- or lower-skilled person assigned to the activity, causing the actual duration to vary from planned duration. These varying skill levels will be both a help and a hindrance to you.

Unexpected Events

Murphy lives in the next cubicle and will surely make his presence known, but in what way, and at what time, you do not know. Random acts of nature, vendor delays, incorrect shipments of materials, traffic jams, power failures, and sabotage are but a few of the possibilities.

Efficiency of Work Time

Every time a worker is interrupted it takes more time to get up to the level of productivity prior to the time of the interruption. You cannot control the frequency or time of interruptions, but you do know that they will happen. As to their effect on staff productivity, you can only guess. Some will be more affected than others.

Mistakes and Misunderstandings

Despite all of your efforts to be complete and clear in describing the work to be performed, you simply will miss a few times. This will take its toll in rework or scrapping semicompleted work.

Common Cause Variation

Apart from all of these factors that can influence activity duration the reality is that durations will vary for no reason other than the statistical variation that arises because the duration is in fact a random variable. It has a natural variation, and nothing you do can really decrease that variation. It is there, and it must be accepted.

Six Methods for Estimating Task Duration

Estimating task duration is challenging. You can be on very familiar ground for some tasks and totally unfamiliar ground for others. Whatever the case, you must produce an estimate. It is important that senior management understand that the estimate can be little more than a WAG (wild a** guess). If you're lucky, maybe it will be a SWAG (the scientific version of a WAG). In many projects the estimate will be improved as you learn more about the deliverables from having completed some of the project work. Re-estimation and re-planning are common. In my consulting practice, I have found six techniques to be quite suitable for initial planning estimates. Remember you have to get it only roughly right so don't spend 30 minutes debating whether it is 2 days or 3 for a task that is way out in the schedule. Those six techniques are:

- Similarity to other tasks
- Historical data
- Expert advice
- Delphi technique
- Three-point technique
- Wide-band Delphi technique

The next subsections take a look at each of these techniques in more detail. By the way, I have listed them in the order in which I would typically use them.

Similarity to Other Tasks

Some of the tasks in your WBS may be similar to tasks completed in other projects. Your or others' recollections of those tasks and their duration can be used to estimate the present task's duration. In some cases, this may require extrapolating from the other task to this one, but in any case it does provide an estimate. In most cases, using the estimates from those tasks provides estimates that are good enough.

Historical Data

Every good project management methodology contains a project notebook that records the estimated and actual task duration. This historical record can be used on other projects. The recorded data becomes your knowledge base for estimating task duration. This differs from the previous technique in that it uses a record, rather than depending on memory.

A simple way to use that historical data is to scan the data and retrieve actual durations of similar tasks. A simple numeric average might be good enough. Alternatively, you might adjust the duration based on local conditions as compared with those in the historical data.

Historical data can also be used in quite sophisticated ways. One of my clients has built an extensive database of task duration history. They have recorded not only estimated and actual duration, but also the characteristics of the task, the skill set of the people working on it, and other variables that they found useful. When a task duration estimate is needed they go to their database with a complete definition of the task and, with some rather sophisticated regression models, estimate the task duration. They build product for market, and it is very important to them to be able to estimate as accurately as possible. Again, my advice is that if there is value-added for a particular tool or technique, use it.

Expert Advice

When the project involves a breakthrough technology or a technology that is being used for the first time in the organization, there may not be any local experience or even professionals skilled in the technology within the organization. In these cases, you will have to appeal to outside authorities. Vendors may be a good source, as are non-competitors who use that technology.

Delphi Technique

The Delphi Technique can produce good estimates in the absence of expert advice. This is a group technique that extracts and summarizes the knowledge of the group to arrive at an estimate. After the group is briefed on the project and the nature of the task, each individual in the group is asked to make his or her best guess of the task duration. The results are tabulated and presented, as shown in Figure F-1, to the group in a histogram labeled First Pass. Those participants whose estimates fall in the outer quartiles are asked to share the reason for their guess. After listening to the arguments, each group member is asked to guess again. The results are presented as a histogram labeled Second Pass, and again the outer quartile estimates are defended. A third guess is made, and the histogram plotted is labeled Third Pass. Final adjustments are allowed. The average of the third guess is used as the group's estimate. Even though the technique seems rather simplistic it has been shown to be effective in the absence of expert advice.

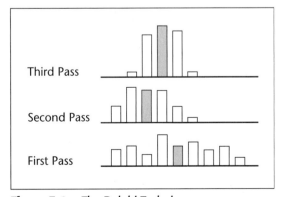

Figure F-1: The Delphi Technique

NOTE

This preceding description of the approach is actually a variation of the original Delphi Technique. The original version used a small panel of experts (say five or six) who were asked for their estimate independently of one another. The results were tabulated and shared with the panel, who were then asked for a second estimate. A third estimate was solicited in the same manner. The average of the third estimate was the one chosen. Note that the original approach does not involve any discussion or collaboration between the panel members. In fact, they weren't even aware of who the other members were.

Three-Point Technique

Task duration is a random variable. If it were possible to repeat the task several times under identical circumstances, duration times would vary. That variation may be tightly grouped around a central value, or it might be widely dispersed. In the first case, you would have a considerable amount of information on that task's duration as compared to the latter case, where you would have very little or none. In any given instance of the task you would not know at which extreme the duration would likely fall, but you could make probabilistic statements about their likelihood in any case.

The three-point technique gives you a framework for doing just that. To use the method you need three estimates of task duration: optimistic, pessimistic, and most likely. The optimistic time is defined as the shortest duration one has had or might expect to experience given that everything happens as expected. The pessimistic time is that duration that would be experienced (or has been experienced) if everything that could go wrong did go wrong and yet the task was completed. Finally, the most likely time is that time usually experienced. For this method you are calling on the collective memory of professionals who have worked on similar tasks but for which there is no recorded history. Figure F-2 is a graphical representation of the three-point method.

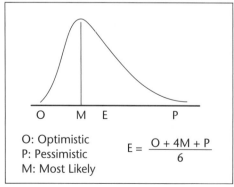

O: Optimistic
P: Pessimistic
M: Most Likely

$$E = \frac{O + 4M + P}{6}$$

Figure F-2: The three-point method

The formula shown in the figure is the formula for calculating the estimated duration. Note that it is a weighted average of the optimistic, pessimistic, and most likely experiences of the expert.

Wide-Band Delphi Technique

Combining the Delphi and three-point methods results in the wide-band Delphi technique. It involves a panel, as in the Delphi technique. In place of a single estimate the panel members are asked, at each iteration, to give their optimistic, pessimistic, and most likely estimates for the duration of the chosen task. The results are compiled, and any extreme estimates are removed. Averages are computed for each of the three estimates, and the averages are used as the optimistic, pessimistic, and most likely estimates of task duration.

Estimation Precision

A word of advice on estimating is in order. Early estimates of task duration will not be as good as later estimates. It's a simple fact that you get smarter as the project work commences. Estimates will always be subject to the vagaries of nature and other unforeseen events. You can only hope that you have gained some knowledge through the project to improve your estimates.

In the top-down project planning model, you start out with "roughly right" estimates with the intention of improving the precision of these estimates later in the project. Management and the customer must be made aware that this is your approach. Give up the habit of assuming that a number, once written, is inviolate and absolutely correct regardless of the circumstances under which the number was determined.

The Project Network Diagram

In every affair consider what precedes and what follows, and then undertake it.

Epictetus
Greek philosopher

Appendix Learning Objectives

After reading this appendix, you will be able to:

◆ Construct a network representation of the project activities

◆ Understand the four types of task dependencies and when they are used

◆ Compute the earliest start (ES), earliest finish (EF), latest start (LS), and latest finish (LF) for every task in the network

◆ Identify the critical path in the network

◆ Analyze the network for possible schedule compression

NOTE Most of the material in this appendix is an abridged version of Chapter 6 of my earlier work *Effective Project Management: Traditional, Adaptive, Extreme, Third Edition* (Wiley, 2003). It is presented here for completeness so that this book may be used as a text for an introductory course in software project management. For courses requiring more detail on these topics, the earlier work may be used as a companion text.

Constructing the Software Development Project Schedule

At this point in the planning of your project, you have identified the set of tasks that must be done and estimated the duration of each task. The next step for the planning team is to determine the order in which these tasks are to be performed. They could certainly be performed one at a time but that would extend the completion of the project beyond the tolerable. Your objective in this step is to determine the minimum time to complete the project by figuring out how to work concurrently on tasks rather than sequentially. The more concurrency you can introduce into the schedule, the shorter will be the completion time of the project.

The Project Network Diagram

The tasks and their duration are the basic building blocks needed to construct a graphic picture of the project. This graphic picture provides you with two additional pieces of schedule information about the project:

- The earliest time at which work can begin on each task that makes up the project
- The earliest expected completion date of the project

This is critical information for the project manager. It will establish the earliest time the project can be completed. Once this is known, the required resources and their availability will be factored in to give a more accurate picture of project completion times.

A *project network diagram* is a pictorial representation of the sequence in which the project work can be done. To establish that network diagram, you need to impose a few simple rules. For each task ask: "What other task or tasks must be complete before this task can be worked on?" Alternatively, you can begin this series of questions with those tasks that can be worked on without the need for other tasks to have been complete and then ask the question: "Now that these tasks are complete, what tasks can be worked on?" Continue this line of questioning, and you will establish the task dependencies needed to construct the project network diagram.

Building the Precedence Network Diagram

The basic *unit of analysis* in the precedence network diagram is the task. Each task in the network diagram is represented by a rectangle that is called a *task node.* Arrows represent the predecessor/successor relationships between tasks. Figure G-1 shows an example network diagram. Every task in the project will have its own task node (see Figure G-2). The entries in the task node describe the time-related properties of the task. Some of the entries describe characteristics of the task such as its expected duration (E), while others describe calculated values (ES, EF, LS, LF) associated with that task. I will define these terms shortly and give an example of their use.

In order to create the network diagram using this format, you need to determine the predecessors and successors for each task. To do this, you ask "What tasks must be complete before I can begin this task?" Here, you are looking for the technical dependencies between tasks. Once a task is complete, it will have produced an output, a deliverable, which becomes input to its successor tasks. Work on the successor task requires only the output from its immediate predecessor task or tasks. What is the next step? While the list of predecessors and successors to each activity contains all the information you need to proceed with the project, it does not represent the information in a format that tells the story of your project. The goal will be to provide a graphical picture of the project; in order to do that, you need to spell out a few rules first. Once you know the rules, you can create the graphical image of the project. In this section you will learn those rules.

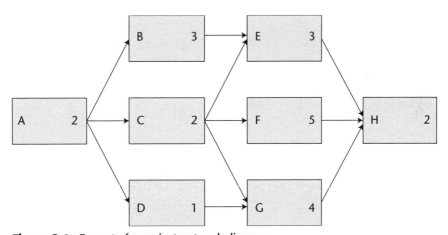

Figure G-1: Format of a project network diagram

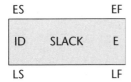

Figure G-2: Task node

The network diagram is logically sequenced to be read from left to right. Every task in the network, except the start and end tasks, must have at least one task that comes before it (its immediate predecessor) and one task that comes after it (its immediate successor). A task begins when its predecessors have been completed. The start task has no predecessor and the end task has no successor. You may have to create dummy tasks with zero duration to meet these conditions. If these conditions are met, you have what is called a connected network. Figure G-3 gives examples of how the variety of relationships that might exist between two or more tasks can be diagrammed.

Dependencies

A dependency is simply a relationship that exists between pairs of activities. To say that activity A depends on activity B means that activity B produces a deliverable that is needed in order to do the work associated with activity A. There are four types of activity dependencies, illustrated in Figure G-4.

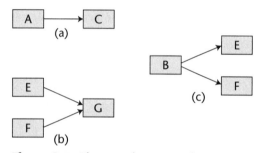

Figure G-3: Diagramming conventions

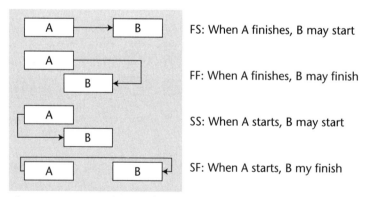

Figure G-4: Dependency relationships

Finish to Start

The finish to start (FS) dependency says that Task A must be complete before Task B can begin. It is the simplest and most risk-averse of the four types. For example, Task A can represent the collection of data and Task B can represent entry of the data into the computer. To say that the dependency between A and B is finish to start means that once you have finished collecting the data you may begin entering the data. I recommend using FS dependency in the initial project planning session. These are the least risk prone and simplest of the four dependency relationships. The finish to start dependency is denoted by an arrow emanating from the right edge of the predecessor task and terminating at the left edge of the successor task.

Start to Start

The start to start (SS) dependency says that Task B may begin once Task A has begun. Note that there is a no-sooner-than relationship between Task A and Task B. Task B may begin no sooner than Task A begins. In fact, they could both start at the same time. For example, you could alter the data collection and data entry dependency: As soon as you begin collecting data (Task A), you may begin entering data (Task B). In this case there is an SS dependency between Task A and B. The start to start dependency is displayed with an arrow emanating from the left edge of the predecessor (Task A) and terminating at the left edge of the successor (Task B). We will use this dependency relationship in the section dealing with schedule compression strategies toward the end of this appendix.

Start to Finish

The start to finish (SF) dependency is a little more complex than the FS and SS dependencies. Here Task B cannot be finished sooner than Task A has started. For example, suppose you have built a new information system. You don't want to eliminate the legacy system until the new system is operable. When the new system starts to work (Task A), the old system can be discontinued (Task B). The start to finish dependency is displayed with an arrow emanating from the left edge of activity A to the right edge of activity B. SF dependencies can be used for just-in-time scheduling between two tasks, but they rarely occur in practice.

Finish to Finish

The finish to finish (FF) dependency states that Task B cannot finish sooner than Task A. For example, if I refer back to the data collection and entry example, suppose data entry (Task B) cannot finish until data collection (Task A) has finished. In this case, Task A and B have a finish to finish dependency. The finish to finish dependency is displayed with an arrow emanating from the right edge of Task A and terminating at the right edge of Task B. To preserve the connectedness property of the network diagram, the SS dependency on the front end of two tasks should have an accompanying FF dependency on the back end.

Creating an Initial Project Network Schedule

As stated earlier, all tasks in the network diagram have at least one predecessor and one successor task, with the exception of the start and end tasks. If this convention is followed, then the sequence is relatively straightforward to identify.

To establish the project schedule, you need to compute two schedules: the early schedule, which you calculate using the forward pass, and the late schedule, which you calculate using the backward pass.

- The **early schedule** consists of the earliest times at which a task can start and finish. These are calculated numbers that are derived from the dependencies between all the tasks in the project.

- The **late schedule** consists of the latest times at which a task can start and finish without delaying the completion date of the project. These are also calculated numbers that are derived from the dependencies between all of the tasks in the project.

The combination of these two schedules gives us two additional pieces of information about the project schedule:

- The window of time within which each activity must be started and finished in order for the project to complete on schedule

- The sequence of activities that determine the project completion date

The sequence of tasks that determine the project completion date is called the *critical path*. The critical path can be defined in several ways:

- It is the longest duration path in the network diagram.

- It is the sequence of tasks whose early schedule and late schedule are the same.

- It is the sequence of tasks with zero slack or float (these terms are defined later in this appendix).

All of these definitions say the same thing: what sequence of tasks must be completed on schedule in order for the project to be completed on schedule.

The tasks that define the critical path are called *critical path tasks*. Any delay in a critical path task delays the completion of the project by the amount of delay in that task. This is a sequence of tasks that warrants the project manager's special attention.

The Early Schedule

The earliest start (ES) time for a task is the earliest time at which all of its predecessor tasks have been completed and the subject task can begin. The ES time of a task with no predecessor tasks is arbitrarily set to 1, the first day on which the project is open for work. The ES time of tasks with one predecessor task is determined from the EF time of the predecessor task. The earliest finish (EF) of a task is calculated as ((ES + duration) – one time unit). The ES time of tasks having two or more predecessor tasks is determined from the latest of the EF times of its immediate predecessor tasks. The reason for subtracting the one time unit is to account for the fact that a task starts at the beginning of a time unit (hour, day, and so forth) and finishes at the end of a time unit. In other words, a one-day task, starting at the beginning of a day, begins and ends on the same day. For example, take a look at Figure G-5. Note that Task E has two predecessors, Task B and Task C. The EF for Task B is the end of day 5 and for Task C is the end of day 4. Therefore the ES of Task E is the beginning of day 6. When there are two or more predecessors, the ES of the successor, Task E in this case, is calculated based on the maximum of the EF dates of the predecessor tasks. The EF dates of the predecessors are the end of day 5 and the end of day 4. The maximum of these is 5, and therefore the ES of Task E is the morning of day 6. The complete calculations of the early schedule are shown in Figure G-5.

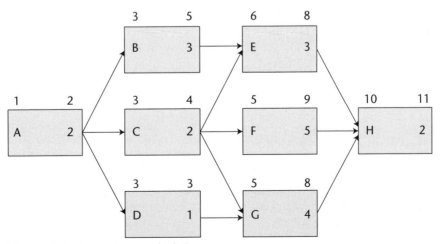

Figure G-5: Forward pass calculations

The Late Schedule

The latest start (LS) and latest finish (LF) times of a task are the latest times at which the task can start or finish without causing a delay in the completion of the project. Knowing these times is valuable for the project manager, who must make decisions on resource scheduling that can affect completion dates. The window of time between the ES and LF of a task is the window within which the resource for the work must be scheduled or the project completion date will be delayed. To calculate these times, you work backward in the network diagram. First set the LF time of the last task on the network to its calculated EF time. Its LS is calculated as ((LF – duration) + one time unit). Again, you add the one time unit to adjust for the start and finish of a task within the same day. The LF time of all immediate predecessor tasks is determined by the minimum of the LS, minus one time unit, times of all tasks for which it is the predecessor. For example, calculate the late schedule for Task E. Its only successor, Task H, has an LS date of day 10. The LF date for its only predecessor, Task E, will therefore be the end of day 9. In other words, Task E must finish no later than the end of day 9, or it will delay the start of Task H and hence delay the completion date of the project. The LS date for Task E will be, using the formula, 9 – 2 + 1, or the beginning of day 7. On the other hand, consider Task C. It has three successor tasks, Task E, Task F, and Task G. The LS dates for them are day 7, 5, and 6, respectively. The minimum of those dates, day 5, is used to calculate the LF of Task C, namely the end of day 4. The complete calculations for the late schedule are shown in Figure G-6.

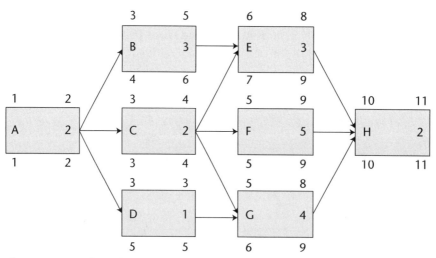

Figure G-6: Backward pass calculations

Critical Path Calculation

The *critical path* is the longest path or sequence of activities (in terms of activity duration) through the network diagram. The critical path drives the completion date of the project. Any delay in the completion of any one of the activities in the sequence will delay the completion of the project. The project manager pays particular attention to critical path activities. The critical path for the example problem used to calculate the early schedule and the late schedule in the previous sections is shown in Figure G-7.

One way to identify the critical path in the network diagram is to identify all possible paths through the network diagram and add up the durations of the tasks that lie along those paths. The path with the longest duration time is the critical path. For projects of any size, this method is not feasible, and you have to resort to the second method of finding the critical path—computing the slack time of a task.

Slack

The second method of finding the critical path requires you to compute a quantity known as the task *slack time*. Slack time (also called *float*) is the amount of delay expressed in units of time that could be tolerated in the starting time or completion time of a task without causing a delay in the completion of the project. Slack time is a calculated number. It is the difference between the late finish and the early finish (LF − EF). If the result is greater than zero, the task has a range of time in which it can start and finish without delaying the project completion date, as shown in Figure G-8.

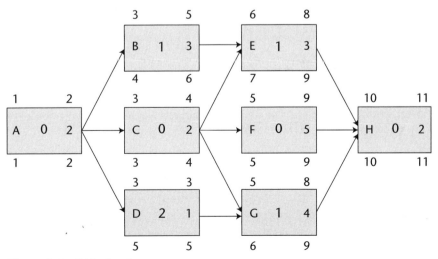

Figure G-7: Critical path

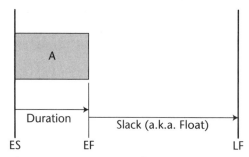

Figure G-8: ES to LF window of an activity

Near-Critical Path

Even though project managers are tempted to rivet their attention on critical path tasks, other sequences of tasks also require their attention. By way of a general example, suppose the critical path tasks are tasks in which the project team has considerable experience; duration estimates are based on historical data and are quite accurate in that the estimated duration will be very close to the actual duration. On the other hand, suppose there is a sequence of tasks not on the critical path for which the team has little experience. Duration estimates have large estimation variances. Suppose further that such tasks lie on a path that has little total slack. It is very likely that this near-critical path may actually drive the project completion date even though the total path length is less than that of the critical path. This will happen if larger-than-estimated durations occur. Because of the large duration variances this is very likely. Obviously, this path cannot be ignored. These are tasks that we call *near-critical path*. The full treatment of near-critical tasks is beyond the scope of this book. I merely introduce it here so that you are aware that there are paths other than critical paths that are worthy of attention.

Analyzing the Initial Project Network Diagram

After you have created the initial project network diagram, one of two situations will be present.

- First, the initial project completion date meets the requested completion date. Usually this is not the case, but it does sometimes happen.

- The more likely situation is that the initial project completion date is later than the requested completion date. In other words, you have to find a way to squeeze some time out of the project schedule.

You will eventually need to address two considerations: the project completion date and resource availability under the revised project schedule. Here I proceed under the assumption that resources will be available to meet this compressed schedule. In Appendix H I look at the resource-scheduling problem. The two are quite dependent on one another, but they must be treated separately.

Schedule Compression

Almost without exception, the initial project calculations will result in a project completion date beyond the required completion date. That means that the project team must find ways to reduce the total duration of the project to meet the required date.

To address this problem, analyze the network diagram to identify areas where schedule compression opportunities exist. You look for pairs of tasks that allow you to convert tasks that are currently worked on sequentially into more parallel patterns of work. Work on the successor task might begin once the predecessor task has reached a certain stage of completion. In these cases the FS dependency is changed to a SS dependency with some delay before the successor task can start. The design-build sequence has that property. Once you have reached a certain stage in the design task you can often begin working on the build part of what has just been designed. The caution, however, is that project risk increases because we have created a potential rework situation if changes are made in the predecessor after work has started on the successor. Schedule compressions affect only the time frame in which work will be done; they do not reduce the amount of work to be done. The result is the need for more coordination and communication, especially between the tasks affected by the dependency changes.

The Resource Schedule

The hammer must be swung in cadence, when more than one is hammering the iron.

Giordano Bruno
Italian philosopher

Appendix Learning Objectives

After reading this appendix, you will be able to:

◆ **Use the whiteboard to create, post, and update the resource schedule**

NOTE Most of the material in this appendix is an abridged version of Chapter 6 of my earlier work *Effective Project Management: Traditional, Adaptive, Extreme, Third Edition* (Wiley, 2003). It is presented here for completeness so that this book may be used as a text for an introductory course in software project management. For courses requiring more detail on these topics the earlier work may be used as a companion text.

Once the initial schedule meets all customer constraints for deadlines, it must now meet the availabilities of the project team and others who will do work on the project. Because people tend to be allocated to more than one project at a time and also have other non-project work to do, creating a schedule that meets the needs of all concerned parties is no small task.

One hint that I can offer is to not get caught in the trap of micro-managing the team. An example will illustrate the point. Suppose you have a task that will require 16 hours of effort from Harry. You will be able to give him the input he needs to do the task 2 weeks from this coming Monday. You need the task to be complete by the end of that week. In other words, Harry has 5 working days to complete a 2-day task. Ask Harry if he can meet your needs? Let Harry consider his other workload during that week and tell you yes or no. Assuming he says yes, do not ask him which days he expects to be working on your task. To do that is to micro-manage.

Building the Resource Schedule

The input to building the resource schedule is the complete WBS and the project dependency network. These are discussed in Appendixes E and G, respectively. The team begins the creation of the micro-level schedule by taking the tasks that make up this project and further decomposing them to the subtask level. This is a top-down whole team exercise. The result is shown in Figure H-1.

Examples of a Resource Schedule

Once the micro-level WBS has been created (see Figure H-1), make Post-it Notes for each of these subtasks and lay them out in a network diagram as shown in the upper portion of Figure H-1. Note that the network diagram is time scaled. This is important. At another spot on the whiteboard (ideally below the network diagram and on the same time scale) lay out a grid that shows the timeline on a daily basis across the columns and have one row allocated to each resource. The resources for this example are Duffy, Ernie, and Fran. Show all 7 days on this grid. For any workdays or half workday in this cycle for which a resource will not be available for cycle build work, put an "X" or some other indicator of unavailability in the corresponding cell or half cell. Half-day units are the smallest unit of time that you are going to build this plan around. Smaller units just create non-value-added work and begin to border on micro-management. This is your resource calendar for this project. The lower part of Figure H-1 gives an example grid for the network diagram shown above in Figure H-1. For this example the tasks were A, B, and C. The subtasks, which are what you are scheduling, are A1, A2, B1, B2, C1, C2, and C3.

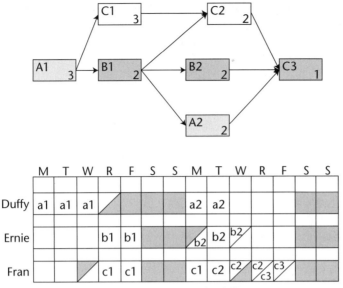

	M	T	W	R	F	S	S	M	T	W	R	F	S	S
Duffy	a1	a1	a1					a2	a2					
Ernie				b1	b1			b2	b2	b2				
Fran				c1	c1			c1	c2	c2	c2/c3	c3		

Figure H-1: An Example micro-level schedule

Before you finalize the micro-level schedule, check to see if the initial schedule and resource assignments will allow the team to complete the project within the allotted. If the current schedule doesn't meet the time constraint, look for alternative resource assignments that will bring the schedule inside the time constraint. Resources that are not assigned for periods of time will be the place to look. They can either take over a task or help another resource complete a task earlier than currently scheduled. What you are doing is manual resource leveling in a way that makes more sense than the approach taken by most software tools.

Once you have met the time constraint, you are ready to finalize the information on the grid. For each resource, simply transfer the information to the grid that shows what task they are working on, what day they expect to start it and what day they expect to end it. Every morning you will have a team status meeting at which time you compare what was completed the previous day with what the grid had scheduled for that day. Any adjustments to the plan are made on the grid. Resources can be moved to meet schedule delays. Since you still have the Post-it Note network diagram on the whiteboard you will be able to see if schedule delays will cause any other delays downstream in the plan and adjust accordingly.

I want to point out a few important points about Figure H-1.

- First, when scheduling a resource, try to keep them busy for consecutive days. That makes it easier if you need to replace an individual on the team.

- Second, notice when a resource is not busy (Duffy is available for a half-day on Thursday of the first week. While this is early in the cycle, it may provide a resource that can help either Ernie or Fran or help the team recover from a slippage or a problem.

- Finally, note that in the second week Duffy and Ernie are available to per-haps help Fran complete c2 when Fran is unavailable on Wednesday after-noon. If that can be scheduled, c3 may be able to be completed early. This means that the project would be completed ahead of schedule. Alterna-tively, that staffing adjustment might provide a way to make up for earlier slippages.

This grid should be permanently displayed in the Team War Room. It will be the focal point of daily team meetings. As status is being reported, the team can refer to this schedule and make any changes to the latter parts of the sched-ule. The most important benefit is that this is visible and accessible to the team. The only negative that you have to worry about is there is no backup for this approach. The fact that the Team War Room is reserved for the exclusive use of the team and is secure will mitigate most of the risk but not all of the risk. I have made it a practice to have one of the team members, when they are not otherwise busy, update an electronic version of the data posted in the Team War Room. Because this is only for backup, it doesn't need to be saved in a high-powered software application. A word processor or a spreadsheet pack-age will do just fine. I have even used Visio on occasion.

The reason that this approach works is that the project duration is short. The example project is only 2 weeks long, but even if it were 3 or 4 weeks long, the same approach would work. Even though I have used project management software packages extensively, I still find this low-tech approach to be far more intuitive than any software display. The entire team can see what is going on and can see how to resolve scheduling problems in a very intuitive manner. Try it.

However, this would never do well in larger projects. For one thing, the net-work diagram would take up too much real estate and is generally not avail-able from the software package. This doesn't mean it can't be generated. It certainly can, but the labor to create it just doesn't justify it. Resource balanc-ing is the other side of the coin. On the whiteboard, it is easy. In a software package, who knows what happen when you try to level resources. We want to see the problem and the software package just doesn't measure up.

A second example of a resource schedule extends the idea given previously to a more sophisticated and complete schedule (Figure H-2).

I have added some other features that you might find as useful as have I. The critical and non-critical paths are identified, as is the slack associated with the non-critical path features. Having that information on the whiteboard schedule makes it intuitive as to what needs to be done to maintain the plan.

	M	T	W	R	F	M	T	W	R	F	M	T	W	R	F	M	T	W	R	F
Archie	A	A				X	X	X	X	X	X	X	X	X	X	X	X	X	X	X
Aaron			A	A	A				X	X	X	X	X	X	X	X	X	X	X	X
Bob	X	X	X			B	B	B			X	X	X	X	X	X	X	X	X	X
Carl	X	X	X	X		C	C	C	C	C	C	→				X	X	X	X	X
Carol	X	X	X			C	C	C	C	C	C	C	→		X	X	X	X	X	X
Donna	X	X	X	X	X	D	D	D	D	D	D	D	D							
Ed	X	X	X	X	X	X			E	E	E	E	E	→		X	X	X	X	X
Fran	X	X	X	X	X	X	X	X	X	X	X	X		F	F				X	X
Gail	X	X	X	X	X	X	X	X	X	X	X			G	G			X		
Harry	X	X	X	X	X	X	X	X	X	X	X	X				H	H	H	H	H

☐ C.P.   ⟶ slack   ■ Not available or PTO   X: Other assignments

Figure H-2: An extended resource schedule

Organizing the Project Team

When a team outgrows individual performance and learns team confidence, excellence becomes a reality.

Joe Paterno
Football Coach, Penn State University

Appendix Learning Objectives

After reading this appendix, you will be able to:

◆ Understand the tools of an effective team
◆ Organize the project team

NOTE Most of the material in this appendix is an abridged version of Chapter 9 of my earlier work: *Effective Project Management: Traditional, Adaptive, Extreme, Third Edition* (Wiley, 2003). It is presented here for completeness so that this book may be used as a text for an introductory course in software project management. For courses requiring more detail on these topics, the earlier work may be used as a companion text.

Every team is different. They may be coming together for the first time and not much more that a group of people, or they may have worked on several projects in the past and are a lean, mean fighting machine. Typically they are somewhere in between these two extremes. In any case it is the project manager that must bring them together into an effective and efficient working team.

Project teams all too often fail to define and agree on the team operating rules. These operating rules define how the team works together, makes decisions, resolves conflicts, reports progress, and deals with a host of other administrative chores.

There are several areas to consider when you create the operating rules that govern how the team conducts itself. Those areas are the subject of this appendix.

Problem Solving

Creativity and problem-solving go hand in hand. A good problem solver will think outside the box. He or she will conceive of approaches that may have been overlooked. The ability to think outside the box and suggest other approaches is the territory of the creative person. As I will discuss next, each of the learning styles relates to a different part of the problem-solving model. That means that the team must have all learning styles represented in order to solve problems effectively. In this section, you will see how the Learning Styles Inventory relates to the problem-solving process.

In his work *Creative Problem Solving and Opportunity Finding* (Boyd and Fraser Publishing, 1995), J. Daniel Couger points out that there are dozens of models for problem solving. The model that seems most appropriate for business problem solving is one put forward by Couger and shown in Figure I-1.

Couger's process begins with an outside stimulus—an event has occurred that creates an out-of-control situation that must be rectified. That launches a series of actions that clarify the situation, identify and assemble relevant data, get a number of ideas and approaches on the table, and analyze the ideas. It then selects the idea that would appear most promising as the way to rectify the situation and return it to normal. Finally an action plan is put in place and executed (the exit point of the model is the action itself). You will see how different learning styles are needed to complete each step in the model. Couger identifies five steps to the problem-solving process.

Step 1: Delineate the Opportunity and Define the Problem

This is a scoping step in which the team members attempt to establish a formulation and definition of the problem and the desired results that a solution to the problem will provide. It helps the team develop the boundaries of the problem—that is, what is in scope and what is out of scope. This step is best performed by team members who have a preference for the assimilator learning style. These individuals will look at the problem independently of any focus on people and try to present the problem at the conceptual level and put it into a logical framework. Their penchant for collecting and concisely reporting data is an early activity in this model.

Stimulus ⇨		Required Learning Style
Step One	Delineate opportunity and define problem	Assimilator
Step Two	Compile relevant information	Assimilator
Step Three	Generate ideas	Diverger
Step Four	Evaluate and prioritize ideas	Converger
Step Five	Develop implementation plan	Accomodator
		⇨ Action

Figure I-1: Couger's creative problem-solving model

Step 2: Compile the Relevant Data

With a definition of the problem in hand the team can now identify and specify the data elements that will be needed in order to further understand the problem and provide a foundation on which possible solutions can be formulated. Again, the assimilator is well suited to this activity.

Step 3: Generate Ideas

This step typically begins with a brainstorming session. The team needs to identify as many solutions as possible. This is the time to think outside the box and look for creative and innovative ways to approach a solution. Ideas will spawn new ideas until the team has exhausted its creative energies. The diverger is well suited to the activities that take place in this step. The job of this individual is to look at the problem from a number of perspectives. Like the assimilator, the diverger also has an interest in data and information with the purpose of generating ideas, but he or she is not interested in generating solutions.

Step 4: Evaluate and Prioritize Ideas

In this step the list of possible solutions needs to be winnowed down to the one or two solutions that will actually be planned. Criteria for selecting the best solution ideas need to be developed (that's a job for the converger), metrics for assessing advantages and disadvantages need to be developed (again, a job for the converger), and the metrics will be used to prioritize the solutions. This is a straightforward exercise that anyone on the team can perform. This individual has the ability to take a variety of ideas and turn them into solutions. His/her work is not finished, however, until he/she has established criteria for evaluating those solutions and makes recommendations for action.

Step 5: Develop the Implementation Plan

The solution has been identified, and it's now time to build a plan to implement the solution. This is a whole team exercise that will draw on the team's collective wisdom for planning and implementation. When it is results that you want, call on the accommodator. His or her contribution will be to put a plan in place for delivering the recommended solution and making it happen. The accommodator is a good person to lead this planning and implementation exercise.

Decision Making

The first operating rule is the establishment of how the team will make decisions. There are three major types of decision-making models.

Directive

In this model, the person with the authority—the project manager for the project and the activity manager for the activity—makes the decision for all team members. While this approach is certainly expedient, it has obvious drawbacks. The only information available is the decision maker's information, which may or may not be correct or complete. An added danger is that those who disagree or were left out of the decision may not carry it out.

Participative

In this model, everyone on the team contributes to the decision-making process. A synergy is created as the best decision is sought. Because everyone has an opportunity to participate, commitment will be much stronger than in the directive approach. Obviously, there are additional benefits to team building—empowerment of the team. Whenever possible, I recommend this participative approach.

Consultative

This middle-ground approach combines the best of the other two approaches. While the person in authority makes the decision, the decision is made only after consulting with all members to get their input and ideas. This approach is participative at the input stage but directive at the point of decision. In some cases, when expediency is required, this approach is a good one to take.

Which model to use in a specific situation is generally a function of the gravity and time sensitivity of the pending decision. Some organizations have constructed categories of decisions, with each category defined by some financial parameters, such as the value of the decision, or by some scope parameters, such as the number of business units or customers affected by the decision. The person responsible for making the decision is defined for each decision category. The more serious the category, the higher the organizational level of the decision maker. Some decisions might be made by an individual team member, some by an activity manager, some by the project manager, some by the customer, and some by senior management. Yet others might require a group decision, using either a participative or a consultative approach.

Decision making is pervasive throughout the life of the project. Consider the following questions from *Managing Project Teams* by Vijay K. Verma (Project Management Institute, 1997) that must be answered at some point in the project life cycle:

- What has to be done and where? (scope)
- Why should it be done? (justification)
- How well must it be done? (quality)
- When is it required and in what sequence? (schedule)
- How much will it cost? (budget/cost)
- What are the uncertainties? (risk)
- Who would do the job? (human resources)
- How should people be organized into teams? (communication/interpersonal skills)
- How will you know if you have done the job? (information dissemination/communication)

The answers to all of these questions require decisions. How will the project team make decisions? Will it be based on a vote? Will it be a team consensus decision? Will it be left up to the project manager? Just how will it operate?

Deciding how to decide is only a piece of the puzzle. Another piece is whether the team can make a decision and, if not, what to do about it. In their book *Organizational Behavior in Action: Skill Building Experiences* (West Publishing Co., 1976), William C. Morris and M. Sashkin propose a six-phase model for rational decision making. The six phases in their approach are as follows.

- **Phase I: Situation Definition**—This phase is one of discovery for the team and clarifying the situation to make sure that there is a shared understanding of the decision the team faces.

- **Phase II: Situation Decision Generation**—Through brainstorming the team tries to expand the decision space.

- **Phase III: Ideas to Action**—Metrics are devised to attach reward and penalty to each possible decision that might be made.

- **Phase IV: Decision Action Plan**—The decision has been made, and the development of a plan to implement it is now needed.

- **Phase V: Decision Evaluation Planning**—This is kind of a post-decision audit of what worked and what didn't work. Some lessons learned will be the likely deliverable as well.

- **Phase VI: Evaluation of Outcome and Process**—The team needs to find out if the decision got the job done and whether another attempt at the situation is needed.

Conflict Resolution

The second operating rule deals with how the team resolves conflicts. Conflicts arise when two or more team members have a difference of opinion, when the customer takes issue with an action to be taken by the project team, or in a variety of other situations involving two parties with different points of view. In all of these examples, the difference must be resolved. Clearly conflict resolution is a much more sensitive situation than the decision-making rule because it is confrontational and situational, whereas the decision-making rule is procedural and structured. Depending on the particular conflict situation, the team might adopt one of three conflict resolution styles:

- Avoidant
- Combative
- Collaborative

Avoidant

Some people will do anything to avoid a direct confrontation. They agree even though they are opposed to the outcome. This style cannot be tolerated on the project team. Each person's input and opinion must be sought. It is the responsibility of the project manager to make sure that this happens. A simple device is to ask each team member in turn what he or she thinks about the situation and what he or she suggests be done about it. Often this approach will diffuse any direct confrontation between two individuals on the team.

Combative

Some avoid confrontation at all costs; others seem to seek it out. Some team members play devil's advocate at the least provocation. There are times when this is advantageous—testing the team's thinking before making the decision. At other times it tends to raise the level of stress and tension, when many view it as a waste of time and not productive. The project manager knows who these team members are and must act to mitigate the chances of these situations arising. One technique I have used with success is to put such individuals in charge of forming a recommendation for the team to consider. Such an approach offers less opportunity for combative discussion because the combative team member is sharing recommendations before others give reason for disagreement.

Collaborative

In this approach, the team looks for win-win opportunities. The approach seeks out a common ground as the basis for moving ahead to a solution. This approach encourages each team member to put his or her opinions on the table and not avoid the conflict that may result. At the same time, team members do not seek to create conflict unnecessarily. The approach is constructive, not destructive.

The choice of conflict resolution styles is beyond the scope of this book. There are several books on the topic that you can consult. Of particular importance will be the variety of collaborative models that might be adopted.

Consensus Building

Consensus building is a process that a team can follow to reach agreement on which alternative to proceed with for the item (action, decision, and so forth) under consideration. The agreement is not reached by a majority vote, or any vote for that matter. Rather the agreement is reached through discussion where each participant in the discussion reaches a point where he or she has no serious disagreement with the decision that is about to be taken. The decision will have been revised several times for the participants to reach the point where they have no serious disagreement.

This is an excellent tool to have in the project team tool kit. In all but a few cases, there will be a legitimate difference of opinion as to how a problem or issue should be addressed. There will be no clear-cut action on which all can agree. In such situations the team must fashion an action or decision with which no team members have serious disagreement even though they may not agree in total with the chosen action. To use the method successfully, make sure that everyone on the team gets to speak. Talk through the issue until an acceptable action is identified. Conflict is good, but try to be creative as you search for a compromise action. As soon as no one has serious objections to the defined action, you have reached consensus. Once a decision is reached, all team members must support it.

If the project manager chooses to operate on a consensus basis, he or she must clearly define the situations in which consensus will be acceptable. The team needs to know this.

Brainstorming

Brainstorming is an essential part of the team operating rules because, at several points in the life of the project, the creativity of the team will be tested. Brainstorming is a technique that can focus that creativity and help the team discover solutions. There will be situations where acceptable ideas and alternatives have not come forth from the normal team deliberations. In such cases the project manager might suggest a brainstorming session. A brainstorming session is one in which the team contributes ideas in a stream-of-consciousness mode, as described in the next paragraph. Brainstorming sessions have been quite successful in uncovering solutions where none seemed present. The team needs to know how the project manager will conduct such sessions and what will be done with the output.

The method for brainstorming is simple and quick. First, assemble together those individuals who may have some knowledge of the problem area. They don't need to be experts. In fact, it may be better if they are not. You need people to think creatively and "outside the box." Experts tend to think inside the box. The session begins with everyone throwing any idea out on the table. No discussion (except clarification) is permitted. This continues until no new ideas are forthcoming. Silence and pauses are fine. Once all the ideas are on the table, you discuss the items on the list. Look to combine ideas or revise ideas based on each member's perspective. In time, some solutions begin to emerge. Don't rush the process, and by all means test each idea with an open mind. Remember that you are looking for a solution that no individual could identify but that, we hope, the group is able to identify. This is a creative process, one that must be approached with an open mind. Convention and *"We've always done it that way"* have no place in a true brainstorming session.

Project Performance Reporting

If two lines on a graph cross, it must be important.

Ernest F. Cooke
University of Baltimore

Appendix Learning Objectives

After reading this appendix, you will be able to:

- ◆ Determine the appropriate reporting plan
- ◆ Measure and analyze variances from the project plan
- ◆ Know how to use milestone trend charts
- ◆ Understand and use cost/schedule control

NOTE Most of the material in this appendix is an abridged version of Chapter 10 from my earlier work *Effective Project Management: Traditional, Adaptive, Extreme, Third Edition* (Wiley, 2003). It is presented here for completeness so that this book may be used as a text for an introductory course in software project management. For courses requiring more detail on these topics, the earlier work may be used as a companion text.

Monitoring and Controlling Software Development Project Progress

"If you can't measure it, you can't manage it" (anonymous). Software development projects are no exception. Whether they are following a tightly controlled plan-driven approach or are developed following a component-driven approach, the progress of software development projects requires some form of performance measurement and tracking.

Progress Reporting System

Once project work is underway, you want to make sure that it proceeds according to plan. To do this, you need to establish a reporting system that keeps you informed of the many variables that describe how the project is proceeding as compared to the plan.

A reporting system has the following characteristics:

- Provides timely, complete, and accurate status information
- Doesn't add so much overhead time as to be counterproductive
- Is readily acceptable to the project team and senior management
- Warns of pending problems in time to take action
- Is easily understood by those who have a need to know

To establish this reporting system, you will want to look into the hundreds of reports that are standard fare in project management software packages. Once you decide what you want to track, these software tools will give you several suggestions and standard reports to meet your needs. Most project management software tools allow you to customize their standard reports to meet even the most specific needs.

Types of Project Status Reports

There are five types of project status reports. Each is discussed in the following subsections.

Current Period Reports

These reports cover only the most recently completed period. They report progress on those activities that were open or scheduled for work during the period. Reports might highlight activities completed and variance between scheduled and actual completion dates. If any activities did not progress according to plan, the report should include a discussion of the reasons for the variance and the appropriate corrective measures that will be implemented to correct the schedule slippage.

Cumulative Reports

These reports contain the history of the project from the beginning to the end of the current report period. They are more informative than the current period reports because they show trends in project progress. For example, a schedule variance might be tracked over several successive periods to show improvement. Reports can be at the activity or project level.

Exception Reports

Exception reports report variances from plan. These reports are typically designed for senior management to be read and interpreted quickly. Reports that are produced for senior management merit special consideration. Senior managers do not have a lot of time to read reports that tell them that every-thing is on schedule, and there are no problems serious enough to warrant their attention. In such cases, a one-page, high-level summary report that says everything is okay is usually sufficient. It might also be appropriate to include a more detailed report as an attachment for those who might wish to read more detail. The same might be true of exception reports—that is, the one-page exception report tells senior managers about variances from plan that will be of interest to them while an attached report provides more details for the interested reader.

Stoplight Reports

Stoplight reports are not really reports but are rather variation that can be used on any of the previous report types. I believe in parsimony in all reporting. Here is a technique you might want to try.

- When the project is on schedule and everything seems to be moving as planned, put a green sticker on the top right of the first page of the project status report. This will signal to senior managers that everything is pro-gressing according to plan, and they need not even read the attached report.

- When the project has encountered a problem—schedule slippage, for example—you might put a yellow sticker on the top right of the first page of the project status report. That is a signal to upper management that the project is not moving along as scheduled but that you have a get-well plan in place. A summary of the problem and the get-well plan may appear on the first page, but they can also refer to the details in the attached report. Those details describe the problem, the corrective steps that have been put in place, and some estimate of when the situation will be rectified.

■ Red stickers placed on the top right of the first page signal that a project is out of control. Red reports are to be avoided at all costs. This means that the project has encountered a problem and you don't have a get-well plan or even a recommendation for upper management. Senior managers will obviously read these reports because they signal a major problem with the project. If this should occur, you might have to find an empty box and pack your belongings in it; your days as project manager might be numbered. However, on a more positive note, the red condition may be beyond your control. For example, there is a major power grid failure on the East Coast and a number of companies have lost their computing systems. Your hot site is overburdened with companies looking for computing power. Your company is one of them, and the loss of computing power has put your project seriously behind in final system testing. There is little you can do to avoid such acts of nature.

Variance Reports

Variance reports do exactly what their name suggests—they report differences between what was planned and what actually happened. The report has three columns: the planned number, the actual number, and the difference, or variance, between the two. A variance report can be in one of two formats.

■ The first is numeric and displays a number of rows with each row giving the actual, planned, and variance calculation for those variables in which such numbers are needed. Typical variables that are tracked in a variance report are schedule and cost. For example, the rows might correspond to the activities open for work during the report period and the columns might be the planned cost to date, the actual cost to date, and the difference between the two. The impact of departures from plan is signified by larger values of this difference (the variance).

■ The second format is a graphical representation of the numeric data. It might be formatted so that the plan data is shown for each report period of the project and is denoted with a curve of one color; the actual data is shown for each report period of the project and is denoted by a curve of a different color. The variance need not be graphed at all because it is merely the difference between the two curves at some point in time. One advantage of the graphic version of the variance report is that it can show the variance trend over the report periods of the project while the numeric report generally shows data only for the current report period.

Typical variance reports are snapshots in time (the current period) of the status of an entity being tracked. Most variance reports do not include data points that report how the project reached that status. Project variance reports can be used to report project as well as activity variances. For the sake of the managers who have to read these reports, I recommend that one report format be used regardless of the variable being tracked. Top management can quickly become comfortable with a reporting format that is consistent across all projects or activities within a project. It will make life a bit easier for the project manager, too.

Measuring Variances

The next subsections go over five reasons why you would want to measure duration and cost variances.

Catch Deviations from the Curve Early

The cumulative actual cost or actual duration can be plotted against the planned cumulative cost or cumulative duration. As these two curves begin to display a variance from one another, the project manager will want to put corrective measures in place to bring the two curves together. This reestablishes the agreement between the planned and actual performance. This topic is treated in detail later in the section "Earned Value Analysis".

Dampen Oscillation

Planned versus actual performance should display a similar pattern over time. Wild fluctuations between the two are symptomatic of a project that is not under control. Such a project will get behind schedule or overspent in one period, corrected in the next, and go out of control in the next report period. Variance reports can give an early warning that such conditions are likely and give the project manager an opportunity to correct the anomaly before it gets serious. Smaller oscillations are easier to correct than larger oscillations.

Allow Early Corrective Action

As just suggested, the project manager would prefer to be alerted to a schedule or cost problem early in the development of the problem rather than later. Early problem detection may offer more opportunities for corrective action than later detection.

Determine Weekly Schedule Variance

In my experience, I have found that progress on activities open for work should be reported on a weekly basis. This is a good compromise on report frequency and gives the project manager the best opportunity for corrective action plans before the situation escalates to a point where it will be difficult to recover any schedule slippages.

Determine Weekly Effort (Person Hours/Day) Variance

The difference between the planned effort and actual effort has a direct impact on both planned cumulative cost and schedule. If the effort is less than planned, it may suggest a potential schedule slippage if the person is not able to increase his or her effort on the activity in the following week. Alternatively, if the weekly effort exceeded the plan and the progress was not proportionately the same, a cost overrun situation may be developing.

Early detection of out-of-control situations is also important. The longer you have to wait to discover a problem, the longer it takes for your solution to bring the project back to a stable condition.

How and What Information To Update

As input to each of these report types, activity managers and the project manager must report the progress made on all of those activities that were open for work during the period of time covered by the status report (in other words, those that were to have work completed on them during the report period). Recall that your planning estimates of activity duration and cost were based on little or no information. Now that you have completed some work on the activity, you should be able to provide a better estimate of the duration and cost exposure. This reflects itself in a re-estimate of the work remaining to complete the activity. That update information should also be provided.

The following subsections comprise a list of what should actually be reported.

Determine a Set Period of Time and Day of Week

The project team will have agreed on the day of the week and time of day by which all updated information is to be submitted. A project administrator or another team member is responsible for seeing that all update information is on file by the report deadline.

Report Actual Work Accomplished During This Period

What was planned to be accomplished and what was actually accomplished are two different things. Rather than disappoint the project manager, activity managers are likely to report that the planned work was actually accomplished. Their hope is to catch up by the next report period. Project managers need to verify the accuracy of the reported data rather than simply accept it as accurate. Spot checking on a random basis should be sufficient. If the activity was defined according to the completion criteria discussed in Appendix E, verification should not be a problem.

Record Historical and Re-estimate Remaining (In-Progress Work Only)

Two kinds of information are reported.

- All work completed prior to the report deadline is *historical information*. It will allow variance reports and other tracking data to be presented and analyzed.

- The other kind of information is *future-oriented*. For the most part, this information is re-estimates of duration and cost and estimates to completion (both cost and duration) of the activities still open for work.

Report Start and Finish Dates

These are the actual start and finish dates of activities started or completed during the report period.

Record Days of Duration Accomplished and Remaining

How many days have been spent so far working on this activity is the first number reported. The second number is based on the re-estimated duration as reflected in the time-to-completion number.

Report Resource Effort (Hours/Day) Spent and Remaining (In-Progress Work Only)

Whereas the preceding numbers report calendar time, these numbers report labor time over the duration of the activity. There are two numbers. One reports labor completed over the duration accomplished. The other reports labor to be spent over the remaining duration.

Percent complete is the most common method used to record progress because it is the way people tend to think about what has been done in reference to the total job that has to be done. Percent complete isn't the best method to report progress, though, because it is a subjective evaluation. When you ask someone, "What percent complete are you on this activity?", what goes through his or her mind? The first thing he or she thinks about is most likely, "What percent should I be?", followed closely by, "What's a number that we can all be happy with?"

In order to calculate the percent complete for an activity, you need something quantifiable. At least three different approaches have been used to calculate the percent complete of an activity:

- Duration
- Resource work
- Cost

Each of these could result in a different percent complete! So when you say percent complete, what measure are you referring to?

If you focus on duration as the measure of percent complete, where did the duration value come from? The only value you have is the original estimate. You know that original estimates often differ from actual performance. If you were to apply a percent complete to duration, however, the only one you have to work with is the original estimated one. Therefore this is not a good metric.

My advice is to never ask for and never accept percent complete as input to project progress. Always allow it to be a calculation. Many software products will let you do it either as an inputted value or as a calculated value. The calculated value that I recommend above all others is one based on the number of tasks actually completed in the activity as a proportion of the number of tasks that currently define the activity. Recall that the task list for an activity is part of the work package description. Here you count only completed tasks. Tasks that are underway but not reported as complete may not be used in this calculation.

Frequency of Gathering and Reporting Project Progress

A logical frequency for reporting project progress is once a week, usually on Friday afternoon. There are some projects, such as refurbishing a large jet airliner, where progress is recorded after each shift, three times a day. I've seen others that were of such a low priority or long duration that they were updated once a month. For most projects, start gathering the information about noon on Friday. Let people extrapolate to the end of the work day.

Variances

Variances are deviations from plan. Think of a variance as the difference between what was planned and what actually occurred. There are two types of variances: positive variances and negative variances.

Positive Variances

Positive variances are deviations from plan that indicate that an ahead-of-schedule situation has occurred or that an actual cost was less than a planned cost. This is good news to the project manager, who would rather hear that the project is ahead of schedule or under budget. Positive variances bring their own set of problems, which can be as serious as negative variances. Positive variances can allow for rescheduling to bring the project to completion early, under budget, or both. Resources can be reallocated from ahead-of-schedule projects to behind-schedule projects.

Not all the news is good news, though. Positive variances also can result from schedule slippage! Consider budget. Being underbudget means that not all dollars were expended, which may be the direct result of not having completed work that was scheduled for completion during the report period. I return to this situation later in the "Earned Value Analysis" section of this appendix. On the other hand, if the ahead-of-schedule situation is the result of the project team's finding a better way or a shortcut to completing work, the project manager will be pleased. This may be a short-lived benefit, however. Getting ahead of schedule is great, but staying ahead of schedule presents another kind of problem—staying ahead of schedule. That means that to stay ahead of schedule the project manager will have to negotiate changes to the resource schedule. Given the aggressive project portfolios in place in most companies, there is not much reason to believe that resource schedule changes can be made. In the final analysis, being ahead of schedule may be a myth.

Negative Variances

Negative variances are deviations from plan that indicate that a behind-schedule situation has occurred or that an actual cost was greater than a planned cost. Being behind schedule or over budget is not what the project manager or his reporting manager wants to hear. Negative variances, just like positive variances, are not necessarily bad news. For example, you might have overspent because you accomplished more work during the report period than was planned. But in overspending during this period, you could have accomplished the work at less cost than was originally planned. You can't tell by looking at the variance report. More details are forthcoming on this in the "Earned Value Analysis" section later in this appendix.

In most cases, negative time variances affect project completion only if they are associated with critical path activities or if the schedule slippage on non-critical path activities exceeds the activity's total float. Variances use up the float time for that activity; more serious ones will cause a change in the critical path.

Negative cost variances can result from uncontrollable factors such as cost increases from suppliers or unexpected equipment malfunctions. Some negative variances can result from inefficiencies or error. I discuss a problem escalation strategy to resolve such situations later in this appendix.

Graphical Reporting Tools

Senior managers may have only a few minutes of uninterrupted time to digest your report. Respect that time. They won't be able to fully read and understand your report if they have to read 15 pages before they get any useful information. Having to read several pages only to find out that the project is on schedule is frustrating and a waste of valuable time.

Gantt Charts

A *Gantt chart* is one of the most convenient, most used, and easy-to-grasp depictions of project activities that I have encountered in my practice. The chart is formatted as a two-dimensional representation of the project schedule with activities shown in the rows and time shown across the horizontal axis. It can be used during planning, for resource scheduling, and for status reporting. The only down side to using Gantt charts is that they do not contain dependency relationships. Some project management software tools have an option to display these dependencies, but the result is a graphical report that is so cluttered with lines representing the dependencies that the report is next to useless. In some cases, dependencies can be guessed at from the Gantt chart, but in most cases they are lost.

Figure J-1 shows a representation of the Cost Containment Project as a Gantt chart using the format that I prefer. The format shown is from Microsoft Project 2000, but it is typical of the format used in most project management software packages.

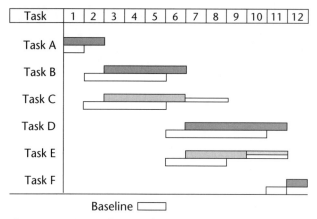

Figure J-1: Gantt chart project status report.

Milestone Trend Charts

Milestones are significant events in the life of the project that you wish to track. These significant events are zero-duration activities and merely represent that a certain condition exists in the project. For example, a milestone event might be that the approval of several different component designs has been given. This event consumes no time in the project schedule. It simply reflects the fact that those approvals have all been granted. The completion of this milestone event may be the predecessor of several build-type activities in the project plan. Milestone events are planned into the project in the same way that activities are planned into the project. They typically have FS relationships with the activities that are their predecessors and their successors.

Take a look at a milestone trend chart (see Figure J-2) for a hypothetical project. The trend chart plots the difference between the planned and estimated date of a project milestone at each project report period. In the original project plan the milestone is planned to occur at the ninth month of the project. That is the last project month on this milestone chart. The horizontal lines represent one, two, and three standard deviations above or below the forecasted milestone date. Any activity in the project has an expected completion date that is approximately normally distributed. The mean and variance of its completion date are a function of the longest path to the activity from the report date. In this example, the units of measure are one month. For this project the first project report (at month 1) shows that the new forecasted milestone date will be one week later than planned. At the second project report date (month 2 of the project) the milestone date is forecasted on target. The next three project reports indicate a slippage to 2 weeks late, then 3 weeks late, then 4 weeks late, and finally 6 weeks late (at month 6 of the project). In other words, the milestone is forecasted to occur 6 weeks late, and there are only 3 more project months in which to recover the slippage. Obviously, the project is in trouble. The project appears to be drifting out of control and, in fact, it is. Some remedial action is required of the project manager.

Certain patterns signal an out-of-control situation. For a complete treatment of milestone trend charts and several examples see Chapter 38.

Earned Value Analysis (a.k.a. Cost Schedule Control)

Earned value analysis is used to measure project performance and, by tradition, uses the dollar value of work as the metric. As an alternative, resource person hours/day can be used in cases where the project manager does not directly manage the project budget. Actual work performed is compared against planned and budgeted work expressed in these equivalents. These metrics are used to determine schedule and cost variances for both the current period and cumulative to date. Cost, or resource person hours/day are not good objective indicators with which to measure performance or progress. While this is true, there is no other good objective indicator. Given this you are left with dollars or person hours/day, which you are at least familiar working with in other contexts. Either one by itself does not tell the whole story. You need to relate them to one another.

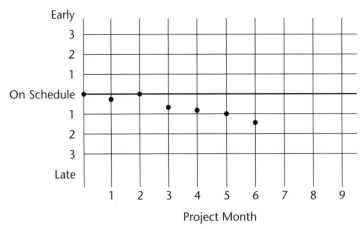

Figure J-2: A run up or down of four or more successive data points

One drawback that these metrics have is that they report history. Although they can be used to make extrapolated predictions for the future, they primarily provide a measure of the general health of the project, which the project manager can correct as needed to restore the project to good health.

The data displayed in Figure J-3 tells the whole story of the project status with respect to both cost and schedule. First, I want to define the terms and then analyze what the data is telling us. First, the BCWS curve (or cumulative budget) shows how costs incur cumulatively for the labor involved in delivering what was scheduled. In this version no capital expenditures are included. While they could be, they usually inflate the data and make it difficult to interpret. Include those costs if you wish. What was actually spent cumulatively is plotted in the ACWP curve. With just the data reflected in these two curves you might come to the conclusion that you are under budget. That would be incorrect. The BCWP curve clarifies the situation. For the work that was done, you are actually overbudget as shown by the Cost Variance. You didn't complete what was planned for the update date, but what you did do you overspent. The gap between the BCWS and BCWP curves tells the schedule story. In this case you are behind schedule. The terminology has changed recently. The legend on the bottom of the graph shows the old terminology (left of the equal sign) and the new terminology (right of the equal sign). For a complete discussion of earned value analysis with several examples see Chapter 38.

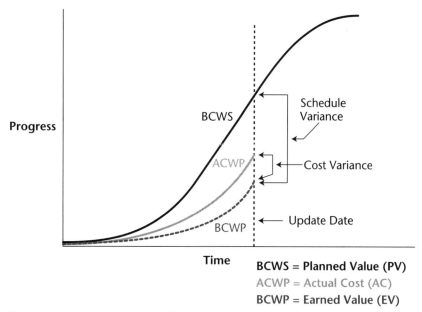

Figure J-3: A typical earned value analysis report

Level of Detail

There are always questions about the level of detail and frequency of reporting in project status reports. Our feeling is that the more you report, the more likely it is that someone will object or find some reason to micro-manage your project. You can examine this issue in more detail by considering the reporting requirements at the activity manager, project manager, and senior manager levels.

Activity Manager

The activity manager will want the most detailed and granular information available. After all, the activity manager is directly responsible for getting the work done. Because he or she manages the resources that are used to complete project work, he or she will want to know what happened, what was scheduled to happen, who did what (or didn't do what), why it happened as it did, what problems have arisen, what solutions are within reach, and what changes need to be made. Reports that reflect very detailed information are of use to the activity manager and the project manager but, because of their very detail, are of little value to anyone outside of the project team.

Project Manager

The project manager is concerned with the status information of all activities open for work during the report period. Just as is the case with activity-level reports, there are reports for the project manager and reports from the project manager to senior management.

Reports for the project manager present data at the activity level and show effects on the project schedule. If project management software is used, the posted data from the activity managers is used to update the project schedule and produce reports on overall project status. Any slippage at the activity level rippled through the successor activities, triggered a new activity schedule, and recomputed project completion dates. These reports display all scheduling information including float and resource schedule data. In effect, they become working documents for the project manager for schedule adjustments and problem resolution. Because these reports are at a very detailed level, they are not appropriate for distribution beyond the project team. In many cases, they may be for the project manager's eyes only.

Senior Management

I recommend using a graphical exception report structure to report project status to senior management. For many projects, reports at the activity level will be appropriate. For large projects, either milestone-level or summary task-level reports are more effective. Senior managers have only a few minutes to review any single project report. Keeping a report to a single page is a good strategy. The best report format, in my experience, is the Gantt chart. These charts require little explanation. Activities should be listed in the order of scheduled start date, a line designating the report date should be given and all percent completed displayed.

If the project is sick, attach a one-page get-well plan to your report. This usually is in the form of a narrative discussion of the problem, alternative solutions, recommended action, and any other details relevant to the issue at hand.

Project Status Meetings

You are no doubt overloaded with meetings. How often do you find yourself saying, "Why am I here? What's the purpose of this meeting?" How many times do you attend a meeting from which no decisions were taken, no action items identified? Doesn't that seem like a big waste of time? Well, it is, and it shouldn't be tolerated. In this section I discuss project status meetings and in the following section problem management meetings. These are the two types of meetings you should attend, meetings with a purpose.

What Is a Project Status Meeting?

In order to keep close track of progress on the project, the project manager needs to have information from his/her team on a timely basis. This information will be given during a project status meeting. At a minimum you need to have a status meeting at least once a week. On some of the major projects on which we've worked, daily status meetings were the norm for the first few weeks, and then as the need for daily information wasn't as critical we switched to twice a week and finally to weekly status.

Who Should Attend?

In order to use the status meetings correctly and efficiently, it's necessary to figure out who should be in attendance. This should be a part of your communication plan, and it's actually very important to know who should and shouldn't be a part of the status meetings.

At first your status team has a tendency to include people who are needed only in the planning phase. If they don't have a need to know information, don't make them come to a meeting and sit there without a good reason. You are going to put out meeting minutes anyway, so those people that aren't needed at the actual meeting will get the minutes in any case.

One other thing about who should be in attendance. There will be times in a status meeting when two people will get into a discussion where the other people in the meeting aren't needed. If this happens, ask them to do a "side-bar" meeting so that your own status meeting can go on. A sidebar meeting is one in which a limited number of people need to participate and these types of meetings can be done more effectively away from your status meeting. Having everyone in the room listen to these sidebar topics isn't useful.

Ask the people who are going to the sidebar meeting to let you know what happens in the meeting, particularly if what they talk about impacts the project. If possible get a meeting summary from the people, even if it's only a sentence or two long. Get this circulated to the rest of the team with your minutes so that everyone on the team is kept up to date.

When Are They Held?

Usually status meetings are held towards the end of the week. Whatever the day, make sure it's the same one time after time. People will get used to preparing information for a status meeting if they know exactly when the meeting will occur.

What Is Their Purpose?

The reason for a status meeting is to get information to the whole team. It may be that on large projects the participants in the status meeting are actually representatives of their department. You can't have all the people on a 250-person project team come into a meeting once a week, so make sure that someone is there to represent the rest of the people in their section. The purpose of the meeting is to encourage free flow of information and that means being sure that the people who need to have information to do their jobs get the information at the status meeting. Remember once again that you are going to send out minutes of the meeting so that will take care of the people who aren't in attendance.

Project size may be the determining factor, but in general I prefer a one-hour limit. This is the maximum, and an entire hour should not be needed at every project status meeting. Good judgment is needed here. Do not waste people's time.

What Is Their Format?

While the format of the status review meetings should be flexible, as project needs dictate, certain items are part of every status meeting. I recommend that you proceed in a top-down fashion:

1. The project champion reports any changes that may have a bearing on the future of the project.

2. The customer reports any changes that may have a bearing on the future of the project.

3. The project manager reports on the overall health of the project and the impact of earlier problems, changes, and corrective actions as they impact at the project level.

4. Activity managers report on the health of activities open or scheduled open for work since the last status meeting.

5. Activity managers of future activities report on any changes since the last meeting that might impact project status.

6. The project manager reviews the status of open problems from the last status meeting.

7. Attendees identify new problems and assign responsibility for their resolution (the only discussion allowed here is for clarification purposes).

8. The project champion, customer, or project manager, as appropriate, offers closing comments.

9. The project manager announces the time and place of the next meeting and adjourns the meeting.

Minutes are part of the formal project documentation and are taken at each meeting, circulated for comment, revised as appropriate, distributed, and filed in the project notebook (electronic, I hope). Because there is little discussion, the minutes contain any handouts from the meeting and list the items assigned for the next meeting. The minutes should also contain the list of attendees, a summary of comments made, and assigned responsibilities.

A project administrative support person should be present at the project status review meetings to take minutes and monitor handouts. The responsibility might also be passed around to the project team members. In some organizations the same person is responsible for distributing the meeting agenda and materials ahead of time for review. This is especially important if decisions will be made during the meeting. People are very uncomfortable if they are seeing important information for the first time, are expected to read and understand it, and then make a decision, all at the same time.

Problem Management Meetings

Problem management meetings provide an oversight function to identify, monitor, and resolve problems that arise during the life of a project. Every project has problems. No matter how well planned or managed the project is, there will always be problems. Many problems arise just as an accident of nature. For example, one of your key staff members has resigned just as he was to begin working on a critical path activity. His skills are in high demand, and he will be difficult to replace. Each day that his position remains vacant is another day's delay in the project. What will you do? Nevertheless, the project manager must be ready to take action in such cases. The problem management meeting is one vehicle for addressing all problems that need to be escalated above the individual for definition, solution identification, and resolution.

This is an important function in the management of projects, especially large projects. Problems are often identified in the project status meeting and referred to the appropriate persons for resolution. A group is assembled to work on the problem. Progress reports are presented and discussed at a problem management meeting.

Change Management

It is difficult for anyone, regardless of his or her skills at prediction and forecasting, to completely and accurately define the needs for a product or service that will be implemented 6, 12, or 18 months in the future. Competition, customer reactions, technology changes, a host of supplier-related situations, and many other factors could render a killer application obsolete before it can be implemented. The most frequent situation starts something like this: "Oh, I forgot to tell you that we will also need . . ." or "We have to go to market no later than the third quarter instead of the fourth quarter." How often have you heard sentences that start something like those examples? Face it—change is a way of life in project management. Be prepared to act accordingly.

Because change is constant, a good project management methodology has a change management process in place. In effect, the change management process has you plan the project again. Think of it as a mini-project planning session.

Two documents are part of every good change management process: a *project change request* and *project impact statement*.

Project Change Request

The first principle to learn is that every change is a significant change. Adopt that maxim and you will seldom go wrong. What that means is that every change requested by the customer must be documented. That document might be as simple as a memo but might also follow a format provided by the project team. In any case, it is the start of another round of establishing Conditions of Satisfaction. Only when the request is clearly understood can the project team evaluate the impact of the change and determine whether the change can be accommodated. Figure J-4 is an example of a change request form that I have found useful.

The change request is submitted by the customer using the form shown in Figure J-4 and forwarded to the manager or managers charged with reviewing such requests. They may either accept the change as submitted or return it to the customer for rework and resubmission. Once the change request has been accepted, it is forwarded to the project manager, who will perform an impact study.

Project Name
Change Requested By
Date Change Requested
Description of Change
Business Justification
Action
Approved By   Date

Figure J-4: Change request form

Project Impact Statement

The response to a change request is a document called a *project impact statement*. It is a response that identifies the alternative courses of action that the project manager is willing to consider. The requestor is then charged with choosing the best alternative. The project impact statement describes the feasible alternatives that the project manager was able to identify, the positive and negative aspects of each, and perhaps a recommendation as to which alternative might be best. The final decision rests with the requestor.

Six possible outcomes can result from a change request. Those are outlined in the subsections that follow.

It Can Be Accommodated within the Project Resources and Timelines

This is the simplest of situations for the project manager to handle. After considering the impact of the change on the project schedule, the project manager decides that the change can be accommodated without any harmful effect on the schedule and resources.

It Can Be Accommodated but Will Require an Extension of the Deliverable Schedule

The only impact that the change will have is to lengthen the deliverable schedule. No additional resources will be needed to accommodate the change request.

It Can Be Accommodated within the Current Deliverable Schedule but Additional Resources Will Be Needed

To accommodate this change request the project manager will need additional resources, but otherwise the current and revised schedule can be met.

It Can Be Accommodated but Additional Resources and an Extension of the Deliverable Schedule Will Be Required

This change request will require additional resources and a lengthened deliverable schedule.

It Can Be Accommodated with a Multiple Release Strategy and Prioritizing of the Deliverables across the Release Dates

This situation comes up more often than you might expect. To accommodate the change request, the project plan will have to be significantly revised, but there is an alternative. For example, suppose that the original request was for a list of 10 features, and they are in the current plan. The change request asks for an additional 2 features. The project manager asks the customer to prioritize all 12 features. He or she will give the customer 8 of them earlier than the delivery date for the original 10 features and will deliver the remaining 4 features later than the delivery date for the original 10. In other words, the project manager will give the customer some of what is requested earlier than requested and the balance later than requested. I have seen several cases where this compromise has worked quite well.

It Cannot Be Accommodated without a Significant Change to the Project

These change requests are significant. They are so significant, in fact, as to render the current project plan obsolete. There are two alternatives here.

- The first is to deny the change request, complete the project as planned, and handle the request as another project.
- The other is to call a stop to the current project, re-plan the project to accommodate the change, and launch a new project.

An integral part of the change control process is the documentation. First, I strongly suggest that every change be treated as a major change until proven otherwise. To do otherwise is to court disaster. That means that every change request follows the same procedure. Figure J-5 is an example of the steps in a typical change process.

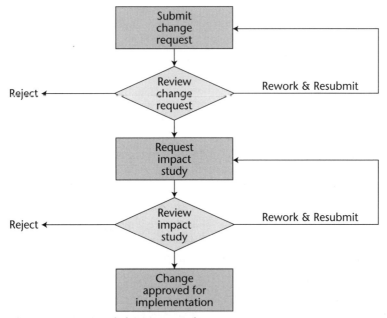

Figure J-5: A typical change control process

The impact study involves looking at the project plan, assessing how the change request impacts the plan, and issuing the impact study, which is forwarded to the management group for final disposition. They may return it to the project manager for further analysis and recommendations or reject it and notify the customer of their action. The project manager reworks the impact study and returns it to the management group for final disposition. If they approve the change, the project manager will implement it into the project plan.

Problem Escalation

Something has happened that put the project plan at risk. Late shipments from suppliers, equipment malfunction, sickness, random acts of nature, resignations, priority changes, errors, and a host of other factors give rise to problems that can affect deliverables, deliverable schedules, and resource schedules. The project manager owns the problem and must find a solution.

This situation is very different for the project manager than the case of a change request. When a change request has been made, the project manager has some leverage with the customer. The customer wants something and might be willing to negotiate to an acceptable resolution. That is not the case when a problem has arisen on the project team. The project manager does not have any leverage and is in a much more difficult position.

When the unplanned happens, the project manager needs to determine the extent of the problem and take the appropriate corrective measures. Minor variations from plan will occur and may not require corrective measures. There are degrees of corrective measures available to the project manager. In trying to resolve the problem, the project manager will begin at the top of the following list and work down the list, examining each choice until one is found that solves the problem.

There are three levels of escalation strategy: project manager–based, resource manager–based, and customer-based.

Project Manager–Based Strategies

If the problem occurs within a non-critical path activity, it can be resolved by using the free float. One example is to reschedule the activity later in its ES to LF window or extend the duration to use some of the free float. Note that this strategy does not affect any other activities in the project. By using total float, you impact the resource schedule for all activities that have this one as a predecessor.

Another approach is to continue the schedule compression techniques employed in defining the original project plan. This can impact resource schedules just as in the prior case.

The last option open to the project manager is to consider the resource pool under his or her control. Are there resources that can be reassigned from non-critical path activities to assist with the problem activity?

Resource Manager–Based Strategies

Once the project manager has exhausted all the options under his or her control, it is time to turn to the resource managers for additional help. This may take the form of additional resources or rescheduling of already committed resources. Expect to make some trade-off here. For example, you might be accommodated now, but at the sacrifice of later activities in the project. At least you have bought some time to resolve the downstream problem that will be created by solving this upstream problem. If the project manager has other projects underway, some trades across projects may solve the problem.

Customer-Based Strategies

When all else fails, the project manager will have to approach the customer. The first strategy would be to consider any multiple release strategies. Delivering some functionality ahead of schedule and the balance later than planned may be a good starting point. The last resort is to ask for an extension of time. This is not as unpleasant as it may seem because the customer's schedule may have also slipped, and the customer may be relieved to have a delay in your deliverable schedule, too.

The Escalation Strategy Hierarchy

Our problem escalation strategy is based on the premise that the project manager will try to solve the problem with the resources he or she controls. Failing to do that, the project manager will appeal to resource managers. As a last resort, the project manager will appeal to the customer.

One thing to note here that is very different from the change request situation discussed previously is the leverage to negotiate. As mentioned, the project manager has leverage when the customer has requested a change but has no leverage when he or she has a project problem to solve. The customer has nothing to gain and therefore is less likely to be cooperative. In most cases, the problem can be reduced to how to recover lost time. There are six outcomes to this problem situation; they are covered in the following subsections.

No Action Required (Schedule Slack Will Correct the Problem)

In this case, the slippage involved a non-critical path activity, and it will self-correct.

Examine FS Dependencies for Schedule Compression Opportunities

Recall that you originally compressed the schedule to accommodate the requested project completion date by changing FS dependencies to SS dependencies. The project manager will use that same strategy again. The project schedule will have changed several times since work began, and there may be several new opportunities to accomplish further compression and solve the current problem.

Reassign Resources from Non-Critical Path Activities To Correct the Slippage

Up to a point, the project manager controls the resources assigned to this project and others that he or she manages. The project manager may be able to reassign resources from non-critical path activities to the activities that have slipped. These non-critical path activities may be in the same project in which the slippage occurred, or they may be in another project managed by the same project manager.

Negotiate Additional Resources

Having exhausted all of the resources he or she controls, the project manager needs to turn to the resource managers as the next strategy. In order to recoup the lost time, the project manager needs additional resources. They may come in the form of added staff or dollars to acquire contract help.

Negotiate Multiple Release Strategies

These last two strategies involve the customer. Just as in the case of a change request, the project manager can use multiple release strategies here to advantage. An example will illustrate the strategy. The project manager shares the problem with the customer and then asks for the customer to prioritize the features requested in the project plan. The project manager then offers to provide the highest-priority features ahead of their scheduled delivery date and the remaining priorities later than the scheduled delivery date. In other words, the project manager asks for an extended delivery schedule, but by giving the customer something better than the original bargain, namely something ahead of schedule.

Request Schedule Extension from the Customer

This is the final alternative. Although similar to the multiple release strategy, it offers the customer nothing in trade. The slippage is such that the only resolution is to ask for a time extension.

The project manager tries to solve the problem by starting at the top of the list and working down until a solution is found. By using this approach the project manager will first try to solve the problem with resources he or she controls, then with resources the resource managers control, and finally with resources and constraints the customer controls.

Business Process Flow Diagramming

I am easily satisfied with the best.
Winston Churchill
British Prime Minister

Appendix Learning Objectives

After reading this appendix, you will be able to:

- ◆ **Define a business process**
- ◆ **Define a business process improvement project**
- ◆ **Construct a business context diagram**
- ◆ **Construct a business process flow diagram**
- ◆ **Define "As Is" and "To Be" business process**
- ◆ **Identify the "As Is/To Be" gap**

Often you will choose to start a software development project by mapping the current ("As Is" process) business process or processes that are going to be affected. You might also want to map the business process after the software products are installed ("To Be" process). Both of these are excellent artifacts to use as input to the requirements gathering process.

Business processes lie at the root of all efforts at software development and process improvement. In this appendix I will explore business process flow diagramming as an add-on to the other topics in this book.

From the systems development perspective the process of gathering requirements often begins with knowledge of the current or "As Is" business process and ends with the "To Be" business process. That gap is filled with a new or enhanced systems project. Having the "As Is" and the "To Be" business process flow diagrams is an invaluable aid in the ensuing systems development effort.

It is an ongoing dictum of today's business that you must continuously improve you business processes. The old saying "If it ain't broke, don't fix it" no longer applies. If you aren't improving your processes and the way that they support your customers, you run the risk of losing market share. Your customer should also be taking the lead in demanding process improvement. On the other hand, they are your customers, and you should be ever watchful for ways to improve the service they deliver to their customers.

All organizations are under pressure to improve. The pressure can come from their customer, their competition, environmental change, or a combination of the three. The improvements can be in their products or their processes. It is all too often the case that the customer doesn't give their business to the business with the best product. If the customer finds that the business is too difficult to deal with, the customer will decide to use second best from a supplier who is easier to deal with.

This also applies to internal organizations. One reason for outsourcing is a belief (frequently inaccurate) that other groups will be easier, faster, or cheaper to deal with. Internal organizations need to counter this belief by clearly demonstrating that they are continuously improving what they can deliver and their methods of delivery.

What Is a Business Process?

A business process is a collection of activities that takes one or more kinds of input from one or more different sources and produces value for the customer (see Figure K-1). The focus of the business must be to ensure that the effort of dealing with the process does not out-weigh the value received from completing the process.

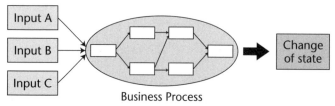

Figure K-1: What is a business process?

For example, order entry/fulfillment is a clear example of a business process. From the customer's viewpoint, the process starts when customer places an order and ends when the customer receives the goods requested. There are numerous activities in between. Credit checks may be run to confirm that the customer can pay for the order. Inventory is accessed to confirm you have what the customer is requesting. A typical list of activities would include:

- Receiving the order
- Logging the order
- Verification of completeness
- Customer credit check
- Determining the price
- Inventory checking
- Production request
- Order picking.
- Order packaging
- Shipment

You will notice that the activity in a high-level business process might be regarded as a process itself by the performing organization. Processes can be decomposed into other processes until you reach the task level where some interim component is produced. The key is to start with the customer as the focus of the original process and define the subprocesses by their contribution to added value.

Characteristics of Business Processes

The more you understand business processes, the more you can improve them. To do that, you must clearly understand several characteristics of business processes:

- **Flow**—The method for transforming input into output
- **Effectiveness**—How well customer expectations are met
- **Efficiency**—How well resources are used to produce an output
- **Cycle time**—The time taken for transformation from input to final output
- **Cost**—The expenses of the entire process
- **Non-value-added time**—The time between process steps when no work is done on the product/service

The items are fairly self-explanatory, except for effectiveness and efficiency, which I want to discuss in more detail.

Process Effectiveness

Process effectiveness is how well the process meets the requirements of the end customer. It measures the quality of the process. Effectiveness is also how well the output of the process meets the input requirements of internal customers and how well the inputs from the suppliers meet the requirements of the process.

The effectiveness of every process can be improved. The direct result of increased effectiveness will lead to happier customers, improved sales, and an increase in market share.

The first step in bringing about an improvement in process effectiveness is to identify the most important effectiveness characteristics. Effectiveness characteristics are indicators of how well the process is functioning. The goal is to be sure that the output meets the customer requirements.

Typical lack of effectiveness indicators are:

- Unacceptable product and/or service
- Customer complaints
- High warranty costs
- Decreased market share
- Backlog
- Redoing completed work
- Rejected output
- Late output
- Incomplete output

During the walkthrough, the team should be constantly looking and identifying effectiveness characteristics.

Process Efficiency

The achievement of process efficiency is for the primary benefit of the customer. Typical efficiency characteristics are:

- Cycle time per unit of transaction
- Resources per unit of output
- True-value-added cost percentage of totals process cost
- Poor quality cost per unit of output
- Wait time per unit of transaction

During the walkthrough the team should be looking for ways to measure efficiency.

NOTE Cost is an extremely important aspect of the process. Every organization should be looking for ways to control costs within their operations. The cost of a process is an accountability issue that should be analyzed. By controlling costs, you will be able to increase your bottom line.

Streamlining Tools

Streamlining is the trimming of waste and excess in order to improve performance and quality. There are 11 tools to streamlining. They are defined below.

Bureaucracy Elimination

Removing unnecessary administration tasks, approvals, and paperwork.

Duplication Elimination

Removing identical activities that are performed at different parts of the process.

Value-Added Assessment

Evaluating every activity in the business process to determine its contribution to meeting customer requirements. Real-value added activities are the ones that the customers would pay you to do.

Simplification

Reducing the complexity of the project.

Process Cycle-Time Reduction

Determining ways to compress cycle time to meet or exceed customer expectations. Typical ways to reduce cycle time are:

- Serial versus parallel activities
- Change activity sequence
- Reduce interruption

- Improved timing
- Reduce output movement
- Location analysis

Error Proofing

Making it difficult to do the activity incorrectly. Error proofing is the process of eliminating the opportunity to create errors. This can be accomplished many ways. For example, you can automate a data entry process to remove the human error factor. Everyone has a tendency to make errors; therefore, the more you can automate a process the greater likelihood that a careless error will not occur.

Upgrading

Making effective use of capital equipment and the working environment to improve overall performance. Upgrading refers not only to improving your technology or office equipment, but also to your personnel. Continuous learning is the norm in today's business world. Organizations that provide training and educational incentives will reap large dividends in the long run due to increased profit and higher employee morale.

Simple Language

Reducing the complexity of the way you write and talk, making your documents easy to comprehend by all who use them. Simplifying the language of your documentation and training manuals will increase effectiveness. Some organizations get burdened by wordy reports and memos. Documentation should be written in simple language to a particular audience.

Standardization

Selecting a single way of doing an activity and having all employees do the activity that way all the time. Standardization of work procedures is important to ensure that all current and future employees use the best ways to perform activities related to the process. When each person is doing the activity differently, it is difficult, if not impossible, to make major improvements in the process. Standardization is one of the first steps in improving any process. This is accomplished by the use of procedures. These standardization procedures should:

- Be realistic, based on careful analysis
- Clarify responsibilities
- Establish limits of authority
- Cover emergency situations
- Not be open to different interpretations
- Be easy to understand
- Explain each document, its purpose, and its use
- Define training requirements
- Define minimum performance standards

Supplier Partnership

The output of the process is highly dependent on the quality of the inputs the process receives. The overall performance of any process improves when its suppliers' input improves.

All outputs require inputs, and in many cases these inputs come from outside suppliers. The first step in this streamlining process is to analyze the inputs to determine their need in the process. An organization can lower costs and increase efficiency by eliminating inputs that are not needed. The next step is to work with suppliers to make sure that the inputs are being delivered on time and are of the highest quality.

Big Picture Improvement

This technique is used when the first ten streamlining tools have not provided the desired results. It is designed to help the process improvement team look for creative ways to drastically change the process. There comes a point in time when you have to be willing to step back and look at the big picture of the process. By looking at the big picture you examine the process form the perspective of what you would do if you abandoned the old way of doing things and started from scratch.

What Is a Business Process Improvement Project?

The continuous improvement of business processes should be a high priority for every contemporary organization. Every time a process is executed there is a wealth of data and information that is produced as a by-product. This data and information has great value in helping the process managers identify and isolate areas where improvement can be made. A business process improvement (BPI) project uses that data and information as input to programs designed to improve the process under consideration. This is represented graphically in Figure K-2.

The goal of a BPI project is to eliminate or at least reduce the effect resulting from one or more process activities that are preventing the process from performing up to its potential.

Figure K-2 shows that a backlog exists at a process activity. From the diagram you might conclude that the backlog is the result of two upstream process activities both delivering output to the single process activity and that process activity is not staffed to handle the volume. What seems like a simple solution, namely, add staff, might solve the backlog problem at that process activity but create another backlog at the following step. The backlog is just transferred, and the efficiency of the total process is not changed at all. This illustrates a common problem—subprocess maximization that may or may not positively affect the total process. In fact, it could reduce the efficiency of the total process. Obviously each of the activities in a business process could make the overall process cumbersome to deal with. The goal of business process improvement is to eliminate (or at least reduce) the pain coming from the activities that are doing the most damage and this also implies that there may be one or more precursor projects that have determined the sources of pain, confusion, and/or chaos.

Beyond a single process improvement project there is a continuous process improvement program. These by definition do not end. They focus on a complete process or process of processes. Their improvement goal is often an ideal end state and for all practical purposes will never be reached but will be a worthy goal to shoot for nevertheless.

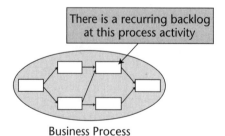

Business Process

Figure K-2: A business process improvement project

Indicators of Needed Improvement

There are several metrics that you will need to define and track in order to discover process improvement opportunities. Some of the situations you will want to detect are as follows:

- Excessive wait time between process steps
- Backlog at a process step
- Idle workstations in the business process
- Frequent re-work
- Excessive non-value-added work
- Errors and mistakes
- Frequent exception situations

For example, an order placement process might have a number of disconnects such as:

- Sales reps take too long to enter orders
- Too many entry and logging steps
- The same level of credit checking is done for existing and new customers
- Credit checking is done before order picking

Any of the preceding is a possible process improvement project.

Business Process Diagramming

How do you diagrammatically represent a business process? You can use the standard flowchart symbols to keep it simple and couched in symbols you are already familiar with. Figure K 3 lists the more commonly used symbols, and the following bulleted list explains them.

- **Operation**—This box denotes that a change has taken place. The input is somehow changed as a result of having gone through this process.
- **Movement**—This symbol denotes the movement of output from one process step to become the input to the next process step.
- **Decision**—This is a decision step. A question needs to be answered. The two flows that emanate from a decision box are either Yes/True or No/False.
- **Inspection**—Someone other than the person producing the output must inspect it for quality, conformance, or some other tangible characteristic. Often an approval is included as a successful inspection.

- **Document**—This denotes a paper document.
- **Delay**—This symbol denotes a wait state in a process. Usually associated with something joining a queue and waiting for the next process step to occur.
- **Storage**—Indicates that an item has been placed in storage and must wait for a release before moving to the next process step. These usually represent wasted time that must be removed from a process.
- **Annotation**—Provides added detail about some process, which is needed for clarification. It might also include the position title of the person responsible for the process.
- **Direction of Flow**—Denotes the order of process steps.
- **Transmission**—The interrupted arrow indicates when information is to be transmitted from one physical or virtual location to another.
- **Connector**—Used to connect flow between two separate locations. Often used as an off-page connector.
- **Boundaries**—Denotes the initiating and closing process of a flow diagram. Usually the words START or BEGIN are associated with the initiating process and STOP or END with the closing process.

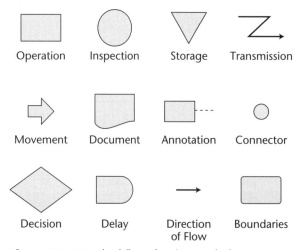

Figure K-3: Standard flow charting symbols

Business Process Flow Diagram Formats

There are three common formats used to render business process flow diagrams. The first (Figure K-4) is the top-down and left-to-right format. It is commonly used in program and system flow charts. The second is the "swim-lane" format (Figure K-5). It identifies the actors who participate in the business process. The third is the linear format (Figure K-6). It can be used to save space but requires that the process being modeled is a linear process—that is, it has no branch on condition situations.

Figure K-4 is the format software developers will be most familiar with. It harkens back to the early days of programming and is the standard they adopted several decades ago. It follows the logical thought patterns of the software developer and is therefore their popular choice.

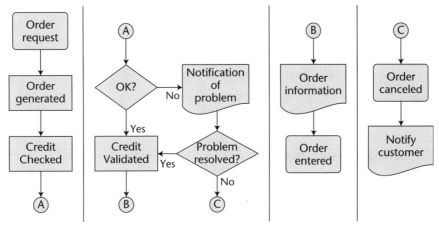

Figure K-4: The top-down left-to-right format

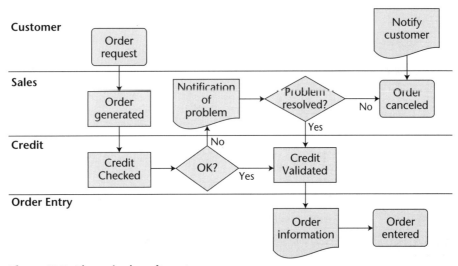

Figure K-5: The swim-lane format

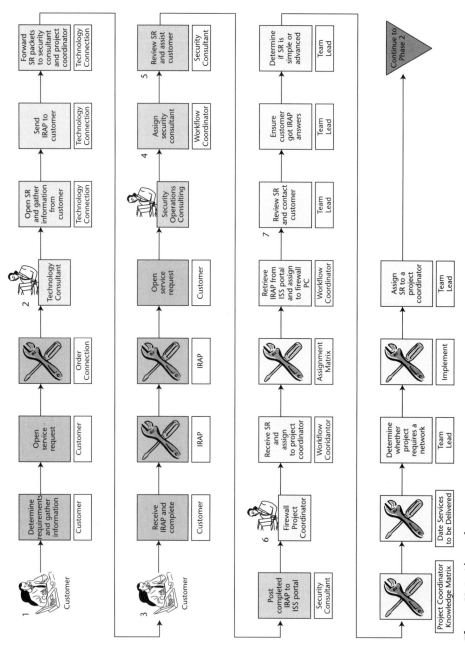

Figure K-6: Linear format

Figure K-5 is the format I prefer when diagramming business processes. For one, it is a customer-facing format. By that I mean it is intuitive to the customer and represents their processes in a way that they can easily understand.

Figure K-6 is most economic of real estate—it uses the least amount of paper to represent the business process. It does have one significant limitation, however; it works only for linear processes. Notice that there are no decision diamonds in the process.

Context Diagrams

One way to describe your process at a very high level is the context diagram. It is a good starting point. A context diagram describes a rough process or a set of processes. It generally has only a few components:

- A stick figure representing the external entity that is triggering the process
- A large circle representing the organization responding to the request
- A text block showing each organization or process acting to fulfill the request
- Arrows showing the rough flow between text blocks

The context diagramming process (Figure K-7) requires that the group identify one or more candidate processes. For example, a process might start with a customer request/action and end with a fulfillment. The modeling activity starts by identifying those two points. You show the process start by using an arrow from the customer to the organization. You show the process end by using an arrow from the organization to the customer. That gives an initial bounding of the process, and the group can decide whether that particular process has enough issues to spend more time diagramming. If the process merits more discussion, the diagramming process continues by identifying the first group to receive the request and the action sequence that the organization goes thru to fulfill the request. Simply put, the group uses Post-it notes and arrows to show what goes on in the organization to fulfill the request. This should be done at a high level and the constrained area of the circle helps keep this high level perspective.

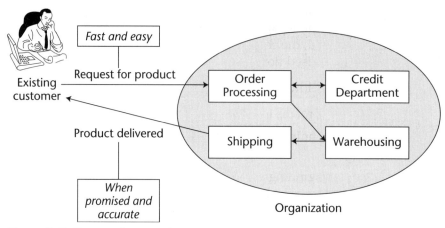

Figure K-7: Context diagramming process

Frequently the group will make refinements as they go. The most common refinements are a clearer identification of the customer being focused upon or the transaction being performed. For example, "customer" might become "existing customer" if the process is different (or should be different) for an existing customer versus a new customer. The group can then annotate the process with success criteria, issues, and so on.

Business Process Work Flow Diagrams

When you need to identify the actual and ideal path that any product or service follows in order to map process quality and identify deviations and improvement opportunities, the flow chart is another tool that can be beneficial in mapping process quality and performance. It is a picture of steps in a process, and can be used to examine the relation and sequence of steps; to identify redundancy, unnecessary complexity, and inefficiency in a process; and to create common understanding of the flow of the process.

Considered one of the simplest tools, the flow chart can be as basic or technically intricate as the process it's used to illustrate. Each type of process step is traditionally identified on the chart by a standardized geometric shape. A flow chart illustrates a process from start to finish and should include every step in between. By studying these charts you can often uncover loopholes, which are potential sources of trouble. Flow charts can be applied to anything from the travels of an invoice and the flow of materials to the steps in making a sale or servicing a product.

In process improvement, flow charts are often used to clarify how a process is being performed or to agree upon how it should be performed. When a process is improved, the changes should be noted on the flow chart in order to standardize the revised flow.

Follow the steps below to create a flow chart:

1. Decide on the process to be diagrammed.
2. Define the beginning and ending steps of the process, also known as boundaries.
3. Describe the beginning step using the Boundaries symbol.
4. Keep asking "What happens next?" and writing each of the subsequent steps in Operations symbols below the Boundaries symbol.
5. When a decision step is reached, write a yes/no question in a diamond and develop each path.
6. Make sure that each decision loop reenters the process or is pursued to a conclusion.
7. Describe the ending step using the Boundaries symbol. Sometimes a process may have more than one ending boundary.

Documenting the "As Is" Business Process

One approach to identifying those goals is to develop a clear understanding of how the process is currently functioning (As Is) and how the process could work in the future (To Be). Knowing the gap between the current and future is input to a plan to change the process (that is, to remove the gap).

The "As Is" is nothing more than a picture of how things are currently working. If you were talking about a hotel, you could build a model of the workflow associated with a guest obtaining a room, using hotel facilities, and checking out of the hotel.

For an old hotel with no automated systems, the steps would be manual and highly dependent upon the accuracy of individuals. Having this set of data alone can make some areas prime candidates for improvement.

There is a tremendous temptation to skip the "As Is." People will say they know the process and what needs to be changed. If you skip this step, the team doesn't get an increased understanding of how the process really works. Without that real understanding, you have a very real chance of negatively impacting the customer.

Envisioning the "To Be" State

This model is a picture of how the process could work. The same work may be done, but the flow might be very different. In some cases, tasks in the "As Is" state might be eliminated entirely. The intent of this model is to get people to talk about how it could be. This is sometimes done by having the subject matter experts tell how they would do things if they were building a brand new process unconstrained by the way you have always done things. This is frequently referred to as the "green field" approach. Another approach is to have people identify those areas where they would like to change the current system to do things differently.

Defining the "As Is" to "To Be" Gap

The difference or "delta" between the "As Is" and the "To Be" shows the opportunities for improvement. It involves building a comparison of the two so that the differences can be categorized. Some tasks might be eliminated entirely. Some tasks might be done faster than they were before. Some tasks that had been sequential might be done in parallel. Others might be done to a higher level of quality. Some opportunities for eliminating the gap might be:

- Eliminate some tasks
- Speed up some tasks
- Introduce parallelism
- Increase quality

Effective Software Project Management